JAPAN'S SECURITY AGENDA

JAPAN'S SECURITY AGENDA

Military, Economic, and Environmental Dimensions

Christopher W. Hughes

LYNNE RIENNER PUBLISHERS
BOULDER
LONDON

Published in the United States of America in 2004 by
Lynne Rienner Publishers, Inc.
1800 30th Street, Boulder, Colorado 80301
www.rienner.com

and in the United Kingdom by
Lynne Rienner Publishers, Inc.
3 Henrietta Street, Covent Garden, London WC2E 8LU

Library of Congress Cataloging-in-Publication Data
Hughes, Christopher W.
Japan's security agenda : military, economic, and environmental dimensions / Christopher W. Hughes.
p. cm.
Includes bibliographical references and index.
ISBN 1-58826-260-X (hardcover : alk. paper)
1. National security—Japan. 2. Japan—Military policy. 3. Japan—Economic conditions—21st century. 4. Human ecology—Japan. I. Title.
UA845.H84 2004
355'.033052—dc22 2003025739

British Cataloguing in Publication Data
A Cataloguing in Publication record for this book is available from the British Library.

Printed and bound in the United States of America

The paper used in this publication meets the requirements of the American National Standard for Permanence of Paper for Printed Library Materials Z39.48-1992.

5 4 3 2 1

For Chiyako

Contents

Acknowledgments

Attempting to write an integrated and explanatory overview of Japan's security policy in East Asia over the Cold War and post–Cold War periods has not been an easy task. Fortunately, I have been helped along in this project by a number of people in Japan and the UK. In Japan, the International Center for Comparative Law and Politics (ICCLP) at the Graduate School of Law and Politics, University of Tokyo, proved to be an excellent base to begin writing this project. I must thank Takahashi Susumu for inviting me there as a visiting associate professor from 2000 to 2001, as well as Wada Keiko and all her staff at the ICCLP for such a warm and supportive welcome.

On the UK side, I have been extremely fortunate to work at the UK Economic and Social Science Research Council's Centre for the Study of Globalisation and Regionalisation at the University of Warwick. Here I have been provided with time and an intellectual environment to explore the links among globalization, regionalization, political economy, and security. Richard Higgott has been a constant source of support in all intellectual endeavors, and I have benefited from working alongside Shaun Breslin and from his insights into the political economy of East Asia. My graduate students, both at the Ph.D. level and in my M.A. seminars, have also given me many stimulating ideas for this book. From Lynne Rienner Publishers, first Richard Purslow and then Elisabetta Linton gave me patient encouragement with the manuscript.

All of the above have helped me greatly, but I alone am responsible for any errors of fact or interpretation contained in this book.

Last, but of course not least, my family has been vital to the completion of this project. Eleanor Aika looked at and then promptly scribbled pictures on all drafts of this manuscript. Chiyako, my wife, has as usual patiently tolerated my fixation on this book and given me the necessary love and encouragement to follow it through to the end.

—*Christopher W. Hughes*

JAPAN'S SECURITY AGENDA

Introduction

The purpose of this book is to analyze Japan's security policy and its contribution to regional security in East Asia from the Cold War period to the present. Japan, despite being a major regional power and a global economic superpower, remains largely unfathomed and underrated as a security actor. Japan has shown signs of enhanced security activity in the post–Cold War period, including its dispatch of military forces to provide logistic support for the U.S.-led war on terror in Afghanistan and Iraq since the September 11, 2001, terrorist attacks. Nonetheless, debate continues within and outside Japan: What type of security actor does it seek to be? What is the dimension of security it should pursue? And how will Japan contribute to East Asian security?

Japan's security policy in East Asia includes a range of roles in the past, in the contemporary period, and in the future. In the military security dimension, Japan has been seen as resistant to an overt and direct role. This has been interpreted as the result of Japanese antimilitaristic sentiment (Katzenstein and Okawara 1993; Berger 1998), a desire to avoid entanglement in U.S. regional military strategy (Green 2001a: 11–14; Welfield 1998), and the contentment to "free-ride" on U.S. military security guarantees (for a description of this type of argument, see Hook et al. 2001: 7; Heginbotham and Samuels 1998). Other observers, particularly East Asian neighbors, have seen Japan as intent on patiently building up its military capabilities to become once again a big, even dominant, power and that it is only the U.S.-Japan alliance that serves as the cork in the bottle of Japanese militarism. Still others envisage a future for Japan as a normal and responsible military power acting in the service of international security (Ozawa 1993). This is to be achieved through a mix of mechanisms, including

It is the convention in Japanese for the family name to precede the given name. This convention is followed in this book. Long vowels are indicated by macrons, except when referring to authors and works published in English and to the names of well-known cities in Japan.

independent use of national military capabilities, expanded military cooperation under the U.S.-Japan alliance, and involvement in United Nations (UN) multilateral military activities.

At the same time, Japan's projected role as a reluctant or resurgent military power needs to be juxtaposed with its role as a major economic power, utilizing official development assistance (ODA) and other forms of economic capacity to achieve stability in East Asia. Japan has long professed a comprehensive security policy that uses military and economic power in equal measures to address military, economic, and environmental threats and their causes. For some, these traditions have offered Japan an alternative route to contributing to regional stability in East Asia, functioning as an "ODA great power," "civilian power," or even "environmental superpower" (Funabashi 1991–1992; Takemura 1994).

This inconclusive debate that has sought to ascribe to Japan a variety of security roles in the Cold War and post–Cold War periods has been matched by a similar debate that has attempted to evaluate the actual application and effectiveness of these roles for Japan's contribution to regional security. Some think that Japan's military role has been valuable to regional security by undergirding the U.S. military presence (Murata 2000). Others believe that Japan's military contribution has been counterproductive by raising regional tensions (Johnson 2000; DiFilippo 2002). Japan's military security policy has also been seen to distract attention from a range of other military concerns that may not affect Japan directly and to have drawn policy energy away from nonmilitary concerns (Hughes 1999).

Thus even though Japan may contribute to regional stability through comprehensive security, its execution of policy has been questioned. Japan's ODA policies have been viewed as ineffective, even heightening economic and environmental insecurity (Wong 2001). Moreover, Japan's commitment to using economic power to pursue security has come into doubt due to a prolonged recession. The jury is still out on Japan's effectiveness as a security actor.

These debates give rise to the two principal objectives of this book. First, it attempts to discern the past, contemporary, and future trajectory of Japan's security policy and to reach a more reasoned judgment on the direction that Japan is heading. It explores the military, economic, and environmental dimensions of Japan's security policy and details the individual state, bilateral, and multilateral aspects of that policy in East Asia. It also looks at how Japan has deployed its military power and whether Japan is indeed moving toward becoming a normal military power or remains wary of assuming such a role. In turn, the book examines individual, bilateral, and multilateral economic and environmental security policies throughout these periods, and looks at how Japan has employed economic power to pursue security interests and whether this approach has been balanced with military power. The hope is that by examining and aggregating Japan's security policy across all dimensions it will then become more fully possible to gauge the extent of its security activity in the East Asia region and to understand its overall military and economic security trajectory.

The second objective is to evaluate Japan's effectiveness as a regional security actor. By examining Japan's activity in these three dimensions (military, economic, and environmental), we may demonstrate the methods Japan has used. We will look at the oversights and contradictions, as well as the successes and positive contributions. This will lead to a broader and more objective understanding of Japan's contribution to regional stability.

The focus is on Japanese concepts and practices of comprehensive security policy in the Cold War period through the present. The analysis will use the broadest possible framework to gather evidence and to analyze Japan's security activity and contribution. Moreover, if Japan adheres to its traditions of comprehensive security, it may adopt a multidimensional approach that is valuable to regional security.

Japan and East Asian Security

Japan's security interaction with East Asia is an important test case. Japan attaches great importance to East Asian security because of the region's proximity and the likely impact on Japanese domestic security. Thus we can assume that Japan's security efforts will be concentrated in this region.

East Asia also presents a complex, multidimensional, multilevel security agenda that has forced changes and has tested Japan's security policy. The regional security agenda is characterized by a range of military threats, including potential interstate conflict between the United States and China; tensions on the Korean Peninsula; the proliferation of weapons of mass destruction (WMD); conventional arms races; and intrastate conflicts and ethnic strife in states such as Indonesia. The potential impact of transnational terrorism and the war on terror in East Asia was demonstrated by the Bali bombing of November 2002. East Asia is prone also to a range of nontraditional security problems such as competition for natural and energy resources; economic crises; large-scale migration; transnational crime; piracy; and transboundary pollution and the destruction of the biosphere. Japan's response should then provide an opportunity to assess its own security policy.

Japan's response to regional security leads us to analyze global security as a whole. The East Asian security agenda reflects and affects global security. Global security after the Cold War and after September 11 is shaped by a range of military, economic, and environmental issues, among a range of state and nonstate actors. Moreover, the sheer scale of the region in terms of geography, population, and economy, as well as the extreme concentration of security issues, arguably makes East Asia more important than any other region to the unfolding global security agenda. If Japan can make an important contribution to regional security, then it can become a major player in global security. Japan's management of its relations with China will be crucial.

Furthermore, the study of Japan's role in regional security highlights the value of policy that Japan has utilized. If it can be demonstrated that Japan's comprehensive security policy has made an important contribution to regional stability, then this points to the inherent worth of Japan's security conceptions in dealing with complex security environments and the necessity of employing similar methods in other regional contexts.

Approaches

This book will employ three interlinked approaches, a combination of conceptual, historical, and political economy approaches. The first conceptual approach derives from international relations (IR), international political economy (IPE), and security studies and seeks to categorize and analyze the security agenda in East Asia and Japan's response. This encompasses military, economic, and environmental security dimensions, as well as the full range of associated security phenomena (e.g., high- and low-intensity military conflict, economic exclusion, disparity, rivalry and dislocation, organized crime, piracy, migration, infectious diseases, natural disasters, and environmental degradation). In addition, this incorporates state, nonstate, societal, organizational, and human actors. The framework enables a comprehensive analysis.

The second approach is based in history. The East Asian security agenda and Japan's response are traced to the early Cold War period through the present. This historical method provides a vantage point from which to map the full trajectory of Japan's security policy.

The third approach is based in political economy. It will evaluate the conceptions behind Japan's security policy, as well as its relevance and effectiveness in the regional security agenda. In order to carry out this task, its causation must be explained. Understanding causation is important to comprehensive security policy because it seeks to address the symptoms of existing problems and to alleviate their root causes. Economic power is often deployed to tackle problems related to economic insecurity that can lead to military conflict.

The book thus asks whether Japan has correctly conceptualized these causes and adjusted its policy accordingly. Certain political and economic conditions have prevailed since the Cold War started. Decolonization, bipolarization, and globalization, and the problems they produced for security, have been the major factors in this context.

Contribution

Japan is unfathomed and underrated as a security actor; it is also understudied. Japan has received minimal attention in mainstream IR, IPE, and security studies. If studied at all, it has been to demonstrate deficiencies, or to point out how its security behavior deviates from what might be expected compared to other major powers. Many have also tried to squeeze Japan into the traditional realist, liberal, and constructivist dichotomies (Katzenstein and Okawara 2002). Japanese studies and East Asian security studies have not always fared better; many critique Japan's military policy. However, the focus is typically on one or two key aspects of Japan's security, such as the bilateral alliance (Muroyama 1992; Green and Cronin 1999; Funabashi 1999); security relations with another East Asian state (Drifte 2002); or security relations with regional states through the prism of the U.S.-Japan alliance (Nishihara 2000; Osius 2002).

Japan's economic and environmental security policies are even more understudied. There are studies of Japan's ODA and environmental policies, but most are limited to the region, and few are within an explicit security framework (Orr 1990; Yasutomo 1996). Surprisingly, despite Japan's constant articulation of comprehensive security and the role of economic power, few studies look at the military, economic, and environmental dimensions of Japan's security policy, and none has looked at this regionally or in the contemporary period (Chapman et al. 1993).

Thus this book seeks to make a distinctive contribution, looking at Japan's security policy from the Cold War to the present. It is the first to examine Japan's security policy in a comprehensive fashion by giving equal attention to its military, economic, and environmental components in East Asia. It takes into account all security actors and all types of security problems in East Asia. It addresses Japan's security policy through the individual state, the bilateral U.S.-Japan alliance, and multilateral security. It includes Northeast and Southeast Asia and covers Japan's key security relations with the United States, China, Russia, the Korean Peninsula, and the Association of Southeast Asian States (ASEAN). Specific issues include Japan's reaction to superpower, great power, and regional power interstate conflict; regional territorial disputes; intrastate conflict and insurgency; human security; the proliferation of WMD; ballistic missile defense (BMD); terrorism; economic collapse in North Korea and Burma; economic disparities in China and Southeast Asia as sources of conflict; regional tensions over food and energy resources; the security impact of the 1997–1998 financial crisis in East Asia; migration as a security issue; transnational crime; piracy; infectious diseases; natural disasters; transborder pollution; the destruction of natural resources; and climate change.

This study is also the first to systematically place Japan's security policy within generic theories of security, and it is the first to outline Japan's response to 9/11 within the context of security policy. Finally, it also seeks to evaluate policy effectiveness and implications for understanding Japan's worth as a regional and global security actor. This holistic approach goes beyond other works currently in existence.

Structure

This book is divided into six chapters. Chapter 1, utilizing generic security theories, generates a robust multidimensional and multilevel framework to help categorize and analyze East Asia and Japan's security agenda. Chapters 2 and 3 employ a historical and political economy approach, concentrating on decolonization, bipolarization, and globalization to outline the development and causation of the East Asian security agenda. Chapter 4 elucidates Japan's conceptions of comprehensive security, then examines the origins, development, strengths, and weaknesses of its military, economic, and environmental security policy during the Cold War. Chapter 5 focuses on Japan's post–Cold War military security policy; its independent military capabilities, the U.S.-Japan alliance, and experiments with multilateral security frameworks; the areas of effectiveness and deficiencies of this military policy; and the debate on Japan's movement toward becoming a "normal" military power. Chapter 6 examines Japan's economic and environmental security policies in the post–Cold War period and their degree of application and effectiveness. Lastly, the Conclusion evaluates the overall trajectory of Japan's comprehensive security policy in terms of the shifting balance between military and other dimensions of security; the overall degree of relevance and effectiveness of Japan's policy for regional and global security; and the future prospects for Japan in maintaining a comprehensive approach.

1

Security Concepts: A Multidimensional Framework

Conceptions of security—definitions, actors, issues, and approaches—are capable of varying across historical (Katzenstein 1996a: 10) and geographical contexts. During the Cold War and the pressures resulting from the U.S.-Soviet confrontation, realist, or Western, conceptions of security were dominant among policymakers and academics. Hence, the traditional policy and intellectual security paradigm of the Cold War focused on the definitions, actors, issues, and approaches in the military dimension and the key role of the nation-state and interstate warfare.

Not all thinking was subject to this security paradigm (Baldwin 1997: 23), especially when the U.S.-Soviet military stand-off relaxed, as well as in regions looking to escape its influence. In these contexts, and away from the somewhat ethnocentric view of security (Booth 1979), it was possible to perceive older, pre–Cold War, nontraditional, or alternative security agendas consisting of differing definitions, actors, issues, and approaches, which coexisted with but were orientated away from Cold War military versions. Certain perspectives from both the developed and developing world emphasized the economic, societal, and environmental aspects of security (Ullman 1983; Thomas 1987; Allison and Treverton 1992; Tickner 1995: 179–184). By and large, however, the Cold War's pervasive influence suppressed and obscured the alternative security paradigm in many policymaking circles and within much of IR and IPE scholarship (Baldwin 1995; Romm 1993).

Consequently, it was not until the 1990s that alternative security concerns were able to reemerge in the mainstream security agenda. In addition, globalization added a new context and complexity to security paradigms. The contemporary world faces intermingling and interlinking security paradigms. The logical outcome is that any attempt to conceptualize and understand the contemporary security agenda must account for and incorporate the range of definitions, actors, issues, and approaches evident from the pre–Cold War, Cold War, post–Cold War, and postglobalization contexts, as well as from different regional contexts.

Such a widened view is becoming increasingly mainstream. But certain schools of thought have challenged this approach and prefer a return to "traditional" and military roots (Tow 2001a: 262–264). Such securitization of issues is inappropriate for a number of reasons. First, it can result in intellectual overload and a lack of analytical focus to perceive and prioritize security problems among the array of others. Second, the securitization of issues can drain resources away from the central agenda: military security and the role of the state (Walt 1991: 213; Gray 1999: 179). Thus broadening the security agenda can be counterproductive by hampering attempts to deploy the intellectual and physical resources necessary. Third, the securitization of a specific issue can lead to the depoliticization of that issue with implications for individual and societal freedoms (Dalby 1997: 12–18). This is because identifying an issue as one of security provides it a rarefied status, demanding concentrated state action that might override normal political conventions and restrictions on state power. Viewed from this perspective, securitizing issues and broadening the security agenda are dangerous.

Although the military and state dimensions remain central, the reality is that security problems are linked to and stand outside the traditional security agenda; these demand an explanation and a response (Booth 1991a: 18). There is a need to look above and below the nation and sovereign state to assess security (a *vertical* extension of understanding) and to look beyond the military dimension to investigate the security problems inherent in other dimensions of human activity (a *horizontal* extension of knowledge regarding security) (Stares 2000a: 15). Therefore, this book will outline a conception of security that incorporates and captures the complexity of security paradigms across different definitions, actors, issues, and approaches, as well as different historical epochs and regions. The inclusion of nonstate actors alongside state actors, and economic and environmental dimensions alongside the military dimension, is justified because each is a substantive and genuine component of the security agenda; each influences the issues posed by the others.

Only then can we look at the dynamics behind the contemporary security agenda in East Asia. All these actors and dimensions are viewed as immediate security concerns that affect everyday lives. In turn, a wider understanding illuminates Japan's broad and comprehensive security policy, as well as its appropriateness, consistency, and effectiveness in responding to the security agenda. Below is an outline of a multilevel and multidimensional analytical framework to elucidate the complexity of the East Asian regional security agenda and Japan's response.

Definitions of Security

The definition of the term *security* has varied from paradigm to paradigm; it is contested and notoriously slippery to nail down (Buzan 1991a: 16). For those concerned with the traditional paradigm and agenda, security refers to the defense of the nation/sovereign state from external military threats (Tickner 1995: 176). For our purposes, security is defined as freeing and protecting human welfare from all forms of potential or actualized threats (Hughes 1999: 32). This definition borrows and combines concepts from critical security theory and peace studies that stress that the achievement of security should not necessarily be equated with the establishment of order and stability per se but in the further goal of the actual emancipation of all objects of security from the threats and structural violence (Galtung 1969; Booth 1991b: 539; Dunn 1991; Devetak 1996: 166). These threats can range from issues of the loss of basic rights, to the deprivation of the conditions of well-being, to concerns about the very ability to ensure life and survival (Väyrycn 1999: 53–54). The military dimension and the role of the sovereign state remain vital. But this more flexible definition makes it possible to gauge global and regional security today, as well as the areas in which actors need to direct their efforts to achieve security.

Security Actors: Referent Objects

Identities and Roles

Security actors can be categorized in three ways according to their identity and role. The first identity is the actor as referent object: the actor is threatened or the focus of insecurity (Buzan et al. 1998: 36–40). The second identity is the actor that imposes threats upon and denies security to other actors. The third identity is the actor as protector of itself or others against threats. In practice, distinguishing these identities is not easy. Depending on the context, actors can assume any or all of these identities. Most obviously, when policymakers and populations of sovereign states feel threatened, they can respond by posing a counterthreat to that actor and by extending protection to other actors. The blurred distinction between victim, aggressor, and protector has increased with globalization, mass media, and the complex channels through which security actors struggle under world opinion. In sum, one person's freedom fighter is another's terrorist.

States as Referent Objects: External and Internal Threats

The nation-state (or, more accurately, the sovereign state) has been the traditional focus and referent object of security. The state has a monopoly of jurisdiction—sovereignty—over a social and territorial area, or "space," delineated by physical geography and human construction. The nation-state has been the basic unit of global and regional space in the modern era. In turn, states exercise sovereign control over all forms of interaction in politics, economics, and security. Thus global and regional spaces have been conceived of as interstate or international social space. Correspondingly, global and regional security space has often been thought of as centered around the interstate and international system, and the sovereign state has been elevated as the principal referent object, denier, and provider of security (Hughes 2001: 409).

This is demonstrated by the fact that national security studies was the progenitor of security studies as a subfield of IR (Baldwin 1995: 121–126). Indeed, the tenets of national security studies have continued to dominate perspectives today. The assumption that sovereign state security can be conflated with the security of the "nation" or general population and citizenry remains strong in security studies. The tendency is to argue that the survival of states is indivisible from the survival of peoples and nations. The result is a view that concentrates not only on states as the key referent objects (Waever 1995: 49) but also on external aspects of state security. For the traditional paradigm, then, security is concerned with external threats to states, especially those threats imposed upon states by interstate conflict—the natural outcome of friction in an international system.

Threats occur on interrelated levels, all of which illuminate the broad overview of the state as a referent object of security. States experience threats from other states through global and regional interstate systems, but those levels also interact. Global interstate conflict is usually the preserve of great powers or superpowers, regional conflict that of medium and small powers. In East Asia, great power conflict has often interacted with regional conflict.

The identity and role of sovereign states is central to our understanding of security, especially for nation-states that associate the security interests of the institution and the national population, and Japan is a good example of this.

In other instances this perspective is inaccurate. The tendency of the traditional security paradigm is to neglect internal threats that arise from a divergence between security interests perceived by states themselves and those perceived by the population. Newer sovereign states encompassing different national and ethnic groups are particularly sensitive to internal threats. It is often the case that such states face small or large ethnic groups who reject the government and are subject to oppression. As a result, these groups seek instead to secure autonomy or to secede; this may launch insurgency movements challenging the integrity and internal stability of the state.

Another internal security problem is any crisis of political legitimacy and leadership. In certain states, the majority of the population may support the cause of national and state integrity yet reject the political legitimacy of the governmental system, the regime, or the elites. The antagonism can center on bad government, mismanagement of the economy, crime and corruption, and the commitment to stable or democratic government. The outcome can be turmoil, violent demonstrations, revolt, and even revolution. If prolonged, political unrest can bring factionalism and civil war. A combination of political crisis and ethnic separatism can lead to the internal disintegration of a state and, in some cases, outright genocide, as in Rwanda during the mid-1990s. Many states in East Asia, especially in Southeast Asia, have been subject to the twin problem of ethnic separatism and lack of political legitimacy. These states have concentrated on dealing with internal/intrastate security threats rather than external/interstate security threats.

However, there is also an inextricable link between intrastate and interstate security dynamics and issues. The diverse ethnic composition of many third world states, and resultant intrastate security problems such as secessionism and irredentism, can often spill over into interstate conflict (Ayoob 1995: 47–48). For instance, a state may interfere in the internal affairs of another to defend an ethnic group with which it has common cause. The state may do so to support secessionist movements and thereby regain sections of territory and population. It may also engage in cynical attempts to play the ethnicity card to focus people's attention on external security issues and thereby respond to and ameliorate internal political stresses. The tensions between India and Pakistan over Kashmir are a long-running example of how secessionism and irredentism can lead to the intermeshing of intrastate and interstate security, even to the point of inducing a nuclear arms race.

Substate and Nonstate Groups as Referent Objects of Security

The focus needs to shift from the nation-state to the security actors and referent objects that are active in social and security spaces, below and outside the state level.

Autonomy, secessionist, and statehood movements can be viewed as the referent object of security due to the perceived repression they experience at the hands of states or other security actors. Such actors may respond by initiating an armed struggle, forming militia and terrorist groups, and undertaking criminal activities. In such instances, societal groups can function as clans and gangs much like the mafia. They may also threaten others. It is difficult to judge whether a societal group is the victim or the aggressor. Those who take a nonviolent approach, and who are mismatched in power capabilities, are often looked at with sympathy. The transnational and transsovereign nature of many such groups means that states face complex challenges due to the limits of their own sovereignty.

Women and children are the final referent group that deserves scrutiny. Traditional security studies, with its ethnocentric (some would claim male gender–centric; see, e.g., Tickner 1992: 1–66) focus upon the state and external interstate conflict, has paid minimal attention to women and children as referent objects. It has become blinkered to the costs of violence borne by women and children as both combatants and noncombatants.

Recent history emphasizes that women have been victims and aggressors in regular, revolutionary, and guerrilla armies and terrorist groups. Recent conflicts have also seen the rise of the phenomenon of child soldiers in Africa and East Asia. According to some estimates, women and children noncombatants comprised roughly 90 percent of all casualties in major conflicts since 1945 (Alexander 1999: 62). Moreover, events in the Balkans since the early 1990s have once again highlighted the deliberate use of rape against women as an instrument of war, ethnic cleansing and impurification, and attacks upon societal identity and security (Kaldor 2001: 52–53; Thakur 2000: 229).

Women as a societal group also have been the object of other indirect forms of violence and insecurity. Those women on the margins of major conflicts have often been the object of military and economic exploitation. But women experience conditions of insecurity even in environments where there is no military conflict. Hence, in many developing states it has been argued that women are the object of structural violence: poor working conditions, unemployment, poverty, and generally low social status (Alexander 1999: 62).

Individuals as Referent Objects of Security

The lowest and most irreducible (Buzan 1991a: 35), but nevertheless the ultimate (Booth 1991c: 319), object of security is the individual. The security of the individual has long been central to liberal political tradition, and it reemerged as an important concept in the 1982 report of the Palme Commission on Disarmament and Security Issues. The report emphasized the need for the economic security of the individual and that state security policy should be framed with the participation of citizens (Rothschild 1995: 56). In the 1990s and early twenty-first century, the individual has received further attention as a referent object due to military, economic, and environmental problems. Many of these problems have impacted individuals disproportionately and have disaggregated the security of individuals from that of their native states. Environmental pollution is one of the most notable examples. Indonesian forest fires and the resulting haze over Indonesia, Malaysia, and Singapore since 1997 have threatened the health and welfare of citizens, even if they do not threaten long-term security.

Moreover, reflecting this shift, the United Nations Development Programme (UNDP) enunciated in 1994 the concept of "human security" (United Nations Development Programme 1994), which attempts to broaden definitions of security outward and downward to the safety of individuals from hunger, disease, crime, and repression (Commission on Global Governance 1995: 81). This extension has been criticized by those who wish to keep the focus of security studies upon the state and because it is next to impossible to frame a policy that would ensure the security of each and every individual within a state (Buzan et al. 1998: 39). However, the acknowledgement of individual security concerns establishes the principle that the security interests of a state and its citizens are not always indivisible and that the concerns of individuals need to be taken into account (Rothschild 1995: 57). Japan's regional security policy has emphasized the individual as referent object and principles of human security. Although Japan's security policy has emphasized basic human needs over human rights, it is not without its inconsistencies.

Organizations as Referent Objects of Security

The final referent objects are organizations in all their forms. In certain regions and contexts, especially in East Asia, it is not always easy to distinguish nongovernmental organizations (NGOs) from official governmental organizations. But in many cases NGOs can be considered as independent and transsovereign security actors. NGOs are capable of denying or providing security to others. Similarly, they can also be the objects of insecurity—as evidenced by the many NGO operatives who have lost their lives in regions of conflict and instability.

National and transsovereign or transnational corporations (TNCs) are another set of referent objects, better known as multinational corporations (MNCs). The common view is that TNCs are more identifiable as providers or deniers in the dimensions of economic and environmental security. Nonetheless, TNCs are also the objects of insecurity during periods of economic crisis.

Last, but certainly not least, another subset is transnational and transsovereign organized criminal organizations. Crime groups, whether Italian-American La Cosa Nostra, Chinese triads, Colombian and Mexican drug cartels, or the emerging Russian mafia usually represent the denial of security to others. But in certain societies, especially in regions where crime supports insurgency movements, these groups are also perceived as providers of security and thus the object of insecurity at the hands of opposing states.

Security Actors: Deniers and Suppliers of Security

External and Internal Levels of Threat

The sovereign nation-state has been considered the most prominent security actor and referent object in the modern era. Likewise, states continue to be responsible for the denial and provision of security to themselves and other actors. Thus states, as the self-proclaimed and sole legitimate authority for the control of the means of violence, both deny and provide external and internal security to others. And despite the erosion of the state's monopoly of violence by actors such as terrorist groups, they retain access to the most powerful weaponry, and they dominate military security through the deployment of military (standing or mercenary) and police forces. In a similar fashion, despite a corresponding erosion in the sphere of economics and the rise of influential competitors such as TNCs, major states continue to be the largest economic actors, individually or in concert, and are the dominant actors in economic security.

States deny security to other actors externally by the initiation of potential or actualized interventions, conflicts, and all-out wars. These threats may occur individually or in combination in the military, economic, and environmental dimensions. The most apparent example of such state activities in the military dimension is interstate conflict on separate or intersecting global and regional levels. But states can also impose threats upon nonstate actors by use of military strikes against terrorist groups, as occurred after the events of September 11 and the U.S.-led campaign in Afghanistan from 2001 onward.

States also impose threats upon other states, nonstate actors, and organizations in the economic dimension. This can occur by the initiation of potential or actual economic sanctions against other states or TNCs and individuals, or by creation of an interstate economic system that imposes threats of economic insecurity upon other states, groups, individuals, and TNCs. For example, a state may assist in the generation of global and regional economic crises, as well as a structure of exploitative dependency relations among developed and developing states.

Many of these same threats may also be utilized by states to deny security internally to societal groups, organizations, and individuals. States can employ military and economic repression against ethnic and separatist minorities within their sovereign territory, even punishing certain individuals for opposition to state dictates. One overt instance was the Iraqi government's use of military force and economic embargoes upon the Kurdish minority. But states may deny security to their citizens in more understated terms, such as the Malaysian government's practice of positive economic discrimination against the Chinese population and in favor of the Malay community.

Conversely, states may provide security to other actors externally and internally. States launch wars, conflicts, interventions, and peacekeeping operations (PKOs) in the military and economic dimensions in the name of providing protection from external threats such as other states, societal groups, individuals, and organizational actors. The most basic function of states has been to provide security to their own populations from external threat; states also work on the individual, bilateral, and multilateral levels to provide security to the populations of other states. Moreover, states utilize their capabilities to supply security internally to various other actors, including their own citizenry, but also specific groups and TNCs. However, this is not to say that states exclusively occupy the identity of provider of security in all contexts and supply "public good" equitably. On the contrary, states will appear as the deniers of security to certain security actors but the provider to others, and even internally states differentiate their security priorities—privileging certain societal groups for protection while discarding others.

Societal Groups and Individuals as Deniers and Suppliers of Security

Societal groups as referent objects may also assume the identities of deniers and providers of security. Ethnic and minority groups can infringe the security of states and other groups and individuals if they are perceived to threaten stability by embarking on a political or military struggle—especially if they become involved in criminal or terrorist activities. But the opposite is also true; that is, groups can be regarded as freedom fighters and the providers of security to minorities subject to repression by states.

Similarly, as many scholars of gender point out, women can in fact assume identities of deniers and providers of security through participation in armed struggle. Moreover, the economic function of women in many societies as the supporters of households means they are also providers of economic security.

In much the same way as individuals can be regarded as the irreducible referent object of security, so they must also be regarded as the irreducible deniers and providers of security functions. Although there is no need to subscribe to a Hobbesian view of a war of "all against all" and individual against individual in the state of nature, individuals retain the capacity to inflict violence and damage upon each other and other security actors. Acts of individual murder and assault remain commonplace, and individuals can pose threats to a society as a whole if they adopt terrorist techniques—as shown by the emergence of one-man bombing campaigns in the United States (the Unabomber) in the 1990s. Individuals in many societies may also feel the responsibility to provide for their own security, especially if the internal policing functions of the state have broken down or where they are perceived to be too severe.

Organizations as Deniers and Providers of Security

NGOs are increasingly seen as providers of security. NGOs, such as aid and development volunteer organizations, can provide immediate security through the supply of basic human needs to societies experiencing famine, disease, and war. Moreover, NGOs are engaged in activities to assist various forms of military, economic, and environmental security to segments of the citizenry. Antinuclear or antilandmine movements have contributed to disarmament and the perceived improvement in security for some actors; NGOs campaigning for fair trade and debt reduction have contributed to the economic security of developing states; and environmental groups have provided improved security on issues of resource depletion, pollution, and environmental degradation. However, care must also be taken in evaluating their contribution. In some cases the counterargument may be made that they lack the public accountability of official interstate organizations such as the World Health Organization (WHO) and United Nations Children's Fund (UNICEF) (Rothschild 1995: 81–82).

TNCs and other business corporations are most usually considered as the deniers of economic, environmental, and even military security. TNCs impose conditions of economic insecurity on states, societal groups, and individuals, as well as other corporations through business activities and competition that can lead to poor working conditions, unemployment and underemployment, poverty, and general economic dislocation. This economic dislocation can provoke external tensions among states, as well as internal tensions within states among societal groups and individuals. The activities of corporations also lead to environmental degradation and can have detrimental effects on military security, not only by the creation of a prosperous or poor economic climate (which can be conducive to increased tensions among security actors and the buildup or reduction of military capacities) but also in terms of the global arms trade (which facilitates these processes).

Nevertheless, TNCs and private businesses can also be a source of security for states, societal groups, and individuals. TNCs can foster ties of interdependence that may promote external security among states or alternatively provide the economic strength to promote independent security. TNCs also provide wealth and employment to segments of a state's population, which delivers general stability and internal security. In addition, TNCs and private firms may provide an income and various welfare benefits and thus economic security to individual workers and their families. Finally, TNCs can provide military security directly through the employment of private armies and mercenaries to protect their business interests, even assisting with the stabilization of sovereign states (Shearer 1998a; Shearer 1998b: 70–72; Singer 2001/2002).

Criminal organizations can be purveyors of security as defenders of ethnic and minority groups. But their primary identity is undoubtedly as deniers of security. Organized crime threatens the security of states by undermining the authority and efficiency of the state, its institutions, and its economy—and thus its capabilities to defend its citizens. In some cases, such as Colombia, criminal organizations may even seek to infiltrate the state and assume its identity. Societal groups are also threatened by organized crime groups that can control segments of the population through violence and exploit women for prostitution. Finally, organized crime directs threats at the individual, as in the narcotics trade, which can subject the individual's economic freedom and damage his or her physical health.

The Interconnection of Security Actor Identities and Levels

This typology of security actor identities establishes different levels of security and demonstrates that the security interests of sovereign states cannot always be equated with those of various societal groups and individuals. However, this is merely an analytical tool designed to assist the understanding of the complex issues, not to suggest that these actors function in isolation from each other. On the contrary, the fate of each level of security actor is firmly bound, negatively or positively, to that of the other levels.

The security of the sovereign state at the top level has a significant impact upon the security of societal groups and individuals at lower levels, either when it itself is threatened as a referent object, or when it imposes threats on its own societal groups or those of other states. Similarly, different security actors are interconnected not only from the top down but also from the bottom up. Hence, if the individual or societal group as the referent object of security experiences a sense of insecurity, then this can also feed into the insecurity of the state, as individuals and groups question the legitimacy of the state and exert political pressure upon it from within. This close interconnection, and the transmission of the consumption, denial, and supply of security among them, is the key to grasping and responding to the complexity of the contemporary security situation.

The Military Security Dimension

Next we examine the different dimensions of security and the related problems and threats that they generate. Specifically, this section concentrates upon three dimensions of security: military, economic, and environmental. The section outlines the types of threat that each dimension can present, as well as the interlinkages among them and to the other dimensions. In addition, it links the analysis of the dimensions of security to the different security actors, examining which level is most dominant in each dimension.

Definitions of Military Security

The military dimension is defined by the imposition of threats of physical violence upon the welfare and security of all security actors. Violent military threats are designed to have a deliberate and eventually destructive impact, either directly or indirectly, upon the human anatomy (crushing, tearing, piercing, burning, poisoning, evaporation) and physiology (denial of air, water, food, movement) (Galtung 1969: 174). In terms of the sheer scale of the concentration of capabilities and technology, it is possible to divide and subdivide the military dimension into nonconventional and conventional threats. These divisions are interlinked.

Nonconventional Military Threats

Nonconventional forms of military threat essentially relate to the use of atomic, biological, and chemical (ABC) WMD. ABC weapons are employed for strategic and tactical purposes on the battlefield; nuclear weapons represent the pinnacle of destructive capabilities within the modern military arsenal. Even though many of these weapons generally involve high-tech expertise in their development, they can be deployed through a variety of high- and low-tech delivery systems, based on land, sea, or air. These systems can include sophisticated ballistic missiles of the short (SRBM), medium (MRBM), long (LRBM), and intercontinental (ICBM) range, launched from fixed and mobile ground sites, from warships and submarines, or from short- and long-range bombers. Alternatively, the miniaturization of many of these weapons has made it possible to deliver them with less sophisticated transports, ships, and aircraft and even by hand, as has been feared after the 9/11 attacks.

The proliferation of certain forms of WMD technology has become a major military security issue. Since the end of the Cold War, the fear, accentuated by 9/11, has been that nonstate terrorist actors may seek to acquire WMD capabilities. The declared legitimization for the U.S.-UK campaign to disarm Iraq in 2003 was in part to prevent the regime from transferring WMD to terrorist groups such as Al-Qaida.

Conventional Military Threats: High-Intensity

Conventional military threats range in terms of the intensity of destructive capabilities and technology employed. At the very top are high-intensity forms of warfare, typically utilizing high-tech weaponry. High-intensity conventional military threats usually involve infantry and mechanized army ground forces (artillery, main battle tanks, and armored personnel carriers); naval sea forces (submarines, missile destroyers, aircraft carriers, and assault ships); and air forces (attack and fighter aircraft, long-range bombers, ballistic missiles tipped with conventional explosive warheads, and reconnaissance and transport aircraft). Ground, sea, and air warfare and weaponry can exist as three separate spheres of military threat, but more usually they exist in combination—airborne operations comprising air and land operations, and amphibious and marine operations involving the use of sea and ground forces, but also support from the air. Indeed, the impulse of modern warfare has been to combine land, sea, and air operations as the three spheres of military activity to concentrate destructive capabilities. In the contemporary period this has been made possible by the role of technology and new battlefield management command, control, communications, computers, and intelligence systems (BMC4^{I}), which allow for the closer integration of ground, sea, and naval forces so as to achieve total domination over the battlefield.

The apogee of this movement is the concept of the revolution in military affairs (RMA) (Freedman 1998; O'Hanlon 2000a; Evans 2000). In theory, RMA enables states to change the face of modern warfare by introducing a fourth sphere of military activity—space—and to obtain the satellite information and weapons stations necessary to instantaneously detect and respond to any threat in any part of the globe. The technology embodied in RMA should allow the United States to strike with land, sea, air, and space forces in a synchronized fashion at any target and to deny an adversary the ability to do the same. The essence of RMA is to offer unprecedented global reach; the ability to selectively commit ground, sea, and air forces and avoid casualties while inflicting damage upon the enemy; and to do all this with near total impunity. In practice, RMA may not produce such results due to its own underdeveloped technology and sheer expense, as well as the ability of asymmetric threats to counter RMA capabilities. But the trend among some military strategists is to avoid the commitment of ground troops, opting instead for stand-off weapons, precision-guided munitions, and smart-bombs.

Not all sovereign states or other security actors with access to conventional military weaponry have the technical or economic resources to impose or defend against the types of military threats that accompany RMA. Many sovereign states aspire to obtain high-tech capabilities; this proliferation is aided and abetted by the developed states, using arms transfers to support proxy wars, or simply for financial gain. But in reality many states use basic techniques of integrated conventional warfare that are reliant upon less-sophisticated technology and land, sea, and air forces in sheer numbers.

Conventional Threats: Low-Intensity

A lower level of technology and intensity may be capable of countering or frustrating the growing sophistication of the developed states, imposing possibly far more hazardous threats upon the entire range of referent object security actors. As commentators point out (Klare 1988; Van Creveld 1991), by far the most significant form of warfare since 1945 has been low-intensity conflict and wars of insurgency, secessionism, and national liberation in Africa, Central Asia, and Indochina. These more traditional postwar and Cold War forms of guerrilla warfare have been added to the mix by a series of more disordered and chaotic guerrilla wars associated with ethnic strife and the breakdown of existing sovereign state structures, as in Somalia, Rwanda, and Bosnia. State and nonstate guerrilla forces have typically fought out these guerrilla wars with low-tech weaponry, ranging from semiautomatic rifles to hand-to-hand combat weapons. In the case of traditional wars of secession and independence, as well as in cases of outside intervention and PKOs in the contemporary period, the adversaries of guerrilla forces have often been the conventional armies of the state, major imperialist powers, or superpowers with access to high-tech and high-intensity capabilities. In many instances, despite the mismatch of raw power capabilities, such forms of low-intensity guerrilla warfare and threat have emerged as victorious.

Low-intensity military threats exist at other levels. The most notable is terrorism. Terrorism is difficult to define, but a workable definition is the use of violence beyond conventions established by a particular society (domestic, international, or otherwise) to instill a climate of fear, to publicize a cause, and to coerce a wider target into submitting to the terrorists' aims. One of the defining characteristics of terrorism is that the violence is often indiscriminate and directed against noncombatants, although individual and collective actors are also targets (Hughes 1998: 41). Hence, terrorist activities employ a mix of violent means and weaponry, ranging in sophistication from prolonged bombing and assassination campaigns against civilian and military targets, to more opportunistic or random hijackings and hostage-taking, to suicide bombings using civilian airliners.

Terrorism follows a variety of causes and is practiced by a variety of security actors. Forms of terrorism include: nationalist terrorists (Irish Republican Army, Basque Fatherland and Liberty); ideological terrorists (Japanese Red Army; Tupac Amaru Revolutionary Movement); religious fanatics (Aum Shinrikyō; Al-Qaida); single-issue fanatics (certain animal rights groups, the Oklahoma City bombing); and state-sponsored terrorism (Hezbollah). In many cases, terrorism can be seen as the extension of guerrilla warfare, as in the instance of the urban tactics of the Shining Path in Peru, the Revolutionary Armed Forces in Colombia, and the Liberation Tigers of Tamil Eelam (Wilkinson 1988: 39–49). Indeed, certain states such as Israel, the People's Republic of China (PRC), and North Korea have employed guerrilla and terrorist threats to achieve independence. In other cases, terrorism is practiced by groups and individuals with no discernible purpose other than the act of destruction itself.

Terrorism is often indistinguishable from the low-intensity military threats presented by organized crime. Organized crime groups such as the Colombian drug cartels, involved in a spectrum of activities including narcotics, piracy on the high seas, arms trading, smuggling, illegal migration, money laundering, gambling, extortion, assassination, and prostitution, have employed assassinations and bombings to achieve their ends (Clutterbuck 1994: 88–94). Guerrilla groups may also employ crime to further their secessionist, nationalist, or ideological struggles, as in the case of the warlords in the Shan state of Burma (known officially as Myanmar since 1989).

Hence, guerrilla, terrorist, and organized crime activities present an interrelated and hazardous set of violent and military threats that affect the security of a range of state, group, and individual actors. These low-intensity security threats are made even more hazardous for two reasons. First, many observers fear that there is a vertical proliferation of capabilities taking place among guerrilla, terrorist, and crime groups. Not only are these actors acquiring more advanced firearms (nondetectable synthetic pistols, high-powered sniper rifles), explosives (semtex), and projectiles (shoulder-fired Stinger missiles); they have shown a propensity to move to qualitatively different levels of destructive power that were formerly the preserve of developed states. The greatest concern, presaged by Aum Shinrikyō's sarin gas attack on the Tokyo subway on 20 March 1995, is that terrorist, guerrilla, and organized crime groups may gain access to chemical, biological, and even nuclear weapons. ABC capabilities in the hands of terrorists would shift these groups from the category of low-intensity conventional threats to nonconventional threats.

Moreover, these groups may inflict damage through nontraditional and nondirect violent means. Cybercrime or cyberterrorism is one example, whereby groups may be able to wreak destruction and cause physical damage to humans by attacking the information and computer systems that support their welfare and security. In many cases, this type of struggle in cyberspace produces economic threats to security. But in others, the damage that could result from interference with power, transportation, emergency services, water, health, sanitation, finance, law enforcement, and food supply systems could also impact human anatomy and physiology (McCardle et al. 2000: 6) and thus constitute military threats.

Second, low-intensity conflicts are hazardous as military threats due to their essential asymmetry. Even though certain guerrilla, terrorist, and crime groups are seeking to proliferate their military capabilities vertically, in most instances they remain at a low level in intensity that is difficult to respond to. The military forces of developed states have been frustrated in the past by the less advanced capabilities of guerrilla movements. The same holds true today. The inability of the United States to defeat smaller and more fluid opponents may sap any enthusiasm for the conflict and lead to the withdrawal of forces. There can exist, then, an essential asymmetry in terms of military threats and possible responses (National Defense Panel 1997: 11; U.S. Department of Defense 2001). Dominated by low-intensity conflicts on the periphery of developed states, today's conflicts suggest that these problems cannot be dealt with by the simple application of overwhelming military firepower. These conflicts may become greater threats to all security actors.

Military Security Actors

Sovereign states are the principal actors in the military security dimension. As referent objects they are subject externally to all forms of nonconventional and conventional threats and are subject internally to conventional low-intensity threats, especially guerrilla warfare and terrorism. In turn, states remain the chief deniers and suppliers of military security externally and internally. At present, states retain the monopoly over nuclear weapons, even if horizontal proliferation is occurring with the transfer of nuclear capabilities to developing states and with the addition of new members of the nuclear club, such as India and Pakistan. The conventional military capabilities of many states also remain unrivaled, with land, sea, and air forces, as well as special operations forces, paramilitaries, and police forces, both imposing and protecting against internal and external threats. Consequently, the threat of external interstate military conflict on the regional and global levels, as well as intramilitary conflict, remain central to the contemporary security agenda.

However, the sovereign state can no longer be regarded as the only referent object of military security. The rise of total war and its associated tactics has meant that military conflicts effect all societal groups. Nonconventional nuclear weapons and the logic of mutually assured destruction (known as MAD) in effect hold hostage the citizenry of states, and conventional warfare, of high- or low-intensity, has generally claimed more civilian than military casualties. The principal casualties of guerrilla warfare, terrorism, and organized crime are societal groups and individuals.

Likewise, not only are societal groups and individuals affected by military threats; they can act as deniers and suppliers of security. Ethnic groups have formed the backbone of certain guerrilla, terrorist, and organized crime activities, and individuals are increasingly gaining access to the technology necessary to produce terrorist bombs and practice cyberterrorism—as demonstrated by computer viruses that threaten to disable networks worldwide. Finally, organizations, including crime groups and TNCs, have become actors in the dimensions of military security.

The Economic Security Dimension

Definitions of Economic Security

Economic security is defined as those threats to welfare that arise from the dynamics of economic activity. Economic welfare threats range from access to basic human needs (food, water, shelter, clothing, education), to more complex questions of growth, income, and employment (Buzan 1991a: 237). Economic activity itself can be divided into production, trade, finance, and aid.

Exactly what constitutes a threat to economic welfare can be dependent upon the level of economic development reached and the type of political-economic system under which it has been achieved (Liew 2000: 193–194). For developed liberal economies, economic threats may be less concerned with basic human needs and more with the maintenance of high levels of income. In developed command and socialist economies, the concentration is more upon the stability of income and employment. In mixed economies there is an attempt to balance the growth of income with a social security system to dampen the impacts of economic change. In developing economies the emphasis may be on basic human needs while attempting to achieve higher growth. Hence, even though some have criticized command economies, some (like China prior to liberalization in the 1980s) can be said to have protected against economic insecurity by alleviating mass poverty and providing for basic human needs. Under conditions of economic restructuring and change, these questions can shift. The current dominance of liberal economic models in the era of globalization, and the subsequent collapse or deterioration of socialist models, has brought into focus the tensions between different conceptions of economic security and the threats that arise in the process of economic adjustment.

Economic Security Actors

As with the other dimensions of security, considerations of economic security affect and interlink the fate of all security actors. Reference to basic human needs carries the implication that the individual is the irreducible referent object of the economic as well as the military dimension of security. However, economic security of individuals and societal groups may also, although not necessarily, be bound up negatively and positively with that of sovereign states. This is because sovereign states are also the object of economic insecurity, both internally and externally, and are involved in attempts, based upon the nature of their production, trade, finance, and aid policies, to impose and defend against economic security threats that affect the security of their own citizens and the citizens of other states.

In addition to individuals and sovereign states, ethnic and other societal groups are economic security actors. Specific ethnic groups may be perceived as experiencing marginalization or the differentially heavy impact of economic activity and thus form the referent object of security. Likewise, women often bear the brunt of substandard working conditions, low incomes, and unstable employment that result in poverty. Conversely, these groups may also be seen as the deniers of providers of security. The overseas Chinese in East Asia dispose of considerable economic resources and are perceived by their own ethnic groups as providers of economic security but often by other ethnic groups in states such as Malaysia and Indonesia as deniers of security due to their believed monopolistic domination of economic opportunity in certain business sectors. The economic security of the state is again bound up with the economic security of all actors. If any of these actors suffers economically, then the economic vitality of the sovereign state is also at risk.

Finally, organizations are crucial economic security actors. Domestic corporations and TNCs can provide economic security through their production, trade, finance, and aid activities, as well as the related benefits of income, employment, growth, and development. Corporations, of course, can be perceived as denying security due to the costs of economic activity, including poor working conditions and wages, unemployment and underemployment, and economic crashes—all of which impact the security of individuals, societal groups, and sovereign states. Another set of important economic security actors are the organized crime groups discussed above. Organized crime is in essence a form of illicit, but nevertheless vigorous, economic activity that supplies and denies security. Individuals, societal groups, and TNCs and sovereign states that are associated with such activities reap the economic security benefits of income and employment. Organized crime also threatens the economic security of similar sets of actors in other contexts, however, due to its ability to disrupt economic welfare through exploitation and corruption.

Economic Exclusion, Disparity, Rivalry, and Dislocation

Economic activity and change can be said to have integrative and disintegrative outcomes with regard to security (Camilleri 1994: 184–185). Viewed from a liberal economic perspective, the closer integration and interdependence of production, trade, finance, and aid links among a range of actors can bring about economic inclusion, equity, cooperation, and stability, all of which are perceived to have positive effects for security. This is the essence of complex interdependence and "democratic peace" arguments (Doyle 1986), and attempts to promote security through economic interdependence are central to comprehensive security policy in general and Japanese security policy in East Asia.

Yet there is also a disintegrative flipside to all forms of economic activity and transition, with correspondingly negative effects on security. Economic inclusion can also be mirrored by a process of economic exclusion for certain actors. Economic security actors may be excluded, of their own volition or involuntarily, from processes of economic development, leading to a deterioration of their economic welfare.

For actors that do embark upon processes of economic restructuring, the negative parallel to economic equity is often economic inequity and disparity. Economic change creates winners and losers among all actors. Individuals and societal groups may experience inequalities of income and welfare, which can produce social discontent that feeds into political instability. Similarly, states may also experience economic disparities, both internally among different societal groups and regions, and externally in comparison to other sovereign states. Internal economic disparities can have unpredictable consequences for security, with wealthier regions pulling ahead of less prosperous ones, raising the specter of political fragmentation and exacerbating internal security threats.

Likewise, economic disparities among states can give rise to the next disintegrative problem of economic security—that of economic rivalry. Governments attach importance to economic development as a means to ensure internal and external security. Development provides sovereign states with economic capabilities to satisfy welfare demands of citizens, to promote social and political stability, and thus to ameliorate internal security threats. This is particularly so in East Asia for states that have relied on economic development to establish their political legitimacy. Development can also provide states with the economic and military capabilities necessary to defend citizens from various forms of external threats. Indeed, traditional security paradigms often tended to ascribe importance to the economic performance of states simply as an indicator of relative military capabilities, and thus as a subset of military security, rather than as a dimension of security in its own right with its own threats and responses (Cable 1995: 307; Naya 1999: 83–85). Hence, if sovereign states perceive themselves as falling behind, losing out to, or even in danger of being subject to domination by other states in the process of economic development (Sorensen 1990: 10), with possible implications for internal and external security, then this may create a zero-sum and neomercantilist impulse to gain exclusive control over economic resources. In turn, this rush to seize scarce economic resources, whether they are natural renewable (fresh water, clean air, fertile soils, forests, fish stocks), nonrenewable (fossil fuels, nonfuel minerals, metals), or human-created (markets), can be seen by other states as threatening their economic security (Maull 1989). Their response may be to initiate an economic or military conflict to retain control over them.

History is replete with examples of sovereign states attempting to seize or regain control over economic resources through economic sanctions and military force. Other security actors are not immune to this rivalry for economic resources. Studies have demonstrated how ethnic conflict and rural and urban unrest have been generated by disputes over scarce natural resources such as fresh water and agricultural land (Gleick 1993; Lowi 1993; Homer-Dixon 1994). In particular, intrastate and cross-border migration has been responsible for such tensions at the substate and societal group levels, but that can also lead to conflict at the interstate level.

Economic dislocation is the final set of economic insecurity issues. Economic integration, particularly the process of adjustment to a liberal market economy (Buzan 1984: 620–621), is usually accompanied by what has been termed by Charles Kindleberger as "manias, panics and crashes" (Kindleberger 2001). These produce sharp falls in income and varying degrees of unemployment and underemployment for individuals and societal groups. The extreme downswings in the business cycle to which liberal capitalism is susceptible can reduce moderately wealthy individuals and societal groups to a condition of poverty quickly, and this dislocative effect is accentuated if sovereign states are slow to react to economic crisis or provide no social safety net for citizens.

Additionally, economic dislocation often gives rise to intra- and interstate migration as individuals and ethnic or socioeconomic groups subject to economic hardship uproot themselves and move elsewhere in search of employment and economic security. In these instances, migration caused by economic dislocation can compound economic rivalry. The social discontent that follows the frustration of hopes for economic advancement brings about social and political upheaval and can worsen ethnic tensions. Migration across borders can also feed into conflict between home and host states. The degree to which migration produced by economic dislocation produces interstate friction may depend upon the relative volume of migrants, their ethnic compatibility with the existing population of the host state, and the economic ability of the host state and its citizens to absorb and support migrants (Weiner 1995: 196–197). But if migrants are perceived as an economic and social burden, and thus an endangerment to the economic security of the host state and its citizens, this may create international tensions, most especially if the home state is thought to be deliberately sanctioning the migration.

Perceived threats to the economic security of a state can also produce other forms of security threats. Migrants may be viewed as a threat to the ethnic identity of a state and its citizens (Buzan et al. 1998: 121), or as an "enemy within"–type threat to social stability, resulting in political and even military tensions within states and along borders in states where migrants are often concentrated.

Organized Crime and Piracy

Finally, the issue of migration focuses attention upon an economic security threat—namely, organized crime—that sits in-between and exploits the integrative and disintegrative effects of economic change (Cusimano 2000: 17–18). Crime, in the same way as any other economic activity, is subject to the laws of supply and demand (Stares 1996: 47). The disintegrative effects of liberal capitalism account for the supply, or "push," factors that promote forms of organized crime. Economic exclusion, disparity, rivalry, and dislocation can produce powerful incentives for individuals, societal groups, and even sovereign states to engage in criminal activities to escape poverty. Hence, it is no coincidence that the major sources of supply for illegal commodities such as narcotics are concentrated in the developing states of Latin America and East Asia.

Piracy is defined by the International Maritime Bureau (IMB) as "an act of boarding or attempting to board any ship with the intent to commit theft or any other crime and with the intent or capability to use force in the furtherance of that act." Piracy is also prevalent in these regions. At the same time, the integrative effects of liberal capitalism produce demand, or "pull," factors, as well as supply factors, that foster a market for the commodities of organized crime. For instance, the wealth of developed states and their citizens encourages the consumption of drugs for remedial and symbolic uses (Stares 1996: 60–63). Globalization, characterized by the growing interdependence and liberalization of the developed economies, enhances the trafficking and supply conditions of organized crime (Andreas 2002; Coker 2002: 48). Deregulation and the declining control of sovereign states over flows of finance, telecommunications, and transportation assist legitimate economic interchange by TNCs, but they are also capable of being utilized by crime groups for illegal activities. Organized crime groups can negotiate deals using cell phones and the latest telecommunications technology, then transfer money via the legitimate banking system to offshore accounts for laundering. The expansion of global air and sea traffic also helps organized crime groups to move increasing volumes of illegal commodities, including human beings for the purposes of prostitution and illegal migration. In essence, organized crime groups are simply mimicking the activities of TNCs (Flynn 2000: 52). Meanwhile, the sheer volume of deregulated economic transactions means that it is harder for authorities to monitor and intercept illegal transactions.

Organized crime groups are thus evading sovereign controls and becoming transsovereign in nature. The business of organized crime is expanding greatly in scale. Estimates of the annual revenue of the global drug trade range from U.S.$100 billion to U.S.$500 billion (Dziedzic 1990: 533; Flynn 2000: 45), the latter figure putting it second behind the arms trade among the world's largest industries. The economic security benefits for those engaged in organized crime are great, especially for those at the very downstream end of the market.

The range of organized crime activities, including narcotics, piracy, arms trading, smuggling, illegal migration, money laundering, gambling, extortion, assassination, and prostitution, also produces negative economic security effects (Godson and Williams 1998: 69). Organized crime activities may compromise the security of the individual through the direct appropriation or embezzlement of wealth, or more indirectly by creating an environment that saps the individual of economic vitality. This may come about through wasteful economic addiction to narcotics. Alternatively, the corruption and diversion of economic resources resulting from organized crime can damage legal frameworks underpinning economic activities and decrease economic opportunity for individuals.

Organized crime also inflicts economic damage on sovereign states, depriving them of tax revenues and complicating general economic management. Crime groups may use financial power to buy bureaucratic and political influence, leading to a distortion of economic policies and an undermining of general confidence in that state's economy.

Lastly, the threat of organized crime extends into the other dimensions of security. Organized crime is an inherently violent activity and poses a military threat to all security actors. States fear organized crime as an internal security threat because it can be perpetrated in support of ethnic separatism. The threat of organized crime also extends threats into the environmental dimensions, including "ecocrimes" involving the dumping of toxic waste and smuggling of endangered flora and fauna (Godson and Williams 1998: 69–70).

The Environmental Security Dimension

Definitions of Environmental Security

Environmental security is defined here as those threats to welfare that arise as a result of drastic change and degradation in the natural environment upon which mankind depends for survival. Hence, for some analysts environmental security represents "ultimate" security (Myers 1993), and the sustainability of the biosphere is the greatest long-term challenge to human survival (Cox 1996: 517). The issue has emerged into the mainstream security debate during the post–Cold War period. Some observers have argued that environmental security is simply a short-term distraction from the long-term agenda of military security afforded by the temporary respite brought about by the end of the Cold War (Deudney 1990). The urgency of environmental degradation threatens to overwhelm the "conditions of human existence on a large scale" (Buzan 1991a: 450) and warrants a detailed examination.

Environmental Threats: Natural and Manmade

Environmental threats consist of two types—natural and manmade—although there is a connection between the causation and outcomes of the two. "Natural" environmental threats refer to those that take effect largely as the result of the functioning of the biosphere without significant human interference or control. These include natural disasters such as volcanic eruptions, earthquakes, tidal waves, El Niño, torrential rains and floods, landslides, drought, and forest fires. This category also includes infectious diseases and epidemics such as malaria, cholera, tuberculosis, yellow fever, Ebola, AIDS (Pirages and Runci 2000; Elbe 2002), and SARS (severe acute respiratory syndrome). These natural disasters and diseases have accounted for a huge number of deaths throughout history, as well as economic dislocation as people flee their path.

The distinction between natural and manmade environmental threats is not always easy to discern, given that the human interference associated with the former often influences the size and speed of impact of the latter. The spread of disease is assisted by increasing social interaction. In particular, humankind's tendency to degrade the natural environment has had an influence upon certain "natural" environmental phenomena such as extremes of climate, drought, and floods. Manmade environmental degradation and disasters can be subdivided into three subcategories. First, there is the depletion of renewable and nonrenewable natural resources, such as animal and fish stocks, agricultural land, and forests. Second, there is pollution of land, sea, and air due to deliberate or accidental release of toxic and hazardous industrial byproducts, such as carbon dioxide, oil, heavy metals, and nuclear radiation. Third, and interlinked with the first two but on a qualitatively more damaging and possibly irreversible level, there is the human interference with and alteration of ecosystems. This includes deforestation; desertification; land degradation and urbanization; loss of biodiversity in species and habitat of flora and fauna; and ozone depletion, global warming, rises in sea level, and climatic changes (Elliott 2000: 159; Wirth 2000; Buzan et al. 1998: 74–75). This last category has produced the most dramatic predictions of the extinction of humankind.

Environmental Security Actors

In one sense the natural environment itself is the most important referent object of security due to its systematic attack by humankind, and it has responded in kind as the imposer of ultimate threats to human survival. However, there is a need to identify a range of human-derived security actors that also occupy the role of referent objects and imposers of and defenders from threats. In traditional security analysis, there has still been an attempt to link the issue to national security studies by viewing environmental problems as the substance of interstate conflicts. Indeed, it is possible to support this view given that environmental problems have raised tensions among states in East Asia. Sovereign states can then be viewed as the referent objects of environmental security if they are deprived of the ability to provide access to vital resources for citizens. Conversely, states are also the imposers of and defenders against environmental security problems depending on their own environmental policies. Hence, some states may largely disregard environmental concerns in the rush to achieve economic development (China at present, for example), whereas developing states may be more concerned with using their capabilities to work for the protection of the natural environment. States may even deliberately inflict environmental damage as a weapon of warfare.

However, the most notable referent objects of environmental security are individuals. The essence of environmental security is that as a natural phenomena it does not respect state borders and can directly impact individuals without regard to government capabilities in the military and economic dimensions. Yet individuals should not be seen as the sole referent objects of environmental security, as they can both deny and supply security in this dimension. Individuals may deny environmental security through individual consumption patterns that lead to environmental degradation, or through patterns of agriculture such as slash and burn that lead to environmental imbalances and destruction.

Finally, organizations also need to be seen as important actors in denying and providing environmental security. TNCs and business corporations of various types (electrical power, chemical, fishing, logging, agricultural) are responsible for much of the environmental destruction affecting the developed and developing worlds. But they can also limit the environmental impact by scaling back or altering their activities through the use of environmentally friendly technologies. NGOs are another important set of actors that work for environmental security. Greenpeace and the World Wildlife Fund are two examples of NGOs curbing certain forms of environmental destruction through a combination of government lobbying, direct action, and the construction of transsovereign environmental advocacy links.

Approaches to Achieving Security

The section above outlined a series of interconnected security actors and security dimensions. The chapter now turns to the various approaches to ensure the provision security. In broad terms, it is possible to conceive of the construction of a viable security policy to meet a variety of security challenges through the capabilities or power of security actors and the frameworks through which that capacity is deployed.

Capacity: Political/Diplomatic, Military, and Economic Power

The distribution of capabilities or power to address security issues is uneven among security actors. Sovereign states still retain the greatest capabilities due to their ability to mobilize other actors—whether societal groups, individuals, or organizations—for security ends. Yet other types of security actors are increasingly acquiring their own capabilities to supply security, and these actors should also be taken into account.

The capabilities most traditionally associated with security policy are those of political/diplomatic power and military power. Sovereign states have been the main gatekeepers of diplomacy in the modern era, responsible for the mediation of state interests and the obviation of conflict to create the conditions for security. In many cases states will attempt to achieve ends through bargaining and negotiation, backed by economic and military coercion. In other cases, states may exercise more indirect forms of power by creating the norms and regimes of the interstate relations that determine the rules of the game for other states to follow, and that thus restrain their behavior. One such example is the principle and norm of sovereignty that gives rise to the practice of nonintervention and hinders the ability of one state to interfere in the internal affairs of another. Sovereign states certainly continue to dispose of the principal forms of military power and are able to coerce other actors through the disposal of military, paramilitary, and police forces. Nevertheless, states are also rivaled increasingly by societal groups, individuals, and organizations with access to military weaponry.

In addition to political/diplomatic and military power, economic power is essential to security policy. Sovereign states use economic power in the areas of trade, investment, and aid to prevent and deal with conflict situations. States may extend positive economic sanctions, such as the provision of financial or food aid, to alleviate economic hardship that can generate conflict.

States also employ more indirect forms of economic power to generate interstate security. "Democratic peace" arguments stress that economic integration among states raises the costs of noncooperation and conflict, which in turn should moderate interstate political and military behavior. Hence, states that can determine the shape of the global and regional economies and integrate other states into it should be able to exercise a degree of economic power for security purposes.

Sovereign states also remain the dominant actors in disposing of economic power. But there is also a strong case for viewing other economic actors such as TNCs as exercising power on similar lines. TNCs can exercise economic power by providing positive (investment and trading links) and negative economic sanctions (withdrawal of investment and trading links). In an age of globalization, TNCs are able to exploit capital mobility, and the concomitant ability to offer positive and negative economic sanctions that affect the economic and political security of a state's citizenry, to exert leverage and secure preferential investment and trading conditions. Moreover, TNCs form an essential element of any attempt to engage other states for security ends. Even though sovereign states can initiate economic interdependence by creating the political environment that reduces barriers to economic interaction, ultimately private-sector TNCs are the principal forgers of closer economic ties among states and citizens. Therefore, sovereign states need to consider how they can enlist the economic power of TNCs to maximize the effectiveness of any security policy that utilizes economic power.

This is not to imply that only one subdivision can be used exclusively to deal with only one security dimension. For instance, diplomatic and military power may be used by sovereign states to deal with military threats. Economic power can also be used to supplement, and even substitute for, military power in certain cases. Economic power assists with the creation of conditions for economic, social, and military stability that prevent the outbreak of conflicts; it can also be used in military conflicts to provide positive and negative sanctions to moderate the threat.

Frameworks for the Deployment of Power

Next this chapter considers the frameworks and channels through which actors deploy capacities to attain security. First, sovereign states, societal groups, individuals, and organizations can deploy power through independent action. Sovereign states have exercised diplomatic, military, and economic capacities independently and unilaterally. Hence, the right of states to self-defense is universally recognized. After 9/11 the United States emphasized its right to act unilaterally in its own self-defense. Societal groups, individuals, and organizations also exercise a degree of independent action in seeking security.

Security actors may also work in concert to establish frameworks for the deployment of capabilities and the achievement of security. States exercise diplomatic and economic power through bilateral arrangements and also may exercise military power through a bilateral military treaty and alliance. Sovereign states may also act in concert to form multilateral security arrangements. The most common ones occur in relation to military threats.

States form international organizations and multilateral alliances to achieve collective security and to facilitate the mutual exercise of military power. The UN Charter recognizes the right of collective self-defense, and the North Atlantic Treaty Organization (NATO) mandates that each member recognize a threat to one as a threat to all and respond accordingly through collective military capabilities. However, sovereign states can also stop short of collective multilateral military arrangements and alliances and approach military security through other common and cooperative multilateral arrangements.

Common security—as first conceptualized by the Palme Commission in 1982, and adopted to some degree by the Organization for Security and Cooperation in Europe (OSCE) during the Cold War as a means to reduce bipolar tensions with the Soviet Union—stresses that even sovereign states in an adversarial relationship share a degree of interdependence and a common security fate (Väyryen 1999: 55–59). This is because in the event of conflict, particularly one involving nuclear weapons, both sides could equally expect to suffer catastrophic damage. *Common security* emphasizes the necessity for adversaries to work with each other and alleviate the conditions and miscalculations that can lead to unwanted conflict, involving steps such as the increased interchange of information on military capabilities and budgets. *Cooperative security* makes no attempt to designate certain states within a region as adversaries and instead stresses the need for all regional states, even those of potential concern, to cooperate to eliminate sources of military conflict. The cooperative security approach involves no military commitment on the part of participants but requires increased interstate dialogue and preventive diplomacy on military issues (Kamiya 1997: 151–152).

Sovereign states therefore do invest much energy in the creation of multilateral arrangements to deal with military problems. But they may also create multilateral frameworks to exercise diplomatic and economic power to deal with threats in the economic and environmental dimensions. Hence, many international summits, institutions, and organizations function as collective security arrangements although they are not often overtly ascribed this function per se. The UN Earth Summit in Rio in 1992 and the Kyoto Summit on Global Warming in December 1997 were charged with preserving the biosphere and the consequent alleviation of the security risk involved in its destruction. Likewise, decisions made by developed states to provide financial assistance to developing states suffering from financial crisis can also be linked to a security agenda designed to alleviate poverty, social and political unrest, and consequently intrastate and interstate military tensions.

Furthermore, states can act in concert with different security actors. In terms of military security, sovereign states may augment their own military power by cooperating with societal groups or organizations within the territory of another state. For example, the United States has supported guerrilla and terrorist movements, and even organized crime, if it is has been perceived to advance its interests.

Conversely, actors below the state level may move beyond self-reliance to cooperate with other actors of the same or different type, as well as with states. For instance, guerrilla, terrorist, and organized crime groups have been known to forge links with similar actors in other regions to enhance their military capacity through the exchange of arms and tactics. Likewise, TNCs forge business alliances with other corporations to increase their economic power capacity.

Conclusion: The Complex Security Agenda and Comprehensive Responses

Security concepts and global and regional security agendas are complex. The security agenda has expanded its conceptual horizons to involve many actors. Security is no longer the exclusive preserve of sovereign states. Sovereign states and their external and internal security concerns remain central. However, societal groups, individuals, and organizations must be considered as referent objects of security and as deniers and suppliers of security to others. Moreover, the security fate of each actor impacts upon and is interlinked with the security of others. The deepening of the levels of security actors has also been accompanied by a widening of the dimensions of security threats beyond just military threats to include economic and environmental ones. In turn, the approaches employed to meet the challenges rely on more than diplomatic and military power and must incorporate economic power. What is more, these forms of power are increasingly at the disposal of many actors and must be deployed through unilateral, bilateral, and multilateral levels.

The picture that emerges is one of mutually interlinked security actors, dimensions of security, and approaches to security. Hence, the ultimate response to security challenges that is needed is one that can also cut across and interlink all actors' threats and responses. This leads logically to the conclusion that the most efficacious form of security policy is one that is comprehensive. Sovereign states as the primary actors will need to take the lead in conceptualizing such comprehensive approaches, but they will also need to address the security concerns of a range of actors, in a range of threat dimensions, using a range of forms of power through a range of frameworks.

Chapter 2 looks at the complexities, characteristics, and causation behind the contemporary security challenges facing East Asia.

2

East Asia's Cold War Security Agenda

In addition to identifying and categorizing the security agenda in East Asia, this chapter aims to explicate the processes responsible for its generation. Specifically, it will argue that it is necessary to examine the evolution and causation of the security agenda in East Asia in tandem with the evolution and characteristics of the political economy of the region from the postwar to the contemporary period. This can be comprehended only with reference to three interlinked processes: decolonization, bipolarization, and proto-globalization (and then globalization). The interrelation and cumulative effects of these three processes shaped the characteristics of the sovereign states and other security actors; created the conditions for military, economic, and environmental insecurity; and determined the range of capabilities and frameworks available to respond to security problems.

This political economy–oriented approach is vital. With it one can evaluate the degree of effectiveness of Japan's security policy. The true quality and worth of Japan's security policy can be ascertained only through an analysis of how far it seeks to address root causes of issues on the regional agenda, which in turn can be ascertained only by an analysis of its origins and causation.

In addition, the historical and political economy approach is crucial for comprehending the methods and tools that Japan has selected. Japan's comprehensive security policy traditionally placed great emphasis on economic alongside military power and on economic stabilization and state-building. Japan's past and continuing predisposition can be understood by reference to its realization that the East Asian security agenda, in the military, economic, and environmental dimensions, has been determined by major shifts in the region's political economy and the challenges of state-building. Finally, the historical and political economy approach is essential to provide the international context and analysis in later chapters.

The section below provides a historical framework for understanding the transformation of the political economy of East Asia as the outcome of decolonization, bipolarization, and proto-globalization. It also explains the impact of these transformations on the regional security agenda, in terms of the military, economic, and environmental threats dimensions, the actors involved, and the types of responses.

East Asian Security Dynamics

Definitions of the Cold War

An examination of the historical phases and processes of political economy that influenced the rise and evolution of the contemporary security agenda in East Asia shows that they continue to influence it. The actual historical periodization of the Cold War is subject to some debate—with "traditionalist" studies locating the start of the Cold War in the immediate postwar period as the irreconcilable nature of U.S. and Soviet Union strategic interests became apparent (Painter and Leffler 1994); whereas "revisionists" trace the Cold War's initiation back to the later stages of World War II, when the United States foresaw "atomic diplomacy" directed at Japan as a means to check future Soviet expansion in Eurasia following Germany's eventual defeat (Sherwin 1994: 77–94; Alperovitz 1994). Almost as controversial are attempts to date the exact end of the Cold War. The fall of the Berlin Wall in 1989 is often taken as the symbolic date, whereas many commentators view the practical end as coming in the period of détente in the 1970s, with the "second Cold War" following the Soviet invasion of Afghanistan in 1979 and stretching into the 1980s and 1990s, marking the last gasp of the Cold War system. Moreover, the problem depends on the regional context, with events in Europe and East Asia in related but not strict synchronization. Hence, some would argue that the Cold War never in fact began at all in East Asia; that the security issues from the late 1940s to the early 1990s were the product of nationalist struggles and thus unrelated to those in Europe; and that the term *Cold War* used with regard to East Asia is a misnomer. Other studies, however, insist that the Cold War in parts of the region such as the Korean Peninsula, with the continuing military standoff between North and South Korea, has been slower to fade or has yet to end.

The term *periodization* is used here in two senses that draw upon the major strengths of the above arguments and bridge the divides by picking up on the common analytical themes.

First, the Cold War is understood as the historical period that runs from late World War II and the immediate postwar years through to the late 1980s and early 1990s; it can be further split into "first" and "second" Cold War phases, divided by the détente of the 1970s. This chronological approach spans the initiation and cessation of the Cold War.

Second, the Cold War is also understood as a historical period that is given coherence and demarcated from other periods by the characteristics, confluences, and relative intensity of processes of political economy that generated certain security problems. Hence, "traditionalist" and "revisionist" views concur despite division over timing and responsibility; the Cold War period was characterized by the intensification of U.S.-Soviet strategic military competition and the imposition of a bipolar political economy.

Nevertheless, there is also the need to acknowledge that the Cold War as a historical period and set of security issues cannot be understood solely as the product of bipolarization. If the Cold War encompasses and encapsulates the period from the late 1940s to the early 1990s, this leads to the danger that other processes of political economy responsible for security problems will be obscured. In the case of East Asia, the Cold War period was characterized by intertwining processes of bipolarization, decolonization, and proto-globalization. Indeed, it is arguable that decolonization was in fact just as important as, or more so than, bipolarization in driving security issues in the Cold War period and has continued to be the underlying security dynamic today.

Bipolarization of the Global Political Economy

During the Cold War, the structure of the global political economy was dominated by great power and superpower confrontation between the United States and the Soviet Union. Superpower confrontation may have originated in ideological divisions over liberal democracy and socialism, but it generated and was subsequently sustained by military, political, and economic competition, giving rise to distinct forms of political economy on the global and regional scales and to the process of bipolarization. The bipolar political economy, by definition, was bifurcated with its respective halves centered upon the dual poles of U.S. and Soviet hegemony. The U.S. hegemonic pole was larger in geographic scope, being centered on the sovereign states of North America and Western Europe and extending into Latin America and East Asia. The U.S. pole was characterized by a system of political economy that promoted liberal capitalism and generated economic interdependence among sovereign states in production, trade, finance, and aid. In a sense, such economic interdependence actually constituted a form of proto-globalization, largely limited to the Northern and Western Hemispheres. It is possible to label the U.S.-dominated pole in the global political economy as the *world of interdependence* during the Cold War.

The Soviet pole existed on a smaller geographical scale, stretching across the Eurasian continent in the Northern and Eastern Hemispheres. The Soviet Union constructed a system of political economy that promoted increased economic interdependence among sovereign states in production, trade, finance and aid, all based upon principles of socialism and planned economy. But the Soviet pole exhibited a lesser degree of economic dynamism with regard to its ability to integrate sovereign-state economies. Consequently, it is more appropriate to label the Soviet-dominated pole in the global political economy as the *world of independence,* resistant to absorption into the U.S.-dominated world of interdependence and proto-globalization.

However, the global political economy in this period was subject to greater complexity. First, the bipolar division of states, as well as the physical boundaries of the system itself, were unclear and fluid. The progression of the Cold War brought about fissures and defections at the regional level from both sides. In East Asia, the system was challenged by processes of tripolarization. The Sino-Soviet split of the 1960s rendered divisions within the world of independence and created a long-term struggle between the Soviet Union and China vis-à-vis one another and the United States for influence.

Second, many sovereign states defy easy compartmentalization into either the U.S. or Soviet camps. Instead, some states remained neutral, sitting on the margins of the bipolar divide or flitting in and out of both the worlds of interdependence and independence. Such states, predominantly developing states concentrated in the Southern Hemisphere, were integrated one way or another into the U.S. and Soviet political economies. The Soviet Union extended preferential production, trade, finance, and aid links to a number of developing states in Latin America, Africa, and East Asia to secure support in the political and economic struggle. In turn, the United States competed to extend similar links to developing states across these regions; it was successful in many cases in establishing a system of center-periphery economic relations that extended outward and gradually integrated states in the South.

Sovereign states accepted or resisted the economic tug-of-war, often seeking political and economic nonalignment and implementing policies of economic autarky such as import substitution. However, many states on the margin acquiesced to one side or carefully balanced their reliance upon the two so as to ensure economic development and survival. In this sense, then, it is important to refine our understanding of the process of bipolarization and to note that there was a third component of the global political economy, located mainly in the Southern Hemisphere. As the Cold War progressed, this *world of dependence* became increasingly merged and subordinated to the worlds of interdependence and independence (Spero 1997).

The section below investigates the process of decolonization, its impact on the ordering of the regional political economy, and its particular characteristics, which in combination with bipolarization were able to help form the security agenda.

Decolonization and the Political Economy

The Western Colonial Legacy

Prior to the end of World War II and the onset of the Cold War, colonization was principally responsible for the ordering of the East Asian political economy. By the middle of the nineteenth century the imperial and great powers of the West (or in the proxy form as trading companies such as the Dutch East India Company and British East India Company) had acquired a series of colonies in Southeast Asia and contributed to the gradual dismemberment of China. The process involved attempts to impose upon and replicate within East Asia a derivative of the modern sovereign state system then found in Europe and the United States (T. Shiraishi 2000: 106–112), although the colonial administrative territories subsequently created were mere adjuncts, dependent upon and oriented politically and economically toward colonial rulers.

More specifically, colonization required that existing political and economic space in East Asia should be reordered, delimited, and subjugated in accordance with the principle of territorial sovereignty. Hence, the ethnicities, religions, and languages that had defined precolonial political and economic space were replaced with or suppressed by the principle of territorial sovereignty. It dictated that the colonial powers exercise exclusive jurisdiction over a tightly demarcated territorial space and control all forms of political and economic interaction within and among sovereign territorial units. The effect was to truncate or redirect the ethnic, religious, and language ties and the forms of political and economic interaction that had existed prior to the imposition of sovereign borders. Moreover, the effects were accentuated when the imperial powers, for administrative convenience or as the result of horse-trading territorial acquisitions, imposed sovereign borders with total disregard for, or in contradistinction to, the precolonial ethnic ties in East Asia.

Colonization can thus be viewed as a process of remapping the political and economic space in East Asia into territorial and administrative units under the control of imperial powers based upon the principles of territorial sovereignty. This is the *territorialization* of the regional political economy. But territorial sovereignty as the ordering principle did not sit well with many in the region and engendered an array of political and economic contradictions and distortions.

First, within the territorial borders of a particular colony there could be forced together two or more hostile ethnic groups. Moreover, the policy of ascribing a distinct and rigid ethnic identity to loosely identified societal groups enhanced the sense of political and economic division among groups. Following their foundation of the new model colony of Singapore in the early nineteenth century, for instance, the British ascribed strict administrative and ethnic identities to Chinese, Malay, Indian, Eurasian, and European populations, obliging them to divide not only physically into different residential quarters in the city but also cognitively into different political, economic, and societal units (T. Shiraishi 2000: 92–102).

Colonial possessions in Southeast Asia most typically consisted of a majority ethnic group accompanied by a variety of minority ethnic groups. In the Philippines, the United States grouped a population that was more than 90 percent Christian Malay, but it also included Muslim Malay minorities in Mindanao and a small Chinese minority; in Burma, the British formed a colony comprised a 70 percent Burmese majority, as well as substantial minorities of Shan and Karen tribes; and the Netherlands East Indies contained a population that was around half Javanese, with large Sundanese, Madurese, and other minorities scattered across the former kingdoms of the Indonesian archipelago. This shoehorning, this raising of the distinct consciousness, had the unintended consequences of laying the foundations of nationalist sentiment in Southeast Asia and creating ethnic tensions. These latent tensions were exacerbated by the political and economic policies of the imperial powers (Godement 1997: 31), which included the immigration of different ethnic groups into the colonies to provide cheap labor, as in the case of the Chinese and Indian traders and laborers encouraged to work in Singapore and the plantations of Malaya and Indochina, as well as the occasional policy of balancing minority against larger ethnic groups as a form of "divide and rule" policy.

The second contradiction was that one ethnic group could be divided physically by two or more colonial boundaries. In such instances, the imposition of colonial borders proved capable of suppressing, rather than extinguishing, precolonial ties, and a strong impulse remained to reunite and restore former political and economic links.

Third, it also hampered economic development in the colonial units. Colonization functioned to reorient the economies of East Asia away from the region, instead connecting them outward to the economic networks of the imperial powers. This incorporation into imperial economic networks brought a degree of economic development in rail and communications infrastructure, plantation agriculture, and heavy industries. Yet colonization also distorted economic development by converting regional economies into captive markets for the manufactures of imperial powers, with the consequent decimation of local handicraft industries. It led to forced reliance upon the exploitation of natural resources as the principal form of exports. And it led to the destruction of flourishing agricultural sectors as production was shifted from the supply of food for local needs to cash crops for export (Ayoob 1995: 34–37).

Colonization thus reordered the East Asian political economy into territorial units under the sovereign control of imperial powers from the seventeenth century to the middle of the twentieth century. The process of colonization created latent political and economic distortions within territorial units, which were often suppressed by military force. The impact of colonization was nearly universal in geographical extent, with only Thailand and Japan escaping subjugation. Thailand evaded direct colonization due to its skillful balancing of diplomatic ties with the imperial powers; Japan became a modern sovereign state and imperialist power in East Asia.

Colonization brought about two intertwined reactions within Japan. On the one hand, Japan's leaders knew, even after the decline of the Chinese world order and the imposition of imperialism, that their country continued to form part of East Asia geographically, ethnically, and culturally. Thus, as expressed in sentiments such as pan-Asianism, Japan, as the first modern sovereign state in the region, had a special responsibility to take the lead in protecting East Asia from the ravages of Western imperialism. On the other hand, this vision of Japan's role in East Asia was counteracted by an awareness that Japan, to survive and prosper in a regional and global order dominated by the imperial powers, required similar physical, economic, and military resources. The outcome was Japanese colonialism in East Asia (Taiwan in 1895, the annexation of Korea in 1910), with the contest becoming one between Japan and the Western imperial powers for control of resources in the region, especially those on the Chinese mainland. Japan's fear that its economic development and imperial ambitions would be suffocated by Western imperial powers led it to challenge head-on the existing colonial order, leading to World War II. The rapid occupation of French (Indochina, 1940), Dutch (Netherlands East Indies, March 1942), and British and U.S. (Malaya, Singapore, Philippines, March 1942) colonial possessions in Southeast Asia, followed by the proclamation in 1942 of the Greater East Asian Co-prosperity Sphere (Daitōa Kyōeiken), enabled Japan to construct under its own imperial auspices a new political and economic regional order centered upon itself.

Japanese Colonialism's Impact

Japan's declared intent in proclaiming the Greater East Asian Co-prosperity Sphere was liberation of East Asia from Western colonial rule and to foster (under Japanese guardianship) regional solidarity and eventual independence (Beasley 1987: 245). The Greater East Asian Co-prosperity Sphere was viewed as a cynical exercise on Japan's part to disguise its intent to supplant Western colonial rule with its own (Dower 1986: 262–290). But regardless of pan-Asian sentiments, the rapid establishment and then collapse of Japanese colonial rule and the Greater East Asian Co-prosperity Sphere were responsible for initiating the process of decolonization. Movements for national independence had been in existence in many East Asian colonies prior to the outbreak of the Pacific War. But Japan's expansion of its presence into Southeast Asia from 1941 onward added momentum to these movements in two ways.

First, Japan's swift defeat of the Western colonial powers destroyed the "myth of white supremacy" (Storry 1979: 6–13). Japan, for instance, established control of French Indochina through the agency of a pro-Vichy administration, and it did not seek to dismantle French colonial rule in Vietnam, Cambodia, and Laos (Ferro 2000: 263–266). Nevertheless, the demonstration of Japanese superiority over the French was to inspire the anti-French and communist movements in Vietnam (Mendl 1995: 113). Second, even though Japan's colonial rule generated a good deal of suffering and anti-Japanese feeling across the region and especially in the Philippines, Singapore, and Malaya, Japanese administrators in some newly acquired colonies were able to ameliorate hostility by encouraging popular national movements. Hence, Japan fomented anti-British feeling in Burma by granting it nominal independence in 1943, and it appealed to mass opinion and nationalist elites in the Netherlands East Indies and the Philippines by holding out the prospect of eventual independence (Leifer 1983: 1–2).

The final consequence of Japan's colonial experience was that it managed to unleash pro-independence and decolonization forces. Japan's defeat in 1945 and the collapse of its empire was thus accompanied not only by a legacy of anti-Japanese sentiment but also by a legacy of anticolonialism that hampered the ability of the Western imperial powers to reassert control. Indeed, in the case of Burma and the Netherlands East Indies, the military training provided by the Japanese enabled nationalist forces to frustrate the return of the Western colonial powers (Lebra 1977). The implications of decolonization, coupled with the onset of bipolarization, are considered below.

Decolonization and Bipolarization

The Emergence of "Weak States"

Japan's expulsion of the Western imperial powers from East Asia during the Pacific War, and its own subsequent defeat and forced withdrawal, opened considerable political and economic space, which was filled and reconstituted by the two interrelated processes of decolonization and bipolarization. The process of decolonization, set in motion by Japan's failed colonial experiment, led to the emergence of new sovereign states. Elite leaders of the majority ethnic groups in the colonies took advantage of the power vacuum to launch or relaunch movements for national liberation (fused with peasant movements for economic emancipation as in China, or movements to halt the socioeconomic advance of Chinese minority groups, as in Malaya; the selective adoption of forms of communist ideology, as in China, North Korea, and Indochina; and elements of religious movements as in early Indonesian and Burmese nationalism) and the creation of independent states (Godement 1997: 42–60; Leifer 2000a: 159–160). Hence, following a struggle of national liberation in the Netherlands East Indies, the Dutch acceded to Indonesian independence in 1949. The United States and Great Britain also granted eventual independence to their colonies in the Philippines (1946), Burma (1948), and the Federation of Malaysia (1955), the latter splitting into Malaysia (1963) and Singapore (1965). In the meantime, France became engaged in a long-term and ultimately futile war against forces fighting for national liberation in Vietnam and Indochina, eventually acceding to the independence of Vietnam, Laos, and Cambodia at the Geneva Conference of 1954.

By the early 1950s the colonial order in Southeast Asia had thus begun to be replaced by newly independent sovereign states. However, in most cases sovereign territorial borders were inherited unaltered from the previous colonial administrations. The result was that policymaking elites inherited the same internal consistencies and distortions left over from the colonial period's partitioning of political and economic interaction into territorial units.

The imperial powers bequeathed to many independent successor states territories comprising different majority and minority ethnic groups forced into uneasy political and economic cohabitation (Acharya 2000: 55–58). The majority ethnic groups in certain former colonies, such as the Malays in Malaysia and the Philippines, and the Thais and Vietnamese, formed a basis for the creation of sovereign states modeled along the lines of the sovereign nation-states of Europe and the United States, marked by cohesion among the territorial borders and the national identities and interests of the bulk of the citizenry contained within. Consequently, many colonies produced strong anticolonial and nationalist movements capable of unifying general populations in pursuit of national independence and statehood, as seen most in the case of the Vietnamese struggle against the French and the United States. At the same time, though, these newly established states also contained significant ethnic minorities, the presence of which mitigated against the formation of fully consistent nation-states. Ethnic and religious minorities in the Philippines, Malaysia, and Burma created the potential for internal ethnic tensions within these states and gave them the qualities of "semi-nation" sovereign states.

Moreover, ethnic divisions and inconsistencies in territorial boundaries and ethnic composition were multiplied many times over in the case of Indonesia; its highly pluralistic makeup of 490 ethnic groups were constantly in tension with attempts of the Javanese majority under the New Order of President Suharto (1966–1998) to create a unified sovereign and nation-state (Vatikiotis 1998: 92–118, 350–351). Furthermore, the independent states also faced the problem that territorial borders had been drawn arbitrarily and carried over from the colonial period. This continued to divide sections of the minority and majority ethnic groups across different states and to lock in within the body politic transmigrant ethnic groups brought in under colonial labor policies. The result was to create the potential for minority ethnic groups to secede and join another state, giving rise to separatist movements; or for a majority ethnic group to demand the reabsorption of similar ethnic groups located within another state, giving rise to irredentism.

Finally, the inherited problems of ethnic composition were compounded by economic weakness. In certain cases, such as the Korean Peninsula (Kohli 1999), colonization laid the infrastructure for the rise of developmental states and future economic growth. But colonization also engendered distortions in economic development that carried over into the postcolonial period and limited the ability of governments to ameliorate disparities of wealth among ethnic groups and thereby dampen internal frictions.

The final outcome of decolonization created a series of newly independent sovereign states in East Asia that were not entirely "natural" or organic political and economic entities; they were systemically "weak" (Buzan and Segal 1994: 16–17; Acharya 2000: 55). Nationalism was undoubtedly an important force in the formation and binding together of these states. Nonetheless, few featured the internal cohesion found in Europe or the United States and thus did not fully approximate the typical model of the nation-state. Instead they were multiethnic in character; marked by internal contradictions between the delineation of sovereign territorial boundaries and the political and economic affiliations of large sections of their populations and citizenry; and consequently preoccupied with a security agenda dominated by ethnic tensions, separatism, and irredentism.

In turn, these sovereign states were to enjoy varying degrees of political and economic legitimacy in the eyes of their citizenries (Alagappa 1995: 56–57). They also reflected a gap dividing the security interests of the state and large segments of populations. As will be seen in later sections of this chapter and in Chapter 3, the test for the policymakers of these Southeast Asian states since independence and continuing into the contemporary period has been to try to resolve or at least ameliorate these contradictions, to moderate the gap between the security interests of states and substantial sections of the populations contained within their borders, and thereby maintain the integrity of these states as territorial, political, and economic units. Government policymakers in Southeast Asia have attempted to achieve these objectives through the assertion of the principles of sovereignty and nonintervention so as to shut out any form of external intervention that could threaten their exclusive control over their citizenry and create alternative ties of loyalty, while also engaging in top-down internal efforts at centralized state-building and state "resilience" (Emmerson 2001: 95) through the promotion of nationalist identities and economic development (T. Shiraishi 2000: 151–174). In short, Southeast Asian governments have been subject to the strictures of "performance legitimacy" and the delivery of economic stability to survive (Stubbs 2001: 38–39).

Sovereign states in Northeast Asia created in the immediate postwar period also were not immune to internal contradictions. China incorporates a large number of ethnic minorities within its borders (including Zhuangs, Hui [or Chinese Muslims], Uygur, Yi, Tibetans, Miao, Manchus, Mongols, Bouyei, and Koreans), accounting for around 8 percent of its total population, and is concerned with the implications of this for territorial integrity, separatism, and internal security (Wang 1995: 163–165). North and South Korea, as former colonies of Japan and as sovereign states newly established in 1948, are ethnically homogeneous, but the existence of a large Korean minority in the autonomous prefecture of Yanbian, Jilin Province, has long raised Chinese concerns about ethnic separatism or Korean irredentism in the event of reunification. Moreover, the entire problem of ethnic groupings, secessionism, and irredentism in Northeast Asia, and in parts of Southeast Asia as well, has been compounded by national division engendered by the onset of the Cold War. Hence, the Chinese government views the Taiwan issue as one of separatism produced by the Cold War, whereas other interpretations label it as one of Chinese irredentism.

Statehood and the Onset of the Cold War

Bipolarization was the second process introduced into the region as a result of Japan's defeat in 1945. In combination with decolonization, it reconstituted the political and economic order and influenced the regional security agenda. Joining the newly independent sovereign states were the two superpowers, which had become functionally regional powers due to their strategic interests and power projection capacities. The superpowers remained engaged during East Asia in the postwar period and initiated the process of the bipolarization due to their intrinsic function both in carrying forward and hampering the process of decolonization. The responsibility that the United States and Soviet Union took for the occupation of Japan and the dismantlement of its empire in Northeast Asia, and the U.S. role in terminating as well as prolonging European colonial rule in Southeast Asia, influenced the course of decolonization across the region. This became the starting point for the interconnection of decolonization and bipolarization.

In Japan, the United States occupied the mainland, as well as the Ogasawara (Bonin), Senkaku, and Ryūkyū (Okinawa) island chains; the Soviet Union took possession of the Kurile Islands (Northern Territories). In Northeast Asia, as mandated in the Cairo and Potsdam Declarations (1943 and 1945), Japan was stripped of its colonies in China, Taiwan, Korea, and the Pacific Islands. The withdrawal of Japan from its colonies on mainland China and Taiwan enabled the Chinese Communist Party (CCP) and Nationalist Party (Kuomintang, or KMT) to resume their civil war—resulting in a communist victory, the establishment of the People's Republic of China in 1949, the decampment of the KMT to Taiwan, and the de facto division of China. Meanwhile, in Korea the original plan had been to restore this former

Japanese colony to full independence through a U.S.–Soviet–British–Republic of China (ROC) four-power trusteeship agreed at the Yalta Conference of February 1945. However, as Japan's defeat approached in August, the United States and Soviet Union hastily agreed to partition the Korean Peninsula at the 38th Parallel into military zones administered by themselves. The division of Korea was meant only as a temporary stage in the decolonization process, and the problem of elections for a united government was entrusted to the UN between 1947 and 1948. Nevertheless, unification was to remain unresolved because of the Korean Peninsula's position as the point of convergence for the processes of decolonization and bipolarization.

The end of Japanese colonial rule and division of the Korean Peninsula released independence and nationalist factions, split into procommunist and anticommunist forces located north and south of the 38th Parallel. In turn, increasing bipolar confrontation in Europe encouraged both superpowers to back either the procommunist and anticommunist forces, leading to the establishment in 1948 of the Republic of Korea (ROK—South Korea) and the Democratic People's Republic of Korea (DPRK—North Korea). The reasons for the eventual outbreak of the Korean War in June 1950 are subject to various historical interpretations. North Korea's decision to reunify the Korean Peninsula by military means was arguably the result of inter-Korean domestic and nationalist tensions (Cumings 1990), and the degree to which the United States and Soviet Union were willing to disturb the status quo in Korea is questionable. Nevertheless, the launch of the civil war, the U.S. pledge to defend South Korea in line with UN mandates, the Soviet Union's support for North Korea, and the entry of China into the war in October 1950 had the effect of interlinking, first on the Korean Peninsula and then throughout the rest of East Asia, the processes of decolonization and bipolarization. From its initiation in 1950, through the armistice of 1953, and finally the Geneva Conference of 1954, which affirmed the armistice and de facto division of the peninsula, the Korean War came to be perceived as a contest of strength between the two superpowers and their respective allies. It transmitted the bipolar pressures on the global level down to Northeast Asia on the regional level.

Likewise, the U.S. response was not only to commit men and matériel to the South; it expanded its security perimeter by signaling its preparedness in 1950 and again in 1954–1955 to interpose the U.S. Seventh Fleet in the Taiwan Strait to prevent any Chinese attempt to invade that island. Hence, Taiwan represented another intersection of U.S. superpower global interests with regional civil and nationalist struggles; this led to the intensification of bipolarization in East Asia along lines of demarcation established by the fall of Japanese imperialism and the process of decolonization.

In Northeast Asia, the intersection of decolonization and bipolarization was solidified by the conclusion of the San Francisco Peace Treaty in

September 1951 and the fuller incorporation of Japan into the U.S. half of the bipolar divide. The treaty completed the formal process of divestment of Japan's colonies by asserting in article 2 that it should renounce control over Korea, Taiwan, and the Pescadores, the Kurile Islands, and the Spratly and Paracel Islands, as well as administrative authority over the Nansei Shotō (Ryūkyū and Daito Islands) and Nanpō Shotō (including the Bonin Islands, Rosario Islands, and Volcano Islands). However, this process of decolonization was affected by bipolar tensions. First, even though Japan renounced its rights to the Kurile Islands, the bipolar tensions that led the Soviet Union to reject the peace treaty meant that the Kuriles issue remained unresolved—thereby reinforcing the territorial dispute over the Northern Territories between Japan and the Soviet Union and later Russia. Second, divisions among the Allied Powers over policy toward communist China meant that the neither the ROC nor PRC were invited to the peace conference, with the result that the treaty did not specify to which country or governmental authority Japan renounced Taiwan and the Spratly and the Paracel Islands (Hara 1999: 523). Third, the U.S. decision to assume administrative control over the Ryūkyūs to ensure continued control of its vital bases on Okinawa and military domination would sow the seeds of a territorial dispute between Japan and China over the Senkaku Islands.

Finally, bipolar pressures were transmitted across to Southeast Asia. In 1949 the United States had pressured the Dutch to grant Indonesia independence; by the 1950s it was providing massive financial aid and military hardware to support French attempts to maintain colonial rule in Indochina. Following France's defeat at Dien Bien Phu in May 1954 (the First Indochina War) and military withdrawal from Vietnam, the Geneva Conference on Indochina agreed to the partition of North and South Vietnam. Although the Geneva agreements on Indochina anticipated that Vietnam would later be united through elections, the final outcome was to establish a communist regime in the North oriented toward China and the Soviet Union, and an anticommunist regime in the South reliant upon the United States. North Vietnamese insurgency in the South, and attempts to reunify Vietnam by military force from the early 1960s onward, led to the increasing U.S. military commitment to defend South Vietnam and the onset of the Vietnam War (also known as the Second Indochina War). Hence, between 1961 and the Kennedy administration decision to deploy U.S. ground troops in Vietnam, and the final withdrawal of U.S. forces under the Nixon administration in 1973, the nationalist struggle in Vietnam was overlain by bilateral pressures and became another outlet for hot war.

The U.S.-Centered Worlds of Interdependence and Dependence

The consequence of East Asia becoming an arena for U.S.-Soviet confrontation introduced the process of bipolarization and "overlaid" the already ongoing process of decolonization and the newly established sovereign states

(Buzan 1994: 133). This would shape the regional political economy and security agenda. The most important feature was to replicate an approximate division of sovereign states into spheres of interdependence and independence, centered on the United States and Soviet Union, with each sphere associated with a third sphere of dependence. In the case of the sphere of interdependence, there was to be a merger with that of dependence into a sphere of asymmetric independence.

Indeed, the only state that appears to defy categorization throughout the Cold War period is Burma. From independence in 1948 onward, the Burmese state maintained a consistent policy of nonalignment. And following the imposition of military rule from 1962 onward, it advocated its own independent ideology of development, a mix of Marxism and Buddhism termed the "Burmese Way to Socialism." The failure of Burma's economic experiment by the late 1980s led to mass protests and challenges to military rule. The military reasserted its control through the bloody suppression in August and September 1988 of the prodemocracy movement led by Aung San Suu Kyi's National League for Democracy, then through the establishment in September 1988 of the State Law and Order Restoration Council (SLORC). SLORC promised free elections but overturned the results of the elections in May 1990 when the population voted in favor of the National League for Democracy. It then subsequently placed Aung San Suu Kyi under house arrest.

During the first Cold War, from the outbreak of the Korean War to détente in the early 1970s, the United States moved to consolidate its position vis-à-vis the Soviet Union by creating combined spheres of interdependence and dependence in East Asia. This sphere was centered on the United States itself, and extended to incorporate Japan, South Korea, and Taiwan in Northeast Asia, then across to the noncommunist states of Southeast Asia. In effect, the sphere was given cohesion through a series of U.S. bilateral security treaties with states in the region. However, it was also held together by U.S. efforts to promote economic interdependence. U.S. plans for ordering the regional political economy during the early phases of the Cold War envisaged a system of economic ties with the United States as the center, Japan as the semiperiphery, and Southeast Asia as the dependent periphery (Cumings 1984: 16–22; Schaller 1985: 178–211; Hook 1996: 173; Gilpin 2000: 54–68).

This system of economic linkages functioned through special U.S. economic dispensations. The United States at the center exported manufactured capital goods to the region and in return opened its markets to Japanese manufactures from the semiperiphery and supported Japanese efforts to enter Southeast Asian economies on the periphery to obtain raw materials. In time, the economies of South Korea and Taiwan, as well as those of noncommunist Southeast Asia, were encouraged to export to the U.S. market. Moreover, in addition to preferential access to its domestic market, the

United States assisted the economic development of these periphery states by providing advanced technology (Strange 1996: 6) and large-scale aid. Japan's economic revival during the early 1950s, for instance, was kick-started through its ability to purchase patents cheaply for U.S. technology (Johnson 1982: 223–227), as well as its receipt of up to U.S.$500 million in annual U.S. military procurement orders to support the war effort in Korea. South Korea and Taiwan also received close to U.S.$4 billion each in U.S. loans and military aid between the early 1950s and late 1960s, enabling both to upgrade their economic infrastructure and to finance trade deficits. South Korea, Taiwan, Singapore, and Thailand were also to gain from an increase in aid and a boom in orders for military equipment from the United States during the Vietnam War (Stubbs 1994: 367–369). Hence, by the late 1960s South Korea, Taiwan, Hong Kong, and Singapore had become the Newly Industrializing Countries (later Newly Industrialized Economies [NIES]).

The political economy of the sphere of interdependence and dependence created under U.S. auspices was certainly not static, and from the late 1960s onward it began to undergo structural changes. These were occasioned by the declining U.S. ability and willingness to single-handedly underpin the costs of its side of the bipolar political economy in East Asia, with the interrelated rise of Japan as the dominant economic actor in the region. The Nixon administration demonstrated the limits of U.S. political and military strength with its announcement on 25 July 1969 of the "Guam Doctrine," which sought to scale back the U.S. military ground force presence and increase the military contribution of its allies to their own defense; and with its announcement on 15 July 1971 of the forthcoming presidential visit to Beijing in February 1972 and the consequent decision to seek rapprochement with China, which ushered in a period of partial tripolarity in East Asia and paved the way for the U.S. withdrawal from Vietnam. The limits to U.S. economic strength were revealed a month later with the New Economic Policy (NEP) and the decision to abandon the gold standard and fixed exchange rates, as well as to impose a 10 percent surcharge on import tariffs, targeted at Japanese textile imports (Schaller 1997: 210–214; Nester 1996: 300–315). In addition, the limits to U.S. power were revealed with the first oil shock in October 1973. In this sense, the United States indicated its diminishing ability to provide special economic dispensations to Japan and other states.

The relative decline in U.S. political, military, and economic dominance in East Asia that produced the NEP was in part the result of and in reaction to the economic ascendance of Japan. By the early 1970s, encouraged at first by the United States, Japan had begun to create within East Asia its own economic order through the extension of trade, foreign direct investment (FDI), and ODA linkages. Japan had risen to supplant the United States as the principal supplier of capital goods, and following the rise in the value of the yen brought about by the "Nixon shocks" and the rise in oil prices in the early 1970s increased its FDI in the NIES-4 (South Korea, Taiwan, Hong Kong, and Singapore) and the ASEAN-4 (Thailand, Malaysia, Indonesia, the Philippines). This investment was driven by the need to produce manufactures for consumption in the domestic markets of these states to circumvent import barriers, as well as for export to markets outside the region in the United States and Europe. In turn, the increased willingness of the NIES-4, and in particular the ASEAN-4, to accept Japanese investment and integration as export platforms into the changing economic structure of the region was the result of the oil crisis—declining revenues from primary exports forcing a switch from import substitution strategies of development to export-oriented industrialization strategies to take advantage of the New International Division of Labor (NIDL) (Higgott et al. 1985: 38–40; Robison et al. 1987: 4–10; Robison 1997: 34–35; Hutchison 1997: 68–70; Hewison 1997: 104–110).

Further upsurges in Japanese FDI in East Asia occurred in the late 1970s and early 1980s, with a massive increase in the mid-1980s, an indirect effect of the onset of the second Cold War and renewed signs of limitations to U.S. economic strength. The heavy military spending of the Reagan administration, accompanied by rising trade deficits with Japan, East Asia, and much of the rest of the world, convinced U.S. policymakers once again of their declining ability to bear alone the costs of supporting the structure of the political economy of interdependence and dependence. Hence, in addition to U.S. demands for Japan to increase economic and military burden-sharing, the United States attempted to reduce its trade deficit with Japan and the NIES through dollar devaluation. The Plaza Accord of September 1985 produced close to a 70 percent appreciation in the value of the yen against the U.S. dollar, compelling Japanese manufacturers to seek low-cost production and export bases in the NIES-4, then increasingly in the lower-wage economies of the ASEAN-4. The rise in Japanese FDI in East Asia from the late 1970s onward helped to produce a distinct pattern of trade within the region. Japan rose to become by the early 1990s the largest individual trade partner for Thailand, Indonesia, and Malaysia and the second largest partner for South Korea and the Philippines after the United States. Japan also increased its share of total exports to East Asia relative to its share of exports to the United States, but the trade relationship with the region has remained asymmetrical, with Japan running trade surpluses with the NIES-4 and the ASEAN-4. These surpluses are largely accounted for by an imbalance in exports and imports of manufactures, such as electronics, transports, and precision machinery (Hook et al. 2001: 195–198). Japan from the 1970s until the end of the Cold War thus became dominant in many sectors of the East Asian economy.

Certain Japanese academic and economic ministries portray this division of labor within the region—with Japan at the top of the production ladder exporting high-tech products to the region, in return for the promotion of low-tech export industries in the NIES-4 and ASEAN-4—as the fulfillment of the "flying geese model" (Akamatsu 1962). However, to a large extent a triangular pattern of trade relations persisted among East Asia, Japan, and the United States. Even though the East Asian states and Japan decreased their share of total exports to East Asia, and intraregional trade increased by the end of the Cold War, the United States rather than Japan still continued to account for the largest individual share of manufacturing exports among the East Asian states. This pattern of trade suggests that Japan's economic activity in East Asia was characterized more by its role as an exporter of technology and capital goods to the region than as an importer of manufacturers, and that the United States continues to serve as a key market for the region (Pempel 1997: 76–82). Indeed, the patterns of Japanese FDI and trade that developed following the Plaza Accord suggest that one of the most important economic functions of states in East Asia for Japan remains as key offshore production bases for export to U.S. and European markets. Japan then possibly served more to create complex production links centered on itself as the source of production FDI, while the NIES-4 and ASEAN-4 functioned as production and export platforms, and the United States functioned as the market of last resort (Mitchell and Ravenhill 1995).

The history of the sphere of interdependence and dependence during the Cold War was characterized by a general decline in the will and ability of the United States to support its superstructure, punctuated by brief attempts in the early 1970s and mid-1980s to reduce its burdens or shift them to partners. Nevertheless, the overriding strategic imperative to maintain U.S. influence and to contain Soviet communism meant that the United States continued to endure the domestic political and economic costs of keeping its markets open to East Asian exports (Johnson 2000: 194–195). The extension of U.S. hegemonic power across its half of the bipolar divide in East Asia, accompanied by the establishment of an overarching framework of preferential market access and economic assistance (even if Japan was increasingly at its core), thus created an environment conducive to the economic development of many of the sovereign states of the region. These states were provided with an important "breathing space" (Cumings 1984: 9) to develop their own distinct forms of capitalism.

During the first phase of the Cold War, they faced only moderate U.S. pressure to liberalize their economies and provide market access to competing foreign imports and TNCs and were instead able to build up domestic industries for import substitution and then for export. Moreover, even as the Cold War waxed and waned in the 1970s and 1980s, and the interdependency of world and regional economies became enhanced, thus speeding globalization, the United States continued to insulate East Asian economies from the full impact of liberal capitalism. U.S. hegemonic power, even if in relative decline throughout this period, thus provided a kind of "hothouse" within which was fostered increased integration among the core, periphery, and semiperiphery economies. This was carried out not only under the overall auspices of the United States but also increasingly through Japan's efforts at regional integration, thus in de facto terms merging the worlds of interdependence and dependence into one of greater interdependence and proto-globalization. However, at the same time, the insulation of these states from the full norms of liberal capitalism ensured that they could pick and choose the benefits of proto-globalization without fully taking on all its entailed economic and political costs.

The opportunities for economic development within this sphere of interdependence also influenced the political development of these states. The policymaking elites of the East Asian states were able to use economic development as a means to strengthen internal institutions, such as the central bureaucracy and military, as well as to diffuse economic benefits to the general population, provide compensation for those sections left out in the drive for development, and thereby ameliorate internal societal tensions and strengthen their political legitimacy. In turn, the internal political strengthening of the states also enabled them to further gain control of and mobilize domestic resources to promote economic development (Ōnō and Sakurai 2000: 184; Huntington 1976: 17–78).

In this way, many of the governments of Northeast and Southeast Asia were able to steer a middle course between the twin dilemmas of technocratic and populist models of development and state-building: the former implying an approach to growth based on strong restrictions of political freedom, which provides for rapid national economic growth but also the expansion of social inequality and consequent political unrest; and the latter implying an approach to growth based on wider political participation, which may handicap national economic growth but also lead to the stagnation of the economy and consequent political unrest. However, the ability to pursue economic growth as a means to secure the legitimacy of the state while restricting the political freedom of large sections of their populations became increasingly limited in the latter stages of the Cold War.

The first reason was that these developmental strategies and the effects of modernization could also generate a backlash in traditional and Muslim societies. The elites in Indonesia and Malaysia attempted to avoid the politicization of Islam and promoted its moderate varieties to prevent civil strife, but from the 1970s onward they faced an increasing resurgence of Islamic movements opposed to the values of modernization. In Malaysia this took form in the emergence of the Muslim Unity Movement as a major opposition party, in Indonesia the United Development Party. In response, in Indonesia the Suharto government sought to utilize the resurgence of Islam for its own political purposes, encouraging the formation of the Association of Indonesian Muslim Intellectuals. The second reason was that the economic success of these states led to the rise of middle-ranking socioeconomic groups, or even a "middle class," more demanding of political as well as economic liberalism, thereby giving momentum to democratic movements less tolerant of authoritarian rule by the political elites (Acharya 1993: 25–26). The third reason was that the economic success of these states also strengthened demands by lower-ranking socioeconomic groups, as well as the middle-ranking groups, for a greater share of the benefits of economic growth. But any failure or economic crisis on the part of the state to provide these could also lead to demands for political change. The developmental strategies of the governing elites thus presented a means to secure their own position and to suppress economic and political instability; they also contained the potential causes of their own downfall.

Hence, the outcome was to provide conditions for the rise of the East Asia developmental states. These were characterized by public-sector and business-sector cooperation in the pursuit of rapid economic development, as well as various forms of "soft" and "hard" authoritarian governments (Johnson 1987: 137–138). Japan was very much the exception, evolving into an advanced democracy within the sphere of interdependence. South Korea and Taiwan were dominated by military dictatorships. In Southeast Asia, Thailand, although a constitutional monarchy and with alternating periods of democratic rule, was also subject to direct military control. By contrast, Malaysia and Singapore were controlled throughout this period by civilian and democratically elected governments, albeit with strong authoritarian tendencies to suppress internal opposition parties and dissident societal groups.

Clearly not all of the states contained within the U.S. half of the bilateral divide benefited equally from the reordering of the regional political economy. The authoritarian regime in South Vietnam until its eventual fall in 1975 failed to achieve significant economic development because of its position on the front lines of U.S. containment policy in Southeast Asia. This meant that it was engaged in civil war with North Vietnam and that its overreliance on U.S. financial aid perpetuated government corruption and a decline in popular legitimacy. Likewise, the Philippines, under democratic government until 1972 and then under the authoritarianism of Ferdinand Marcos (1972–1986), despite feigning attempts to build a strong centralized state, failed to shake off political and economic corruption and lagged behind its Southeast Asian neighbors in terms of development (T. Shiraishi 2000: 167–173). Moreover, economic development not only among but also within the region was uneven. Economic growth was concentrated away from the rural interiors and toward coastal and urban areas, often controlled by political and economic elites.

Furthermore, other states resisted integration into the political economy of interdependence. Indonesia under President Sukarno promoted the

Non-Aligned Movement (NAM) (its progenitor, the Asian-African Conference, was held in Bandung in April 1955) in an attempt to steer clear of incorporation into either the U.S. or Soviet camps during the early stages of the Cold War. But while maintaining a policy of nominal nonalignment, Sukarno also attempted to attract support from the Soviet Union and China in the late 1950s before finally siding with China at the time of the Sino-Soviet split in the mid-1960s. Sukarno's Indonesia following the imposition of the Guided Democracy in 1959 also embarked on the Konfrontasi (Confrontation) process and coercive diplomacy with neighbors. First, Indonesia pressed successfully its anticolonial campaign to recover Irian Jaya (the western half of the island of New Guinea) from the Dutch between 1960 and 1962, then later unsuccessfully tried to prevent the formation of Malaysia and its extension to border Indonesia in Borneo in 1963 (with a British-backed Malayan proposal to merge the Federation of Malaysia, Singapore, and the British colonies of Sarawak and North Borneo, and the British protected sultanate of Brunei). Consequently, Sukarno's Indonesia relied on policies of economic nationalism and "socialist" planning (Robison 1985: 303–304).

However, Sukarno's increasing reliance on the Partai Komunis Indonesia (PKI, the Communist Party of Indonesia), its abortive coup in 1965, and the subsequent fall from power of Sukarno and the rise of Suharto in 1966 (backed by the Indonesian armed forces and its violent suppression of communism) transformed the orientation of Indonesia within the regional political economy. Indonesia maintained its principles of nonalignment and a careful distance from China but also ended Konfrontasi with Malaysia and took a leading role in the establishment of ASEAN in 1967 (Leifer 1995: 17–19). Added to this, Suharto's New Order sought to integrate Indonesia more fully into the regional economy and NIDL, ending import-substitution industrialization policies and moving toward export-oriented industrialization. The result was the conversion of Indonesia into one of the quasi-developmental states of the ASEAN-4 and to demonstrate the inexorable economic pull of the sphere of interdependence for states in Southeast Asia. Much as with the other ASEAN states, the economic benefits of integration into the regional economy were used to construct a strong centralized state and thereby compensate for the weaknesses in the political legitimacy of the Indonesian state.

The Worlds of Independence and Dependence

The counterpart to interdependence and dependence was independence centered initially upon the Soviet Union and then on the Soviet Union and China. The Soviet-centered world of independence was given cohesion following the outbreak of the Korean War due to a series of bilateral mutual security treaties and the provision of military aid. In addition, the Soviet

Union extended economic and technical aid and preferential trading relations to sponsor the creation of dependent forms of communist political economies in the newly independent states of the region. China, North Korea, and Vietnam were all recipients of substantial Soviet aid (even if it did not always measure up to Chinese expectations, or was on a par with U.S. aid to other parts of the region) (Chandler et al. 1987: 449).

Soviet plans to mold the sphere of independence and dependence in East Asia went awry with the rise of China as a regional competitor and the Sino-Soviet split from the late 1960s onward (Yahuda 1996: 170–173). Although elements of Soviet capitalism continued to influence China's efforts at modernization, the latter pushed toward its own independent development programs, as did North Korea, which continued to pursue a hazardous middle path between accepting aid and trade assistance from both the Soviet Union and China, and seeking to secure autarchy in both economic and political development based on the principles of self-reliance, or *juche* (Hughes 1999: 117–119). North Vietnam (and later the successor state of a reunited Vietnam), having adopted Chinese collectivization and economic development strategies during the 1950s, did accept increased Soviet military and economic assistance in planning for modernization (Yahuda 1996: 203; Godement 1997: 134–136). In the meantime, Cambodia failed to navigate a path of neutrality during the Vietnam War and was subject from 1975 until 1978 to the extreme revolutionary and socialist ideology of the Khmer Rouge. Vietnam's fears of encirclement, resulting from the tacit alignment of the Khmer Rouge with China, caused it to initiate the Third Indochina War and to invade and occupy Cambodia between 1978 and 1989. The Chinese response in seeking, in Deng Xiaoping's words, "to teach Vietnam a lesson," and to prevent perceived Vietnamese attempts to dominate Indochina with the cooperation of the Soviet Union, was a punitive military expedition across its own borders into North Vietnam in February 1979. China's intervention failed to dislodge Vietnamese forces from Cambodia, although it did signal another open internal rift in the socialist bloc in East Asia and produced a China-ASEAN-U.S. anti-Vietnam coalition opposed to its occupation of Cambodia and the expansion of its influence in Indochina. As a consequence, the Khmer Rouge, provided with territorial sanctuary by Thailand and military supplies by China, rehabilitated itself as a guerrilla force and continued its war in Cambodia against Vietnam. In the meantime, Laos came under communist rule in 1975 and followed domestic and international economic and political strategies in line with its Vietnamese neighbor.

Hence, by the mid-1970s the world of independence was subject to internecine rivalries and displayed a wide range of forms of socialism. The orthodox Marxist-Leninism of the postrevolutionary Soviet Union clashed with the antirevisionist, revolutionary, and nationalistic communism of

China, which proved capable of the extremes of the Great Leap Forward of 1958–1959 and the Cultural Revolution of 1966–1969. By means of further contrast, North Korea produced a model of developmentalism based on an extraordinary amalgam of the principles of revolutionary socialism, anti-colonialism, Confucianism, and *juche* ideology. Nonetheless, it can be argued that these states did share sufficiently common characteristics in the makeup of their political economies to constitute a sphere of independence and that, despite the regional strategic competition between the Soviet Union and China, it was still Soviet military power, and to some degree its economic power, that underwrote the viability of these systems and their autarchy from the U.S.-centered sphere of interdependence. Moreover, even though the Soviet Union (in the same way as the United States) experienced difficulty in bearing the costs to support the political economy in East Asia, it continued to possess sufficient strength not only to provide economic dispensations to Vietnam and North Korea throughout the Cold War but also to attempt to extend communist influence in the period of the second Cold War from the late 1970s. Thus, the Soviet Union expanded its military at former U.S. naval ports of Cam Ranh Bay and Danang in Vietnam and embarked on a buildup of its fleet in the Soviet Far East (Leifer 1983: 20–21).

The diverse socialist systems of the sphere of independence engendered mixed results in economic development for the states within its ambit. Rigid socialist dogma produced costly mistakes in development, such as the Great Leap Forward in China and "millennarian" collectivization in Cambodia under the Khmer Rouge. Regional conflict also squandered the valuable resources of Vietnam and Cambodia. The structural limitations of the North Korean economy in terms of agriculture and production also became increasingly clear toward the end of the Cold War (Noland 2000: 172). However, at the same time, for long periods the sphere of independence also provided its newly independent states the opportunity to evolve their own forms of political economy, to achieve economic development, and to advance state-building. China's economic development during the Cold War may not have been spectacular, but it did ensure a general rise in living standards and the "iron rice bowl" social safety net for the bulk of its population.

Likewise, Vietnam's economic growth was slow, assisted by access to Soviet assistance. North Korea was able to exceed South Korea's economic growth until the mid-1970s, and its own efforts, combined with preferential economic access to the socialist economic sphere, enabled it to achieve relatively high standards in the development of infrastructure, industrialization, urbanization, education, and health. In this way, the states in the sphere of independence were still capable, after rejecting capitalism, of achieving internal legitimacy and internal economic and political success, even if ideological rivalries were capable of generating tensions.

Security Actors, Threats, and Responses

The next section examines the specific types of security actors, threats, and responses that the three processes of political economy generated during the Cold War. The description is brief but is necessary to understand the dynamics of the security agenda in East Asia. The roots of many security problems, and Japan's response, can be traced to this period.

Military Security: Threats and Actors

The superimposition of the three processes of decolonization, bipolarization, and proto-globalization produced a range of military threats and provided states with the identity of the referent objects and deniers of security.

U.S.-Soviet superpower interstate military conflict. First, these three dynamics, especially bipolarization, generated U.S.-Soviet great power and superpower military confrontation in East Asia, manifested in the form of nonconventional and conventional high-intensity threats. U.S.-Soviet bipolar strategic competition led both superpowers throughout the Cold War to upgrade, in both quantitative and qualitative terms, their land-, air-, and sea-based strategic and tactical nuclear arsenals. The United States deployed strategic nuclear weapons capable of striking Soviet allies in continental East Asia and provided an extended nuclear deterrent, or "umbrella," to its own allies; it also maintained tactical nuclear weapon stockpiles in South Korea and elsewhere in the region. Similarly, the Soviet Union targeted strategic nuclear weapons, including the SS-20, at U.S. allies and provided some form of implicit extended nuclear deterrent to China (until the Sino-Soviet split) and also to North Korea and Vietnam. A major part of the Soviet strategic nuclear arsenal was deployed on submarines from the Soviet Pacific Fleet.

The military position of the superpowers was further buttressed by the forward deployment of conventional land, sea, and air forces. U.S. deployments fluctuated greatly in accordance with the intensity of its involvement in the wars in Korea and Vietnam. Nevertheless, the periodic resurgence of Cold War pressures, and the onset of the second Cold War in the late 1970s, ensured that the United States continued to deploy some 350,000 personnel in the region until the early 1990s (Weeks and Meconis 1999: 31). U.S. Air Force, Army, Marine Corps, and Navy assets were concentrated in bases in the Philippines, South Korea, and Japan. In comparison, the Soviet Union deployed a large number of ground troops in the Soviet Far East to counter threats from the United States and its allies as well as from China, and from the late 1970s onward it undertook a major buildup of its air and naval forces in East Asia. The Soviet Union increased its combat aircraft in the region and introduced technologically advanced models, such as the Foxbat fighter and the nuclear-capable Backfire fighter-bomber. In addition to its force of nuclear and conventional submarines, the Soviet Union deployed missile cruisers and Minsk-class vertical/short takeoff and landing (V/STOL) aircraft carriers—thereby demonstrating its intent to acquire an oceangoing fleet and challenge the dominance of the U.S. Seventh Fleet in East Asia and the Pacific (Kimura 1998: 286–289).

Superpower–major regional power interstate military conflict. Nonetheless, despite the deployment of extensive nonconventional and conventional arsenals in the theater, as well as fluctuating bipolar tensions, the United States and Soviet Union (with the possible exception of air combat during the Korean War) did not become involved in direct military clashes in the region. Rather than direct superpower-to-superpower conflict, there was greater potential for involvement in other forms of interstate military conflict in the region. The first was direct superpower and regional major power conflict, specifically a conflict involving either one of the superpowers and China, or the Soviet Union and Japan. In the case of the potential Soviet-Japanese conflict, the issue was the Soviet occupation of the Northern Territories and Japan's demand for the return of the four disputed islands of Habomai, Shikotan, Kunashiri, and Etorofu (Braddick 2001: 210). During the Cold War, the Northern Territories dispute never looked like it would provoke a direct conventional or nuclear conflict. The Soviet Union did use the issue to pressure Japan to detach from its U.S. alliance and also engaged in provocative military behavior (e.g., stationing of troops in the territories in 1978) (Hara 1998: 149–150). Japan was not overly intimidated by Soviet actions as long as the U.S.-Japan security treaty was in place, and it had no intention of attempting to recover the islands by force.

The conflicts involving the superpowers and China were primarily conventional in nature, but they also involved nuclear threats by both superpowers toward China at different times, as well as China's response: the development of its own small nuclear deterrent. China conducted its first successful test of an atomic bomb in October 1964, then a nuclear missile in October 1966, and then a hydrogen bomb in June 1967.

In the case of Sino-U.S. relations, China's ideological opposition to the U.S. sphere of political economy and hegemony, and China's alignment with the Soviet Union in the early stages of the Cold War, provided grounds for direct conflict. Hence, the Korean War marked a period of direct Sino-Soviet conventional military conflict, and threatened nuclear conflict, as the United States sought to extricate itself from the war (Foot 1988–1989). Following the conclusion of the Korean armistice in 1953, the strategic interests of the United States and China on the Korean Peninsula, and their consequent support for the South and North Korean regimes respectively, ensured that Korea remained a potential site for conventional and military conflict throughout the rest of Cold War. In addition, from the mid-1950s onward, the principal focus of Sino-U.S. tensions shifted to Taiwan, the most likely theater for a direct Sino-U.S. military conflict. Nevertheless, Korea and Taiwan need to be seen as security issues that originated in the process of decolonization subsequently overlain by the process of bipolarization. Hence, Taiwan can be viewed as an interstate military security issue that is not so much a direct military power issue but rather the result of an unfinished civil war, drawing in the United States.

In contrast to Sino-U.S. relations, Sino-Soviet relations did give rise to direct interstate military conflict. The Sino-Soviet split, relating to issues of global communist ideology, combined with their rivalry to achieve regional influence in Indochina and their contiguous borders in Northeast Asia, led to the clash of Soviet Union and Chinese conventional military forces over the disputed islands in the Ussuri River on the Manchurian border in March 1966. Thereafter, the disposition by both sides of large military forces along the Sino-Soviet border produced a situation capable of triggering conflict at any time during the Cold War.

Superpower–major regional power–regional power interstate military conflict. Direct military nuclear and conventional war between the United States and China, and between the Soviet Union and China, was thus always a calamitous possibility during both the first and second phases of the Cold War. However, the most destructive forms of potential or actualized military conflict were those involving the two superpowers, China as a major regional power, and the smaller regional states, focused in and around the Korean Peninsula, Taiwan, Vietnam, and Cambodia.

Inter-Korean disputes coupled with bipolar and superpower pressures were to produce a situation in which the Korean Peninsula became one of the most heavily militarized areas in the world. On one side, South Korea embarked on an extensive buildup of conventional forces, backed by U.S. security pledges and the physical presence of U.S. troops in South Korea and close by in Okinawa and mainland Japan, as well as the U.S. tactical and extended nuclear deterrent. On the other side, North Korea, increasingly concerned with its existing security guarantees from the Soviet Union and China, devoted ever greater national resources to large conventional forces (the North's famed "1 million man" army), as well as the acquisition of biological and chemical weapons and ballistic missiles. North Korea's military assets provided it the capability to conduct various forms of high- and low-intensity warfare and to inflict significant physical damage and casualties on South Korea and the United States. In this way, a rough military balance was established on the Korean Peninsula for much of the Cold War; although this balance began to tilt toward the South in the later stages of the Cold War, leading to renewed instability.

Taiwan, Vietnam, and Cambodia were sites for potential or actual interstate war involving the superpowers, major regional powers, and smaller regional powers. Hence, Taiwan from the early 1950s onward had the potential to involve China, Taiwan, and the United States in a military confrontation. China in 1954–1955 and again in 1958 shelled the islands in the Taiwan Strait to deter the government of Taiwan and its international supporters from attempting to separate Taiwan from the mainland. In turn, the United States deployed the U.S. Seventh Fleet in the Taiwan Strait to demonstrate its determination to defend those waters and to signal that it would not accept a military resolution to the Taiwan issue. This brought the United States and China relatively close to direct military conflict.

Superior U.S. military power ensured that China was unable to really challenge Taiwan's security. Moreover, Sino-U.S. rapprochement from the early 1970s onward, U.S. acceptance of the "one China" principle (Taiwan being an integral part of the February 1972 Shanghai communiqué), and the U.S. abrogation of its defense treaty with Taiwan (replaced in part by the Taiwan Relations Act of 1979, which committed the United States to retain the capacity to resist any force that jeopardized the security of the people of Taiwan), neutralized Taiwan as a bilateral security issue in the latter half of the Cold War. Nevertheless, Taiwan remains a latent and potentially explosive security issue, with the potential to draw in Taiwan, China, the United States, and Japan.

Finally, the Third Indochina War involving Cambodia also needs to be viewed within this framework. The guerrilla war of the Khmer Rouge in Cambodia following the Vietnamese invasion, and the group's expulsion from Phnom Penh, was in part intrastate in nature but was also a struggle backed by China, ASEAN, and the United States as a means to check Vietnamese and Soviet influence, giving it the character of a bipolar struggle.

Regional major power and regional power interstate military conflict and territorial disputes. Interstate conflicts between the major regional powers, or between the major regional powers and smaller regional powers, or between just the regional powers themselves, were few and far between during the Cold War. But it was not because bipolarization and decolonization failed to generate sufficient latent security issues in the North and Southeast Asian subregions.

In Northeast Asia, the process of decolonization generated a potential territorial dispute over the sovereignty of the Senkaku Islands between China and Japan. Japan had incorporated the Senkaku Islands in January 1895 as part of the Nansei Shotō after surveys confirmed that the islands were uninhabited and had not been under the control of China. The Senkaku Islands were not part of Taiwan or the Pescadores Islands that were ceded to Japan by China in accordance with the Treaty of Shimonoseki of May 1895, and so they were not included in the colonies and territories that Japan renounced under article 2 of the San Francisco Peace Treaty of 1951. Instead the islands were placed as part of the Nansei Shotō under U.S. administrative control in accordance with article 3 of the peace treaty. Japan regained administrative rights over these islands, Okinawa, and the rest of the Nansei Shotō in accordance with the U.S. Japan agreement concerning the Ryūkyū Islands and Daito Islands signed in June 1971. In 1969 the Economic Commission for Asia and the Far East reported the possibility of large oil and natural gas deposits in the seabed in the vicinity of the Senkaku Islands (Kamiya 2000: 236; Takubo 1999: 31). This was followed by the assertion of both Chinese and Taiwanese claims to the islands, the former putting forward the argument that its vessels had first charted the islands in 1534.

China and Japan agreed to set aside territorial claims during the normalization of relations in 1972 (Yahuda 1996: 271), and at the conclusion of the Sino-Japanese Treaty of Peace and Friendship in August 1978 Deng Xiaoping stated that territorial problems could be left to the "next generation" to resolve (Roy 1998: 167–170). However, the right-wing Japan Youth Federation (Seinenkai) had raised popular Chinese ire earlier in 1978 when it erected a lighthouse on one of the islands (Downs and Saunders 1998–1999: 126). The U.S. government indicated in October 1996 that under the U.S.-Japan security treaty it does possess some obligations in relation to the defense of the Senkakus, but it also stated officially that it supported the position of neither side on the issue of territorial sovereignty. That September, the U.S. ambassador to Japan, Walter Mondale, indicated that the U.S.-Japan security treaty would not apply to the Senkakus (Ebata 1999: 197–198). This statement was again countered by the U.S. Department of Defense, which stated that the security treaty *did* cover the Senkakus (Green 1999: 162).

In addition to the Senkaku Islands, Japan became engaged in another territorial dispute with South Korea generated by the effects of decolonization. Japan had incorporated the two tiny uninhabited Takeshima Islands (Tok-do in Korean, Liancourt Rocks on navigation charts), totaling just 23 square kilometers in the Sea of Japan, into Japanese territory in January 1905. During the Japanese occupation, the Supreme Command Allied Powers (SCAP) issued an order in January 1946 placing the Takeshima Islands outside operational limits for Japanese fishermen, although it noted that this order did not constitute a final ruling on the issue of sovereignty. No specific mention of sovereignty was made in the San Francisco Peace Treaty. However, President Syngman Rhee declared South Korean sovereignty over the Takeshima Islands in January 1952, basing his claim on the exclusion of the islands from Japanese jurisdiction in accordance with the SCAP order of 1946. South Korea, in accordance with the declaration of the so-called Rhee Line, also unilaterally extended its territorial sovereignty over the continental shelf surrounding the Korean Peninsula for up to 200 nautical miles in places. This reserved for South Korea the right to exploit the rich fishing resources of this zone in the Sea of Japan and Yellow Sea. The Japanese government protested, and South Korea responded by occupying the Takeshima Islands with a small garrison in 1954. Japan proposed to bring the territorial dispute to the International Court of Justice in 1954, a move rejected by South Korea.

The 1965 Basic Treaty on normalization between Japan and South Korea and related economic agreements resolved to some degree the issue of fishing rights, with the abandonment of the Rhee Line and provisions for cooperation and arbitration of disputes in this area. The issue of sovereignty over Takeshima, though, was not resolved, with both Japan and South Korea accepting that the issue should be left to future negotiations. Although the Takeshima issue was not mentioned specifically, both sides agreed that remaining bilateral differences should be settled by diplomacy and third-party mediation. Nevertheless, the issue remained a thorn in Japan–South Korea relations, with periodic incidents in February 1977, May 1978, and August 1981 and clashes between the Japanese Maritime Safety Agency (the Japan Coast Guard since 2000) and South Korean fishing and Fishery Agency boats. Most of these incidents were fueled by periodic deterioration in bilateral relations over fishing rights and the colonial past (Mendl 1995: 69–70), as in the first "textbook controversy" of 1982 (Hook et al. 2001: 176).

In Southeast Asia, latent military conflicts among the major regional powers and smaller regional powers, in particular over territorial sovereignty, were considerable during the Cold War period. The most notable was over the Spratly Islands (Nansha in Chinese, Truong Sa in Vietnamese) among China, Taiwan, Vietnam, the Philippines, Malaysia, and Brunei, and the Paracel Islands between China and Vietnam. The Spratly Islands, a dispersed group of more than 400 tiny islands, reefs, shoals, and sandbanks in the South China Sea, are located some 1,300 kilometers south of the Chinese mainland, 500 kilometers southeast of Vietnam, 500 kilometers west of the Philippines, and close to offshore Malaysian Borneo. The islands have never supported continuous human settlement or been subject to the continuous sovereign jurisdiction of any single state (Leifer 1995: 221). Nevertheless, since the Cold War they have become of crucial importance in East Asia security for two reasons. First, rival claimants have sought to gain control of potentially large reserves of oil and natural gas, as well as rich fishing grounds, in and around the islands. The conclusion of the United Nations Convention of the Law of the Sea (UNCLOS) in 1982 potentially provides territorial rights to establish Exclusive Economic Zones (EEZs) extending up to 200 nautical miles (approximately 370 kilometers) and thus exclusive access to sea and seabed resources. Second, the Spratly issue and the need for stability are also of concern to regional states such as Japan, as they are located across major sea lines of communication

(SLOCs) that link the Indian and Pacific Oceans. The Paracel Islands are a cluster of 130 barren islands located 165 miles southeast of China's Hainan Island and 225 miles west of Vietnam. They are of less resource and strategic importance than the Spratlys but are of considerable symbolic importance to China and Vietnam.

China, Taiwan, and Vietnam lay claim to all of the Spratly Islands, the Philippines to a concentration of islands west of Palawan, Malaysia to several islands off the coast of Borneo, and Brunei to Louisa Reef on the periphery of the island chain. China, Taiwan, and Vietnam's claims to the Spratlys originate from the process of decolonization (Lin 1997: 323–339). France, as the colonial power in Indochina, established domination over the Spratlys and Paracels from the late nineteenth century, then was displaced in part by Japan during the Pacific War for submarine bases. Following the end of the war, Nationalist China challenged France's attempt to reestablish colonial control over the Spratlys and the Paracels by occupying some of the islands, although the KMT lost control over all the Paracels when it withdrew from the mainland in 1949. China and Vietnam subsequently registered claims to the Spratlys and Paracels at the San Francisco Peace Conference, where Japan was forced to relinquish its own colonial control over the islands, but again without specifying to which country it renounced these territories. From the mid-1950s onward China and South Vietnam competed to occupy both island groups. South Vietnam's attempts to incorporate the Paracels into its territory in September 1973 resulted in China's forced expulsion of South Vietnam from the islands and its full occupation of them from January 1974 onward. Following North Vietnam's absorption of South Vietnam in 1975, the Vietnamese government reasserted its claim to the Paracels, also occupying twenty-one of the Spratly Islands. China again responded by establishing footholds on a number of islands, and in January and March 1988 a clash between Chinese and Vietnamese naval forces led to the former taking control of six islands (Valencia 1995: 13). Meanwhile, Malaysia and the Philippines occupied a number of the islands and have maintained a limited military presence there (Acahrya 1993: 33–34).

The slow unwinding of the process of decolonization also gave rise to a series of other territorial disputes with military implications. The most notable was the Konfrontasi produced by Indonesia's successful campaign to recover Irian Jaya from the Dutch between 1960 and 1962, then its failed attempts to prevent Britain from merging the Federation of Malaysia, Singapore, and the British colonies of Sarawak and North Borneo. The latter dispute produced armed incursions into northern Borneo and peninsular Malaysia, fended off by the Malaysians and British, with support from Australia and New Zealand under the terms of the Anglo-Malayan/Malaysian Defense Agreement.

The next dangerous bilateral territorial dispute centered on the rival claims of Malaysia and the Philippines to Sabah (North Borneo). Again this claim was generated by the process of decolonization and Britain's decision to transfer sovereignty to the Federation of Malaysia at the time of its formation in 1963, in the face of Philippine objections that they were traditionally part of the Sulu Archipelago. The rival claims to Sabah produced deep tensions in bilateral relations throughout the 1960s and 1970s, with Malaysia fearing the infiltration of Philippine-trained guerrillas into Sabah. President Corazón Aquino attempted unsuccessfully to persuade her country's legislature to revoke its claim to Sabah in 1987, and the dispute remained unresolved. Finally, Malaysia has been engaged in territorial disputes with Singapore over Pedra-Branca Island (Horsburgh Light) in the Singapore Strait (with an eventual agreement to refer the matter to the International Court of Justice), and with Indonesia (Sipadan and Ligtigan Islands) in the Sualwesi Sea near the Sabah-Kalimantan border (eventually resolved in 2002 in favor of Malaysia), again related to the demarcation of sovereign boundaries that took place during the periods of British and Dutch colonial rule.

Intrastate military conflicts. For many states in East Asia during this period the intrastate and domestic security agendas were more dominant. Given the importance of intrastate conflict as a force to feed interstate conflict, the following section examines the potential and actualized intrastate conflicts that occurred in East Asia during the Cold War, the dynamics behind them, and their continuity into the post–Cold War period. The bundling together of different ethnolinguistic and religious groups within the same sovereign territorial units, and the consequent lack of cohesion between the apparatus of the state and sections of its citizenry, created security problems with intra- and interstate implications.

The division and incorporation of ethnic groups across and within sovereign state territorial boundaries has produced both irredentist and separatist movements, often taking the form of armed guerrilla struggles. In the case of Indonesia, attempts by the Javanese majority to create a centralized nation-state have been resisted by separatist movements across the vast Indonesian archipelago. The population of the province of Aceh in northern Sumatra has long been resentful of the central government's exploitation of its local natural resources, leading to the growth of a separatist movement from the 1970s onward, which then drew the response of military repression from the central government (Sukma 2001: 379–380). The central government in Jakarta also faced separatist movements at various times in central and West Sumatra (the Pemerintahan Revolusioner Republik of Indonesia). Meanwhile, the central government's need to satisfy nationalist demands among the Javanese majority produced an irredentist impulse to incorporate more territory into the Indonesian republic during the post-colonial and Cold War periods. However, this irredentism only served to fuel ethnic tensions and separatist movements. Indonesia's determination to acquire Irian Jaya during the Konfrontasi era satisfied irredentist demands but also produced the armed separatist Free Papua Movement by Melanese inhabitants. Likewise, Indonesia's irredentist urge, and its concern over the spread of communism, which led to its intervention in and eventual occupation of the former Dutch colony of East Timor between 1975 and 1976, also generated a separatist movement and intrastate military conflict. Indonesia's invasion and pacification of East Timor is believed to have accounted for up to 200,000 Timorese deaths (Candio and Bleiker 2001: 66) and met continued armed resistance from the Fretilin (Frente Revolucionária do Timor Leste Independente). For instance, a political protest in the East Timor capital of Dili in November 1991 was crushed by the Indonesian security forces with considerable loss of life.

Meanwhile, in the Philippines the central government faced an armed insurgency from the Moro National Liberation Front (MNLF), consisting of Muslims in the southern island of Mindanao resentful at domination by the Christian majority of the Filipino state (producing a conflict that cost an estimated 120,000 lives from 1972 to 1996 [*Financial Times*, 4 May 2000: 12]); in Thailand, the state was confronted by the militant Muslim group of the Pattani United Liberation Organization (PULO), which railed against Buddhist assimilation and conducted a number of bomb attacks; and in Burma the government was engaged for much of this period in separatist and autonomy struggles against the Chin, Kachin, Shan, and Karen minority groups, all of which formed individually and collectively significant military threats to the integrity of the Burmese state (Lintner 1999).

The process of decolonization also led to economic inequality and a general lack of political legitimacy in central governments. The combination of these factors could be explosive, as with the larger indigenous but relatively economically disadvantaged Muslim populations of Malaysia and Indonesia and the usually more prosperous overseas Chinese minorities, manifested most strongly in the interracial rioting directed against the Chinese in Malaysia in 1969.

In many cases the lack of political legitimacy within the states of Southeast Asia could be overlain by the process of bipolarization, giving rise to the challenge of armed communist insurgency. The Communist Party of Malaya (CPM) launched an armed struggle first against the British colonial government and then against the independent Malay government during the period of the Emergency from 1948 to 1960, and continued its struggle until 1989; in Thailand, the pro-Beijing Communist Party of Thailand comprised a guerrilla force of up to 10,000 in the mid-1970s before entering into a decline by the late 1980s; and in the Philippines, the New

People's Army (NPA) from the late 1960s onward recruited up to 22,500 guerrillas and posed a major threat to the enfeebled Marcos regime before declining in numbers during the Aquino presidency (Acharya 1993: 18).

In most instances, insurgency threats were met with fierce internal repression. Moreover, the overlapping of decolonization and bipolarization created another threat in terms of the lack of political legitimacy, the perceived threat of communism, and ethnic divisions. In these instances the internal security effects were explosive. Thus some states, such as Indonesia and Malaysia, perceived the Chinese ethnic minorities as synonymous with communism as sources of economic inequality for majority groups; this intensified violent crackdowns by authorities. This is evidenced by the bloody elimination of the PKI in Indonesia upon the fall of Sukarno in 1966, which accounted for the deaths of thousands of Chinese and Javanese suspected of being communist sympathizers (Vatikiotis 1998: 34).

Societal group and individual level military conflicts. Groups in East Asia can be the referent objects of and perpetrators of conflicts. Ethnic minorities in Southeast Asia were subject to repression by central governments yet inflicted considerable damage on states or other societal groups in irredentist and secessionist struggles. Hence, most of the ethnic groups listed above were engaged in low-intensity guerrilla struggles, and many practiced terrorist tactics, as in the case of the PULO in Thailand and NPA in the Philippines (Chalk 1999: 189–192). Some were also engaged in criminal activities, such as the Shan minority under the leadership of Khun Sa's Shan United Army (Mong Tai Army), which financed its insurgency movement against the Burmese state through the opium trade (Dupont 1999: 441–442; Stares 1996: 41; Lintner 1999: 297–337).

Finally, all the inter- and intrastate military conflicts elucidated so far had significant costs for the security of individuals. The citizens in East Asia bore the costs of all forms of nuclear and conventional high-intensity conflict, as well as low-intensity conflict in the form of guerrilla warfare, terrorism, and piracy. The doctrine of nuclear deterrence, in particular MAD, ensured that citizens of the United States, Soviet Union, and China, and those under the U.S. nuclear umbrella, were held hostage by these weapons and would have borne the brunt of casualties in any major nuclear conflict. High-intensity warfare during the Korean War and high- and low-intensity conflict during the three Indochina wars claimed millions of noncombatant casualties, including women and children; and intrastate conflicts, often marked by internal repression and pogroms, claimed a large number of casualties as well.

Moreover, all these conflicts produced refugees and displaced persons. The collapse of the South Vietnam regime in 1975 generated an outflow of Vietnamese boatpeople for more than a decade (Hitchcox 1994: 202); large numbers of refugees sought sanctuary in Thailand from conflicts in Cambodia and Burma (Maley 2000: 151); and Indonesian military repression in Irian Jaya produced at least 10,000 refugees fleeing to Papua New Guinea in 1984–1985 (Anwar 2001: 358). Indeed, Indonesia has one of the largest populations of displaced people in East Asia.

Organizational group military conflicts. A range of other organizational actors are involved in conflicts. The most prominent terrorist organizations in East Asia originated in Japan. Driven by a complex mix of Marxist-Leninist and Maoist ideology—espousing anticolonialism and Marxism—Japanese terrorist organizations conducted bombing and shootings in Japan before heavy police pressure obliged one faction, the Japanese Red Army (JRA), to move to the Middle East in 1970. The terrorist activities conducted by groups in Japan were of limited destructive potential due to their inability to obtain modern weaponry (with the exception of the East Asian Anti-Japan Front's bomb attack against Mitsubishi Heavy Industries in August 1974, which claimed eight lives and wounded 376). However, the JRA, supported by the People's Front for the Liberation of Palestine, was able to engage in a number of highly destructive shootings, bombings, and hijackings in Europe, the Middle East, South Asia, and East Asia, including an attack on an oil refinery in Singapore in 1974, the seizure of the U.S. and Swedish consulates in Kuala Lumpur in 1975, and possible kidnappings and rocket attacks in the Philippines and Jakarta in 1986 (Hughes 1998: 41–43; Katzenstein and Tsujinaka 1991).

The other organizations also involved in crime were the transnational networks of ethnic Chinese located outside mainland China. These groups included Sino-Burmese and Sino-Thai growers, refiners, and distributors, and Triad groups in Macao, Hong Kong and Taiwan. In addition, the Japanese *boryokudan,* or organized crime syndicates (also known as Yakuza), appear to have developed some links to these groups.

Military Security: Responses and Frameworks

Responses to interstate military conflict. During the Cold War, the principal response of East Asian states to the interstate conflicts described above was to deploy military power individually, bilaterally, or multilaterally, creating a balance of military power that both generated and suppressed potential or actualized military conflicts.

Following the outbreak of the Korean War, the United States constructed a chain, or "great crescent," of bilateral and trilateral security treaties across the region intended to stifle communist expansion. Japan served as the fulcrum of this alliance system (8 September 1951), which stretched across from South Korea (27 July 1953), and down to the Philippines (30 August 1951) and Australia and New Zealand (1 September 1951). The United States displayed sporadic interest from the 1950s onward in the creation of a multilateral collective self-defense system modeled along the lines of NATO in Western Europe and involving Japan and other key East Asian allies. Its plans eventually foundered due to Japan's resistance to shouldering new defensive responsibilities in the postwar era and the lack of shared security interests and identity among the East Asian states (Hughes and Fukushima 2003). The United States did succeed in establishing the South East Asia Collective Defense Treaty (the Manila Pact) in September 1954, followed by the creation of the South East Asia Treaty Organization (SEATO) in February 1955, with the participation of itself, Britain, France, Australia, New Zealand, Pakistan, the Philippines, and Thailand. However, this multilateral security treaty failed to function effectively due to internal disputes among its members and was dissolved in June 1977, although the United States maintained a bilateral commitment to the defense of Thailand under the Manila Pact.

The installation in East Asia of a bilateral "hub and spokes" alliance system during the Cold War centered on the United States, confirmed U.S. military hegemony in Pacific East Asia, and provided essential bases for projecting power across to continental East Asia. The system of bilateral security treaties also provided the United States the ability to regulate the pace and scale of military buildups among its treaty partners. Hence, the United States facilitated Japan's rearmament following the Korean War through the provision of aid under Mutual Security Assistance provisions, followed by requests for more "burden-sharing" in the defense of the region. This was viewed as a restraint on the unbridled buildup of Japanese military strength, famously described by Lieutenant-General Henry Stackpole, commander of the U.S. Marines in Okinawa, in 1990 as the "cork in the bottle" of Japanese militarism (Hook et al. 2001: 125). Similarly, the United States regulated the buildup of South Korea's military forces and supplied military aid and technology to allies in Southeast Asia.

In opposition to the United States, the Soviet Union and China jointly, and then separately following the Sino-Soviet split, formed the other half of the bipolar balance of power. The Soviet Union and China's deployment of military power was also accompanied by a system of bilateral security treaties. The Soviet Union and China both signed Treaties of Friendship, Cooperation, and Mutual Assistance with North Korea in July 1961; and the Soviet Union signed the Treaty of Friendship, Cooperation, and Mutual Assistance with Mongolia in January 1966, and the Treaty of Friendship and Cooperation with Vietnam in November 1978. However, China's split from the Soviet Union in the mid-1960s meant that it was to advocate a multipolar world without alliance systems as the preferable model for East Asian security.

These contending superpowers and their respective alliance systems produced tensions during the Cold War that could spill over into highly destructive "hot wars," as in Korea, Vietnam, and Cambodia. Nevertheless, the fragile balance of power established by alliance systems also gave a measure of stability in most major military theaters in East Asia. In the Northeast Asia subregion, the Korean Peninsula retained a military flashpoint, shown by North Korea's agitation against the United States with the seizure of the USS *Pueblo* information-gathering ship in January 1968, and the tensions along the Demilitarized Zone (DMZ) following the axe-killing of a U.S. serviceman at Panmunjon in August 1976 (Oberdorfer 1997: 74–83). But at the same time, contentment with the status quo meant that the superpowers reined in the hostility of the two Koreas toward each other. The Soviet Union refused to supply the technologically advanced conventional weaponry that would tip the military balance in the North's favor, and the Soviet Union and China made it clear that they did not wish to see the North acquire nuclear weapons, and they pressed it to join the Non-Proliferation Treaty (NPT) regime in 1985. Likewise, the United States continued to arm South Korea with conventional weapons but pressured Seoul to halt its nuclear program in the early 1970s and to accede to the NPT in 1974.

In regard to Taiwan, the superior U.S. military presence, and China's need to enlist U.S. support in the Sino-Soviet split, ensured that it was largely suppressed as a security issue. The U.S. military presence suppressed other potential problems arising from territorial disputes. The U.S. military presence in Japan ensured that neither the Soviet Union nor Japan would contemplate resolving the Northern Territories issue by force; and although the United States was noncommittal in the Senkaku Islands dispute, its administration of the islands until 1972, and then its continued military presence in Okinawa from that time onward, discouraged any Chinese attempt to utilize force to pursue its territorial claim. Similarly, the U.S. military presence in the Philippines and interest in the freedom of navigation of the South China Sea (although the United States never extended the U.S.-Philippines Mutual Defense Treaty to cover the Spratlys) also discouraged any power that would seek to upset through military force the status quo. And the U.S. commitment to the defense of Thailand restrained Vietnam's military ambitions beyond Indochina. In turn, the influence and presence of the Soviet Union in Vietnam restrained it from further military expansion.

Hence, the security architecture of East Asia during the Cold War was characterized by a near total lack of multilateral security institutions. Instead there was a bipolar balance of power, which did little to alleviate the causes of interstate conflict generated by decolonization and bipolarization and prolonged them to maintain the status quo. Nevertheless, the superpower military presence and their alliance systems in effect neutralized these problems. They discouraged military rivalries and weapons proliferation among their client and satellite states, even without addressing the root dynamics of conflict. They were a source of continued, if fragile, stability.

In Southeast Asia, the superpower presence was supplemented by the conclusion of the Anglo-Malayan/Malaysian Defense Agreement, which was revised as the Five Power Defense Arrangements in November 1971, and committed Britain, Australia, and New Zealand to the external defense of Malaysia and Singapore. Although the arrangements were originally intended as transitional to overcome any power vacuum following Britain's military disengagement and the buildup of Malaysia's and Singapore's armed forces, and have been subject to tensions between these two powers, the defense treaty has persisted, and the Five Powers continue to hold joint military exercises.

Southeast Asian states value the external security links provided by the Five Powers' defense arrangements, and the presence of the United States, as a means to balance against external intervention by the Soviet Union and especially China. They themselves have limited ability to create subregional frameworks to prevent interstate regional power conflict among their own. The establishment of ASEAN in 1967 (originally comprising Indonesia, the Philippines, Thailand, Malaysia, and Singapore; then joined by Brunei in 1984) did lead to the proposal for the recognition of the subregion as a Zone of Peace, Friendship, and Neutrality (ZOPFAN), which would limit the influence of the Soviet Union, United States, and China and leave management of Southeast Asian security affairs to states in the subregion (Haacke 2003: 54–61). The divisions of opinion among ASEAN states about the strategic necessity of maintaining defense links with external powers ensured that the concept, although official ASEAN policy since 1976, has never fully functioned with practical effect. Moreover, ASEAN has consciously avoided the institutionalization of any form of bilateral or multilateral defense cooperation. Hence, following Vietnam's invasion of Cambodia in 1978, ASEAN formed a political and diplomatic counterweight to the expansion of Vietnamese influence in Southeast Asia, but its members remained dependent for military security upon their own individual military capabilities and guarantees of security from the external powers (Acharya 2001: 82–90).

Response to intrastate military conflicts. ASEAN's greatest security utility for its member states during the Cold War period, and indeed one of its most important founding motivations, was in enabling the management of those subregional military conflicts described above that fell between the inter- and intrastate categories. The experience of the Konfrontasi obliged Southeast Asian states to search for ways to contain and resolve territorial disputes through the organizational structure of ASEAN. ASEAN was intended to provide a forum for discussion and conciliation of contentious intramural subregional issues, and this role was confirmed with the conclusion of the Treaty of Amity and Cooperation (TAC) in February 1976 (Acharya 1992: 150). This treaty stressed the principles of sovereignty, territorial integrity, and noninterference in the internal affairs of ASEAN members; thus disputes among them would be resolved through direct negotiations or by a high council (Henderson 1999: 16–17). Even though the provisions of the treaty were never invoked during the Cold War, and tested only by the Malaysia-Philippines dispute over Sabah, the TAC was a statement on how to conduct subregional affairs and indicated that members would not disturb the existing sovereign state system. Certain observers thus see ASEAN's development as leading to the establishment of a nascent Southeast Asian "security community" within which members rule out the use of force to solve disputes among themselves (Khong 1997: 320–321).

The principle of noninterference governing interaction among ASEAN members, known as the "ASEAN way," thus enabled them to manage and suppress intrastate ethnic conflicts without fear of intervention from neighboring states. The principle is not entirely satisfactory and could lead to clashes between the military and police authorities of different states as they accuse each other of harboring insurgency factions or as they attempt to engage in "hot pursuit" of groups across borders (Simon 1978: 416–426). Hence, in some instances the principle of noninterference was made more flexible, allowing for bilateral cooperation of security authorities across borders to suppress intrastate military threats, especially threats from communist insurgency groups on the Thai-Malaysia and Indonesia-Malaysia borders (Acharya 1993: 27–28).

Nevertheless, the principle of noninterference held fast in ASEAN during the Cold War. This principle enabled states to keep a lid on potentially explosive intrastate threats of ethnic and communist insurgency. In most cases in Southeast Asia, the principal actor responsible for the suppression of intrastate conflicts has been the military. In Indonesia, the military "dual function" (*dwi fungsi*; the protection of the state externally and the right to intervene in internal political affairs) has led to the suppression of insurgency movements against the Indonesian state. The Thai and Philippines military also fulfilled this function to some extent (Hernandez 1996: 67–71). Malaysia and Singapore have depended more on professional and nonpoliticized police forces (Khoo 1997: 47). Meanwhile, in addition to brute military force, governments used other means to integrate dissident ethnic groups, such as the transmigration of Javanese to Irian Jaya and Christian Filipinos to Mindanao, also attempting to prove their legitimacy by spreading the benefits of economic growth.

The ASEAN way also enabled members to tolerate neighbors dealing with other forms of internal political dissent. Again, the military and internal police forces were prominent in suppressing forces seeking to challenge the dominance of the governing elite, such as the prodemocracy movements in the Philippines during the period of the Marcos regime, in Thailand during much of the postcolonial and Cold War periods, and Burma from 1962 onward.

However, the governing elites in Southeast Asia have attempted to strengthen control over the state and its citizens through developmental policies. The ASEAN regimes in particular placed their faith in the trickle-down effect of rapid economic growth as a means to achieve political stability. Greater prosperity and equity, it was hoped, could eradicate socioeconomic and urban-rural divides, remove the conditions that made their societies prone to insurgency and subversion, and enhance the legitimacy of the authoritarian structures over which they presided (Acharya 1992: 153). This recipe for political and military intrastate stability was not unique to Southeast Asia: The governments of Taiwan and South Korea employed military-backed authoritarianism in tandem with economic growth as a means to promote stability, liberalization, and eventually democratization; and China also employed a combination of authoritarian rule, based on the principles of nonintervention from external powers, and economic growth as means to contain political instability from the latter stages of the Cold War onward.

These principles of managing internal political instability have become increasingly untenable in the post–Cold War period. The new security agenda has produced a range of issues that can no longer be contained by and that cut across sovereign territorial borders; they demand a transsovereign response. Moreover, the economic success of East Asia under globalization has also produced further demands for democratization, as well as a transformation in civil-military relations that removes the military's role from internal politics.

Economic Security

Despite the vital significance of military issues during the Cold War, economic security was of considerable concern to all levels of security actors.

Economic exclusion, disparity, rivalry, and dislocation. The division of East Asia into two spheres of interdependence and dependence was marked by economic inclusion that guaranteed economic security to states, societal groups, and individuals. Hence, in the sphere of interdependence, the extension outward from the United States, and then increasingly from Japan, of investment, trade, and aid links ensured that few states were excluded from the regional production system and were thus unable to reap the benefits of economic growth. Likewise, in the sphere of independence, the preferential access to trade and aid in the socialist sphere ensured that states such as Vietnam and North Korea remained economically secure to the extent that the stability of their regimes was unchallenged.

The greater inclusion than exclusion offered by the two spheres of political economy also provided grounds for attempts to minimize economic disparities. In the sphere of interdependency, the developmental orientation of the states of Northeast and Southeast Asia, and the dash for economic growth, produced considerable internal domestic disparities among socioeconomic groups and between rural and urban areas. Nevertheless, high-speed growth also produced some benefits in the equalization of incomes. Japan was the outstanding example of this, but in maintaining average growth rates of around 4–8 percent from 1970 to 1985, the NIES-4 and ASEAN-4 (with the exception of the Philippines) also managed to close the income gap on a par with many developed states (World Bank 1993: 31). In addition, Indonesia, Thailand, Malaysia, and Singapore managed to reduce the percentage of the population below the poverty line by around 20–40 percent and to raise life expectancy (World Bank 1993: 33–34), thus guaranteeing an enhanced degree of individual economic security. Still, these reductions in inequalities were insufficient to satisfy all sectors of the population in East Asia. For instance, in Malaysia and Indonesia the disparities in wealth and economic opportunity between the Malay and Javanese populations and the Chinese minority were a constant source of internal friction. As a result the Malaysian government, following the race riots of 1969, embarked upon the New Economic Policy in an attempt to redistribute wealth to the Malay community (Horii 1991; Khoo 1997: 52–59).

The sphere of independence also functioned to level income inequalities for the bulk of citizens in the states associated with it. China was able through central planning to redistribute economic resources from the wealthier coastal provinces to those on the periphery, as well as to provide a higher and more secure living standard for much of its population. Meanwhile, North Korea was also able to increase and secure standards of living, even if the pace was slow and bought at a high cost in labor suffering. In turn, this economic stability and regime security in both spheres helped alleviate internal political unrest and military conflict.

Economic rivalry over natural resources was also limited during the Cold War period. All states in the region were concerned to secure access to resources. Japan, feeling itself to be resource-poor, was constantly concerned to secure access to raw materials in Southeast Asia and the security of SLOCs for the import of oil from the Middle East. Furthermore, all the states were impacted by the oil shock of 1973, with Japan in particular embarking upon "resource diplomacy" in the Middle East and the diversification of energy to secure vital supplies. Nonetheless, the limited growth of the other East Asian states during the Cold War restricted their appetite for resources beyond their own established territorial borders and minimized potential conflict. For instance, China remained self-sufficient in oil throughout most of the Cold War (Salameh 1995–1996: 133).

Economic dislocation was another factor for conflict during the Cold War. The oil shock engendered a structural crisis in the economies of the sphere of interdependence in the mid-1970s, accompanied by the rise of potential social crises. However, the ability and choice of the states of this sphere to join the NIDL presented them with opportunities to restructure and resume economic growth while heading off worst-case scenarios of economic and political instability. In the meantime, the economies of the sphere of independence such as North Korea were affected by the fall in commodity prices that accompanied the oil shock and were obliged to experiment with a certain degree of unsuccessful restructuring, burdening the North with external debt and laying the grounds for its economic crisis in the post–Cold War period. But the North's continued access to aid and trade from the rest of the sphere also ensured that it was able to stave off economic and political crisis. In the same way, China's disastrous experiment at forced development during the Great Leap Forward induced a homegrown economic crisis, but for much of the Cold War period, due to its nonparticipation in the global economy, it was insulated from external economic shocks.

Migration. Refugee flows resulting from military conflict were relatively common in East Asia and a threat to individual security. Migration as the result of economic change was also commonplace within the sphere of interdependence as investment and trade links between its constituent states deepened throughout the Cold War. Japan's economic expansion into Southeast Asia also brought in a reverse flow of migrant workers, especially female workers from Thailand and the Philippines, many of whom faced exploitation in the Japanese sex industry. Illegal economic migration also occurred among ASEAN states, with a large inflow of Filipinos into the Malaysian province of Sabah—an estimated 400,000 of a total 1.4 million population—further fueling Malaysian concerns about separatism. However, on the whole, economic migration was limited during this period (Skeldon 1999: 3), and its motive force of economic growth and the provision of the demand for labor ensured that inter- and intrastate conflict was also limited.

Organized crime and narcotics. For much of the eighteenth and nineteenth centuries, the European colonial powers promoted the production, trade, and consumption of opium as an important cash crop in East Asia (Trocki 1999), creating up to 15 million addicts in China alone (Dupont 1999: 439). The movement toward the prohibition of the opium trade in the early twentieth century led to a drop in supply, although the KMT and Japan remained engaged in a deliberate attempt to promote opium consumption as a means to consolidate control over their respective portions of China.

The Pacific War, followed by the onset of the processes of decolonization and bipolarization, produced major changes in the narcotics trade in East Asia. The effect of the war was to reduce the supply of heroin. Then the removal of Japanese and KMT influence from mainland China and the assumption of power by the CCP ensured that the narcotics trade was virtually eliminated from this part of the sphere of independence (Stares 1996: 21). The barriers erected to the drug trade in China, coupled with the breakdown of the colonial economic system and resistance of many of the newly independent states to involvement in narcotics, produced a shift in the production of opium. It relocated to territories on the margins of the spheres of independence and interdependence, where state authority was weakest or restrictions on trading activity the most liberalized, thereby placing the trade out of the control of individual sovereign states and international authorities (Flynn 2000: 47).

Even though many of the traditional transnational networks for the overseas trade in narcotics centered on the Chinese diaspora remained in place, production moved to the "Golden Triangle" of Laos, Thailand, and Burma. The Shan tribesmen under the warlord Khun Sa used the narcotics trade to fund their insurgency struggle against the Burmese government (Dupont 1999: 441), as did remnants of the KMT army that fled from Yunan Province to Burma and the Burmese Communist Party (BCP). Opium production in the Golden Triangle was further boosted by the coincidence of decolonization and bipolarization processes, as the Vietnam War increased the demand for heroin from U.S. combat forces. Following the end of the war, opium producers and distributors began to seek other markets in the United States, Europe, and East Asia itself.

Piracy. Like the narcotics trade, the practice of piracy was not a new phenomenon in East Asia. Piracy had long been practiced around the Strait of Malacca and Singapore Strait from the sixteenth to nineteenth centuries, but it had been suppressed to a degree by colonial naval power. During the Cold War, piracy continued in limited form in the Strait of Malacca/Singapore Strait zone, concentrating at the central "choke point" of the Phillip Channel (often less than 5 kilometers wide and no more than 20 kilometers from land, offering hiding places to pirate groups), which formed the fastest transit point for shipping on the SLOC from East Asia to the Middle East and Europe. In most cases, pirate groups carried limited numbers of firearms and boarded ships, ranging up in size to supertankers, to seize cash and safe valuables, even to unload cargo. According to IMB figures, the number of attacks from 1981 to 1988 was no more than a dozen per year (Vagg 1995: 69). Piracy was an important problem during the Cold War, often practiced by corrupt local state authorities and economically poor islanders in Indonesia and Malaysia. Nevertheless, the growing prosperity of local communities, and the projection of U.S. sea power from bases in the Philippines, acted as disincentives to engage in piracy.

Environmental Security

There are three broad categories of environmental security threats: depletion of renewable and nonrenewable resources; pollution of land, sea, and air; and the fundamental alteration of the ecosystem. Regarding the first category, the East Asian states had already embarked on considerable environmental destruction during the Cold War. Efforts at autonomous development in the sphere of independence produced considerable damage to agricultural land and forests. China, for instance, denuded around 40 million hectares of farmland since the 1950s; and North Korea's attempts at self-sufficiency in rice production led to an intensive program of deforestation to create stepped rice fields. The sphere of interdependence and its drive for economic growth also began the depletion of its agricultural and forestry resources, fueled in part by Japan's insatiable demand for natural resources. For example, the destruction of rainforests in Kalimantan, Sumatra, Irian Jaya, and Sulawesi began in earnest in the 1970s (Dupont 1998: 11). Moreover, the competition for territory and fish stocks was also initiated in this period.

East Asia began to increase its pollution of the natural environment during this period. Industrialization in the ASEAN states during the 1970s produced a significant decline in air quality. Policies of industrialization in the post-Mao period also initiated the same process in China (Breslin 1997: 499). Major oil tanker pollution occurred in the East Sea with the spillage of 6,400 tons of oil from the *Juliana* in November 1971 and the grounding of the *Shōwa-maru* in the Strait of Malacca in 1973. The Soviet Union also began dumping of 13,150 containers of radioactive waste from eighteen decommissioned nuclear submarines in the Sea of Japan from 1978 onward (Valencia 1997: 100–101). Russian nuclear dumping was to draw Japanese objections, but its own environmental record was questionable. From the 1970s onward, Japan shifted much of its heavy-polluting industry offshore to Southeast Asia, causing environmental damage through the dispersal of chemicals and heavy metals. Meanwhile, in the sphere of independence, Chinese and North Korean industries continued to pollute unchecked by environmental concerns.

The cumulative effect was to set much of East Asia on the path toward the third environmental security threat: the destabilization of ecosystems. However, the limited economic development of states within the spheres of interdependence and independence restricted their ability to bring environmental threats to their own citizens and those of their neighbors. The onset of globalization has fully realized these environmental threats in the post–Cold War period.

Conclusion: East Asia and Japan's Emerging Comprehensive Security Agenda

This chapter has demonstrated that East Asia's security agenda in the Cold War period was shaped by the overlapping forces of decolonization, bipolarization, and nascent globalization. This produced an agenda that was highly complex, ranging across the military, economic, and environmental dimensions, and affecting the security of states, individuals, societal groups, and organizations. In turn, this understanding of the complexities of the East Asian regional security agenda provides a context for the evolution and current status of Japan's security policy during the Cold War and post–Cold War periods. These complexities and the emerging comprehensive nature of the regional security agenda explain how Japan was forced to respond with a comprehensive security policy during the Cold War, involving the use of military and economic power across all dimensions of security. The fact that the roots of these complex security dynamics were also implanted during the Cold War, and continue to dominate into the post–Cold War period, also explains Japan's continued attachment to notions of comprehensive security in the contemporary post–Cold War era.

3

East Asia's Contemporary Security Agenda

This chapter examines the East Asian security agenda and Japan's place within it during the post–Cold War period. Using the political economy approach, it will demonstrate how the security agenda has been determined by the continued influence of decolonization and bipolarization and is now increasingly affected by full-scale globalization. It considers the three dimensions of military, economic, and environmental security; their impact on all levels of security from the state to the individual; the interrelationship between all dimensions and levels; and the variety of individual state, bilateral, and multilateral responses. The security agenda is complex and comprehensive.

East Asian Security Dynamics

The Retreat of Bipolarization and the Onset of Globalization

Soviet disengagement and U.S. supremacy. Bipolarization waned in East Asia during the period of Sino-U.S. rapprochement in the 1970s. The Soviet Union attempted to reassert a bipolar order from the late 1970s to mid-1980s with its military buildup. However, the task proved largely futile, as it was unable to maintain control over its own sphere of independence, or to compete with the open economies of the proto-globalized sphere of interdependence. As George Kennan, the architect of containment, had predicted in the early stages of the Cold War, the socialist regimes of the states of Eastern Europe and East Asia were simply "unable to stand the comparison" (cited by Cusimano 2000: 16). President Mikhail Gorbachev's initiation of limited reforms in the mid-1980s soon revealed the parlous condition of the Soviet economy, unleashed demands for further restructuring and liberalization, and ultimately induced the collapse of the Soviet Union and its sphere of independence in Eastern Europe and East Asia.

The effective defeat of the Soviet Union and sphere of independence—

battered by pressures from the sphere of interdependence—led to weakening bipolarity in East Asia and globalization (Camilleri 2000: 40–42). The Soviet Union (and successor state Russia from 1991), with its own internal problems, was obliged to seek rapprochement and to some extent disengagement. Hence, Gorbachev reduced Soviet troops in Mongolia and the Russian Far East and normalized diplomatic relations with China in May 1989, then with South Korea in September 1990. The Soviet Union also curtailed military and economic assistance to Vietnam and North Korea (Yahuda 1996: 179–180). Gorbachev sought to improve relations with Japan with initiatives over the Northern Territories and to improve economic and security cooperation. Subsequently, Russia under the presidency of Boris Yeltsin was a founding member of the ASEAN Regional Forum (ARF) in 1994 and joined the Asia-Pacific Economic Cooperation (APEC) Forum in 1997. However, the decline of the Soviet economic and military presence spelled the decline of Russian influence.

The United States was the sole remaining superpower. But sustaining the sphere of interdependence also meant relative economic and military decline. Nevertheless, despite speculation about the rise of Japan as a superpower contender in the early 1980s (Vogel 1986), the United States still possessed supreme military and resurgent economic capabilities in East Asia. However, the willingness of the United States to sustain the costs of hegemony has been on the decline during the post–Cold War period.

Merging the spheres of interdependence and independence. The retreat of bipolarity did not create new dynamics to resolve security issues. Yet the Soviet collapse and the U.S. emergence as sole superpower merged the sphere of independence into that of interdependence, and globalization raised implications for regional security.

The combination of U.S. trade deficits, market incentives and investment access, the opportunity to exercise leverage due to the decline of bipolar pressures, and the perceived necessity to underwrite the sphere of interdependence through economic dispensations meant that the United States became more assertive in pursuing its own economic interests and reciprocity on the part of the East Asian states (Strange 1996: 7; Camilleri 1994: 195; Pempel 1999: 178). The United States pressed for increased liberalization of trade and investment in the region, as in the case of bilateral U.S.-Japan trade negotiations; and to create, through multilateral regional bodies such as APEC (Ravenhill 2001: 93–97) and international economic institutions such as the International Monetary Fund (IMF), World Bank, and World Trade Organization (WTO), the conditions for neoliberal economic development in East Asia.

Definition and implications of globalization. Liberalization within the sphere of interdependence reduced East Asia's insulation from the impact of liberal market economics and globalization. This had significant implications for development and security. But globalization should not be understood solely as the process of economic liberalization; it is also a process that can generate fundamental change to the political economy. Just as decolonization and bipolarization impacted the interstate system in East Asia during the Cold War, globalization contains the potential to alter the function of the state and its role in security today. Globalization represents a qualitatively different process from decolonization due to its essential deterritorialization or, stated in reverse, supraterritorialization of social interaction (Scholte 1997: 431). That is to say, globalization is a process that reconfigures social space away from and beyond notions of delineated territory and *transcends* existing physical and human borders. For instance, global financial transactions, facilitated by information technology (IT), can now often operate without reference to physical distance or human-imposed barriers. It is important to avoid the type of hyperglobalization thesis that views the region and world as moving toward a condition of being totally borderless. For it is apparent that there is considerable territorial drag upon the free flow of globalization forces; that not all forms of economic interaction (such as trade and labor migration) are as fully globalized as finance; that there are disparities in the degree of globalization across different regions; and that there is both resistance to and reversibility in the process. Nevertheless, globalization as supraterritorialization is undoubtedly influencing most regions of the world, especially East Asia.

However, the inherent nature of globalization as a process that transcends and overrides territoriality poses a fundamental challenge to the sovereign state. East Asian states must contend with the free flow of social forces on a global scale. The increasing irrelevance of state borders, and the relative decline in the sovereign authority of states, increases exposure of internal societal groupings to external forces. In these circumstances, even though the apparatus of the state may remain intact, societal groups and individual citizens may view the state as a redundant framework; this translates into a crisis of legitimacy for nation-states. Globalization's impact can thus be to heighten the potential security gap dividing the sovereign state and its internal societal elements. In the East Asian context, this lack of cohesiveness was a major source of instability during the Cold War; globalization highlights systemic weaknesses in states—a recipe for conflict.

Decolonization and Globalization Overlain During the Post–Cold War Period

Expansion of the sphere of interdependence. The states in the sphere of interdependence have deepened their economic linkages. Although the United States undergirds economic interdependency by keeping its market open, Japan has also forged complex production links and fostered the integration of the NIES-4, the ASEAN-4, and China into the regional production ladder.

China for its part embarked on significant economic reforms in the post-Mao era, but the collapse of the Soviet Union and weaknesses in the socialist economy, as well as concern over the reassertion of U.S. technological, economic, and military dominance, convinced its leadership of the need for full-scale economic reform since the end of the Cold War. The liberalization effort that began with agricultural reform, joint ventures, and the establishment of Special Economic Zones (SEZs) in the late 1970s (Wang 1995: 264–270, 308–310) has gathered momentum with China's membership in APEC since 1991 and its accession to the WTO in 2000. The extent of Chinese economic development beyond the coastal regions is still limited. Nevertheless, economic reform has set China on the path to greater economic and military power in the twenty-first century.

Similarly, Vietnam since 1986 has embarked upon the policy of *doi moi* (economic renewal) to encourage market economics and FDI while attempting to preserve the basis of the socialist economy. North Korea has remained largely resistant to economic restructuring; the loss of special dispensations from the Soviet Union, along with its own policy mismanagement, have engendered a deep economic crisis. Nevertheless, the North has experimented with joint ventures and Special Economic Zones since 1984. These include the creation of the Rajin-Sonbong Free Economic and Trade Zone on its northeastern borders with Russia and China since 1991; participation in the UNDP Tumen River Area Development Program (TRADP) in conjunction with Russia, China, Mongolia, and South Korea since 1992 (Hughes 2002); and the establishment of the Kaesong industrial park and Sinujiu Special Economic Zone in 2002. All this indicates that the North perceives that economic autarky is no longer a viable strategy and that it is essential to join the sphere of interdependency in East Asia (Hughes 1999: 124–131).

Globalization's impact on the East Asian political economy. The diffusion of globalization forces across the region has presented states with opportunities to address weaknesses and related security problems, as well as dilemmas that have led to their exacerbation.

First, economic liberalization accompanying globalization offers a powerful tool for many East Asian states to alleviate and suppress intrastate security problems. During the Cold War, many states in Southeast Asia sought economic growth to strengthen internal state-building efforts and to counter separatism, irredentism, and political illegitimacy. In turn, economic liberalization under globalization presented opportunities for supercharged economic growth and internal stability. The growth rates of certain Southeast Asian states from the mid-1980s to the late 1990s (up to 10 percent) created wealth that could be diffused to key constituencies in the elite and middle ranks of society, as well as to lower socioeconomic groups. Moreover, governments in states such as Malaysia embraced globalization and were able to use the benefits of growth to alleviate economic disparities among ethnic groups and thus one source of interethnic conflict (Welsh 1999: 265–270). This use of economic growth to assuage internal societal discontent has not been unique to Southeast Asia. In Northeast Asia, South Korea and Taiwan achieved relative internal political stability through economic growth and integration into regional and global economies. Likewise, in China the CCP sought to use economic growth and consumer goods to offset the decline of communist ideology, to maintain its legitimacy, and to preserve internal political stability.

Second, economic liberalization is a double-edged sword that can work both for and against intrastate security. Economic liberalization and development, as well as increased contact with other political cultures, leads to the growth of middle-ranking socioeconomic groups critical of authoritarian governments and desirous of greater political freedom and democracy. Over the longer term, democratization can produce intrastate stability if governments are able to demonstrate a popular mandate and thereby close the potential security gap dividing the state and its citizens. Over the shorter term, popular struggles for democracy and resistance by governing elites can generate political instability, as in the case of Indonesia since 1997 and the fall of the Suharto regime. Moreover, rapid economic development can raise expectations among middle- and lower-ranking socioeconomic groups, with disappointment following the failure of trickle-down growth. If majority ethnic groups view this as an erosion of their economic position in relation to a minority ethnic group, as in the instance of Javanese resentment toward the Chinese community in Indonesia, it can lead to violent intrastate ethnic tensions. Since the late 1990s, it has become clear that the decision to buy into economic liberalization to access the benefits of globalization exposed states to the violent downturns that characterize global capitalism.

The East Asian financial crisis beginning in 1997 is graphic evidence of this. The exact causes of the crisis are described in detail elsewhere (Hughes 2000a). The crisis was precipitated by the East Asian dash for higher economic growth, which in turn was based on increased liberalization of domestic financial markets, greater dependence on FDI, and the outflow of exports to the United States, Europe, Japan, and elsewhere. A downturn in key export markets, coupled with fears among investors in the United States, Europe, and Japan about the growing imbalance in East Asia's current account deficits, set off a chain reaction that led to the withdrawal of FDI, a declining ability to obtain investment to maintain exports, further declines in investment, and finally an economic crash. The financial crisis brought an abrupt end to the "East Asian miracle" and raised doubts about the future viability of the once-vaunted developmental state model of growth. Economic growth in the NIES-4 and ASEAN-4 plummeted more or less across the board in the aftermath of the crisis; unemployment doubled in Hong Kong, Malaysia, and Thailand and tripled in South Korea and Indonesia (Table 3.1) (Skeldon 1999: 2). Only China and Taiwan escaped relatively unscathed due to the nonconvertible currency of the former and the limited capital liberalization of the latter (Chu 1999; Naughton 1999).

The East Asian financial crisis indicated the limits of globalization, as well as the political and security problems of economic slowdown. Middle-ranking socioeconomic groups become more hostile toward governments and intensify their democratization movements. The failure of economic growth also frustrated lower-ranking socioeconomic groups and threatened to increase interethnic rivalries. Economic crisis can also weaken the apparatus of the state, leaving it unable to cope with separatism, irredentism, and organized crime. In these cases, it is possible to see that economic liberalization under globalization can widen the security gap dividing the state and its citizens, which then proves so destabilizing in the East Asian context (Murphy 1999: 235–236).

The increased integration into a globalized regional economy, in conjunction with decolonization, carries implications for interstate security. Domestic changes can threaten to spill over into intra- and interstate conflict. For example, China's transition toward a market economy is accompanied by downturns in the global economy, as well as internal disparities in economic growth between the coastal zones and interior China.

In this instance, the CCP faces the dual problem of the declining ability to provide economic benefits to the general population and to control the political economy of its provinces. The CCP's response has been to utilize the ideology of nationalism to substitute for communism, to supplement economic growth (Unger 1996: xi), and thereby to preserve political

Table 3.1 GDP Growth Rates in East Asia, 1996–2000

Country	1996	1997	1998	1999	2000
China	9.7	8.8	7.8	7.1	6.5
NIES-4					
South Korea	7.1	5.5	–6.7	10.7	7.5
Taiwan	5.7	6.8	4.6	5.7	6.3
Hong Kong	4.7	5.3	–5.1	2.9	5.0
Singapore	7.0	7.8	1.5	5.4	5.9
ASEAN-4					
Thailand	6.4	–0.4	–10.4	4.1	4.5
Malaysia	8.2	7.7	–7.5	5.4	6.0
Philippines	5.5	5.2	–0.5	3.2	3.8
Indonesia	7.8	4.9	–13.2	0.2	4.0

Source: Japan External Trade Organization (JETRO) (various years). *Sekai to Nihon no Bōeki*. Tokyo: JETRO.

control. The decision of the CCP to stake its legitimacy on the promotion of nationalism also means that it has to pursue irredentist claims to the Senkakus and in the South China Sea (Downs and Saunders 1998–1999: 118), and cannot tolerate Taiwanese independence. In the case of Taiwan, globalization and decolonization pitted democratization and nationalism against the other with unpredictable consequences for regional security.

Globalization's differential impact on economic growth has other implications for intrastate security: access to resources and sovereign state economic survival. The thirst for economic growth can intensify the scramble for natural resources to fuel it. China's decision to integrate into the global economy, and its potential conversion into an economic great power, has raised competition among China, the ASEAN states, and Japan for scarce energy and other resources.

Meanwhile, globalization has increased the concerns of North Korea about its own economic survival. Since the collapse of the sphere of independence, North Korea has lost access to special economic dispensations from the Soviet Union and faced a decline in preferential trade, energy, and aid policies from China. Moreover, North Korea's inability to join the globalizing sphere of interdependence forced it to use military power and brinkmanship to extract new economic dispensations from the United States, South Korea, and Japan. Globalization has overlaid many of the preexisting problems of bipolarization and decolonization and intensified security problems on the peninsula.

Security Actors, Threats, and Responses

Military Security: Threats and Actors

Superpower-interstate military conflict. The decline of bipolarization and Cold War pressures virtually eliminated the conditions for military conflict between superpowers. The Soviet Union and then Russia disengaged from East Asia, their strategic imperatives turning toward Europe and Central Asia. The Soviet Union withdrew its military forces from Cam Ranh Bay in 1991, and Russia formally announced in September 1995 that it would not seek to renew the security aspects of the 1961 Treaty of Friendship, Cooperation, and Mutual Assistance with North Korea. Russia does station military forces in the region, including its strategic nuclear deterrent, and has made some efforts to reengage. Sino-Russian rapprochement in the post–Cold War period enabled the formation of a bilateral strategic partnership on issues such as the formation of regional alliances (NATO enlargement for Russia, the strengthening of the U.S.-Japan alliance for China) and opposition to missile defense programs. This partnership is aimed at preventing U.S. global domination. President Vladimir Putin visited North

Korea in July 2000 in an attempt to renew Russian influence on the peninsula, help resolve issues, and thereby counter U.S. claims for the necessity of missile defense programs. Secretary General Kim Jong-Il paid a return visit to Moscow in August 2001.

Russia has in effect lost its status as a global and regional superpower. In contrast, the United States has preserved its hegemony. But the end of the Cold War also called into question the need for the United States to maintain a forward-deployed military presence and its system of bilateral alliances. The reduction of the Soviet military threat enabled the United States to announce in its 1992 East Asia Strategic Initiative a 12 percent reduction in U.S. forces in East Asia, from 135,000 to 120,000 (Acharya 2001a: 168) and to comply by November 1992 with Philippine requests to withdraw from Clark Air Base and Subic Bay.

However, rising concerns over North Korea and China from the early 1990s onward convinced the United States of the need to maintain its military presence and alliance relationships. The 1995 East Asian Strategic Review (EASR) (Office of International Security Affairs 1995: 23), with a successor version in 1998, confirmed that the United States would stabilize its military presence at around 100,000 troops for the foreseeable future. In addition, the United States and Japan strengthened security cooperation from the mid-1990s onward; and Singapore, Malaysia, and Indonesia offered port logistics and repair facilities for the U.S. Seventh Fleet to replace those lost in the Philippines (Acharya 1993: 57–58; Leifer 2000b: 105). Therefore, the position of the U.S. military remains central to regional security in the post–Cold War period.

Superpower–major regional power military conflicts. The Soviet disengagement brought about by the decline of bipolarization has reduced the sources of possible superpower–major regional power conflicts. Russo-Japanese rapprochement provided opportunities to tackle the legacies of the Cold War, including the lack of a bilateral peace treaty and disputes over the Northern Territories. As of late 2003, Japanese and Russian initiatives to resolve the issue of the Northern Territories and to conclude a peace treaty have been unsuccessful. Nonetheless, peaceful negotiations ensured that the Northern Territories ceased to be a source of military tension in Northeast Asia. Similarly, rapprochement between Russia and China has not removed all suspicions regarding security intentions, but the Sino-Russian border and more generally the region are now no longer sources of bilateral military tensions.

Superpower–major regional power–regional power military conflicts. The increased fluidity in the interstate system shifted the focus to potential superpower–major regional power–regional power conflicts. In Northeast Asia, security problems over the Korean Peninsula and Taiwan have increased.

North Korea, if exposed to the full force of economic globalization, could see the collapse of its totalitarian regime. The North has become progressively weaker economically and militarily in comparison to the South. South Korea has continued to upgrade its conventional forces, negating North Korea's traditional quantitative military advantage. The economy of the South has far outstripped that of the North since the late 1970s.

The consequent reaction of North Korea has been to break out of its diplomatic and economic isolation and to restore some semblance of balance. To execute this strategy, North Korea has attempted to utilize its remaining military power to exert pressure on surrounding powers and to extract diplomatic, economic, and military concessions. In particular, the North has employed brinkmanship designed to increase the threat and to raise security tensions to the maximum before indicating its willingness to back down and moderate its behavior in return for concessions (Hughes 1999; Sigal 1998: 207–254).

From the early 1990s onward, North Korea has used a combination of conventional low- and high-intensity conventional and WMD military threats against surrounding powers. North Korea's conventional high-intensity military threat has been manifested in its ability to launch an attack across the DMZ (Bermudez 2001: 14–16). Such an offensive would almost certainly end in defeat for the North (O'Hanlon 1998). Nevertheless, the devastation it could cause gives North Korea leverage. In addition, in the event of military conflict North Korea is also thought likely to employ low-intensity guerrilla warfare against the South, as well as possibly launching attacks on nuclear power stations in Japan along the Sea of Japan coast. Any conflict on the peninsula would result in many refugees who might cross the Sea of Japan.

North Korea's "chaos power" and related ability to precipitate unwanted and costly military conflicts in Northeast Asia are brought into focus by its development of nuclear weapons. From the late 1980s onward, the North deliberately played on the concerns of surrounding powers that it was producing plutonium for nuclear weapons. U.S. determination to counter nuclear proliferation, its demands that North Korea should accede to International Atomic Energy Agency (IAEA) inspections of its Yongbyon nuclear plant, and the North's subsequent threats to withdraw from the NPT in 1993 and 1994 heightened tensions on the peninsula. The crisis peaked in mid-1994 with U.S. plans to impose, in conjunction with South Korea and Japan, economic sanctions upon the North for its refusal to accept inspections, and the North's response that such an action would be tantamount to a declaration of war.

The military forces of the United States, South Korea, and North Korea were placed on high alert, but the diplomatic and military standoff ended with the visit of former U.S. president Jimmy Carter to Pyongyang in June 1994, with North Korea agreeing to freeze its nuclear program in exchange for new negotiations with the United States. These negotiations produced the so-called Agreed Framework between the United States and North Korea, under which the North confirmed that it would freeze its nuclear program in return for U.S. promises to create an international consortium that would supply it with two lightwater reactors (LWRs) to be completed by 2003 at an estimated cost of U.S.$5 billion. The United States also agreed to supply heavy fuel oil to make up for energy shortfalls in the interim period before the LWRs were operational. Even more important, the United States confirmed its promise not to use nuclear weapons against the North; to move toward full diplomatic normalization; and eventually to lift economic sanctions (Mazaar 1995). The Agreed Framework's provisions on the LWRs and energy were put into effect with the creation of the Korean Peninsula Energy Development Organization (KEDO) in December 1995, with the participation of the United States, South Korea, Japan, and the European Union (EU).

The motivations for North Korea's suspected development of nuclear weapons have been subject to debate. Some commentators during the early stages of the crisis viewed North Korea as irreversibly bent on developing its own nuclear weapons. However, given the negotiations over the Agreed Framework, and the pattern of behavior both prior to and following the nuclear crisis, others argue that North Korea's prime objectives have been diplomatic recognition and economic concessions. In this way, the North was prepared to freeze its nuclear program in return for possible recognition from the United States, energy assistance, and the tantalizing promise of ending sanctions and expanding economic ties.

Following the crisis, the North continued its brinkmanship and indicated its willingness to bargain military assets for diplomatic and economic concessions. The fact that North Korea's economic crisis drove military crises has become clearer since 1994 with its admission that it is experiencing severe food and energy shortages. Hence, one of the concerns of regional policymakers has been that internal economic problems could lead to an implosion of the regime, with unpredictable consequences for regional security. The United States, South Korea, and Japan provide food aid on humanitarian grounds and to maintain internal stability.

At the same time, the North Korean ballistic missile program is another means to extract economic assistance from neighbors. The North had been engaged in the development of ballistic missiles since the late 1970s; was involved in the proliferation of missile technology with its export of SCUD-B missiles to the Middle East; and test-fired its SCUD-C/Nodong-1 missile in the Sea of Japan in May 1994, estimated to have a range of 1,000–1,300 kilometers, enough to strike Japan and deep into China. North Korea conducted another test-launch of a suspected Taepodong-1 missile over Japanese airspace on 31 August 1998. This was viewed by Japan as a highly provocative military act and raised U.S. anxieties about missile proliferation and the development of the Taepodong-2, capable of striking the U.S. mainland. In many ways, the missile test confirmed the fact that Japan is vulnerable to ballistic missile attack. Nevertheless, the "Taepodong-shock" induced a hard-line approach in Japan, including the possible suspension of Japanese funding for the KEDO project, the imposition of economic sanctions, and the decision to move toward the acquisition of strategic surveillance satellites for military purposes and cooperative research with the United States into ballistic missile defense (Hughes 2000b).

However, the United States sought to resolve the crisis through bilateral negotiations and diplomatic and economic concessions. Former secretary of defense William Perry was appointed as the U.S. North Korean policy coordinator in November 1998. His visit to Pyongyang in May 1999 and continued U.S.–North Korea negotiations culminated in the North's eventual agreement in September—once again in return for concessions—to suspend indefinitely its missile launch program. Perry also produced the *Review of United States Policy Toward North Korea* that October; the report recognized the economic problems and the need to sustain the regime in the North and advocated a flexible mix of military containment and economic engagement.

In the meantime, this evolving strategy paralleled the so-called Sunshine Policy of President Kim Dae Jung in South Korea from 1998 onward. The administration sought to encourage private-sector exchange with the North, and North-South rapprochement reached new levels with the first summit meeting between President Kim and Kim Jong-Il in Pyongyang in June 2000. This was followed by the visit of the U.S. secretary of state, Madeleine Albright, to North Korea in October 2000 and the potential agreement to suspend the missile program in return for economic assistance. Japan also moved toward engagement, agreeing to restart negotiations for normalization and food aid in August 2000. These moves to engage North Korea have been loosely coordinated through the Trilateral Coordination and Oversight Group (TCOG) composed of senior officials.

During the early stages of the George W. Bush administration, and especially following the events of 9/11, new fears have arisen. The Bush administration made it clear in 2001 that it expected greater North Korean reciprocity on nuclear issues, the missile program, and conventional weapons. In February 2002, President Bush identified North Korea as one of the members of the "axis of evil." North Korea responded by demanding compensation for the late progress of the LWRs. U.S. officials were prepared to visit the North for new bilateral talks in July 2002, but these were postponed due to a military patrol boat clash between the North and South the previous June. U.S.–North Korea bilateral talks finally took place in October 2002, when the United States confronted the North with the information that it was aware of a second secret program to enrich uranium. North Korea admitted to the program, then stated its intention to reactivate its Yongbyon reactor and that only a nonaggression pact with the United States could prevent conflict. The United States and North Korea declared that the 1994 Agreed Framework was effectively dead. In January 2003, North Korea announced its withdrawal from the NPT and began to conduct surface-to-ship missile tests in the Sea of Japan. Meanwhile, the United States remained reluctant to engage the North, as it was preoccupied with the war in Iraq.

Japan and South Korea were alarmed by a possible second nuclear crisis. Japan undertook a bold diplomatic initiative with the visit of Prime Minister Koizumi Junichirō (2001–) to Pyongyang on 17 September 2002 for talks with Kim Jong Il. The visit produced the Japan-DPRK Pyongyang Declaration whereby the North admitted responsibility for the abduction of fifteen Japanese citizens in the 1970s and agreed to abide by international agreements on its nuclear program and its own moratorium on missile tests. Japan promised to provide significant economic cooperation to North Korea for restructuring its economy. Japan's initiative was designed to demonstrate to North Korea its solidarity with the United States on the issue of WMD, as well as to demonstrate to the United States the importance of dialogue in attempting to resolve these issues. Japan–North Korea normalization talks resumed in October 2003 but ultimately stalled over the fate of the Japanese abductees. Japan still hopes for a resolution on the nuclear issue through bilateral U.S.–North Korea talks, but its security concerns vis-à-vis the North mean that it supports the hard-line U.S. approach. In the meantime, South Korea under Kim Dae Jung, then under President Roo Moo-Hyun, continued to pursue engagement.

As of August 2003, Japan and South Korea were attempting to restrain the United States and North Korea from blundering into an unnecessary military conflict. But the North's fears that the Bush administration is totally unwilling to negotiate absent disarmament, and that the United States may be intent on regime change in the North, may harden the North's resolve to acquire nuclear weapons to guarantee its own security. In talks involving North Korea, the United States, and China in Beijing in June 2003, the North declared that it possessed nuclear weapons and that it was close to reprocessing its plutonium stocks. The prospect of a nuclear North Korea further destabilized the military balance in Northeast Asia and forced Japan to consider acquiring BMD.

In tandem with this stabilized but volatile security situation in and surrounding the Korean Peninsula, there are renewed concerns about Taiwan. As in Korea, decolonization, territorial division, the retreat of bipolarization, and globalization revitalized Taiwan as a regional security issue. The decline of bipolarization and the collapse of the Soviet Union provided China greater strategic freedom and the reduced need to tolerate U.S. military hegemony as a counterweight to Soviet influence. Meanwhile, the onset of globalization set China on the path toward potential great power economic and military status. The expansion of Chinese economic power also led to the perceived expansion of its military power. Following the end of the Cold War, and having witnessed the ability of the United States to crush Iraqi opposition with modern technological weaponry during the Gulf War of 1990–1991, China's military leadership increased defense expenditures and qualitatively upgraded the People's Liberation Army's (PLA).

China is believed to have a small arsenal of around twenty ICBMs and is seeking to increase that number and acquire technology for the multiple independently targetable reentry vehicle (MIRV). In addition, it is building up its SRBM and IRBM forces. China has also sought to reduce conventional forces while upgrading its combat capabilities. Hence, it has procured Russian-designed Su-27 advanced fighter aircraft and acquired for the first time a bluewater navy, including Russian-built Sovremennyy-class destroyers and Kilo-class submarines, and may even acquire an aircraft carrier. China thus began a gradual shift from fighting the traditional "people's war" in defense of the Chinese interior toward fighting modern technological and regional wars beyond its immediate borders (Godwin 1996; Asano 2000). However, the overall objective is to coerce Taiwan and to obtain an asymmetric strike power against the United States and its allies to deter any intervention there (Christensen 2001).

China's actions have paralleled the reunification of Hong Kong (1997) and Macau (1999) pursuant to Deng Xiaoping's "one country, two systems" formula. It has sought to apply the same formula to Taiwan, or at least to prevent it from moving toward independence. In turn, China's interest in Taiwan has only increased with the changes wrought by globalization. Globalization has promoted democratization in Taiwan, President Lee Teng-hui's formula for equal relations, and the election in March 2000 of President Chen Shui-bian of the Democratic Progressive Party (DPP), which is known to favor independence. All these increased the fears about a Taiwanese breakaway. In response, China has reserved the right to use military force if necessary to prevent independence.

Thus from the mid-1990s onward tensions across the Taiwan Strait increased. There is the potential for a military clash between China and Taiwan, which could also involve the United States and Japan. China's March 1996 ballistic missile tests and military exercise were an attempt to intimidate Taiwan and influence the outcome of presidential elections. China's military activities drew a similar U.S. response to the crises in the Taiwan Strait of 1954–1955 and 1958 with the dispatch of two aircraft carriers to waters off Taiwan to deter further escalation. China at this time was practicing its own form of brinkmanship and had no intention of launching a direct attack against Taiwan. Moreover, China's leadership was fully aware that the PLA's capabilities were inferior to those of the U.S. military and that it lacked sufficient air and naval power to mount an amphibious assault against Taiwan.

Nonetheless, China could project military power beyond its borders with SRBMs and thereby compensate for its conventional weaknesses vis-à-vis the United States and its allies. And over the longer term, some estimate that China can increase the pressure on Taiwan with the ability to blockade the SLOCs around Taiwan and the potential to achieve eventual air superiority between 2005 and 2010 (U.S. Department of Defense 1999). Eventually it might even acquire the ability to launch an amphibious invasion. Some still view China as unable to "conquer" Taiwan militarily for the foreseeable future (O'Hanlon 2000b).

If any of these scenarios become reality, the United States might feel it necessary to intervene to defend Taiwan; the conflict would affect Japan due to possible U.S. demands for logistical support and Chinese violations of Japanese territorial waters near Taiwan. Clearly, the preferred U.S. policy on Taiwan has been its declared "one China policy" coupled with strategic ambiguity (Nakai 2000: 82–83), whereby it preserves military capabilities to defend Taiwan but makes no overt commitment to do so. China is thus uncertain whether it could attempt to retake Taiwan militarily without a military U.S. response, and Taiwan is fearful of declaring independence for the lack of certainty that the United States will come to its defense. This preserves the status quo and encourages China and Taiwan to resolve their differences peacefully. However, under the Bush administration this policy may be shifting, with the president's declaration in April 2001 that he would do "whatever it took" to defend Taiwan. U.S.-China tensions were heightened by the midair collision of a Chinese fighter and a U.S. EP-3 spy plane over Hainan Island in April 2001.

Thus, the Korean Peninsula and Taiwan stand as two interstate security problems involving the lone superpower, major regional powers, and a regional power that have reemerged in the post–Cold War era in Northeast Asia. However, it is not the case that the end of the Cold War has meant entirely negative effects on interstate security. For instance, in Southeast Asia the disengagement of the Soviet Union and the cessation of Sino-Soviet and U.S.-Soviet rivalries produced a willingness on all sides to resolve the conflict in Cambodia (Acharya 2001a: 90–94). The decline of Soviet military support for Vietnam persuaded it to withdraw from Cambodia; China and the United States also lost the need to support the Khmer Rouge to check Vietnamese and Soviet expansion. Hence, Vietnam withdrew its forces from Cambodia in September 1989, and the International Conference on Cambodia held in Paris in October 1991 concluded an accord whereby the UN would take responsibility for implementing a peace plan and elections in 1993. The United Nations Transitional Authority in Cambodia (UNTAC) was put in place to supervise PKOs and the conduct of elections.

These elections established a fragile coalition government composed of the Cambodian People's Party (CPP), the successor to the Kampuchean People's Revolution Party that had formed the previous Vietnamese-backed government, and FUNCIPEC (translated, the National United Front for an Independent, Neutral, Peaceful, and Cooperative Cambodia) led by Prince Norodom Ranariddh, son of the reinstated monarch Prince Norodom Sihanouk. Ranariddh and Hun Sen, CCP leader and former prime minister, resolved to join the coalition government due to their common fear of the Khmer Rouge, which despite signing the 1991 Paris accord had refused subsequently to cooperate with UNTAC. The final result was the gradual decline of Cambodia as a problem of regional security; it was now a subregional interstate and intrastate security issue. Vietnam's withdrawal from Cambodia also lessened its presence as a threat to ASEAN and paved the way for Vietnam, Laos, and Cambodia to enter ASEAN (in July 1995, July 1997, and April 1999, respectively).

Regional major power and regional power interstate military conflict and territorial disputes. The retreat of bipolar pressures opened up territorial disputes in the Northeast and Southeast Asia subregions, with the onset of globalization giving further momentum and thus placing them at the fore of the regional security agenda.

China's and Japan's interest in the exploitation of energy resources in the Senkaku Isles reemerged as a contentious bilateral issue. Sino-Japanese friction came in the wake of the Japan Youth Federation's repair of its lighthouse in 1988–1989 and the JCG's reported willingness to recognize it as a navigation point in 1990. However, the problem was largely suppressed when the Chinese government sought engagement with Japan in the wake of the Tiananmen Square incident. In February 1992, the Chinese government adopted the Law on Territorial Waters that laid formal claim to sovereignty over islands in the East China Sea and South China Sea, including the Spratlys, the Paracels, and the Senkakus. This was followed in August 1996 by the attempt of rightists from the Japan Youth Federation to construct another lighthouse on the Senkakus, which then drew private ships from Hong Kong and Taiwan to demonstrate support for Chinese and Taiwanese territorial claims.

At the time, both governments attempted to keep it from spiraling into a major dispute. The Chinese government was muted and constrained; the Japanese government attempted to control its own domestic pressure groups (Downs and Saunders 1998–1999: 132–138; Deans 2000: 124, 126), although it was forced to dispatch JCG ships to patrol the Senkakus. Since 1996 the issue has quieted, but it still contains the potential for conflict. China has sent more than twenty-five survey missions into the Senkaku area and Japanese EEZ to search for oil, and the Japanese Self-Defense Forces (SDF) continue to monitor the incursions of Chinese vessels. China, for instance, sent thirteen and then ten ships to the area in May and July 1999, respectively (Bōeichōhen 2000: 55), compared with only two in 1998 (McNally and Morrison 2001: 89). Japan for its part wishes to preserve its sovereignty without provoking a conflict with China. Hence, Japan has maintained a low profile but also insists that the U.S. Department of Defense state that the security treaty extends to cover the Senkakus to deter any Chinese move to disturb the status quo (Green 1999: 161–162).

Japan's territorial dispute with South Korea over the Takeshima Islands also flared up. The indeterminate status of the islands following Korea's decolonization, and the desire for both Japan and South Korea to acquire productive fisheries and possible mineral resources for economic development, have been the principal causes. South Korea's construction of a wharf on Takeshima in February 1996 led to statements by Foreign Minister Ikeda Yukihiko that it represented an infringement of Japanese sovereignty, with domestic protests following in reaction in South Korea. The Japanese and South Korean governments, wishing to avoid conflict and sharing concerns over North Korea, deescalated the dispute. Hence, the governments negotiated a bilateral agreement in October 1998 to establish a joint fishing zone around the islets 64 kilometers from their respective shores (Paul 1999: 135–136; Green 2001a: 131–133).

However, sovereignty over the Spratly Islands has figured as the most prominent conflict in East Asia. This was heightened by the combination of globalization, increased demand for natural resources, and the retreat of bipolarization and the U.S. military presence. China and the ASEAN states have an interest in the oil and mineral resources there, and the withdrawal of the U.S. military from the Philippines provided them with the motivation to expand military capabilities in the South China Sea in pursuit of territorial claims.

China announced in August 1990 that it was prepared to set aside the issue to concentrate on joint resource development. However, China's declaration of its Law on Territorial Waters in February 1992 indicated renewed determination to exert sovereignty over the Spratlys. This was followed in May by China awarding a U.S. oil company exploration rights in the South China Sea just 160 kilometers from Vietnam's coast, with the apparent pledge that it would protect these concessions with military force (Valencia 1997: 96). The ASEAN states responded by issuing in July 1992 the Declaration on the South China Sea that called on all claimants to resolve issues of sovereignty without resort to force. The Indonesian government also sponsors the annual Workshop on Managing Potential Conflicts in the South China Sea. This produced the Bandung Statement stressing that interested parties should not resort to unilateral actions that could increase tensions. China has exercised caution, but this has not prevented a gradual buildup in tensions (Whiting 1997). Vietnam has continued to demand that China remove its drilling rigs, and the Philippines discovered in 1995 that China had occupied its claimed territory in Mischief Reef. In March 1995 the first violent clash between China and an ASEAN state occurred when a Chinese fishing boat was fired upon by Malaysian naval vessels when it was discovered in waters that Malaysia claimed (Acharya 2001a: 135).

Periodic clashes have also occurred between the Philippine navy and Chinese fishing vessels around Mischief Reef and other areas; and China further strengthened its structures on Mischief Reef in 1998. In the meantime, Indonesia was concerned that China's territorial claims could conflict with its own control of the oil-rich Natunas Islands to the south (Dupont 1998: 33); all the ASEAN states involved moved to build structures on various reefs within the islands to stake claims against China and each other. The potential for intra-ASEAN disputes was demonstrated in October 1999 when Vietnamese troops on Tennent Reef fired on Philippine air force reconnaissance aircraft (Baker and Morrison 2000: 132).

ASEAN and China have sought to address the problem in bilateral and multilateral contexts. China has not been prepared to discuss the issue but negotiated a bilateral agreement with Vietnam in October 1993 on the nonuse of force, and with the Philippines in August 1995 on negotiated settlement. The strength of these agreements in restraining China's behavior has been in doubt. But the ASEAN states have placed the Spratlys issue on the multilateral agenda of ARF since 1995. The ASEAN states have also increased their military capabilities to counter China's increasing strength in the South China Sea (Gallagher 1994: 138–145).

Beyond the Spratlys, Malaysia and Singapore continue to contest Pedra Branca, and Malaysia and the Philippines Sabah. Interstate tensions bordering on violence can occur (Acharya 2001a: 130).

Intrastate military conflicts. In Southeast Asia, intrastate security conflicts have declined in significance. Weakening communist insurgency movements play a part (e.g., the CPM surrendered to Thai and Malaysian authorities), but some continue their guerrilla struggles, as in the Philippines.

Likewise, following the establishment of the coalition government in Phnom Penh in 1993, the Khmer Rouge continued its insurgency movement. Devoid of external support, the group largely disintegrated and surrendered by 1999. The focus of internal conflict shifted to political tensions between the coalition government partners. New elections were held in July 1998 and a power-sharing compromise was established whereby Hun Sen assumed the sole premiership and Ranariddh the presidency of the National Assembly.

In contrast, separatist and irredentist intrastate conflicts rose during the post–Cold War period. The process of decolonization, political contradictions, systemic weaknesses, and the security gap dividing states and citizens, especially minority ethnic groups, led to separatism during the Cold

War. However, separatism could also be suppressed by a strong and centralized state using the benefits of accelerated economic growth through proto-globalization. In the post–Cold War period, though, constructing centralized sovereign states, economic growth, and social contracts between government and populations were undermined by other forces (Dibb et al. 1998: 15). The economic crises from 1997 onward produced a corresponding crisis of "embedded mercantilism" and its mechanisms for compensating dissident socioeconomic and ethnic groupings with the body politic of many Southeast Asian states (Jayasuriya 2001: 41). In addition, globalization spurred processes of democratization. Sovereign states can no longer easily paper over the cracks in their multiethnic societies and contain intrastate military conflicts.

The most prominent example is Indonesia, where the financial crisis led to political crises (Huxley 2002: 14), the fall of President Suharto in May 1998, the ouster of his successor, President B. J. Habibie (1998–1999), and then the impeachment of President Abdurrahman Wahid (1999–2001). The political paralysis and wider instability led to the enfeeblement of the apparatus of the state and control over its provinces (Wee and Jayasuriya 2002: 478). In turn, this has reduced its ability to suppress separatist movements either through economic benefits or through brute force and intimidation (Anwar 2001: 356–366).

Hence, a referendum on independence for East Timor in August 1999, overseen by the UN, produced a decisive 78.5 percent in favor. The refusal of Indonesia's military to accept the vote led the government to sponsor local militias to sack the East Timorese capital of Dili. Internal conflict in East Timor forced close to three-quarters of its total population of 890,000 to seek refuge in West Timor and neighboring islands; 90 percent of the province's physical infrastructure was destroyed. This raised international concerns about humanitarian impacts and any actions in contravention of UN mandates, as well as the possible breakup of Indonesia. The international community chose to intervene in September 1999 through the Australian-led and UN-authorized International Force in East Timor (INTERFET) PKO mission. The strength of this force eventually reached 11,500 troops, and the UN Transitional Authority East Timor (UNTAET) took responsibility for East Timor's move to independence by May 2002.

Meanwhile, other independence movements occurred, such as the Gerakan Aceh Merdeka (GAM, Free Aceh Movement), which stepped up its armed insurgency in Aceh. The Indonesian military's attempts to suppress the rebellion led to a cycle of human rights abuses and hundreds of civilian deaths (Sukma 2001: 383–390); GAM struck liquefied natural gas plants and interrupted energy supplies to the region. The Indonesian provinces of Riau, South Sulawesi and Irian Jaya (Papua) have also become restive (Baker and Morrison 2000: 86), with a number of deaths resulting from clashes between civilians and police (McNally and Morrison 2001: 79).

President Wahid endeavored to address the Aceh intrastate conflict through talks with the GAM and the negotiation of a "humanitarian pause" between late 2000 and early 2001 as an opportunity to deliver assistance to populations affected by the conflict. This and other peace initiatives have failed to stop the conflicts in Aceh and elsewhere, and the Indonesian government has had few answers other than the preparation of special regional autonomy bills introduced in early 2001. The demands for independence in the provinces appear to be incompatible with a unitary state; political instability following Wahid's impeachment may increase centrifugal secessionist pressures, raising the prospect of Indonesian *disintegras* (Huxley 2002).

Moreover, separatist conflict has continued elsewhere in Southeast Asia. Despite the negotiation in September 1996 of an agreement between the Philippine government and MNLF to establish the Autonomous Region of Muslim Mindanao, the breakaway Moro Islamic Liberation Front (MILF) continued and intensified its guerrilla war (Putzel 2000: 182), inspired by East Timor and the opportunities to achieve an independent Islamic state in Mindanao (Baker and Morrison 2000: 130). In May 2000, the MILF conducted bomb attacks and hostage-takings across Mindanao (McNally and Morrison 2001: 133). The Abu Sayaf Group, a breakaway group of the MNLF established in 1991 and committed to the region's independence, also conducted bombings and high-profile kidnappings of foreign tourists in 2001 in Mindanao. The Philippine government responded with an all-out and costly military offensive, with support from the United States. Meanwhile, the Burmese government continues its cycle of conflict and accommodation with a range of ethnic separatist groups.

Societal group and individual military conflicts. The security gap dividing the state and its population can affect the societal and individual levels. Consequently, the major referent objects, as well as in many cases deniers, of security in conflicts accentuated by globalization have been societal groups. The disastrous economic performance of many states in Southeast Asia and the scrabble for employment and basic human needs tend to increase economic frictions between different groups. In particular, the ethnic Chinese in Indonesia, long perceived to have accrued wealth at the expense of the Javanese majority, became a target immediately following the financial crisis. The result was the outbreak of urban and intercommunal violence directed at ethnic Chinese and, in many cases, the flights of these groups overseas. In total the riots in Jakarta and other urban areas of Java claimed up to 1,200 ethnic Chinese and Javanese lives (Johnson 2000: 75; Anwar 2001: 359).

These forms of intercommunal violence have not been limited to ethnic Chinese. Long-term economic tensions between Dayaks and transmigrant Madurese, heightened by the impact of the economic crisis, produced violent clashes, up to 3,000 fatalities, and thousands of refugees in West Kalimantan Province in 1999. Similar tensions in Central Kalimantan led to some 2,000 deaths in 2001 (Huxley 2002: 62–64). The economic crisis also formed a backdrop to social instability and the promotion of religious violence. For instance, from 1999 onward, Muslims and Christians have been involved in intercommunal violence in Ambon, the capital of the Indonesian province of Maluku, resulting in up to 10,000 deaths, 500,000 refugees (out of a population of 2.4 million), and widespread destruction of property (Huxley 2002: 56; Camilleri 2000: 270–271).

Malaysia saw intrastate conflict during this period, albeit on a far more limited scale than in Indonesia. Differences over economic policy triggered an elite power struggle between Prime Minister Mahathir Mohamed and Deputy Prime Minister Anwar Ibrahim from 1997 to 1999 (Milne and Mauzy 1999: 155–157), which spilled over into civil violence between police authorities and rival support groups. The effect has been to reexpose differences in economic status among the Malay majority and Indian and Chinese minority groups, leading to renewed religious and ethnic tensions and occasional intercommunal violence, as in Kuala Lumpur in March 2001.

Therefore, even though it is possible to argue that the decline of bipolarization has reduced the risk of major interstate war and nuclear conflict, and thus reduced the risk of violent conflict, the burden has shifted to certain ethnic and minority groups. The ability or inability of states to respond to these problems is discussed later in this chapter.

Organizational group military conflicts. The final level of security is the organizational group; terrorism and organized crime top the agenda. The retreat of bipolarization and onset of globalization have had mixed effects on terrorist threats. The diminishing strength of communist ideology has weakened terrorist organizations espousing revolutionary causes. In Japan, radical organizations such as the JRA have been reduced in strength to the point of near total elimination or irrelevance. Indeed, the JRA had become relatively inactive since the mid-1980s, and the remnants of its members, including its leader Shigenobu Fusako (arrested in late 2000), have been forced to abandon safe havens in Lebanon and been brought back to Japan to face trial.

But the continuing threat of terrorist groups in East Asia was demonstrated most strikingly by the Aum Shinrikyō (Supreme Truth) cult's sarin attack on the Tokyo subway on 20 March 1995. Aum showed itself to be capable of developing chemical WMD, to have ambitions to obtain biological and atomic WMD, and to purchase and mass-produce conventional weapons such as automatic rifles. The decline of bipolarization has been a significant factor in the formation of Aum because the collapse of the Soviet Union provided it with a potential arms market in Eastern Europe. Even more significant, globalization, the spread of IT, and reduced barriers to the movement of people enabled the group to acquire know-how in the production of WMD, to fund activities through various business enterprises, and to move with relative freedom on a global scale (Mackinlay 2002: 17–24). Moreover, Aum's involvement in the production of hallucinatory drugs and its business activities also made it an organized crime group. In many ways, Aum was unable to fulfill its more destructive visions and to master the development of all forms of ABC WMD. Nevertheless, its activities do indicate a qualitative leap in destructive potential that terrorist groups can possibly wield (Hughes 1998).

Other terrorist groups will continue to operate in East Asia on a lower technological basis but can nevertheless wreak destruction. Bomb attacks against civilian targets in Manila in December 2000 killed fourteen people; traditional terrorist organizations believed to have been responsible are the Muslim separatist NPA and the Abu Sayaf Group (Clamor 1999). The events of September 11, 2001, have also given impetus to terrorism in Southeast Asia and revealed the connections with Al-Qaida; the Bali bombing claimed close to 200 lives. Tibetan and Muslim separatists in Xinjiang have mounted bomb attacks against Chinese authorities from the mid-1990s onward. Narcotics traffickers and pirates also pose a major threat to all levels of security in the post–Cold War era.

Military Security: Responses and Frameworks

Responses to interstate conflict: augmentation of individual state capabilities. During the post–Cold War period, the traditional responses have continued, although with an emphasis on individual capabilities, the U.S.-Japan and regional bilateral alliances, and experimentation with multilateral security dialogue.

One of the most striking features is the buildup of individual sovereign state military capabilities, marked by increases in defense expenditures and modernization programs, leading to the horizontal and vertical proliferation of certain forms of conventional weapons and WMD. Defense expenditures in Northeast Asia are far greater than in the ASEAN states (U.S.$10–35 billion for Japan, China, South Korea, and Taiwan, compared to U.S.$1–5 billion annually in Southeast Asia). And during the 1990s, all states in this subregion, with the exception of Japan, increased their spending substantially (Ball 1993–1994: 80). Among ASEAN states, defense spending rose sharply between 1985 and 1996. In Indonesia, expenditures increased 44 percent; in Malaysia 47 percent; in Burma 61 percent; in Thailand 65 percent; in the Philippines 125 percent; and in Singapore 144 percent (Huxley and Willett 1999: 15). Among ASEAN states, only Vietnam decreased its spending (by 70 percent) due to the decline of Soviet military aid.

These increases in defense spending have been fueled on the supply side by the collapse of the Soviet Union and the Soviet threat; shrinking defense markets in Europe and North America have encouraged defense contractors to seek new customers in East Asia. Meanwhile, the United States faces competition in East Asian markets from the Russian arms industry, desperate to exploit export markets to survive and willing to sell high-tech weaponry at bargain prices. Hence, Russia has become the largest arms supplier to China and has enabled South Korea, Malaysia, and Indonesia to diversify its arms suppliers. On the demand side, globalization has provided the ASEAN states with the "largesse" to procure modern weapons systems (Ball 1993–1994: 80). Democratization, economic liberalization, and reform have also meant that the more liberal branches of the armed forces in East Asia, in particular naval forces, received funding for arms acquisitions for supporting such policies (Heginbotham 2002).

At the same time, the concerns described above, relating to the potential reduction of the U.S. military commitment in the region following the end of the Cold War, and the range of security problems that have been generated by the overlap of decolonization and globalization, have spurred arms acquisitions. The onset of the financial crisis, the need to reduce defense expenditures, and declining currencies restrained defense spending in Southeast Asia, with many ASEAN states canceling or postponing military procurement programs (Umbach 1998: 26). Nevertheless, China, Taiwan, and Singapore have been left relatively unscathed by the financial crisis in terms of defense expenditures (Huxley and Willett 1999: 21–22); other states of the region, despite the growth of democratic regimes less beholden to the military, intend to increase spending following economic recovery.

China concentrated on the qualitative upgrade of its conventional forces and WMD. North Korea focused on its nuclear and missile programs. South Korea responded with the procurement of a multirole fighter, new maritime power projection capabilities, and the development of its own 300-kilometer SRBM. (Japan's post–Cold War defense capabilities are described in Chapters 4 and 5.) In Southeast Asia, the military buildup has concentrated on restructuring defense forces from counterinsurgency to modern high-tech forces, with maritime (sea and air) power projection capabilities. The air forces of many ASEAN states have acquired multirole fighters with air-superiority capabilities as well as maritime attack capabilities (U.S.-built F-16s in Singapore, Thailand, and Indonesia; U.S.-built F/A-18s in Malaysia; British Aerospace Hawks in Malaysia, Brunei, and Thailand; Russian-built MiG-29s in Malaysia; and Russian-built Su-30s in Indonesia), as well as maritime reconnaissance aircraft. The ASEAN states have expanded their navies beyond coastal defense, acquiring modern surface and submarine combatants (missile-equipped large patrol craft in Brunei and the Philippines; corvettes and frigates in Thailand, Malaysia, and Indonesia; submarines in Singapore and Indonesia; and the subregion's first aircraft carrier in Thailand [capable only of leaving port once a month due to the declining Thai defense budget]) to protect SLOCs and maritime territorial interests. Finally, Singapore, Malaysia, and Indonesia have sought to create rapid-reaction forces, equipped with amphibious assault ships, transport aircraft, medium-lift helicopters, light tanks, and amphibious infantry vehicles (Ball 1993–1994: 102–103; Acharya 2001: 137–138; Huxley 2000: 60).

Responses to interstate military conflict: bilateral and multilateral security frameworks. In the post–Cold War period, the Soviet-centered alliance system and half of the bipolar balance of power collapsed, leaving the United States as the principal security guarantor in Northeast and Southeast Asia. In the mid-1990s and continuing today there have been doubts about the reliability of the U.S.-inspired San Francisco system as a means to guarantee security. The disappearance of the Soviet threat, and the U.S. withdrawal from bases in the Philippines, raised concerns of a possible power vacuum and destabilization. However, states of Northeast and Southeast Asia continue to view the United States as the essential balancer against North Korea and, more seriously, an irredentist China. Hence, despite problems in their alliances with the United States, both South Korea and Japan have sought to strengthen their military ties with the United States in the 1990s; and certain ASEAN states have been willing to offer facilities (Tow 2001b: 197–200).

The ASEAN states do not regard the U.S. presence as a guarantee against Chinese ambitions in the South China Sea. But the U.S. presence certainly represents insurance and deterrence. Consequently, the continuing limitations of the ARF process and U.S. concerns about China's reluctance to adhere to a code of conduct in the South China Sea have meant that it and the ASEAN states have increased security ties (Tow 1999: 10–17). The United States and the Philippines reimplemented the Visiting Forces Agreement (first ratified in May 1999) in January 2000 by conducting a joint exercise involving 5,000 troops. U.S. warships, as part of the exercise, also visited Palawan, the Philippine port closest to the Spratlys. These exercises were followed in February and June by joint U.S.-Philippines ground and naval exercises (Valencia 2001: 533); and in July 2000 by discussions between Admiral Dennis Blair, U.S. commander in chief of Pacific Command (CINCPAC), and Philippine counterparts over the right to use Subic Bay and Clark Air Base for servicing and repairs.

Following 9/11 and the Bali bombing in 2002, the United States and key ASEAN states drew closer together on antiterrorism. In November 2001, the Philippines secured U.S.$100 million in military aid, including one C-130 transport aircraft, eight UH-1 helicopters, fast patrol boats, trucks, and 30,000 M-16 rifles. In January 2002, the United States deployed 1,200 troops to the southern Philippines, including 160 U.S. special forces advisers, to assist the armed forces of the Philippines in combating the Abu Sayaf Group. In November 2002, the United States and Philippines signed the new Mutual Logistics Support Agreement, which granted the United States the right to stockpile military equipment in the Philippines. Indonesia has been more reluctant to accept U.S. military assistance for fear of domestic Muslim sentiment, but as of August 2002 the United States planned to provide U.S.$50 million in counterterrorism assistance to Indonesia (Capie and Acharya 2002: 10–11, 14–15).

At the same time, ASEAN states place high value on the continuation of the Five Power Defense Arrangements. Australia and Indonesia also experimented with the Agreement on Maintaining Security, signed in December 1995. This reversed Indonesia's long-standing opposition to formal security arrangements with external powers and was designed as a confidence- and security-building measure (CBM); it was abrogated in 1999 as a result of Australia's intervention in East Timor (Acharya 2001a: 181).

China has resolutely opposed all bilateral alliances, arguing that they promote U.S. hegemony and that a multipolar balance of power would be more stable. Instead, China put forward its "new security concept" at the ARF in 1997, arguing that no state should seek military superiority over others, that military cooperation between states should not be aimed at third parties, and that there should be no doctrine of military interference in other states' affairs (Shambaugh 1999–2000: 67). Nevertheless, even though China undoubtedly fears the continued U.S. presence, it also seems to perceive some benefits in the U.S.-Japan alliance by restraining further expansion of Japanese military power (Wang and Wu 1998).

The perceived necessity to look to external powers can be explained in part by the reluctance or failure to develop functioning frameworks for intraregional bilateral and multilateral defense and security cooperation. Japan and South Korea, with encouragement from the United States and with common concern over North Korea, have sought to improve bilateral defense contacts in the post–Cold War period and succeeded in overcoming some of the suspicions of the colonial past and Japanese militarism. But these efforts are concentrated mainly in CBM-style defense exchanges and fall far short of an effective bilateral defense framework. Moreover, ASEAN states have conducted bilateral military exercises among themselves. But defense ties have been hampered by interregional rivalries, the desire not to provoke China, and lack of interoperability of military equipment and thus never transformed ASEAN's status from diplomatic and security community to "defense community" (Acharya 2001a: 146–151).

In multilateral security cooperation, there has been remarkable progress in the initiation of institutions and dialogue, but also considerable retreat in the perceived ability of multilateralism to prevent interstate conflict. During the Cold War East Asia was characterized by the total absence of multilateral security arrangements. However, in the post–Cold War period conditions have begun to emerge for initiation of multilateral security dialogues.

President Gorbachev proposed in a speech in Vladivostok in 1988 the creation of a Pacific Ocean conference similar to the OSCE in Europe (then the Council for Security and Cooperation in Europe [CSCE]); this was followed by separate proposals from the foreign ministers of Canada and Australia in 1990 for the creation of a CSCE-like Conference on Security and Cooperation in Asia (CSCA). The military powers in East Asia at first were against multilateral security arrangements. The U.S. viewed them as ineffective in this region, preferring its bilateral hub and spokes system; China was concerned that multilateralism could undermine its territorial claims; ASEAN was concerned that any multilateral security arrangement defined by external powers could weaken its role in managing intrasubregional conflicts in Southeast Asia and undermine the bilateral alliance system of the United States (Acharya 2001a: 170).

Nevertheless, by June 1991 the ASEAN Institutes of Strategic and International Studies (ASEAN-ISIS) had begun to consider proposals that the ASEAN Post-Ministerial Conference (ASEAN-PMC) be utilized as a forum for multilateral dialogue, concerned as they were to consider some security framework that could hedge against any possible decline in U.S. military commitment to the region, or the growing military assertiveness of China. ASEAN-ISIS proposals became the basis for ASEAN's agreement to create the ARF in July 1993. Since July 1994, the ARF has met annually after each ASEAN-PMC; is committed to a three-stage evolution from CBMs, to preventive diplomacy (Tay 1999), and to conflict resolution; and takes an evolutionary approach stating that progress from one stage to the next is dependent on the consensus of all ARF members. The ARF intergovernmental process is also supported by the "track-two" process of contacts between academics and government officials from across the region in bodies such as the Council for Security Cooperation in the Asia-Pacific (CSCAP) founded in June 1993 (Ball 2000). By the time of the sixth ARF in 1999, membership had grown to encompass the ASEAN-10, Japan, China, South Korea, Mongolia, Russia, Papua New Guinea, Australia, New Zealand, Canada, and the United States. North Korea was admitted in 2000, but China has objected to the inclusion of Taiwan. The United States since the Clinton administration has been in favor of the ARF as a means of supplementing, rather than substituting, its bilateral alliance network. China has supported the ARF to influence the process from within and has attended all the ARF meetings since 1994. ASEAN has continued to support the ARF to preserve its role in facilitating regionwide cooperation and to keep the United States engaged as a balancer in regional affairs, even if preserving an arms-length relationship in defense cooperation. As of 2003, the stage of preventive diplomacy had not been reached, although its completion had been blocked by China's refusal to accept the working definitions of preventive diplomacy (Acharya 2001a: 177).

The ARF has significant limitations as a cooperative security arrangement. Cooperative security relies on the concept that no partner is a potential adversary. But in many instances China has felt targeted and constrained by the ARF. In addition, the ARF has been unable to discuss fully some key issues of regional concern, China vetoing discussion of Taiwan on the basis that it is an intrastate political problem (Yamakage 1997: 302), and with North Korea not joining until 2000. Discussion of the South China Sea has also been problematic. The Philippines drafted a code of conduct on this issue between ASEAN and China for discussion at the July 1999 ARF. China was reluctant to discuss the issue but after some pressure accepted that it should be referred to a working group (Valencia 2001: 529–530). China hosted the working group on a code of conduct for the South China Sea in Dalian in August 2000. Nevertheless, ASEAN's united position on the South China Sea was undermined to some degree by Malaysia's occupation just prior to the ARF of Erica and Investigator Reefs, also claimed by China, Taiwan, the Philippines, and Vietnam.

The ARF has also been hampered by its modes of conduct, modeled on ASEAN, meaning that decisionmaking can take place only on the basis of consensus and can thus easily be impeded by certain members (Narine 1997). But even though the ARF is not yet a multilateral alternative to the bilateral alliance system and balance of power, it does represent important progress in starting multilateral security dialogue and provides an arena and set of norms to conduct intraregional relations, thus making it harder for major powers to exercise military power unilaterally. Recent moves to enhance the capacity of the ARF to deal with regional conflict and to move toward preventive diplomacy offer additional hope. The ARF has also been proactive in response to 9/11 and the threat of transnational terrorism. The August 2002 ARF meeting introduced a program of action to prevent terrorist financing and fund-raising. This ARF agreement, unlike previous ones, was not voluntary and actually stated what was required of members (Capie and Acharya 2002: 17).

The difficulties of the ARF process have forced states to fall back on bilateral security ties with the United States and to experiment with various forms of "quasi-multilateral" security arrangements (although usually with the United States still playing a central role). On the macroregional level, APEC has increasingly discussed questions such as North Korea's missile program, East Timor, and 9/11. ASEAN+3 (ASEAN-10 plus China, South Korea, and Japan, instituted since 1999) has also discussed rapprochement on the Korean Peninsula, Indonesia, and nontraditional security issues, including transnational crime, contagious diseases, and the environment.

In Northeast Asia, there was the idea of forming the Northeast Asian Security Forum and six-party talks to include Russia, China, North and South Korea, Japan, and the United States; the first of these fora intended to supplement the four-party peace talks on the Korean Peninsula (Green

2001: 220–221). The United States also sponsored the creation of KEDO—perhaps the region's only true multilateral security institution, albeit one designed to use economic cooperation to deal with the military problem of WMD proliferation. As mentioned above, the United States, South Korea, and Japan have also been engaged in the TCOG to cooperate on policy toward North Korea. In July 2001, Australia proposed a new form of trilateral talks on security cooperation among itself, the United States, and Japan. In terms of military cooperation, the United States has organized the Rim of the Pacific (RIMPAC) exercises with the participation of a number of Asia-Pacific states (including Australia, Japan, and South Korea) since 1971. However, these exercises fall short of multilateralism, with the United States retaining the central coordinating role and conducting in essence a series of simultaneous bilateral exercises with each participant separately.

Indeed, the RIMPAC exercises reflect the continued U.S. predilection for "serial bilateralism" across East Asia. From the U.S. point of view, this serial bilateralism, or "multiple bilateralism," as a substitute for true multilateralism is advantageous in that it keeps security partners isolated from each other, handicapped in any quest to collectively organize against U.S. dominance (Leaver 2001: 31). Instead, as long as the United States provides a perceived guarantee of security, states in the region are likely to acquiesce in the prolongation of the San Francisco system and merely work to improve their marginal position with the system.

Frameworks for managing intrastate military conflicts. During the post–Cold War period, the militaries in many states in East Asia retain an important intrastate security function against political dissent and insurgency. Hence, for example, the Indonesian military, despite its gradual reorientation toward an external military role and the increasing check on its ability to deploy force without civilian consent, is still structured for internal security.

The ASEAN states along with China have also attempted to preserve the principle of noninterference as a means to provide a freer hand to deal with internal security threats. However, this principle has come under increasing stress as states face internal problems that cannot be easily contained within sovereign borders, threaten to spill over into regional problems, and demand that neighboring states take some form of action in response. ASEAN's position was first tested with its decision to admit Burma in 1997, which brought a host of security problems, including refugee flows and drug production. The difficulty of ASEAN turning a blind eye to problems that threatened its own organization, and concerns about the repressive nature of the SLORC regime and its suppression of the prodemocracy movement under Aung San Suu Kyi, led it to practice a form of constructive engagement to moderate the situation in Burma. Moreover, ASEAN also was forced to practice a form of intervention in delaying

Cambodia's entry to express dissatisfaction at Hun Sen's political coup in July 1997. Furthermore, ASEAN's norm of nonintervention was tested by the crisis in East Timor, where certain members were unable to ignore the humanitarian cause and, even more important, the risk of disintegration. Hence, Brunei allowed Gurkhas from its British garrison to be deployed to East Timor, and Thailand, Malaysia, and the Philippines contributed troop contingents to INTERFET. Indonesia did agree to accept the INTERFET force but only under international duress, meaning that these states had in effect breached ASEAN's principles on nonintervention (Singapore Institute of International Affairs 2001: 11). It is true, though, that ASEAN played only a minor role in managing the outcome of the East Timor crisis; outside military intervention by Australia and other states, provided with logistical support from the United States, ensured East Timor's independence from Indonesia (McDougall 2001: 174).

The role of economic development remains crucial. The cessation of the economic miracle in 1997 opened a Pandora's box of intrastate security problems in Southeast Asia. Efforts to restart economic growth will continue to be one of the keys to internal stability in the post–Cold War and postglobalization periods.

Economic Security

Stripped of the insulation and protective cocoon of the bipolar system, states in East Asia have been able to ride the globalization wave to achieve rapid economic growth to assist state-building. But they have also been exposed to violent downswings in the global economy, which in turn has opened long-suppressed security issues.

Economic exclusion. In the post–Cold War period, North Korea illustrates how the collapse of the bipolar system led to economic exclusion and the resulting security problems. North Korea's loss of access to socialist dispensations, and its reluctance to reform the economy and thereby risk undermining the regime, has led to economic decline and fears of total collapse. North Korean gross domestic product (GDP) is estimated to have declined at the rate of around 5 percent annually in the 1990s. Industrial production has broken down due to its overemphasis on state planning and heavy industrial instead of consumer goods. In agriculture, large sections of the population have experienced famine conditions due to the fixation on collectivization and clearing forests to create arable land; soil erosion was compounded by flooding from 1995 to 1997 (Hughes 1999: 124–125). The UN World Food Programme (WFP) estimated in 1997 that up to 800,000 North Korean children were malnourished (Dupont 1998: 48), and other sources have claimed that in certain rural regions food shortages have accounted for up to 2 million fatalities (Reese 1998: 30; Eberstadt 1999: 46; Noland 2000: 192).

North Korea's economic problems are accentuated by its accumulated foreign debt (up to U.S.$11.5 billion) (Hughes 1999: 135) and by the decline in its trading position. For instance, North Korea's trade with the Soviet Union and Russia plummeted from U.S.$2.7 billion in 1990, to U.S.$365 million, and then to U.S.$65 million by 1996 (Hughes 1999: 143). North Korea also saw the cessation of oil imports from Russia, a declining ability to exploit its own substantial coal reserves, and structural weaknesses in its energy generation and transmission infrastructures (Hughes 1999: 151). Hence, KEDO from 2002 onward was to play a vital role in meeting the North's energy needs. Finally, the North has been deprived of vital economic aid from the Soviet Union believed to be close to U.S.$2 billion between 1948 and 1980 (Hughes 1999: 155). In turn, the security implications are manifest: economic desperation, the risk of military conflict on the Korean Peninsula, food shortages, malnutrition, and an entire "lost generation" of physically and mentally stunted children (Smith 1999: 458–462).

Burma is another example. The failure of the "Burmese Way to Socialism" and its isolationist policies became apparent by the early 1980s. One of the most resource-rich states in East Asia had sunk to being one of its poorest, with an annual average per capita income of only U.S.$250 (Callahan 1995: 203). SLORC (renamed the State Peace and Development Council since 1997) has attempted to jumpstart its economy by encouraging foreign investment in oil and extractive industries and through promoting tourism. But the regime's political repression and hesitant economic reform has meant that external aid and FDI have been limited. Moreover, much of the foreign exchange gained has been channeled into arms procurements. The effects have been internal political strife between SLORC and the prodemocracy movement, which has intensified since the rearrest of Aung San Suu Kyi in May 2003; the further weakening of central government authority over its regions and secessionist movements; reduction of the government's ability to control the narcotics trade; and environmental destruction.

Economic disparity. Globalization's onset has also raised concerns about economic disparities, with possible consequences for regional security. In China, fears have grown that continued economic liberalization and WTO accession will accelerate disparities among its population and between the coastal and interior provinces. The gradual erosion under globalization of social guarantees and job security may be one cause of political tension. These could feed into political unrest and destabilization, with concerns about human security for the vast bulk of China's population yet to benefit from economic reform.

In addition, the rapid economic development in China's coastal provinces has raised concerns about the political disintegration, or "deconstruction"

(Segal and Goodman 1994), of China during the era of globalization. Such concerns may be exaggerated, as China's political system has shown considerable flexibility and resilience. However, the pressures of globalization are mounting, and the Chinese leadership has used nationalism to compensate for the decline of communist ideology and to hold the state together. The outcome is to exacerbate problems related to interstate security and the scramble for territory and resources.

Economic rivalry. Economic rivalry also intensified under globalization as states compete for access to the resources vital to rapid economic development and try to compensate for systemic weaknesses. The quantitative and qualitative decline in fresh water supplies in East Asia is troubling. The quantity of water available per capita in Asia is estimated to have dropped between 40–65 percent since 1950, and the quality of the water has declined due to deforestation, damming, soil erosion, and pollution. Major cities such as Beijing and Jakarta suffer from water shortages, and the Chinese minister for water resources admitted in 1993 that more than 83 million people in rural areas were finding it difficult to obtain fresh water (Dupont 1998: 61–64). The problem raises concerns over individual and human security, as well as interstate security. For instance, Singapore remains dependent on Malaysia for 50 percent of its water supplies and has a water-sharing agreement with Indonesia. The Singapore government fears that Malaysia's growing demand for water could lead it to reduce cross-border supplies; it also reacted sharply to President Wahid's comment in November 2000 that one way to prevent Singapore's profiteering from the economic woes of neighbors was to cut off the water supplies. Moreover, hydropolitics over drinking, irrigation, fishing, and transport could also increase among states in the Mekong Basin, Cambodia, Laos, Vietnam, Thailand, and China (Goh 2001). Although the first four states signed the Agreement on Cooperation for the Sustainable Development of the Mekong River Basin in April 1995, clauses therein enable them to divert water resources and construct dams, thereby affecting the water security of the others. China, controlling the source of the Mekong River and able to control water supplies to these states, is not a party to the agreement (Dupont 1998: 71).

Pressure on global food supplies due to population expansion and dietary changes is also increasing. The land becoming available for arable cultivation has declined since the 1970s, and some existing farmland has become less productive due to overcultivation, the overapplication of chemical fertilizers, and soil erosion. The possible food shortage coming to the region is symbolized by the fact that states such as Indonesia went from net food exporters to net importers, as well as the famine in North Korea. States such as Indonesia and China may be able to overcome future food shortages through the improvement of agricultural techniques (Li 2000:

178). But the issue of food supply will remain a constant concern for human security and interstate security if states become dependent on, and compete for, external food sources.

The third concern is fish stocks. Fish is a vital food resource, the principal protein source for some 1 billion people in East Asia. However, fish stocks have fallen, and aquaculture may not be a sufficient substitute for marine fishing. The competition to secure fish supplies has driven small-scale conflict in Northeast and Southeast Asia. Armed fishing vessels from Thailand have intruded into the EEZs of other ASEAN states and clashed with the naval forces of Malaysia, Vietnam, and Burma. For instance, in 1992 Burmese patrol boats sank ten Thai fishing vessels, accounting for the deaths of 200 crewmen (Ganesan 2001: 514); and in May 1995 Thai and Vietnamese gunboats exchanged fire after the Thai navy attempted to defend Thai fishing vessels from being seized by the Vietnamese navy. The Philippines regularly conducts arrests on Chinese and Taiwanese trawlers. In Northeast Asia, the South Korean navy has been placed on alert against Chinese fishing ships, and Russia has regularly impounded Japanese vessels around the Kurile Islands. Added to these low-intensity conflicts is the possibility of interstate military conflict over territorial claims in the Northern Territories, Takeshima, the Senkakus, and the Spratlys.

However, the fourth concern with implications for regional security is increasing rivalry for energy resources. The acceleration of economic growth in East Asian states, even allowing for the financial crisis, greatly expanded energy demands. From 1990 to 1996, total energy demand in East Asia grew at an annual average rate of 5.5 percent, compared to the global average of 1.5 percent (Stares 2000b: 19). East Asian states by 1996 accounted for more than one-fifth of global energy production and had doubled their consumption of oil. China is set to record the largest increase in the demand for energy supplies and since 1990 has been a net importer of oil (Salameh 1995–1996: 133). Japan imports 88 percent of its primary energy needs and 90 percent of its oil; despite its policy of diversification of supply, it still imports 80 percent of its oil from the Middle East. South Korea is in a similar position to Japan; North Korea has potentially greater but underdeveloped energy resources, leading to an energy crisis; and Taiwan has no energy resources at all. The states of Southeast Asia have also increased energy consumption, and even Indonesia, Malaysia, and Vietnam, formerly oil exporters, may soon become importers of oil (Dupont 1998: 28). The inability of states to provide for energy demands means that they will look to the Middle East as the major supplier.

This increased energy dependency need not necessarily lead to a frantic scramble for energy resources and increased insecurity. Global energy markets and reserves may adjust to meet the increased demand; technological improvements may lead to energy saving and better exploitation of existing energy resources; and many states are prepared to increase energy stockpiles. In addition, East Asian states are increasing interregional cooperation and diversifying energy sources. China has potentially rich and untapped oil fields in Tarim Basin in the Xinjiang Autonomous Region (Salameh 1995–1996: 138–139; Andrews-Speed, Liao, and Danreuther 2002: 53–58). The Russian Far East and Central Asia, with enhanced investment, may be able to meet many of Northeast Asia's energy needs, and there are plans to construct gas pipelines linking these energy resources with the subregion. Included among these are Russia's Vostok plan, running a pipeline from Yakutsk via Seoul to Fukuoka in Japan; China's Energy Silk Route Plan, linking the gas fields of Central Asia with China, South Korea, and Japan; and the Irkutsk plan, linking North and South Korea and Japan (Valencia 1997: 88–89; Dupont 1998: 30). All these plans, however, involve massive investment in infrastructure. The diversification of energy needs in Northeast Asia has taken form in plans to better exploit coal reserves and solar and geothermal power but above all to increase reliance on nuclear power. Japan operates fifty-three nuclear reactors and doubled its generation of nuclear power between 1985 and 1996. China constructed three nuclear reactors between 1992 and 1997 and is set to increase its dependency on this form of power (Gao 2000: 50–51); Taiwan operates three nuclear power plants; North Korea was set to acquire two LWRs under the KEDO project; and South Korea intends to build sixteen new nuclear plants by 2010 (Dupont 1998: 36). None of the ASEAN states as yet operates a nuclear plant, but rising energy demands caused Indonesia to consider the feasibility of introducing nuclear power (Zamzam 2000: 131).

Despite all the possibilities for alleviating future rivalries, the struggle for energy resources remains a major concern for the East Asian security agenda. Competing claims for EEZs, seabed oil, mineral resources, control of SLOCs to the Middle East—competition for such resources may be the key to dealing with interstate conflict (Calder 1996, 1997: 43–61).

Economic dislocation. The financial crisis of 1997 affected intrastate security by revealing the security gap dividing the state and citizenry. The financial flows engendered by globalization penetrate and transcend state borders and render ineffective the traditional role of the state in providing security for its citizens. Many states in the region, lacking any form of social safety net to cope with economic crisis, or gradually dismantling it by default, as in the case of China, have proved unable to absorb or to redistribute the costs of economic dislocation (Hill and Chu 2001: 14–18). The outcome for many citizens has been exposure to the effects of globalization and a view that the state is irrelevant to their personal security. The effect has been to threaten the livelihoods and human security of individuals.

For instance, following the outbreak of the 1997 financial crisis, the proportion of the Indonesian population in poverty rose from 11 percent to

17 percent; household per capita incomes fell an average of 33.9 percent in urban areas, 17 percent in rural areas. Indonesian households also experienced food insecurity due to panic-buying of key commodities and the removal of government subsidies under pressure from the IMF (Haggard 2000: 192–195, 203–204), as well as concerns about basic health and medicine (Yue and Bhanu 1999: 68–69). Economic dislocation also reopened intrastate conflicts by enfeebling the apparatus of the state and revealing ethnic differences in society, fueling democratization and the short-term convulsions that can result.

Migration. Economic exclusion, disparities, and dislocation generated intrastate and interstate migration during the post–Cold War era. North Korea's economic exclusion and gradual slide produced fears in China, South Korea, and especially Japan of mass migrations of refugees. Already 100,000–200,000 North Koreans are believed to have sought illegal sanctuary in China (Gurtov 2002: 36). China's gradual integration into the global economy, the accompanying freedom of movement for labor, and economic disparities among provinces led to internal migration and as many as 100 million migrant workers seeking employment in the Coastal Economic Zones (Skeldon 1999: 8).

Meanwhile, the financial crisis also produced labor migration and interstate friction in Southeast Asia. The growth of economic interdependence under globalization prior to the crisis had produced a relative rise in intrasubregional labor flows, with migrant workers coming to account for 20 percent of the labor force of Singapore and 20 percent in Malaysia (Skeldon 1999: 4). The financial crisis caused Malaysia to expel 500,000 Indonesia migrant workers, often forcibly, and raised political tensions between the states (Welsh 1999: 279). Thailand also expelled 300,000 migrant workers (Skeldon 1999: 6). In addition, Thailand has been the recipient of around 100,000 ethnic Karen refugees from Burma. These refugee flows were produced by the Burmese government's attempts from the late 1980s onward to suppress Karen insurgency movements within its borders (Ganesan 2001: 517).

Organized crime and narcotics. The decline of bipolarization, combined with the onset of globalization and continued impact of decolonization, accentuated the security problems associated with organized crime and narcotics in East Asia. The economic liberalization and integration, and the sustained economic growth that it has produced, generated new wealth for the consumption of narcotics. In turn, the supply has risen to meet the demand, facilitated by the ability of organized crime groups to mimic TNC behavior and to exploit global transportation and telecommunications links and weakening interstate barriers to transactions (McFarlane 2001: 198–199).

The Golden Triangle has been subsumed within a wider triangle that links Burma, Thailand, and Laos with the liberalizing economy of southern China, opening new opportunities for the organized crime groups of Hong Kong and Bangkok (Dupont 1999: 449). The onset of globalization also boosted demand and supply through economic integration, as well as economic disintegration and exclusion. The effect of the 1997 financial crisis and increased unemployment has been to persuade citizens that narcotics offer an economic lifeline. North Korea's exclusion from the region and its need for hard currency led government officials to conspire to export narcotics to surrounding states, including Japan. Finally, the process of decolonization, with its legacy of intrastate ethnic conflicts, has continued to undergird the narcotics industry in certain East Asian states. The BCP in 1989 and then Khun Sa in 1995–1996 surrendered to the Burmese military, raising hopes for an end to the involvement in narcotics (ODCCP 2001: 57). However, the suspicion is that in return for ending the insurgency these groups were allowed to continue drug trafficking (Dupont 1999: 443–445) and that government elements have been co-opted by organized crime groups, thus making Burma a so-called narcostate.

These processes brought about expansion in opium production in Southeast Asia from the late 1980s to the first half of the 1990s, stabilizing in the latter 1990s (Burma accounting for 23 percent of world production in 2000 [ODCCP 2001: 68]), with a massive increase in the use of amphetamine-type stimulants (ATS) in the 1990s (based on seizure rates, increasing on average 48 percent annually from 1990 to 1996). Opium and heroin use expanded in Thailand and China, as has ATS use in Thailand, Philippines, and Taiwan. ATS users total around 30 million in East Asia (Dupont 1999: 438) and account for 2.2 percent of the Philippines population and 1.1 percent of the Thai population (ODCCP 2001: 272). The security effects of the expansion of drug trafficking are readily apparent in East Asia. At the interstate level, the flood of drugs from Burma into Thailand has raised bilateral security tensions between these states and the rest of ASEAN since 2000. Japan–North Korea security relations also worsened with the latter's suspected export of ATS to Japan. At the intrastate level, the narcotics trade threatened to produce endemic corruption in the Philippines. At the societal group level, farming communities can become overdependent on the production of opium, undermining access to food supplies. At the human security level, drug addiction has a serious effect upon the health of individuals and risks the spread of HIV through intravenous drug use.

Piracy. Globalization and economic liberalization have led to a major expansion of sea traffic through the South China Sea SLOCs, increasing at an annual rate of 8 percent (Paul 1999: 124). At the same time, the financial crisis increased the attractiveness of piracy as an alternative economic activity, and a shortage of funds for regional coast guards and navies enhanced the ability of pirate groups to operate. Indeed, it may be the case that police and military authorities in Indonesia have cooperated with pirates to supplement their own incomes (Chalk 2000: 133). Decolonization's influence in this area is seen in the fact that separatist groups such as MILF and the Abu Sayaf Group in the Philippines and GAM in Indonesia are believed to practice piracy (Abbot and Renwick 1999a: 187–88; Huxley 2002: 82–83).

According to IMB figures, pirate attacks in Southeast Asia increased from fifty-six in 1991 to ninety-four by 1997 (Abbot and Renwick 1999b: 13), with the majority of attacks concentrated at the "choke points" around Indonesia. Pirates may rob the crew of the ship, hijack and steal the cargo, or even take the ship for resale. These attacks can involve the use of firearms and considerable violence toward individuals. For instance, between 1991 and 1997, 856 crew were taken hostage, 75 injured, and 106 murdered (Abbot and Renwick 1999b: 14); and in 1998, 35 sailors were injured and 67 killed in regional piracy incidents (Weeks 1999: 8). Piracy poses a threat not only to individual human security and the economic security of TNCs, their employees, and states; there are also concerns that pirate groups could seize or sink ships with cargoes potentially hazardous to human life and the environment, such as oil tankers. Japanese shipments of nuclear waste could be hijacked (Paik and Bergin 2000: 185); new Japanese antipiracy initiatives were worked out with ASEAN in the late 1990s.

Environmental Security

The gradual globalization of the sphere of interdependence, and then the acceleration of its effects across the merged spheres of interdependence and independence from the late 1980s onward, pushed environmental security concerns to the forefront of the post–Cold War security agenda.

HIV/AIDS, infectious diseases. In 1999, more than 2 million people were reported to have contracted HIV. The heaviest incidents were in Thailand (740,000), Burma (510,000), China (500,000), Cambodia (210,000), Vietnam (99,000), Indonesia (52,000), Malaysia (48,000), and the Philippines (26,000). Japan has 10,000 recorded cases of HIV. For Cambodia (4 percent), Thailand (2.2 percent), and Burma (2 percent) these incidences were particularly high in terms of the percentage of the adult community with HIV (Brandt 2001: 13). Intravenous drug abuse, the spread of the narcotics trade, and the commercial sex trade—all fueled by globalization—are contributing factors to the spread of HIV/AIDS. The impact of HIV/AIDS in East Asia is similar to other regions: disruption of family life and social stability, interruption of children's education, and the stimulation of other diseases such as tuberculosis. The disease also saps the economic vitality of many East Asian states by diverting resources to health care and by weakening the labor force. Thailand in 2001 was estimated to undergo a 9 percent contraction in GDP due to the disease (Brandt 2001: 20).

East Asia in 2003 also experienced an outbreak of SARS (severe acute respiratory syndrome), which by May had claimed 282 lives in China (WHO 2003: 10), thirteen in Hong Kong, and smaller numbers in other East Asia states (*Financial Times,* 1 April 2003: 17). SARS is expected to have a major impact on the East Asian economy as domestic consumption and foreign travel declines.

Environmental degradation. The high-speed economic growth of many of East Asian states, and the thirst for natural resources, generated new concerns about the depletion of renewable and nonrenewable resources. The rapid economic growth of many ASEAN states produced massive deforestation on an unsustainable scale. Indonesia (–10 percent), Malaysia (–18.4 percent), Thailand (–28.8 percent), and the Philippines (–28.8 percent [Contreras 2000: 351]) all lost significant areas of natural forest from 1980 to 1990; the Philippines and Vietnam are estimated to have lost about 70 percent and 50 percent of their mangrove forests, respectively; around 40 percent of land that is capable of sustaining tropical forest has lost its forest cover; and forest cover is declining at a rate of around 1 percent annually (Asian Development Bank 2001: 5). Land is under increasing pressure across East Asia, and the implications of forced agriculture development policies in North Korea have become clear with the onset of famine and the creation of "environmental refugees" (Lee 2000: 204). Fish stocks in the Yellow, South, and East China Seas are in decline as a result of increased demand from wealthier East Asian consumers (Dupont 1998: 50), leading to concerns of conflict over marine resources. Similarly, fresh water resources in Southeast Asia and China are increasingly under stress, again raising concerns that competition for supplies could lead to military conflict.

The depletion of renewable and nonrenewable sources is a result not only of increased demand but also the shrinking stock available due to environmental pollution. Deforestation in Cambodia, Laos, Burma, Thailand, the Philippines, Indonesia, China, and North Korea has affected the water cycle in those states (Dupont 1998: 62), producing soil erosion, water pollution, and in extreme cases, such as North Korea, desertification. Drinking water supplies in urban areas in Thailand, Indonesia, and China are in jeopardy due to pollution. The water supply available for agricultural usage is also declining. For instance, in the late 1980s it was estimated that 82 percent of China's major rivers were polluted, 20 percent to the point where the water was useless for irrigation. Marine pollution is increasing in the Gulf of Thailand, Manila and Jakarta Bays, the South China Sea, the Mekong Delta, and the waters off China, Japan, and South Korea. The overuse of chemical fertilizers and the increase in shipping has contributed to pollution in the Yellow, East, and South China Seas; increased tanker traffic also increased the probability of oil spills and related environmental destruction in areas such as the Strait of Malacca (Paul 1999: 124). For example, the Russian tanker *Nakhodka* broke up off the Japanese coast in January 1997, causing damage to fish and aquaculture in the area (Dupont 1998: 15).

There are also increased concerns about the risks of pollution from nuclear power generation and waste material. Japan demanded that Russia stop dumping liquid nuclear waste into the Sea of Japan in 1997 and is anxious about possible leaks of nuclear material from Russian nuclear submarines rusting at anchor in Vladivostok. For its part, Japan runs the risk of contributing to nuclear pollution. The Japanese government has continued to emphasize nuclear power generation to limit dependence on external supplies, resulting in the stockpiling of plutonium and mixed-oxide (MOX) material. Apart from the concerns of its East Asian neighbors that the stockpiling of plutonium represents a potential Japanese nuclear weapons program (Kim 1996), Japan's reliance on nuclear power raises environmental safety concerns. This was illustrated by the accident at the Tōkai Mura fuel conversion plant in September 1999, which led to the irradiation of plant workers. Japan's shipment of nuclear waste to Europe for recycling since 1993 has also created fears of a hijack or sinking that could lead to a nuclear environmental catastrophe.

Such fears surrounding land and water pollution have been matched by fears over air pollution. In Northeast Asia, China's drive for economic growth and expanded use of fossil and nuclear fuels engendered major environmental concerns. South Korea and Japan are concerned that China's increased output of sulfur dioxide (SO_2) from coal-burning power stations (already accounting for around 50 percent of totals [Dupont 1998: 14], and making it the largest emitter of this gas in the world [Gao 2000: 52]) will only intensify the current problems of cross-border acid rain deposition (Kojima 2000: 56). These states also harbor concerns that China's intention to enhance its reliance on nuclear power will lead to Chernobyl-like scenarios on their doorstep.

In Southeast Asia, the security impact of environmental air pollution was revealed by the forest fires across the Indonesian archipelago during 1997 and 1998. The fires in Kalimantan and Sumatra were the product of high-speed development policies that allowed unregulated logging and forest clearing and generated a haze that affected the health of literally millions of Indonesian, Malaysian, and Singaporean citizens (Cotton 1999). In many ways, the fires represented the apogee of the globalization-security nexus: they threatened human security, completely transcended sovereign-state borders, and revealed the inability to compartmentalize international and domestic security during the era of globalization (Weatherbee 2001: 159). In both Northeast and Southeast Asia, rapid economic growth is also affecting urban air quality. In addition, East Asia's output of greenhouse gases is contributing to the overall degradation of the biosphere. It is estimated that China is currently the second largest producer of carbon dioxide (CO_2) and will be the largest by 2020–2030 (Gao 2000: 52–53).

Finally, environmental destruction is accentuating the impact of natural environmental disasters upon security. The periodic flooding in North Korea that has contributed to poor harvests since 1995 has been the result of heavy rains and deforestation. The record flooding of the Yangtze River in China in 1998, which reportedly cost 2,100 lives and U.S.$30 billion, was also exacerbated by deforestation (Van Ness 1999: 330).

Environmental security: responses and frameworks. States in Northeast and Southeast Asia responded at the individual, bilateral, and multilateral levels. In Northeast Asia, there are a number of forms of environmental cooperation in place. These include the Memorandum of Understanding on Environmental Principles Governing the TRADP (China, North and South Korea, Russia, and Mongolia, signed in 1995); and the subregional Northeast Asian Conference on Environmental Protection, the Northeast Asian Regional Environment Program, the Northwest Pacific Action Plan, and the Economic and Social Commission for Asia and the Pacific. In Southeast Asia, the ASEAN Environmental Program was established in 1978 to promote sustainable development. ASEAN produced its first declaration on the environment in 1981, then the Kuala Lumpur Accord on the Environment and Development in 1990 (Hernandez et al. 2000: 127), reaffirming the organization's commitment to sustainable development. ASEAN also produced the 1992 Singapore Resolution on the Environment, the 1994 Bandar Seri Begawan Resolution on the Environment and Development, and the 1995 ASEAN Cooperation Plan on Transboundary Pollution. At the macroregional level, APEC encouraged dialogue on maritime transport of hazardous substances and marine pollutants, holding the first APEC environment ministers' conference in 1994. The Environment Congress of Asia and the Pacific was also established for APEC to monitor acid rain (Shouchuan 2000: 221). In addition, many states are party to global conventions on maritime pollution (Weeks 1999: 13).

Despite encouraging signs of reinforcing environmental cooperation, state responses have been complicated by territorial disputes, economic rivalries, and modalities of noninterference that hamper the effective functioning of environmental regimes. The clearest instance was ASEAN's reaction to the Indonesian forest fires. ASEAN established the Haze Technical Task Force in 1995, but it proved largely ineffective. This was in part the result of ASEAN's norms of noninterference, which did not prevent the creation of cooperative environmental regimes but meant that they could not be imposed without the consensus of members (Acharya 2001a: 155–156; Cotton 1999: 17). Instead, individual Southeast Asian governments were forced to criticize Indonesia outside the framework of ASEAN.

Conclusion: A Comprehensive Security Agenda

This chapter has analyzed the emergence and reemergence of military, economic, and environmental security problems in East Asia due to decolonization, bipolarization, and globalization. During the Cold War and post–Cold War period, these formed a multifarious and complex security agenda that demands an equally sophisticated response. In the post–Cold War period in particular, there has been a multiplication of security actors. The sovereign states of East Asia remain key and powerful actors, but the security agenda of the region is also set by nonstate actors such as TNCs and transnational crime groups, especially in the dimensions of societal and individual military and economic security.

At the same time, the frameworks involving these actors, and for addressing the range of extant security problems, are insufficient. The response of states as the principal providers of security on the individual and bilateral levels is still crucial, but there is a need for multilateral frameworks of cooperative, common, and collective security to deal with problems that cut across boundaries. Moreover, security actors can be under no illusion that the deployment of military power will be sufficient, or even relevant, to address the array of security problems they face. Military power is central, but there is also a need for economic power to supplement military power in dealing not only with military insecurity due to economic disintegration but also real security problems associated with economic disintegration and environmental degradation.

Hence, the final conclusion from assessing the security agenda in East Asia is that a truly effective approach must account for multilevel actors; it must be multidimensional to encompass military, economic, and environmental security; and it must include multiple and combined forms of military and economic power. In short, the agenda and response of the East Asian states must be comprehensive. As will be seen in Chapter 4, Japanese traditions of comprehensive security mean that Japan may be uniquely equipped to deal with the regional security agenda.

4

Japan's Comprehensive Security Policies in the Cold War Era

Japan as a security actor in East Asia has an identity problem. Security actors can be deniers, suppliers, and referent objects of security. Japan's predominant identity has been that of denier. This identity in East Asia was a threat to regional security, originating in Japanese colonialism from the Meiji period to the end of the Pacific War. Japan's unusually harsh program of emulating and supplanting Western modes of colonization left a historical legacy of mistrust. That legacy is strongest in China and the Korean Peninsula in Northeast Asia, and varies in strength across Southeast Asia.

This continuing antipathy was revealed by the textbook controversies of 1982 and 1986 (Hook et al. 2001: 168–169), and again in 2001 with renewed textbook controversies and Prime Minister Koizumi Junichirō's decision to visit Yasukuni Shrine (devoted to Japan's war dead and including Class A war criminals). Economic penetration of the Northeast and Southeast Asia by TNCs during the postwar period perpetuated this threat perception, demonstrated by anti-Japanese riots over "economic imperialism" during Prime Minister Tanaka Kakuei's (1972–1974) visit to Southeast Asia in 1974 (Hook et al. 2001: 187).

Japan still poses security threats to its neighbors, especially in the dimension of economics. The Japanese state and TNCs are involved in globalization processes and their associated security problems. Moreover, Japan's identity as a denier of security constrained its ability to function as a regional security actor. The identity of Japan as a potential military threat is an international structural constraint on its ability to project military power. Likewise, the atomic bombings and defeat in the Pacific War created powerful norms of anti-militarism that constrain Japan's utilization of military power for security ends (Hook 1996b; Katzenstein 1996b; Berger 1998).

Japan's identity as a denier of security will not be overlooked. However, the principal focus is to evaluate Japan as a referent object and provider of security. In the case of Japan as a referent object of security, the concentration will be upon analyzing security at the individual state level. Some critics argue that Japan, throughout the process of nation-building from the mid–nineteenth century to today, has exercised actual and structural violence over minorities within its borders, such as Okinawans, Ainu, and Koreans. Moreover, the period of ultranationalism and the Pacific War culminated in total defeat and the atomic bombings of Hiroshima and Nagasaki. In these instances, the security interests of the state and general population became unbundled, the casualties being viewed as victims of state policy. Furthermore, the security interests of many Japanese citizens diverged from state policy during the revision and extension of U.S.-Japan security arrangements in 1960 and 1970 and in the antinuclear movement since the mid-1950s. Nevertheless, despite potential divisibility, national unity produced a correlation of security interests. Hence, the use of the word *Japan* as a referent object of security means "national security" or the security of the Japanese "nation."

Japanese Conceptions of Security

Levels of Security

Japanese policymakers and citizens, especially following the Pacific War and Cold War, have possessed a multilevel and multidimensional "holistic" conception of security (Hughes 1999: 33). The role of the state as the referent object and provider of security has remained central, a perspective derived from Japan's drive to achieve nation-state status and the government's self-appointed role as gatekeeper of security.

However, Japanese security conceptions range above and below the level of sovereign state. Japanese policymakers have been concerned with the condition of the interstate security system. Japan's self-perception as a weak newcomer to the system, coupled with the trauma resulting from defeat and incorporation under U.S. hegemony, mean that policymakers understand that Japan's security fate is linked to stability at the interstate level. Thus, Japan has participated in bilateral and multilateral frameworks to achieve security at that level.

Below the interstate system and individual state, Japan has also concentrated on intrastate security. In the body politic, as in other developing states, some societal groups' security interests may diverge from those of the state. Japan has managed to overcome this fact through economic development and state-building, but other states in East Asia are undergoing similar developmental processes that may lead to insecurity. Ironically, Japan's understanding at this level is reinforced by its experience of imperialism and the knowledge that states in the region have diverse ethnic and social makeups. Thus, policymakers recognize that East Asia is subject to internal systemic weaknesses and intrastate conflict.

Thus we see Japan's response of economic development and state-building programs to achieve domestic and interstate stability. Japan's approach, evolutionary and pragmatic, emphasizes securing basic human needs, then gradually moves toward securing higher levels of human rights, especially political rights. For Japan, securing basic human needs means a peaceful and healthy environment, with access to humanitarian assistance. The next stage, after such economic rights, is to progress toward higher levels of human rights, including political freedoms. All of these stages presuppose a minimum political and legal order, which in turn requires economic development (Watanabe 2001: 76).

The result is muted criticism from the government, actively or passively supporting "soft" and "hard" authoritarianism if it leads to a process of developmentalism for economic and political benefit. Japan's faith in developmentalism and state-building reflects its view that authoritarianism and containment of internal conflict can be an unsavory but necessary stage in the progression toward stronger sovereign statehood and stability especially when facing conditions of globalization.

Japanese perceptions extend downward to the individual level as well, again derived from the experience of defeat, specifically the atomic bombings. These experiences produced the view that true peace could be achieved only through individuals contemplating the destructive effects of direct and structural violence (Takahashi and Nakamura 1979). In this sense, the individual became the essential component of state and interstate security—the experience of each individual acting as a check upon further violence at higher levels by states.

Human Security

The importance of the individual as a referent object and actor in security has strengthened the Japanese concept of "human security" with regard to military threats, but particularly economic and environmental security threats. Japan's conception of human security emphasizes threats to human life, livelihoods, and dignity generated by globalization: poverty and debt relief, environmental degradation, illicit drugs, transnational crime, infectious diseases such as HIV/AIDS, health care, refugees, and the proliferation of small arms and antipersonnel landmines (Gaimushōhen 2001: 61; Paris 2001: 90; Kurusu 2001: 138–139). Japan's focus on human security is humanitarianism, emphasizing the most basic level of human rights.

As will be seen in Chapter 6, the Japanese government's human security priorities have involved providing access to humanitarian assistance and the immediate securing of human health. However, the concept can be seen to link with those concerned with societal level security in that it presupposes over the longer term that the true conditions for securing human health and livelihoods, and thus preventing and resolving conflict conditions, can be ensured only through staged and interlinked economic and political development. The Japanese government has stressed human security in the wake of the East Asian economic crisis, which demonstrated in states such as Indonesia the links among economic poverty, declining health care, political instability, and human and intrastate security. Prime Minister Obuchi Keizō (1998–2000) established a U.S.$80 million (later expanded by U.S.$100 million under Prime Minister Mori Yoshirō) United Nations Trust Fund for Human Security in late 1998 to support UN human security agencies, and the government established the Commission for Human Security in January 2001, charged with deepening understanding of the concept. The commission produced its final report in May 2003, and it reemphasized many of the basic human needs and development priorities of Japan's human security agenda. But the report also indicated future flexibility in the concept by stressing the need for "empowerment" and achievement of greater political rights (Commission on Human Security 2003).

Hence, the Japanese view of security exists at multiple levels, with sovereign states as the central building blocks of security, matched by the recognition that the stability of states is dependent upon addressing internal security problems at the societal group and individual levels. Japan's intuitive understanding of the dynamics of inter- and intrastate security conflicts provides useful approaches and notable successes in domestic and regional security, especially based on norms and modes of developmentalism.

Nevertheless, this position leads to contradictions and inconsistencies. The idea that the state is the principal building block of regional security can undercut the human security issue. For example, Japan has tolerated the regime in Burma despite its human rights violations and supported the territorial integrity of Indonesia and the Indonesian military. This support continued even when it became clear that the human and societal group interests of Indonesia's minorities could not be reconciled with a state apparatus that was failing in state-building and developmental objectives. In this sense, Japan's tendency to emphasize more "freedom from want," in terms of the provision of basic human needs and material livelihood, can sit uncomfortably with conceptions of human security that prioritize "freedom from fear," in terms of the provision of human rights and political freedoms (Acharya 2001b: 460).

Military, Economic, and Environmental Dimensions

Japanese conceptions of security are also multidimensional, encompassing military, economic, and environmental issues. Japan's role in the military dimension has been one of the least salient and most constrained in comparison to the major powers. The traumatic experience of war and defeat, and the constitutional prohibitions placed upon the exercise of armed force, constrained Japan's participation in military conflicts and its use of military power as a legitimate instrument of state policy (Hook et al. 2001: 12). In the immediate postwar period, Japanese policymakers were quick to realize that military power and Japan's role as a regional military security actor had been discredited in the eyes of its own citizenry and neighboring states. In the future Japan would be obliged to search for alternative, nonmilitary means to guarantee its own security and contribute to regional stability (Hughes 1999: 21).

Japan's policymakers and citizenry have remained innately suspicious about the utility of military power for security ends and the associated risks, but Japan has not ignored the military dimension entirely. Japan's policymakers perceive a range of regional and global military threats and have attempted to counter them by retaining bilateral and individual military options. Hence the so-called Yoshida Doctrine (*Yoshida rōsen*) of Prime Minister Yoshida Shigeru (1946–1947, 1948–1954), seen as responsible for laying out the basic line of Japanese diplomacy during the postwar era (Edström 1999: 169–179). It emphasized not only economic reconstruction (*keizai to tsūshō no jūshi*) but also acceptance of the need for light rearmament (*keigunbi*) and alignment with the United States (*anzen hoshō no taibei izon*) through the bilateral U.S.-Japan security treaty in September 1950 (Iokibe 2000: 15). Japanese military security policy during the Cold War and post–Cold War period emphasized a twin-track approach: the incremental buildup of Japan's military capabilities, and the incremental expansion of bilateral security cooperation with the United States. This expansion of Japan's individual and bilateral military security roles in East Asia are parallel, complementary processes. Japan's experiments with multilateralism in military security during the post–Cold War period will be outlined later in this chapter.

This has not obscured the lessons of the Pacific War and other aspects of the Yoshida Doctrine, which emphasize alternative and nonmilitary dimensions of security. Japanese interest in economic dimensions of security can be traced to the long-held conception of its position as a resource-poor and economically vulnerable state (Samuels 1991: 47–48). Japan's need from the Meiji period onward to secure access to the economic resources to sustain state-building explains in part its imperial expansion in the late nineteenth and early twentieth centuries, as well as its desperate bid for outright regional hegemony to control the energy resources of Southeast Asia. In the postwar era, Japan's policymakers in line with the Yoshida Doctrine concentrated on economic reconstruction and reengagement with regional and global economies to prevent further domestic economic disintegration and to generate conditions for political stability in Japan and peaceful coexistence with neighboring states and the major powers. Japan has become an economic superpower in the postwar era, yet it is conscious of the importance of economic security, particularly in access to energy resources and overseas markets. Japan was forewarned by the two oil shocks of the 1970s (Soeya 1998: 208) and the Nixon administration's NEP, which involved import restrictions on Japanese textile products. In the contemporary period, Japan's dependency on overseas energy supplies and access to markets and production bases remain major security issues.

Japan, based on its own history and recent regional events, has long recognized that economic exclusion, disparity, disintegration, and rivalry are capable of generating insecurity and conflict at the interstate and intrastate levels. Consequently, its regional security agenda devotes considerable attention to tackling economic security threats that impact Japan's own security and that of its neighbors. Such security problems threaten individuals, societal groups, sovereign states, and the interstate system by denying access to various forms of welfare, ranging from basic human needs to growth and development. Japan is also aware that economic security concerns were compounded by the onset of globalization. In turn, they perceive that economic insecurity is linked to military insecurity for all security actors. For example, as in the case of prewar Japan, threats of economic disintegration, exclusion, and rivalry imposed upon individuals, societal groups, and sovereign states can have a multiplying effect that can feed into interstate conflict.

Hence, Japan's response has been to deploy its economic power to deal with economic insecurity as a root cause of intra- and interstate military tensions. Japan's ODA programs and the emphasis on human security as aspects of regional security policy are intended to address economic and military security threats.

Japan has long demonstrated concern over environmental security threats as well. In part, this is derived from Japan's vulnerability to natural disasters—typhoons, floods, landslides, earthquakes, tidal waves, and volcanic eruptions. In part, it also reflects Japan's developmentalism and the costs of environmental degradation. Japan did suffer from self-inflicted environmental pollution in the prewar period, and rapid economic growth in the 1960s and 1970s ensured that many industrialized areas became the most polluted in the world (Barrett and Therivel 1991: 27–38). Japan's disregard for the environment produced notorious pollution (*kōgai*) security threats (Ohta 2000: 97).

Japan succeeded in reducing environmental pollution through new technologies and by moving heavy industries to East Asia from the 1970s onward. Japan can thus be accused of taking an "out of sight, out of mind" attitude to pollution and foisting environmental threats upon others in the region. Nevertheless, Japan's intimate knowledge of the costs of developmentalism can, at the very least, lead to awareness of the importance of environmental security. Hence, Japan has sought to contribute to regional security by converting itself into an "environmental superpower." Japan has attempted to carry out this role through economic power in the form of ODA to support environmental protection programs in East Asia. Many of these programs have been implemented on the individual state, bilateral, and multilateral levels.

Japan and Comprehensive Security Policy

Japanese conceptions are articulated best by its comprehensive national security strategy (*sōgō anzen hoshō senryaku*). This first emerged during the administration of Prime Minister Ōhira Masayoshi (1978–1980), with the commissioning of the National Institute for Research Advancement to produce the *Report on Comprehensive National Security*. The successor administration of Prime Minister Suzuki Zenkō (1980–1982) adopted elements of the report as national policy and established the Comprehensive National Security Council in December 1980 (Chapman, Drifte, and Gow 1983).

The adoption of these concepts reflected the uncertainties of the 1970s and perceived changes in the global and regional systems. The report noted the relative decline in U.S. hegemony and the rise of Soviet power, as well as the increasing political and economic demands of the developing world. Given these adjustments in the international system, and the likelihood of conflict over energy resources, the report advocated that Japan adopt a comprehensive strategy across multiple dimensions, levels, and frameworks. As the report stated:

> [Previously] the problem of security was considered essentially as one of the question of dealing with military threats. . . . However, the oil crisis has demonstrated that other threats exist which can threaten people's lives. In addition, viewed from the medium and long-term perspective, food shortages are a distinct possibility. In this way, there exist many serious threats other than in the military realm, and it is necessary to employ a comprehensive approach to security encompassing all these areas. . . . Non-military means should not be ignored, such as peace diplomacy to ease or eliminate conflict, or economic cooperation to remove the causes of conflicts. (Sōgō Anzen Hoshō Gurūpu 1980: 25–26; author's translation)

Consequently, in the military dimension, the report advocated increased cooperation at the international level through arms control and CBMs; increased cooperation with the United States via the framework of the bilateral security treaty to enhance global and regional stability; and the augmentation of Japanese military power. In the economic dimension, it stressed that Japan could ensure a more peaceful interstate system through cooperation at the international level to undergird the liberal trading order and alleviate North-South tensions. It stressed also the importance of Japan's own efforts to ensure a certain measure of self-sufficiency in food and energy supplies and to maintain economic competitiveness (Sōgō Anzen Hoshō Gurūpu 1980: 7–44).

Japan thus articulated early on the security implications of economic exclusion, disparity, rivalry, and dislocation, as well as the link between Japanese security and the economic security of the developing world and surrounding region. In this sense it laid the groundwork for conceptions of human security after the onset of globalization.

The environmental dimension is probably the least developed component of comprehensive security. The report focuses on Japan's need to improve its crisis management capabilities to respond to natural disasters (Sōgō Anzen Hoshō Gurūpu 1980: 79–87). But the articulation of the environmental dimension did provide scope to conceptions of security and foreshadowed the interest in environmental security.

Comprehensive security policy has been influential in Japan and in East Asia. The concept has been criticized in elements on the right and left. Those on the right view the emphasis on economic factors as a way to evade international military responsibilities; those on the left see economics and security as a means to legitimize Japan's mercantilistic penetration of East Asia, or as camouflage for the buildup of its own military forces (Hughes 1999: 23; Kimura 2000: 36–37). Comprehensive security is not without flaws, but it has strengthened multidimensional and multilevel approaches to security policy making. The concept was embraced by Prime Minister Nakasone Yasuhirō (1983–1987), the successor to Suzuki and known for supporting the buildup of Japan's independent military capabilities and increased cooperation with the United States.

The concept has been rearticulated since in key reports, such as that of the prime minister's Advisory Group on Defense in August 1994, known as the Higuchi report, which considered the future of Japanese security policy in the post–Cold War context. Although the report emphasized that Japan should strengthen its military contribution to regional and international security in areas such as PKOs, it also stressed that Japan should follow a comprehensive policy, employing a balance of military, economic, and diplomatic means (Advisory Group of Defense Issues 1994: 7). Similarly, a blue-ribbon commission on Japan's goals in the twenty-first century, established under Prime Minister Obuchi Keizō and producing its report in January 2000, reiterated the concept that Japan's security policy should be comprehensive and multilayered. The report saw human security as one part of the comprehensive agenda and recommended that Japan should seek its place as a global "civilian power," deploying economic power to fulfill international responsibilities (Prime Minister's Commission on Japan's Goals in the Twenty-First Century 2000: 45). In turn, comprehensive security has been taken up in many states in East Asia that also see the links between the different dimensions of security as well as the need for a holistic approach.

Japanese ODA policy puts much of this into action. Economic aid is used as a multilevel and multidimensional tool to address the interlinked problems of military, economic, and environmental security. Japan's 1992 ODA Charter (ODA Taikō) supplied the first explicit enunciation of ODA principles, stressing that further development in the developing world is essential to the stability of the entire interstate system. The ODA Charter committed Japan to provide ODA for basic human needs and basic human rights and for environmental conservation, taking into account recipient countries' policies on WMD, arms exports, and the devotion of resources to economic and social development in ways that strengthen peace and stability.

Japan's Regional Security Role and the Continuing Importance of Comprehensive Security

These conceptions of comprehensive security appear well-suited to the complexities of the multilevel and multidimensional military, economic, and environment challenges in East Asia. Hence, it is important to evaluate the nature and effectiveness of Japan's contribution to regional security within the framework of comprehensive security. Japan has consistently employed a multifaceted and comprehensive approach to regional security, a meaningful contribution to stability in the region and global security. Japan can thus provide a unique contribution to future security. This is especially so in light of globalization, the shifting power balances among major powers, and renewed economic tensions among developed and developing states.

Japanese Security Policy in the Immediate Postwar Period

Japan's defeat in World War II, and its consequent withdrawal from an overt security role in East Asia, was total in physical and psychological terms. Japan's military power was spent, and it was promptly stripped of its colonial possessions by the return of Allied powers in Southeast Asia. Its colonies in China and Taiwan were divided between the CCP and KMT, and in Korea between the U.S. and Soviet superpowers. Ironically, Japan was subject to a form of colonization with the Soviet occupation of the Northern Territories and the U.S. acquisition of Okinawa. The loss of its colonies removed Japan's physical military and security presence from East Asia; it also detached Japan psychologically from its security role. Although Japan was to be obliged under the San Francisco Peace Treaty of 1952 to provide reparations to many former colonies, the fact was it had been relieved of any direct responsibility for its colonial past and rebuilding relations with the newly independent states in the region. Thus Japan's history of colonialism has not been fully confronted, even today.

In turn, this physical and psychological separation was reinforced by the rejection of Japan by many of its former colonies themselves. Anti-Japanese sentiment in the region during the postwar era was widespread. Consequently, East Asian states view an active security role for Japan, especially in the military sphere, with a mix of ambivalence and outright hostility.

The process of decolonization and the legacy of colonialism thus led to Japan's isolation from East Asia after its defeat; this separation from the region was compounded by bipolarization. Japan's defeat spelled its withdrawal from East Asia, as well as subjugation at home due to the U.S.-led occupation (1945–1952). The U.S. superpower also had designs for remaking Japan, first in the wake of decolonization, then in the face of bipolar pressures. The Supreme Command for the Allied Powers under General Douglas MacArthur implemented the initial phase of U.S. postwar strategy for Japan, which sought to ensure that Japan could never emerge again as a regional imperial power through a three-pronged reform package of demilitarization, democratization, and economic deconcentration. Japan's demilitarization and the removal of its ability to project power was ensured by disbanding the Imperial Japanese Army and Imperial Japanese Navy in November 1945 (Welfield 1988: 61), then the promulgation (3 November 1946) and adoption (3 May 1947) of a new constitution containing the so-called peace clause (article 9), which renounced the maintenance of military forces and resorting to war as an instrument of state policy.

U.S. and SCAP strategy was then thrown into reverse (*gyaku kōsu*) with the onset of the Cold War and the outbreak of the Korean War on 25 June 1950. Korea, coupled with the crisis over Taiwan, heightened U.S. perceptions of the threat from communist expansion and persuaded U.S. policymakers to convert Japan into a friendly client state that would serve as a bulwark against communism. From 1950 onward, the United States concentrated on the economic rehabilitation of Japan, and on 8 July that year MacArthur ordered the establishment of the National Police Reserve Force (Keisatsu Yobitai) to preserve internal security; minesweepers from the Maritime Safety Force would also perform secret duties during the early stages of the Korean War. Japan's indispensable role as a platform for U.S. power projection was demonstrated by the U.S. amphibious landings at Inchon from bases in Japan in September 1950. And in talks with Prime Minister Yoshida in January and February 1951, Secretary of State John Foster Dulles requested that Japan rearm (including building an army of up to 350,000) (Welfield 1988: 51). Yoshida rejected the request, citing fears over renewed Japanese militarism in East Asia, the Japanese public's memories of the devastation of the Pacific War, and the need to concentrate on economic recovery. However, in a secret memorandum submitted to the United States on 3 February 1951, Yoshida conceded to Dulles that Japan would create land and sea security forces totaling 50,000 (Katahara 2001: 72).

Japan's emergence as a U.S. client led to reengagement in regional security affairs, but it was heavily influenced by the U.S. bilateral relationship and Cold War strategy. The next stage was the simultaneous signing of the San Francisco Peace Treaty with the Allied powers and the bilateral U.S.-Japan security treaty in September 1951. The Korean War gave impetus to these efforts. Even though the treaty restored Japan's independence and reentry into the regional community, this was only partially due to the Soviet Union's refusal to sign the treaty and the U.S. decision to invite the ROC instead of the PRC to the peace conference.

These events determined the future path of Japanese regional security policy. It ensured that Japan was incorporated into the U.S. side in the bipolar divide and that its contribution to regional stability would be indirect by providing bases for U.S. power projection. But the conclusion of the security treaty opened the way for rearmament, with the establishment of the National Safety Agency (NSA) (Hōanchō, the agency charged with the control of the National Security Force [NSF, or Hōantai, a de facto army and predecessor to the Japan Self-Defense Forces (SDF)]) in August and October 1950; and the expansion of the Maritime Safety Force to become the Maritime Patrol Force (MPF) (Kaijō Keibitai). Japan also agreed to accept U.S. military aid in the form of mutual security assistance in 1953; enacted in June 1954 the Defense Agency Establishment Law to create the Japan Defense Agency (JDA, the successor to the NSA) and the Self-Defense Forces Law (June 1954) to create the SDF (as the successor of the NSF and MPF); and then enacted the Law Concerning the Structure of the National Defense Council (July 1956) to create the National Defense Council (later National Security Council of Japan [NSC]) responsible for planning Japanese defense policy.

Japan's decision to accept the partial peace of San Francisco and the bilateral security treaty led to its integration into the U.S. camp and consequent political and security isolation from the region. Japan was thus incorporated into the sphere of interdependency centered on the United States, which allowed for economic relations with U.S.-aligned powers in Northeast and Southeast Asia. The Soviet satellites were another matter altogether. Japan normalized diplomatic relations with the Soviet Union in October 1956, normalized relations and concluded a peace treaty with China in September 1972 and August 1978, and has yet to normalize relations with North Korea.

Japanese policymakers thus continued to see the region as of utmost importance for security. But they never fully shared U.S. threat perceptions in East Asia, and so Japan sought to circumvent the restrictions of the U.S. bilateral relationship, avoided overcommitment and conflicts not in its state interests, and pursued quiet diplomacy with Soviet satellites to improve regional security. These initiatives were driven by Japan's knowledge that East Asia is vital for resources, markets, and production bases. Consequently, even while aligning with the United States, Japan undertook a delicate balancing act to reconcile its global interests with the United States and its regional interests in East Asia. It is within this context that Japanese security policy was constructed.

Japan's Cold War Strategic Security Interests

The Korean Peninsula

Japan has geostrategic and security interests throughout Northeast and Southeast Asia. The Korean Peninsula was a key influence upon Japan's security policy makers, as it is a point of geostrategic convergence for regional and global powers. All the regional powers—China, the Soviet Union, the United States, and Japan—sought to defend their security interests on the peninsula and bring it into their respective spheres. History has witnessed a repeating of this process, marked by diplomatic and military competition between great powers that spilled over into armed conflict, with destabilizing consequences for regional and international security (Hughes 1999: 52).

Japan saw Korea as an invasion route to and from Japan and continental Asia. Historically and into the modern era, Japan's strategic aim has been to prevent the domination of the Korean Peninsula by a hostile power. Japan fought for control of it during the Sino-Japanese War of 1894–1895, and again during the Russo-Japanese War of 1905, which led to Japan's eventual annexation of Korea in 1910. Japan's subsequent wars in China were also motivated by the desire to create a buffer zone between hostile powers and its key Korean colony.

In the postwar era, Japan's concerns are similar. The outbreak of the Korean War demonstrated that the most immediate threat came from Korea and that the peninsula could embroil Japan in another costly land war in East Asia. However, Japan's security position was complicated by its own weakened capabilities; it would have to rely on other regional powers and the U.S. security guarantee. Japanese policymakers concluded that the U.S. presence in and around the peninsula, underpinned by Japan's provision of military bases, would establish a balance of power and minimize the risk of renewed conflict among North Korea, China, South Korea, and the United States. Japan therefore made an indirect contribution to Korean security and tolerated the continued division of Korea. Japan also improved economic relations with South Korea—despite the prevailing anti-Japanese feeling in the South and tensions over other issues—to stabilize it economically and politically and thus strengthen it against the external pressures from North Korea and its Cold War allies.

Japan's strategic interest has often been portrayed as the perpetual division of the Korean Peninsula. This view is not entirely accurate, as Japan's goal has been to achieve stability within the prevailing regional balance of power; the division of Korea is one part of that balance. Japan did not applaud the division of Korea, and there were residual feelings about Japan's responsibility for the postcolonial condition of North and South Korea. Japan's incapacity to alter the situation meant it acquiesced to the status quo. But policymakers were aware that the North-South divide could create destabilizing tensions that even the balance of power could not contain. Hence, during the 1970s Japan was prepared to improve relations with North Korea. Again, these moves were portrayed as a policy of "equidistance," designed to play one Korea off against the other and to restore the hostile balance of power between North and South. Japan's real intent, though, was to improve conditions for renewed North-South relations and to alleviate the worst tensions of the bipolar balance. However, the difficulties that emerged between Japan and North Korea, in tandem with renewed Cold War hostilities by the late 1970s, largely put paid to Japan's efforts in this period (Hughes 1999: 57–61).

Today Japan above all desires a stable Korean Peninsula that is not dominated by a hostile power. Japan continues to identify more closely with the United States and South Korea in opposing perceived North Korean aggression that could threaten Japan. It also recognizes that given the end of the balance of power, resulting from the collapse of the Soviet Union and the condition of the North Korean regime, new political and economic security mechanisms must be found. Japanese policymakers accept that the North-South divide is essentially destabilizing and that rapprochement and eventual reunification, the optimal solution, will reduce the threat.

China

The transformation of mainland China into a communist state, and its alignment with the Soviet Union against the United States in the early stages of the Cold War, raised concerns. International communism could influence Japan's domestic stability, especially during the immediate postwar era, when the weakened economy left Japan susceptible to political radicalism.

However, Japan's policymakers doubted that China harbored aggressive intent toward Japan, arguing that Chinese leaders were pragmatists too preoccupied with internal problems to risk unprovoked conflict with the United States and Japan. Japan's leaders generally remained unconvinced of China's communist credentials; Yoshida Shigeru famously remarked that he did not care "whether China was red or green. China is a natural market, and it has become necessary for Japan to think about markets" (Welfield 1988: 41). Yoshida and others also doubted the strength of the Sino-Soviet alignment and correctly predicted the split between the two powers. There was also skepticism as to the ability of China to threaten Japan as long as U.S. security guarantees remained in place. Hence, China's periodic denunciations of the U.S.-Japan security treaty, and China's acquisition of nuclear weapons from 1964 onward, were met with calm confidence in Tokyo, secure under the U.S. nuclear umbrella.

Japanese and U.S. threat perceptions were closer with regard to the Taiwan issue. Japan's policymakers were less concerned about the demise of the KMT on the mainland, and less committed to its subsequent defense on Taiwan. Japanese policymakers were certainly concerned about the implications of a China-Taiwan conflict, aware that the first Taiwan Strait crisis prompted the United States to follow the "reverse course," seek the rearmament of Japan, and conclude the U.S.-Japan security treaty. Moreover, the security of Taiwan was important to SLOCs running to the South China Sea. Japan also committed itself, although under some duress from the United States (Welfield 1988: 53), to sign a peace treaty with the ROC in April 1952 to demonstrate its general support for U.S. containment policy vis-à-vis China. Hence, Japan was certainly supportive of the status quo in Taiwan as the most viable option for ensuring stability and was prepared to provide political and indirect military support via the U.S.-Japan treaty. Japan was also willing to provide economic support to the regime in Taiwan in line with U.S. interests. In this way, Japan's role in buttressing U.S. hegemony in East Asia largely suppressed the Taiwan issue during the Cold War. Likewise, Japan's dispute with China over the Senkaku Islands remained inert due to the U.S. administration of the islands until their return along with Okinawa in 1972.

But there were also limits to Japan's willingness to preserve the status quo and to uphold U.S. security commitments to Taiwan. Japan wished above all to see a peaceful resolution to the Taiwan issue and viewed the U.S. presence as the principal bulwark. Simultaneously, Japan was intent to influence the United States. Japan avoided making explicit commitments to the security of Taiwan. Japan's hope was to create some sense of equivocation on its position, so that it would be difficult to prejudge Japan's level of commitment in either opposing China or supporting the United States. This device would check the actions of both sides in a potential conflict and reduce the risk of Japan being sucked in.

Consequently, even though Japan was obliged to partially accommodate U.S. containment policy toward mainland China, its doubts about the actual threat, as well as its desire to avoid any escalation, meant that it also sought to exploit the international structure to engage China economically and moderate its security behavior. Japan, throughout the first Cold War, pursued an informal policy of engagement and the separation of politics and economics (*seikei bunri*) and built a valuable trading relationship with the mainland to establish a basis for peaceful bilateral relations. Japanese expectations of the Sino-Soviet split, and that China would seek a less hostile attitude toward the capitalist world, were borne out by Sino-U.S. rapprochement from 1972 onward. Although Japan was surprised by the U.S. strategic about-face (Hook et al. 2001: 166), it exploited the opportunities to achieve normalization with China in September 1972 and to push ahead with economic and political engagement. During this period of détente, Japan and China were able to conclude the Treaty of Peace and Friendship in August 1978, and China toned down criticism of the U.S.-Japan security treaty—aware that it restrained the Soviet Union.

Japan's principal security concern was to support economic and political reform efforts in China. The lessons of the prewar era still held: there was only one threat greater to Japan than a strong China, and that was a weak China, one with civil strife and unpredictable external relations. In the post–Cold War period, Japan now encounters a stronger China striving to cope with economic change. Japan's preferred security option remains economic engagement, but it is also considering upgrading its own independent military capabilities.

The Soviet Union

In terms of intent and sheer destructive capacity, the greatest threat emanated from the Soviet Union. Beyond the pitfalls of communist ideology for society, a full-scale regional or global war between the United States and Soviet Union was not out of the question. The Soviet Union did not view Japan as a serious regional competitor (Kimura 2000), but it was prepared to intimidate Japan due to its U.S. alliance and support for containment of Soviet power. Japan's geostrategic position, between the Soviet Far East and Pacific Ocean, meant that the U.S. bases it provided were ideally situated for projecting U.S. power onto the Eurasian continent; forces based in Japan could also hinder deployment of the Soviet nuclear submarine fleet from the Sea of Okhotsk. Japan's preferred strategic option throughout the Cold War, especially during the first phase, was to seek rapprochement with the Soviet Union. Japan achieved normalization of relations under a Japanese-Soviet joint declaration of October 1956 and entered economic arrangements in areas such as energy development in the Soviet Far East. The Soviet Union was prepared to make diplomatic overtures toward Japan to coax it away from the United States (Kimura 2000: 79).

Fluctuations in U.S.-Soviet tensions, and Japan's alignment with the United States in opposing Soviet communism, placed Japan at the front line of a potential superpower conflict. Following the Soviet invasion of Afghanistan and the initiation of the second Cold War, Soviet-Japanese security tensions intensified. Japan responded by increasing the capabilities and scope of action of its forces to contain the Soviet Union.

The Northern Territories were not considered a sufficient casus belli, but they did generate deep Japanese suspicion over Soviet intent. Japan's hostility toward the Soviets drove Japan further into the U.S. strategic sphere.

Southeast Asia

Japan's strategic interests stretched as far as Southeast Asia during the Cold War even though it was expelled from the subregion following World War II. The Southeast Asian states remained important to Japan for raw materials and markets and their geographic position along the SLOCs that connect Japan to oil supplies in the Middle East (with up to 80 percent of its oil shipments passing via the Strait of Malacca). Nevertheless, physical separation, combined with the U.S. hegemonic military presence in the subregion, meant that Japan could stand aloof from Southeast Asian security affairs. Japan's principal contribution was again indirect, via the U.S.-Japan security treaty; direct involvement was limited to the economic dimension.

The communist threat in Southeast Asia was also downplayed in Japan. Japan was certainly willing to resist the spread of communism and promote general stability, but Japanese policymakers engaged in *seikei bunri* (the separation of politics and economics) with communist states in the subregion. Japan's policymakers sought recompense for the colonial past and to gain access to material resources, but also saw that it was important to establish a basis for integration of the communist and capitalist camps. This, it was felt, would create a more complete regional unit to promote economic interdependence and stability.

Japan's dual-track policy toward Southeast Asia was seen in its reaction to the Vietnam War. Japan, in line with U.S. interests, maintained diplomatic relations with the anticommunist regime of South Vietnam. During the height of the war, from the mid-1960s onward, the Japanese government continued to support the U.S. war effort and South Vietnam. The Japanese government expressed public support for U.S. bombings, many of them carried out from bases in Okinawa. Japan also provided economic aid to the South Vietnamese regime. Nonetheless, many Japanese policymakers were dismayed at the modern technological response to what they viewed as a brave independence movement, doubted the likelihood of U.S. success, were concerned about the destabilizing effects for the United States, the Soviet Union, and China, and feared that Japan could be dragged in (Hook et al. 2001: 210). Opposition was incapable of overcoming the government's steadfast public support, but this did not mean that Japan avoided all attempts to engage North Vietnam. Japan maintained a small trading relationship with North Vietnam even during the height of the war; following the cease-fire in 1973 it recognized both governments of the South and North—finally transferring sole recognition to the North following the collapse of the South in 1975 (M. Shiraishi 1990: 51–53).

Japanese and U.S. views toward the threat of communism coincided in intrastate security. They shared the concern that states such as Indonesia would drift into the sphere of independence. Japan devoted considerable energy to the engagement of Sukarno's Indonesia, despite the latter's proclaimed leadership of the NAM and its anti-U.S. sentiment in the 1950s, as well as its shift toward the communist bloc and the Konfrontasi policy toward the Western-backed Malaysian Federation in the mid-1960s (Welfield 1988: 216–219). Following Sukarno's fall in 1965, the Japanese government switched its support to the anticommunist Suharto, thereby falling more into line with U.S. policy. However, Japan's policy was designed to support authoritarian regimes with the best hopes of achieving economic modernization leading to more liberal forms of government. Japan's willingness to engage authoritarian regimes in Southeast Asia during the Cold War, such as Burma, and to eventually throw its weight behind the fledgling ASEAN, should be viewed within the context of developmentalism. Japan's belief was that economic engagement fostered intra- and interstate security.

The changing nature of the interstate system in and around Southeast Asia forced Japan to think about the military aspects of subregional security. The U.S. defeat and withdrawal from Vietnam by 1973, followed by the Vietnamese invasion of Cambodia in 1978, indicated the limits of U.S. military power and protection. Vietnam's seeking of hegemony in Indochina had a disruptive effect on ASEAN's stability, and raised tensions with China. Japan's response was the so-called Fukuda Doctrine, announced by Prime Minister Fukuda Takeo in August 1977: Japan would not seek a major military role and would not step into the vacuum created by declining U.S. military power. Japan would endeavor to make a direct contribution to ASEAN security through diplomatic and economic means. Japan was thereafter to push for resolution in the Cambodia problem and extend economic assistance to ASEAN states to assist state-building.

Japan's Cold War Military Security Policy

Limitations to Japan's Exercise of Military Power

External factors (the legacy of anti-Japanese sentiment in the wake of decolonization; Japanese demilitarization; the bilateral security treaty with the United States; the "peace constitution") constrained Japan's exercise of military force for security ends. Internal and self-imposed constraints, formal and informal, also shaped Japan's response to security challenges. Domestic constraints define and legitimize Japanese military security activities, the scope of these actions for defense planning, the acquisition of capabilities, and the projection of power.

The starting point for understanding the fundamental nature of Japan's regional security policy is the 1946 constitution. The preamble states its ideals with regard to security:

> We, the Japanese people, desire peace for all time and are deeply conscious of the high ideals controlling human relationship, and we have determined to preserve our security and existence, trusting in the justice and faith of the peace-loving peoples of the world. We desire to occupy an honored place in an international society striving for the preservation of peace, and the banishment of tyranny and slavery, oppression and intolerance for all time from the earth. We recognize that all peoples of the world have the right to live in peace, free from fear and want.

Chapter 2, article 9 (Renunciation of War) states:

> Aspiring sincerely to an international peace based on justice and order, the Japanese people forever renounce war as a sovereign right of the nation and the threat or use of force as means of settling international disputes.
>
> In order to accomplish the aim of the preceding paragraph, land, sea, and air forces, as well as other war potential, will never be maintained. The right of belligerency of the state will not be recognized.

Original drafts prohibited offensive warfare and using force in self-defense (*jieiken*) and maintaining any type of military establishment. However, amendments ("to accomplish the aim of the preceding paragraph") opened the door to military forces for other purposes, as long they were not designed to settle international disputes. Consequently, Japanese governments since the 1950s have interpreted article 9 as permitting Japan, in line with its status as a sovereign state, to exercise the right of individual self-defense (*kobetsuteki jieiken*) and to maintain the SDF for that purpose. The SDF's legitimacy, though, has not gone unchallenged. The main opposition Social Democratic Party of Japan (SDPJ; the Japan Socialist Party [JSP] during this period) argued until 1994 that the existence of the SDF should be interpreted under article 9 as unconstitutional. The constitution has set the parameters for Japan's military security policy, but its role is also dependent on the prevailing political situation and how far the government is willing to stretch interpretations of the constitution.

Exclusively Defense-Oriented Defense

The Japanese government has pursued an exclusively defense-oriented policy (*senshū bōei*) and elaborated other constitutional prohibitions on Japan's exercise of military power. The first is that Japan should limit its military capacity to the minimum necessary for the purposes of self-defense (*jiei no tame no hitsuyō saishō gendo*). The government stresses that the minimum limit depends on the prevailing international situation and standards of military technology. It also stresses that the SDF should not possess "war potential" as prohibited in article 9; the calculation of what constitutes such potential looks at the total strength of the SDF. Hence, this leaves the possibility for certain types of very powerful weapons for self-defense, including nuclear weapons, as long as they do not represent the accumulation of war potential. The Japanese government does regard as unconstitutional offensive weapons used for the destruction of other states, since they exceed the minimum necessary level for self-defense. In the past, this meant that the SDF eschewed power projection capacities such as ICBMs, ballistic missiles, long-range strategic bombers, in-flight refueling aircraft, and aircraft carriers.

The second prohibition relates to the conditions of the right of self-defense. The Japanese government defines these as an imminent and illegitimate act of aggression against Japan; the absence of an appropriate means to deal with the aggression other than the resort to the right of self-defense; and the use of armed force confined to the minimum necessary level. The third constraint defines the geographic scope of self-defense. The government argues that it is not necessarily confined to Japanese territory and is difficult to evaluate, as it may vary according to conflict conditions. However, since 1980 the Japanese government has regarded as unconstitutional the dispatch of the SDF overseas, because that would exceed the minimum force necessary for self-defense. Japan has always had the potential under the constitution to dispatch its forces overseas within the limits of the minimum necessary force for self-defense. In practice, Japan refrained from this during the Cold War. This was in part due to its desire to avoid overseas entanglements, and the law on the SDF prohibited overseas dispatch. Hence, until the law was amended in June 1992 to allow limited SDF participation in UN PKO missions, the overseas dispatch of the SDF was not unconstituional but illegal.

Collective Self-Defense

The fourth prohibition is the ban on collective self-defense (*shūdanteki jieiken*). The Japanese government recognizes that as a sovereign state and under article 7 of the UN Charter it has the inherent right to collective self-defense. However, since the 1950s onward, the government has taken the position that its actual exercise would exceed the minimum necessary force for self-defense and is therefore unconstitutional. Japan does not regard SDF support for the military forces of other states as unconstitutional if the actions do not involve military combat (Asagumo Shimbunsha 2001: 575–576). The range of actions possible include logistical support such as transport, supply, maintenance, medical services, guard duty, and communications (Nagashima 2001: 32).

During the Cold War, Japan was never asked to exercise collective self-defense in support of its U.S. ally. This was due to the fact that Japan-U.S. defense cooperation was concentrated around Japan; any action it potentially took would be to defend its own territory and U.S. troops based there, both justified under the right of self-defense (George Mulgan 1997: 145–146). Japan has been prepared to provide the United States with logistical support in areas outside Japanese territory such as the Korean Peninsula or the war on terror in Afghanistan. However, from the U.S. perspective, this is increasingly seen as an insufficient alliance commitment, especially because the United States envisages that the scope of U.S.-Japan defense cooperation will move further beyond Japan's own territory, so forcing a distinction between Japanese military actions designed to defend Japan itself under the right of individual self defense, and Japanese actions designed to defend the United States and other states, which are necessitated under the right of collective self-defense. As a result, there is a vigorous debate in Japan regarding the need for the government to revise its interpretation to permit the exercise of collective self-defense.

Restrictions on the Use of Force

In addition to the above constitutional prohibitions, Japan's exercise of military force for security ends has been governed by a range of antimilitaristic principles and policies, many derived from the spirit if not the letter of the preamble and article 9.

First, the government repeatedly pledges not to become a military great power. It gives no strict definition of the criteria for that but stresses that it will not acquire military capabilities above the minimum necessary. Second, since the administration of Prime Minister Satō Eisaku in 1967, the Japanese government has maintained the three nonnuclear principles—not to produce, possess, or introduce nuclear weapons into Japan—preferring instead to rely on the U.S. nuclear umbrella. The first two principles have been strengthened by Japan's ratification of the NPT since 1976. (Although it should be noted that the Japanese government does not regard nuclear weapons as unconstitutional if used for the purposes of self-defense.) The third principle has arguably been breached by the introduction into or transit through Japanese ports of nuclear weapons on U.S. naval vessels.

Third, Japan restricts the export of arms and defense technology. Prime Minister Satō's administration enunciated restrictions on arms exports to communist states, countries under UN sanctions, and parties to international disputes. Prime Minister Miki Takeo's administration then extended this to all states and prohibited the export of all weapons-related technology (Drifte 1983: 81–143). These restrictions have largely held, even though Japan has exported certain dual-use technologies with civilian and military applications.

Fourth, the Japanese National Diet in May 1969 passed a resolution stating that Japan's activities in outer space should be limited to peaceful purposes (*heiwa no muokuteki ni kagiri*), interpreted as nonmilitary activities (*higunji*). Japan's development of spy satellites and a BMD system since the 1990s has challenged this principle.

Finally, Miki's administration established the principle that defense expenditures should be limited to 1 percent of gross national product (GNP) from 1976 onward. In effect, this principle was breached by Prime Minister Nakasone Yasuhirō, who pushed defense spending just above 1 percent in 1986. Nonetheless, successive administrations have kept Japanese defense spending at around 1 percent.

Civilian Control and Security Policymaking

Japan's exercise of military power for national security ends has also been restricted by the memory of prewar militarism and the system of civilian control (*bunmin tōsei*) subsequently imposed on the SDF. Article 66 of the constitution stipulates that all ministers of state must be civilians. In addition, the 1954 Defense Agency and SDF establishment laws decree that the civilian prime minister is the commander in chief of the SDF (article 7 of the SDF law), and that the prime minister directs the civilian director general of the JDA (articles 8 and 9 of the SDF law), who then gives orders to uniformed chiefs of staff of the three services of the SDF. The prime minister is expected to act on behalf of the cabinet and in consultation with the NSC of Japan (article 2 of the Security Council Establishment Law). The prime minister, in issuing orders for the mobilization of the SDF in case of external aggression, must obtain prior or ex post facto approval from the Diet (Article 76 of the SDF Law) (Katahara 2001: 73–74; Gow 1983: 24–26), which also exercises civilian control over the SDF via budgetary and legislative decisions on composition and organization, with loose oversight of security planning occurring in special committees. In the postwar period the Diet has been dominated by the Liberal Democratic Party (LDP), which has given its politicians and committees a role in overseeing military policy.

This framework of constitutional-legal civilian control has been buttressed by bureaucratic dominance over the military. Japan's Ministry of Foreign Affairs (MOFA) has traditionally been at the top of the pecking order with regard to other ministries in devising security policy. MOFA's National Security Division, within the Foreign Policy Bureau, along with other functional and regional bureaus, has overall responsibility for guiding Japan's policy. In part, it has been able to maintain this position through the Security Consultative Committee (SCC), the principal coordinating mechanism for the Japan-U.S. military alliance.

The JDA, in contrast, was regarded as a junior partner in the security policy making process due to its lack of full ministerial status and incorporation into the prime minister's office. JDA bureaucrats were considered, and many of its top administrative positions were "colonized" by MOFA officials or officials on secondment from the other big ministries, such as the Ministry of Finance (MOF) and the Ministry of Economy, Trade, and Industry (METI). For example, the JDA's administrative vice minister and the top bureaucrat is generally a METI or MOF official. The JDA headquarters were also exiled until the late 1990s to the Roppongi district of Tokyo, far away from the center of power in the Kasumigaseki district.

In turn, the JDA exerted a similar structure of civilian bureaucratic dominance (*bunkan tōsei*) over the SDF. The internal bureaus (*naikyoku*) of the JDA, staffed by civilian bureaucrats, advise the director general of the JDA; draft legislative bills and orders of the cabinet and prime minister's office; and draft the director general's instructions to the Joint Staff Council (JSC), composed of the three chiefs of staff responsible for SDF operation plans, and examine these plans before they are sent to the director general for approval. In essence this means that the JSC of the SDF has only an advisory role to the internal civilian bureaus. The result has been friction between bureaucrats and uniformed officers, the latter feeling that they are sidelined when it comes to making crucial decisions about potential military operations. Indeed, the suspicion of many SDF officers is that the JDA's internal bureaus have been more concerned with keeping watch on Japan's military to deflect civilian criticism from the politicians and Diet (*kokka taisaku*) than with devising practical measures for the defense of Japan.

Japan's Cold War Military Security Policy

During the Cold War period, the principal security threats that Japan faced ranged across the superpower–major regional power–regional power levels, although it was also concerned with intrastate, societal, individual, and organizational group conflicts. Japan's response was comprehensive in nature. But Japan was obliged to respond to threats in the military dimension with military power in varying degrees across state, bilateral, and multilateral frameworks.

The U.S.-Japan Alliance and Bilateral Policy

The constraints placed upon Japan during the early Cold War period, and its dependency on the United States for military security, inevitably dictated that the principal Japanese response was indirect via the 1951 Security Treaty Between the United States and Japan. Under article 1 of that treaty, along with article 5 of the revised 1960 Treaty of Mutual Cooperation and Security Between the United States and Japan (extended in perpetuity in 1970), the United States was obligated to protect against an external attack of Japanese territory. Japan in the revised 1960 security treaty was explicitly obliged to defend U.S. forces on its territory. However, Japan avoided any formal commitment to collective self-defense (defending U.S. forces on Japanese territory was considered individual self-defense), and the treaty contained no provision for the defense of U.S. forces outside Japan or the United States itself. So, even though the security treaty was mutual, the Japanese emphasized cooperation rather than security and were not formally bound to collective security and mutual defense, as was South Korea (Hughes and Fukushima 2003). Japan's most important obligation was to provide U.S. military bases for the purpose of "contributing to the security of Japan and the maintenance of international peace and security in the Far East" (article 6).

According to the 1960 security treaty (article 4), and the exchange of notes between Prime Minister Kishi Nobusuke and U.S. secretary of state Christian Herter, Japan and the United States would consult regarding implementation of the treaty, major changes in U.S. force dispositions in Japan, and use of U.S. bases in Japan for military operations other than those designated in article 5. The mechanisms for this were the SCC (consisting of the U.S. ambassador, the CINCPAC, the Japanese minister of foreign affairs, and the director general of the JDA), and the Security Subcommittee on Defense Cooperation of the SCC (composed of working-level officials) (Giarra and Nagashima 1999: 96–97), established in July 1976.

The Japanese government has thus claimed since 1960 that its rights of "prior consultation" provide the ability to veto U.S. military actions from Japan that it opposes (Welfield 1988: 141–142). In practice, any such ability has been questioned. There is little evidence that the United States has sought prior consultation with Japan, or that Japan has the political will to refuse, dependent as it is on the United States for its own security (Hook et al. 2001: 129). The scope of the Far East and the range of action of the U.S.-Japan security treaty was defined by Prime Minister Kishi in Diet interpellations in February 1960. The official position was that even though the Far East was not necessarily a designated geographical region to which the treaty could be restricted, it included the areas north of the Philippines and surrounding Japan (*Nihon no shūhen*), and the areas under the control of South Korea and Taiwan (Asagumo Shimbunsha 2001: 619–620).

The treaty provided for the immediate defense of Japanese territory by allowing U.S. forces on its territory. On the Japanese mainland, the U.S. Air Force has maintained bases at Misawa (Aomori Prefecture) and Yokota (Chiba Prefecture), the Navy Seventh Fleet at Yokosuka and Atsugi (Kanagawa Prefecture) and Sasebo (Nagasaki Prefecture), the Marines at Iwakuni (Yamaguchi Prefecture), and the Army at Camp Zama (Kanagawa Prefecture); on Okinawa, under U.S. administration and then returned to Japan in 1972, there have been concentrated substantial forces from all four service branches (Weeks and Meconis 1999: 90–94). In addition to conventional military forces, the United States provided a "nuclear umbrella" (*kaku no kasa*) against neighbors. The Japanese government regarded these U.S. commitments as a formidable security guarantee during the Cold War, in particular against the Soviet Union. However, the U.S. commitments did expose Japan as a target in any global or regional military conflict between the superpowers.

The integral position of the U.S.-Japan security treaty within the U.S. bilateral "hub and spokes" alliance system was seen to function for the security of the region around Japan in the Cold War. Japan's provision of bases under the security treaty for the projection of U.S. military power in and around the Korean Peninsula was clearly designed to reinforce the deterrent functions of the U.S.-South Korea alliance and to augment the balance of power against North Korea. South Korea was included within the scope of the security treaty as defined in 1960; and the joint communiqué between President Nixon and Prime Minister Satō in November 1969 (agreed to by the Japanese side as a first step toward the United States agreeing to the reversion of Okinawa) stated that the "security of the ROK was essential to Japan's own." Japan's support for U.S. containment policy versus North Korea thus ensured that it was largely neutralized as a major security threat to Japan in this period.

Similarly, the security treaty was perceived as important for stabilizing security relations with China. The Chinese government condemned the treaty in 1951, 1960, and 1970 as an attempt to perpetuate the division of

China and to revive Japanese militarism in support of U.S. hegemony. The pivotal role of the security treaty in U.S. military strategy vis-à-vis China was highlighted by Prime Minister Kishi's statement in the Diet in February 1960 that Taiwan was included within its scope; and by the Nixon-Satō communiqué that stated that alongside South Korea "the Taiwan area was also a most important factor for the security of Japan." China also viewed the announcement of the Guam Doctrine in 1969, on the need for East Asian states to take a greater burden for their own defense, as a U.S. ploy to utilize Japan as its regional policeman (Wang and Wu 1998: 13). This carried implications for political and economic relations with China and meant that military containment was not the only option to be pursued. Even Japan's staunch anticommunists viewed China's threat as small compared to that of the Soviet Union, and were prepared to use economic engagement to ensure that China did not become a destabilizing factor in East Asia. Still, Japan's leaders were aware that the obligation to provide U.S. bases could drag Japan into a costly and unwelcome conflict between the United States and China over Taiwan.

However, despite the alternative policies to military containment and the risks of hosting the U.S. military, the overall calculation of Japan's leaders was that the security treaty fostered stability between Japan and China. The sheer weight of U.S. military hegemony guaranteed it. Thus, China's development and deployment of nuclear weapons from 1964 onward was not perceived in Japan as a significant strategic threat due to their faith in the U.S. nuclear umbrella (Welfield 1970). In addition, overwhelming U.S. naval and air power barred any attempt by China to threaten Taiwan militarily and ensured that Taiwan was an inert security issue, and that Japan's resolve to support the U.S. military was never tested. Similarly, U.S. control prior to 1972 of the Senkaku Islands, part of Okinawa, and its continued military presence there kept a lid on this territorial dispute.

Japan was able to distance itself from events in Southeast Asia during much of the Cold War. Nevertheless, Japan was still involved in the military security of this subregion through the framework of the U.S.-Japan security treaty. During the Vietnam War, much of the U.S. bombing was carried out from bases in Okinawa (Gallicchio 2001: 129–130); bases on mainland Japan were used for logistical support (M. Shiraishi 1990: 37). Moreover, Japan's integral position within the bilateral alliance reinforced U.S. military hegemony in East Asia and Southeast Asia that suppressed potential territorial disputes along the SLOCs in the South China Sea. Japan continued to remain dependent on U.S. military power in Southeast Asia even following its withdrawal from Vietnam and the announcement of the Guam Doctrine. The 1977 Fukuda Doctrine, stressing that Japan would not seek a military role in Southeast Asia and would not compensate for declining U.S. military power, made this a certainty. Thus Japan would contribute to regional stability through political and economic cooperation with ASEAN and the states of Indochina (Hook et al. 2001: 187).

Japan's Individual Military Security Policy

Japan's principal involvement in regional security during the Cold War was an indirect one via the framework of the U.S.-Japan security treaty. Japan also engaged in the incremental expansion of its military security policy to augment its defense capabilities and to enhance its role in support of that treaty.

Japan's first statement of its individual military security policy was the Basic Policy for National Defense (BPND; Kokubō no Kihon Hōshin), announced in May 1957. The Japanese government declared that it would support UN activities and promote international cooperation for world peace; establish the welfare and domestic stability necessary for internal security; develop capabilities necessary for self-defense with due regard to national resources and the prevailing domestic situation; and confront external aggression based on the U.S.-Japan security arrangements in the absence of an effective UN for deterring and repelling such aggression (Keddell 1993: 38). Hence, the BPND established that Japan's defense policy would be predicated upon the incremental expansion of its own individual defense capabilities, but it would be carried out with regard to developments in the U.S.-Japan bilateral security relationship It is noteworthy that the BPND has remained unchanged as the foundation of Japan's security policy since 1957 (Tanaka 1997: 158–159).

The BPND opened the door to the quantitative and qualitative buildup of SDF military capabilities. Japan's First Defense Build Up Program (1958–1960) (Daiichiji Bōeiryoku Seibi Keikaku) produced a quantitative increase in Ground Self-Defense Force (GSDF) strength to compensate for the phased withdrawal of U.S. ground troops from its territory. The Second Defense Build Up Program (1962–1966) (Dainiji Bōeiryoku Seibi Keikaku) augmented the Maritime Self-Defense Force (MSDF) and Air Self-Defense Force (ASDF) through increased weapons procurements and stated that the SDF's mission was to deal effectively with aggression lower in scale than a local conventional war and fairly large-scale aggression without U.S. help during the initial period (Katahara 1990: 125). The Third Defense Build Up Program (1967–1971) (Daisaniji Bōeiryoku Seibi Keikaku) concentrated on qualitative improvements in Japan's naval defense in its periphery waters and to air defense in vital territories (Asagumo Shimbunsha 2001: 61). This plan indicated efforts by Japan to provide for its own defense and to assist U.S. military strategy by increasing SDF capabilities in areas such as antisubmarine warfare (ASW) (Katahara 1990: 125; Keddell 1993: 41).

Japanese government initial proposals for a Fourth Defense Build Up Program (1972–1976) (Daiyoji Bōeiryoku Seibi Keikaku) encountered domestic opposition. Nakasone Yasuhirō, director general of the JDA, noting the Nixon Doctrine of 1969 and declining military support for East Asia, argued that Japan should pursue a more autonomous defense posture (*jishu bōei*) and that the BNDP should be replaced with a principle that stated, among other things, that the U.S.-Japan security arrangement should merely *supplement* Japan's own defense capabilities. Nakasone subsequently proposed a near doubling of defense expenditures in the new program. Nakasone's plans were defeated by opponents inside and outside government who forced his replacement and pared back the final program. These opponents feared that an autonomous defense posture and the new program would undermine the U.S.-Japan security treaty and lead to a major expansion of the SDF and Japanese remilitarization.

The period of détente at the end of the first Cold War produced further developments in Japan's buildup of its individual capabilities in relation to its security ties with the United States. Japan's policymakers concluded that there were increasing limits to U.S. power and the degree to which Japan could rely on the United States for security, and this appeared to reinforce the arguments of those seeking greater efforts by Japan in its individual framework of military security policy. Nevertheless, as détente proceeded, marked by U.S.-Soviet rapprochement, as well as by Japan-China normalization, it became harder to increase already weak domestic support for enhanced Japanese military efforts. Japanese policymakers concluded that even if the trend in interstate superpower and regional power relations was toward détente and the declining role of military force, the factor that had contributed to this situation and would perpetuate it was the role of the United States in establishing the balance of power between the communist and capitalist spheres. In turn, their perception was that the U.S.-Japan security arrangements had and would continue to be an integral part of maintaining this international structure, and that these bilateral arrangements still formed the ultimate safeguard for Japan's security, especially given the particular political, economic, and strategic circumstances of Japan that necessitated that it could not fully defend itself independently. Hence, policymakers resolved that, despite expected domestic opposition and constraints in an era of détente, they should continue to seek to increase Japan's individual defense capabilities and to support the U.S. security position in the region.

The Japanese government—forced as it was to juggle the varying demands of the continued strengthening of individual defense capabilities, the maintenance of U.S.-Japan security arrangements, and to simultaneously restrain any excessive buildup of the SDF—produced the National Defense Program Outline (NDPO) (Bōei Keikaku no Taikō) in 1976 as the next step in military security policy planning (Gow 1983: 65–71; Ōtake 1983: 127–132; Katahara 1990: 135–149; Keddell 1993: 59–65; Tanaka 1997: 244–264; Sebata 1998: 57–73). The NDPO represented the first attempt to set out principles for defense alongside the military force structure necessary to achieve them. It assumed that the United States and Soviet Union would avoid nuclear war and large-scale conflict; that there was a rough military equilibrium in East Asia among the United States, Soviet Union, and China; and that security arrangements and the superpower balance would prevent large-scale aggression against Japan from Korea and elsewhere.

The NDPO stated that Japan would maintain a force structure to repel limited direct aggression; if that aggression proved too powerful, it would employ a force structure capable of effective resistance until U.S. cooperation could be obtained (Bōeichōhen 1995: 316). The necessary denial capabilities (*bōshiryoku*) for the defense of Japan were defined as the *standard defense force concept* (*kiban teki bōeiryoku kōsō*). This was intended to form the nucleus of a qualitatively improved and minimum defense posture during a period of détente and peace, but it could be adapted to various types of aggression. The standard defense force concept differed considerably from that of the *required defense force concept* (*shoyō bōeiryoku*) upon which previous quantitative and qualitative buildups had been predicated. The required defense force concept dictates that force levels be capable of matching, in balance-of-power fashion, the existing capabilities that could be employed against Japan. In the case of Japan and East Asia, the *required* defense force structure, if continued, would have meant a relentless buildup to match the capabilities of the Soviet Union. In contrast, the *standard* defense force factored in the existing capabilities *and* the intentions of potential aggressors. Consequently, the political judgments in the NDPO necessitated a modest expansion of the SDF.

The NDPO essentially stabilized SDF expansion in the short term and focused the buildup on quality in light of the prevailing international environment and likely security contingencies. The NDPO had considerable utility for Japan's defense planners, who could pursue quality and emphasize the continuing importance of U.S.-Japan security arrangements. At the same time, the standard defense force concept restricted a potentially endless quantitative buildup of the SDF and defense expenditure for which there was little domestic support. Hence, the NDPO was accompanied by the 1 percent GDP limit on defense expenditures in return for opposition parties' support for the program (Calder 1988: 437). But the NDPO was subject to harsh criticism from elements of the SDF who argued that its assessment of the regional security environment was overly optimistic and that the standard defense force concept was unrealistic by attempting to establish Japan's defense posture without calibrating it against the capabilities of potential regional aggressors.

The Evolution of the U.S.-Japan Alliance

The defense buildup programs and the NDPO were predicated on the U.S.-Japan security treaty as guarantor of Japanese security. The United States had exerted pressure on Japan to develop its own defense capabilities, even if only to support the U.S. military position. The willingness of the SDF to cooperate with the United States on domestic and subregional defense was revealed by the Three Arrows Incident (Mitsuya Kenkyū) of February 1965. The SDF had secretly devised plans to assist the United States in the event of a military crisis in Northeast Asia provoked by a North Korean or Chinese invasion of South Korea. The plans stated that Japan would act as an integral part of U.S. strategy in the Far East to contain the crisis; that U.S., Taiwanese, South Korean, and Japanese troops would conduct joint training exercises; that Japan's MSDF would assist the United States to blockade the eastern coast of China; and that the SDF could be dispatched as a reserve force in South Korea and Manchuria. Prime Minister Satō first denied the existence of the plan, then later acknowledged its existence and defended it as merely a theoretical study (Hook et al. 2001: 211–212).

The onset of the second Cold War obliged Japan to concentrate on the qualitative upgrade of the SDF, to consider more direct military security cooperation with the United States, and to contemplate military cooperation within the framework of the security treaty that would function not just for the immediate defense of Japan but also for the surrounding region. Japan was alarmed at the rise in Soviet military power and opposed plans for the withdrawal of U.S. ground troops from South Korea—both developments challenging the assumptions underlying the NDPO. Japan's response was comprehensive security and economic security; it also acted on U.S. calls for burden-sharing by expanding its own defense capabilities and directly cooperating with the United States.

Despite the existence of the bilateral security treaty since 1951 and Japanese defense plans that called for the SDF to cooperate with U.S. forces against large-scale aggression, there were few established mechanisms for direct coordination of Japanese and U.S. military forces. Japan's policymakers had relied on the U.S. shield, and indeed shied away from close integration at the operational level for fear that it would lead to entrapment in U.S. regional strategy and conflicts (Welfield 1988: 354). Japan's policymakers, though still reticent about close military cooperation, in the mid-1970s recognized the pressing need to increase military support for the United States, leading to the establishment under the SCC of the SDC in 1976. The SDC subsequently began to formulate the Guidelines for Japan-U.S. Defense Cooperation (the "Defense Guidelines") that were approved by the NSC of Japan in November 1978.

The 1978 Defense Guidelines were designed to give definite shape for the first time to U.S.-Japan military cooperation, including combined tactical planning, information exchanges, and logistical support. The Defense Guidelines maintained the SDF's role in self-defense, not collective self-defense, and envisaged three scenarios. In accordance with article 5 of the security treaty (immediate defense of Japan), the first two scenarios of the Defense Guidelines provided for U.S.-Japan cooperation to deter aggression and in the event of actual aggression against Japan (*Nihon Jitai*, or *Nihon Yūji*). In accordance with article 6 of the security treaty, the third scenario provided for U.S.-Japan cooperation in regional contingencies in the Far East (*Kyokutō Jitai* or *Kyokutō Yūji*), which would have an important influence on Japan's security. Japan in the case of the first two scenarios restated that it would repel small-scale aggression by itself and seek assistance from the United States if this proved impossible. GSDF operations were defined as cooperation with the United States to check and repel aggression, and the MSDF was to conduct operations with the United States for the defense of surrounding waters and SLOCs. Japan and the United States made considerable progress into joint research for the first two scenarios (Hook 1996: 50). The third scenario came under study in 1982 but yielded few concrete results as the Japanese side adhered to its policy of *senshū bōei* and resisted any explicit commitment to support the United States in a regional contingency for fear of entrapment. This lack of planning for regional contingencies was to engender major frictions in the bilateral relationship during the post–Cold War period.

Nevertheless, the 1978 Defense Guidelines and their legitimization of U.S.-Japan defense planning established precedents for enhanced strategic military cooperation against the Soviet Union with the onset of the second Cold War (Green 2001b: 140). The Japanese government's response to the increased Soviet naval presence in East Asia, and the Reagan administration's expectations for burden-sharing, took the form of Prime Minister Suzuki's announcement on his visit to Washington, D.C., in May 1981 that the MSDF would take responsibility for the defense of Japan's own SLOCs up to a range of 1,000 nautical miles. The defense of SLOCs had first been acknowledged as an MSDF mission in the 1978 Defense Guidelines and was designed to relieve the burden of the U.S. Seventh Fleet and to help control the three narrow "choke points" of the Soya, Tsugaru, and Tsushima Straits (Katahara 1990: 191) and thereby bottle up Soviet conventional and nuclear submarine fleets. Japan's responsibility of SLOC defense was accompanied by a quantitative and qualitative buildup of the SDF's military capabilities to complement U.S. military deployments and support the overall regional security strategy. The GSDF acquired larger numbers of tanks and shifted the weight of its deployments to Hokkaidō to counter Soviet power in the north. The ASDF's purchases of E-2C early-warning aircraft and F-15 fighters in the 1980s were justified to defend Japanese airspace against Soviet T-26 Backfire bombers, but in the event of a conflict they would clearly be used to defend U.S. bases in Japan from Soviet air strikes and release U.S. military units from defensive responsibilities to concentrate on combat outside Japanese territory. The MSDF procured large numbers of destroyers, minesweepers, and P-3C aircraft to assist ASW and SLOC defense and built a close working relationship with the U.S. Navy.

By the end of the Cold War in 1991, Japan had acquired 300 short-range interceptors, a greater number than all U.S. fighter deployments in East Asia; and 60 destroyers, three times the number of the U.S. Seventh Fleet (Keddell 1993: 154). Japan also decided in the late 1980s to acquire costly but highly advanced airborne warning and control system (AWACS) aircraft and Aegis-class destroyers—weapons systems designed to support the United States through SLOC and ASW defense and to provide air defense for U.S. carrier task forces (Katzenstein 1996b: 36). The SDF's defense structure became skewed to the point that it lacked the balanced capabilities necessary to defend Japan independently. Indeed, it could be argued that Japan's force structure in this period began to shift back to the required defense force concept to match and supersede Soviet capabilities (Katahara 1990: 123). Moreover, Japan's new weapon systems, its increased responsibility for SLOC defense, and the complementary role of the SDF meant, despite the fact that it did not acquire overt offensive capabilities, it could be perceived as gravitating away from an exclusively defense-oriented posture to one that could be construed more as "offensive defense." Japan had now shifted from a position where it envisaged the role of the SDF with the U.S.-Japan security arrangements was purely for the defense of Japan's immediate territory and was now serving as the shield for the U.S. to project power regionally.

U.S.-Japan military cooperation expanded during the second Cold War. The SDF increased its combined exercises with U.S. forces following the 1978 Defense Guidelines; and in 1980 it participated in RIMPAC for the first time, justified as a peacetime exercise and thus not collective self-defense (Hook 1996: 52). Japan was also careful to demonstrate that it was conducting a bilateral exercise with the United States in close proximity to other U.S. bilateral exercises (Midford 2000: 371). In November 1983, the Exchange of Technology Agreement Between Japan and the United States made an exception to the 1976 ban on arms exports. In accordance with this agreement, the United States was able to gain access to Japanese technology in possession of the JDA, including technology that had been originally provided by the United States and then improved by the Japanese government and private sector, as well as technology developed independently by the private sector. Japan in 1986 also signed an agreement with the United States for participation in the Strategic Defense Initiative (SDI, the so-called Star Wars missile shield proposed by President Ronald Reagan). Japan imported U.S. "black box" technology for its advanced fighters and Aegis-class destroyers. U.S.-Japan friction over technological cooperation came to a head with the Fighter Support Experimental (FS-X) dispute, where the Japanese attempted to develop indigenously (*kokusanka*) its next generation of fighter; the United States proposed joint development to enhance interoperability of the ASDF and U.S. Air Force and to prevent the disclosure of advanced U.S. technology to Japan. The FS-X "techno-nationalism" dispute was eventually settled with a joint program for the development of the F-2 fighter (Samuels 1994: 231–244; Green 1995: 86–107).

Japan also saw robust increases in defense expenditures. Japan instigated the Mid-Term Planning Estimate (Chūki Gyōmu Mitsumori) in 1978 and 1981 (for the periods of 1980–1984 and 1983–1987, respectively) to bring the SDF up to NDPO levels. These were then followed by a Mid-Term Defense Plan (1986–1990) (Chūki Bōeiryoku Seibi Keikaku). Japanese defense expenditures increased at between 21 percent and 10 percent between 1975 and 1979, then between 5 percent and 8 percent between 1980 and 1991 (Keddell 1993: 149). Japanese defense expenditures exceeded the 1 percent limit of GNP for the first time between 1987 and 1989, before falling back just under the limit. Japan also assumed increasing responsibility for the costs of U.S. bases in Japan from the late 1970s onward. These were dubbed by Kanemaru Shin, the director general of the JDA, as "sympathy payments" (*omoiyari yosan*) to compensate for costs associated with the rise in value of the yen and general defense burden on the United States, but they are termed officially host-nation support (HNS) (*zainichi Beigun chūryū keihi futan*). The payments included salaries of Japanese workers at U.S. installations and the construction of amenities for U.S. personnel, runways, ammunitions magazines, and other upgrades of U.S. military facilities. The United States and Japan signed the Special Measures Agreement in 1987, which obliged Japan to provide 40 percent of the costs of U.S. deployments in Japan (excluding the salaries of U.S. personnel). Japan and the United States entered two additional special agreements for 1991–1995 and 1996–2000. Under these agreements Japan came to assume by the mid 1990s 100 percent of the costs for Japanese civilian workers, fuel, water, and lighting at U.S. facilities, and two-thirds of the total costs for basing U.S. forces in Japan (Nishihara and Tsuchiyama 1998: 46; Maeda 2000: 163–162; Bōei Mondai Kenkyūkai 2000: 137; Hook 1996: 63–64; Bōeichōhen 2001: 183).

Alliance Asymmetries

Japan's expansion of its individual military capabilities in conjunction with the United States allowed Prime Minister Suzuki, during his May 1981 visit to Washington, to describe the U.S.-Japan security arrangements as an "alliance relationship" (*dōmei kankei*). Japan further emphasized its newfound alliance during the Nakasone administration and the famed "Ron-Yasu" relationship between the Japanese premier and President Reagan.

But despite the gradual transformation into an alliance, there were limits on how closely the two partners were bound together. Japan and the

United States had developed a highly asymmetrical alliance, with Japan providing the conventional defense of its own territory and U.S. bases, the United States using its nuclear deterrent and forward deployments to guarantee security. Japan developed an SDF force structure skewed toward complementary and increasing interoperability with U.S. military forces and the support of their power projection role.

However, even within this bilateral alliance framework and with the SDF's declining ability to defend Japan independently of the United States, Japan was still reserved in the degree of support it would extend to the United states in the event of a regional contingency. Japan's ban on the exercise of collective self-defense remained in force, it had shied away from making any explicit commitment under the 1978 Defense Guidelines to assist the United States, and the SDF maintained separate command structures and military roles. This functioning but loose alliance relationship was to be challenged with the end of the Cold War and the decline of the Soviet threat. In this environment, it has become harder for Japan to justify SDF activities in support of the United States regionally, raising questions about collective self-defense. In turn, the emergence of regional contingencies during the postwar period has created pressure for an expanded role for Japan, the revision of the Japan-U.S. Defense Guidelines, and calls for tighter integration between the SDF and U.S. military roles and command structures.

Multilateral Security Frameworks

Japan during the Cold War deliberately avoided regional and multilateral frameworks for security cooperation. Japanese policymakers, fearing entrapment, resisted U.S. attempts to create a collective security arrangement along the lines of SEATO and incorporating Japan (Welfield 1988: 48). Japan's increasing commitment to U.S.-Japan security cooperation as the Cold War progressed also meant that it rejected any multilateral security arrangement that could undermine the bilateral security treaty. Japan was unenthusiastic toward ASEAN's ZOPFAN concept, which appeared to be designed to undermine U.S. influence. Japan subsequently rebuffed Soviet Union president Leonid Brezhnev's proposal in 1969 for a collective security community in East Asia, then President Gorbachev's proposal in 1988 for a regionwide security community. These were perceived as Soviet attempts to drive a wedge between the United States and its partners (Fukushima 1999: 140). Moreover, even when Japan's defense expansion caused security concerns for states in Northeast and Southeast Asia, it was carried out within the U.S.-Japan bilateral framework (Hughes 1996a: 231).

Organizational Group Military Conflicts

Japan perceived significant terrorist threats from two sources: the JRA, and the North Korean community in Japan under its umbrella organization,

Chōsensōren (General Association of Korean Residents in Japan). Japanese authorities believed both to be capable of fomenting communist revolution inside Japan, although the JRA and associated factions proved to be the most violent. Japan responded through police efforts. In Japan counter-terrorism is coordinated by the National Police Agency (NPA), the Tokyo Metropolitan Police Department (Keishichō), and prefectural police forces. These organizations possess their own security bureaus for surveillance of subversive groups and can call on riot police (*kidōtai*). In addition, the Public Security Investigation (PSIA) of the Ministry of Justice (MOJ) is responsible for implementation of the Subversive Activities Prevention Law (Habō Katsudō Bōshihō or Habōhō), designed to target communism in Japan and that if fully applied would allow the compulsory dissolution of groups deemed to be engaged in the repetition of violent actions for political ends. Finally, Japan was able to call on the SDF to counter terrorism. In practice, the temptation to dispatch the SDF to respond to terrorist acts was resisted throughout the Cold War due to constitutional constraints and antimilitaristic norms (Hughes 1998: 47–49).

Indeed, Japan's civilian police institutions proved effective in countering terrorism; they were able to push the JRA offshore and lessened their threat to Japan itself. However, Japan's success met criticism internationally for merely exporting terrorism to other regions. Moreover, Japan was criticized for its soft line against terrorist threats outside its borders. Japan's antimilitaristic norms and reluctance to use force against terrorists meant that the JRA was able to extort cash payments and the release of radicals held in Japan and other countries as the price for the release of hostages in the 1975 incidents in Kuwait, The Hague, and Kuala Lumpur. Furthermore, Japan's cooperation in the multilateral policing of terrorism was seen as inadequate. Japan attempted toward the end of the Cold War to extend horizontal linkages between the NPA and other East Asian security institutions. Such efforts were undercut by the vertical nature of Japanese decisionmaking structures and the reluctance of the Japanese government to cede sovereignty to multilateral organizations (Katzenstein and Tsujinaka 1991: 106–113; Okawara and Katzenstein 2001: 174).

Japan's Cold War Economic Security Policy

Japan's main concern during the Cold War was interstate security, and it played a major role in establishing the regional military balance of power and a measure of stability. Japan was also concerned to make a more direct contribution to regional security in the economic dimension. Japan's limited ability to deploy military power for security ends necessitated this; it viewed economic assistance and development as vital to state-building, to assuage societal group and intrastate conflicts, and to address potential sources of instability.

Japan utilized its economic power in response to U.S. requests for burden-sharing (so-called aid to U.S. aid [Pharr 1993: 251]) and to buttress U.S. hegemony and its bilateral alliance system in East Asia. In many instances, this led Japan to provide support for U.S.-backed authoritarian regimes of various ilks. Japan's economic support of such regimes was not simply a response to U.S. demands and the exigencies of the bipolar order. Supporting authoritarian regimes was part of a long-term process of developmentalism under conditions of bipolarization and decolonization. Hence, Japan sought to provide economic support not only to U.S.-aligned states but also to states on the opposite side, such as China and Vietnam, based on the belief that economic engagement would ultimately lead to cooperation and stability.

Japan deployed economic power through direct economic sanctions, private-sector trade, and FDI. The Japanese government's preference has been for the "carrot" of positive incentives rather than the "stick" of sanctions to punish behavior (Hughes 1999: 24; Wan 2001: 102). Japan's principal tool for the deployment of economic power has been the provision of ODA.

Japan's total ODA increased from approximately U.S.$160 million in 1960 to U.S.$11.5 billion by 1992. Japan from 1991 onward displaced the United States as the top ODA donor in the world and was now spoken of as an "ODA great power" (*enjo taikoku*) (Orr 1990; Pharr 1994; Igarashi 1990; Yasutomo 1986; Arase 1995; Rix 1993). Japan channeled aid bilaterally and multilaterally via the Asian Development Bank (ADB) in East Asia (providing close to 50 percent of its funding by the early 1990s [Wan 1995–1996: 513]). Japanese ODA has traditionally been concentrated in East Asia, although the proportion to that region has fallen from around 90 percent in the 1960s to around 60 percent in the 1990s. Japan became the top ODA donor to Thailand, the Philippines, Malaysia, Indonesia, Laos, Vietnam, and China (Hook et al. 2001: 194–195).

The Economic Security of Southeast Asia

Japan's economic reengagement with East Asia began with its obligations under the 1952 San Francisco Peace Treaty and other treaties to provide reparations to the newly independent states of Southeast Asia. Japan negotiated settlements with Burma (November 1954), the Philippines (April 1954), Indonesia (January 1958), and South Vietnam (May 1959) (Mendl 1995: 98; Sudo 2002: 57). Japan also compensated Thailand (1955), Laos (1958), Cambodia (1959), Singapore (1968 and 1970), Malaysia (1967), and Micronesia (1969) (Wan 2001: 76). The start of Japan's ODA activities came with its provision of technical assistance as part of the British Colombo Plan in 1954.

Japan's principal objective at this stage was more economic than overtly political. The provision of aid was designed to forge new economic links between Japan and the subregion, in the form of machinery and loans, which led to dependency on Japanese corporations for spare parts, related products, and technical assistance (Nester 1992: 122). Japan's re-entry into Southeast Asia was encouraged by the United States in order to boost its economic recovery, to counter communism in Japan itself, and as a counterweight to communist influence in Vietnam. During the course of the 1960s and escalation of tensions in the Vietnam War, Japan was pressed to buttress the U.S. position in the region through economic aid to South Vietnam. However, Japan was not averse to attempts to engage North Vietnam on the other side of the bilateral divide. Japan maintained a small trading relationship with North Vietnam during the Vietnam War and later pledged aid for reconstruction (Hook et al. 2001: 186). Japan's assistance for Vietnam was again motivated by potential commercial private sector gains but also by the belief that efforts to build economic interdependence would over the longer term lead to the reintegration of the Indo-China states and a more complete Southeast Asia subregion.

Japan deepened economic ties with the capitalist-oriented ASEAN states. The Japanese economic penetration of Southeast Asian markets facilitated by the extension of ODA sparked anti-Japanese protests in 1974. Japan thus came to be viewed as an "economic animal," primarily a purveyor, rather than a defender, of economic security threats. The Fukuda Doctrine in 1977 was one response. Following Vietnam's invasion of Cambodia in 1978 and renewed bipolar pressures in Southeast Asia, Japan buttressed U.S. security strategy by increasing burden-sharing in the subregion. Japan, in a rare example of using the stick, severed all aid to Vietnam in 1979 and instead increased ODA to U.S. allies and other states "bordering on areas of conflict," including Thailand, Indonesia, the Philippines, and Malaysia. Japan continued to support ASEAN opposition to the Vietnamese occupation throughout the remainder of the Cold War and to deepen its political and economic ties with the organization. Nonetheless, Japan demonstrated diplomatic independence throughout the 1980s as an intermediary between ASEAN and Vietnam and succeeded in incorporating the Cambodia issue into the G7 summit statement in 1981 (Hook et al. 2001: 187).

The Economic Security of the Korean Peninsula

Japan's economic reengagement with the Korean Peninsula was complicated by the legacy of decolonization. Issues included Japan's reluctance to accept the South as the only lawful government of Korea; its refusal to negotiate reparations with the South for its colonial and wartime actions; and the territorial dispute over the Takeshima Islands.

The result was a series of acrimonious Japan–South Korea normalization talks that were suspended six times between 1952 and 1965. The United States increased pressure on both sides for normalization as it wished to see enhanced cooperation between its allies to help contain communism in East Asia. In June 1965, Japan and South Korea signed the Treaty on Basic Relations (the Basic Treaty). Japan recognized South Korea under the Basic Treaty and, in accordance with UN resolutions, as the only lawful government on the peninsula. Japan provided no official apology or compensation for the period of colonial rule; instead both governments forged a political compromise and under separate agreement Japan provided South Korea with U.S.$500 million in "economic cooperation." Japan and South Korea defused bilateral fishing disputes under another agreement by establishing 12-mile exclusive fishing and joint operation zones. However, this agreement did not settle all fishing disputes or the sovereignty of the Takeshima Islands.

The economic aid helped South Korea become a bastion against communism as well as promote economic opportunities for Japanese business interests, and over the longer term to stabilize South Korea's regime economically and politically in order to moderate its authoritarian nature. Relations progressed toward economic interdependence, although they were not untroubled, especially due to the South's concerns of Japan moving toward a possible policy of "equidistance" between North and South during détente. Japan continued to prioritize bilateral relations with South Korea as a member of the sphere of interdependence and strengthened economic ties in the second phase of the Cold War. President Chun Doo-Hwan demanded in 1981 that Japan provide a U.S.$6 billion aid package to help South Korea serve as a "bulwark" against North Korean communism (Bridges 1993: 15). Japan's policymakers resisted this due to the size of the package and the direct links drawn between the security of the two states. Nevertheless, Prime Minister Nakasone's administration, seeking to display greater burden-sharing to the United States, pledged U.S.$4 billion to the South in 1983.

The flipside was Japan's relative isolation from North Korea. Normalization of relations with the South and the alliance with the United States compounded the legacy of the colonial period, precluding any chance for normalization with the North. Japan did maintain some trade links with the North, but the first opportunity for a substantial improvement in relations did not come until private trade expanded in the mid-1970s, with North Korea in dire need of Japanese capital and technology. However, relations deteriorated with the onset of the second Cold War and a series of bilateral disputes, including North Korea's failure to repay debts to Japanese companies; emerging allegations surrounding the abduction of Japanese citizens; and involvement in terrorist bombings in Rangoon in October 1983 and of a South Korean airliner in November 1987 (Hughes 1999: 56–61). Hence, Japan was unable to bring its economic power to bear to engage North Korea as with China and other communist states.

The Economic Security of China

Japan, believing that China was not a potent communist threat, and wanting to assist in its gradual reintegration into the region, engaged its neighbor through a process of *seikei bunri* during the first Cold War period. During the period of détente, Prime Minister Tanaka traveled to Beijing in September 1972. Japan and China produced a joint communiqué whereby Japan recognized the PRC as the sole legitimate government of all China, accepted the indivisibility of Chinese territory and Taiwan as a province of China, and abandoned diplomatic ties and the 1952 peace treaty with Taiwan. China renounced all claims for war indemnities from Japan, but it declined to discuss the issue of the sovereignty of the Senkaku Islands. Japan and China eventually signed a peace treaty in 1978; during negotiations China indicated privately that it was prepared to tolerate the U.S.-Japan security treaty (due to its deterrent function against the Soviet Union) and to shelve the issue whether the 1960 treaty covered Taiwan and the sovereignty of the Senkakus.

Japan-China relations during the period of the second Cold War were affected by a series of bilateral disputes concerning suspicions of revived Japanese militarism. The first (1982) and second (1986) textbook controversies occurred as a result of claims by liberal and left-wing groups in Japan, as well as by pressure groups in China and South and North Korea, that school textbooks had been revised to distort the true nature of Japanese colonial aggression (Rose 1998). Prime Minister Nakasone's visit to Yasukuni Shrine in 1985 generated further friction. Japan's growing trade surplus with China in the mid-1980s also provoked frictions, as it appeared to the Chinese side as an "economic invasion."

However, the principal trend was toward deepening political and economic ties, facilitated by the coincidence of the strategic interests of Japan, China, and the United States in countering Soviet power. China did become nervous about expanded Japan-U.S. military cooperation during the Nakasone-Reagan era and Japan's potential rise as a major military power. Japan launched its ODA program in China with pledges of ¥350 billion in loans to support Deng Xiaoping's Five Year Plan for 1979–1984. Japan pledged a second loan package of ¥470 billion for 1985–1990 (Zhao 1993: 239). The Japanese ODA program was designed to support reformers within China, to assist internal stability, and lessen the risks of an economically and politically weak China (Tanaka 1991: 110–113).

Japan's Cold War Environmental Security Policy

Japan's principal involvement in the environmental security of East Asia for much of the Cold War—to some degree matching its image of an "economic animal" or "economic invader"—was as a purveyor of threats. Rapid economic growth in the 1950s and 1960s led to domestic pollution problems. Japan reacted by tightening environmental protections and by "exporting" polluting industries offshore to sites in East Asia where pollution controls were looser or nonexistent (Ui 1989: 399). For instance, in 1977 Kawasaki Ironworks, harassed by environmental protest groups in Chiba, moved its sintering process to Mindanao Island in the Philippines. In the same year, the Japanese companies Marubeni, Sumitomo Shōji, and Itōchū established the Basar Copper Smelting Plant in the Isabela Region of Leyte Island in the Philippines, which resulted in complaints from residents about the pollution of fishing resources (Sumi 1995: 160–161). The Japanese private sector also created environmental security threats through resource extraction. The major trading companies were involved in tropical rainforest logging in Sumatra and Papua New Guinea. Mitsubishi Kasei Corporation established the joint-venture Asia Rare Earth Company in 1982, located in a suburb of Ipoh City in Malaysia. The plant's waste products included radioactive thorium that impaired the health of workers and local residents (Tsuru 1999: 214).

In certain cases these projects were supported indirectly by Japanese ODA, criticized for overemphasizing capital- and technology-intensive projects designed to assist the Japanese private sector (Potter 1994: 207). The recipient state governments tended to accept this transfer of Japanese industrial plants and attendant environmental costs as a necessary stage of economic development and part of the growth-environment dilemma.

However, toward the latter stages of the Cold War Japan began to shift from a denier to a supplier of environmental security as it searched for a nonmilitary means by which to contribute to regional security (Ohta 2000: 96). Japan's status as a major developed power provided it leeway to limit the environmental costs of economic growth. Japan's perception of environmental security moved from localized pollution (*kōgai*) to a more holistic understanding of the regional and global environment (*kankyō*). Japan established the Environment Agency in July 1971, took full part in the UN Stockholm Conference on the Environment in 1972, and in the World Commission on Environment and Development (Bruntland Commission) between 1984 and 1987. The Tokyo Declaration that came out of the Bruntland Commission's final meeting in February 1987 called for "sustainable development." In the Environmental Agency's annual white paper for 1988, global environmental issues were chosen as the main theme for the first time. Japan hosted the Tokyo Conference on the Global Environment and Human Response in September 1989 and supported the Earth Summit in

1992. Japan's rising environmental consciousness, among both its policymakers and its citizenry, was to lead to the launching of its environmental ODA policy in the late 1980s.

Conclusion: Japan's Emerging Comprehensive Security Policy

Japan's Cold War security policy was multilevel and multidimensional. Japan's security perceptions ranged from the interstate level to the societal and individual levels. These perceptions also spanned the military, economic, and environmental dimensions. The ultimate manifestation of Japan's complex view was its articulation of comprehensive security policy during the 1980s.

Japan's total defeat and the legacy of colonialism ensured that its military role during the Cold War was circumscribed. Japan's principal contribution was as a partner in the U.S.-Japan security treaty, which eventually evolved into an asymmetric alliance relationship. Japan built up its own individual military capabilities to complement the United States but avoided multilateral military security frameworks. All this laid the groundwork for Japan's expanded military role in the post–Cold War period.

Japan was wary of assuming too great a military commitment, however. Japanese policymakers feared becoming entrapped in U.S. military strategy; any deployment of military power had limitations in scope and effectiveness in dealing with the regional security agenda. Instead, through comprehensive security Japan sought to balance and even supersede military power with economic power. Economic instability needed to be addressed over the longer term through economic engagement, even with communist states. Likewise, it recognized that economic and environmental threats fed military instability and were important threats in their own right. Japan was in many ways farsighted. Japan's deployed economic power in deliberate attempts to support state-building projects regionally in the hope it would generate greater security at all levels.

Japan's comprehensive security policy thus involved the joint application of military and economic power, with considerable effect on the East Asian security agenda. Its alliance with the United States contributed to stability in the interstate system, if not the resolution of many problems among regional superpowers and great powers. Meanwhile, its utilization of economic power cut to the heart of the security agenda, centering on state-building and societal and individual security. It was a highly relevant response to the political economy processes of decolonization, bipolarization, and proto-globalization. In these ways, it can be argued that Japan, within its own sets of domestic and international policy constraints, understood and responded to the East Asian security agenda by developing comprehensive security.

Chapter 5 considers how Japan's comprehensive security policy has fared in responding to the East Asian security agenda during the post–Cold War period. Japan's comprehensive approach and use of economic power remain relevant despite the shifting balance between the military and economic components of the policy.

5

Japan's Contemporary Military Security Policy

Japan's security policy has displayed continuity but also changes since the end of the Cold War and its related security dynamics. The end of the Cold War accelerated fundamental shifts in the interstate system and global and regional political economies. Japan, due to its central position in the regional economy was integrally involved in shaping the outcomes of these dynamics. In East Asia, the cessation of bipolarity pressures led to the gradual merging of the spheres of interdependence and independence, the spread of globalization and the resurfacing of the unaddressed problems of decolonization. Territorial sovereignty in Northeast and Southeast Asia became an emerging issue; disputes related to the Korean Peninsula and Taiwan have continued to be influenced by the legacy of bipolarization. Globalization also produced a complex and fluid security environment, involving a variety of actors beyond the state and cross-cutting military, economic, and environmental security dimensions.

A comprehensive approach to security is capable of encompassing all levels and dimensions. Japan has become a more active player in East Asian security in the 1990s, and comprehensive security has framed its response to security issues in all dimensions. Comprehensive security has been supplemented by its conception of human security, which enabled it to make a distinct contribution to regional security.

This role has been comprehensive but not fully balanced. Japan boosted its economic and environmental input into regional security at the state and nonstate levels, but its principal focus has been the military dimension at the interstate level.

Japanese Security Debates in the Post–Cold War Period

The Impact of the Gulf War

Japan's quest for an enhanced role in East Asian security has been driven by a combination of events at the regional and global levels since the end of the Cold War. The domestic debate has been reinvigorated at the regional level by the collapse of the USSR and concomitant questioning of the raison d'être of the U.S.-Japan alliance, as well as by the regional crises centered on the Korean Peninsula and Taiwan. The debate has also been fueled by wider global security issues, including especially the Gulf War of 1990–1991. Following Iraq's invasion of Kuwait in 1990, Japan was under pressure from the United States and its allies to participate in the multinational coalition in some other way than providing economic assistance. Japan provided a total of U.S.$13 billion to the war effort (estimated to represent more than 20 percent of the total cost of the war [Wan 2001: 33–34]), but this came to be perceived as merely another example of "checkbook diplomacy"—Japan acting as a "cash dispenser" (Funabashi 1994) in lieu of exposing its own military and citizens to physical risk. The government of Prime Minister Kaifu Toshiki began to look for ways to make a "human contribution" within the constraints of the constitution. Japan's defense-oriented posture, and its prohibition on collective self-defense, meant that it was unable to dispatch the SDF on missions overseas that would involve the threat or use of force unless strictly for its own self-defense. Hence, the Japanese government attempted to pass through the Diet in October 1990 the United Nations Peace Cooperation Bill, sponsored by Ozawa Ichirō, the LDP secretary general; it would have involved sending volunteers from the SDF and JCG to support noncombat UN activities in the Gulf. The Bill failed to pass the Diet due to poor preparation, SDPJ opposition, and a general lack of public support. The Japanese government was thus frustrated in its efforts to dispatch the SDF overseas during the Gulf War. Instead it had to be content with sending minesweepers to the Persian Gulf after the cessation of hostilities, on the basis that the clearance of mines from SLOCs during peacetime did not represent the exercise of force (Woolley 1996).

These events strengthened the determination of some to amend the SDF law and even possibly the constitution to allow the dispatch of the SDF to support UN PKO missions. The government established the Special Study Group on Japan's Role in International Society under the chairmanship of Ozawa, which concluded that it would be possible for Japan to participate in multilateral and UN military operations by adopting the concept of "international security"—coded language for Ozawa's own concept of collective security (Tanaka 1995: 94–95). Ozawa sought to draw a distinction between the right of collective self-defense and collective security. Ozawa argues that there is common ground for this among Japan's constitution, the UN Charter, and the U.S.-Japan security treaty. The preamble of the Japanese constitution states that Japan will cooperate with other states to "preserve [its] peace and existence" and to "occupy an honored place" in international society. Article 9 of the Japanese constitution states that Japan aspires to "international peace based on justice and order." The U.S.-Japan security treaty commits both states to "strengthen the UN so that its mission of maintaining international peace and security may be discharged more effectively." Ozawa's emphasis on such internationalist-centered statements is designed to support the notion that Japan should not be concerned exclusively with its own security in *senshū bōei* terms but that it should seek to contribute to international security through the UN as its highest representative. Japan's support for UN-centered security activities should not, according to Ozawa, necessarily be limited by article 9. Ozawa reads the first clause of article 9 and its statement that Japan renounces "war as a sovereign right of the nation and the threat or use of force as means of settling international disputes" as prohibiting only the use of force abroad by the Japanese government based on its own sovereign decision. Therefore, Japan should not be barred from the use of force by article 9 if it was in accordance with UN decisions or commands, and Japan's actions would be sanctioned by the UN and article 9 itself, the preamble, and the U.S.-Japan security treaty. Ozawa stressed that Japan could participate in UN PKO and peace enforcement activities (Mochizuki 1997: 58).

This concept of collective security differs from the right of collective self-defense, in that the latter is an inherent sovereign right recognized by the UN but for which no UN sanction for its exercise is necessary, whereas the former can be exercised only when legitimized by the UN and places an international constraint on Japan's exercise of military force. But Ozawa's vision was countered by others who preferred a more straightforward reinterpretation on the ban on collective self-defense to enable a fuller contribution to global and regional security.

The UN PKO Law

However, after the Gulf War the debate shifted from participation in multilateral coalitions to UN PKOs; Japan would not return to the issue of collective security until after the events of 9/11. Instead, the government's energies were concentrated on revisions of the SDF law and the formulation of the International Peace Cooperation Law (IPCL; often referred to as the UN PKO law), which passed the National Diet in June 1992. The SDF's dispatch on UN PKOs was enabled as long as missions did not involve the use of force and fulfilled the "five PKO principles" that: agreement on a cease-fire should have been reached by all parties in the conflict; the parties involved in the conflict should give their consent to the deployment of PKO forces and the participation of Japan in the operation; the PKO force shall remain impartial and not favor any party in the conflict; should any of the proceeding guidelines be broken, Japan may withdraw its contingent; and the use of weapons is limited to that necessary to protect directly the lives of personnel. In addition, to assuage concerns about Japan's possible involvement in military conflicts, the government froze the "core" (*heiwa ijitai hontai gyōmu*) PKO missions—monitoring cease-fires, patrolling cease-fire zones, inspecting the transport and disposal of weapons, and assisting the exchange of prisoners—until such time as a revision to the law was introduced to "unfreeze" these missions.

These activities were unfrozen in December 2001. In the meantime, SDF PKO activities were restricted to logistical support activities: medical care, transportation, communications, and logistics. The law also designated a range of non-PKO-related SDF humanitarian relief activities, including the rescue of refugees, the provision of food, clothing, and medical supplies, and the construction of refugee camps (Bōeichōhen 2001: 205). The PKO law led to the overseas dispatch for first time of the SDF to participate in noncombat PKOs in Cambodia between October 1992 and September 1993. Although the PKO law placed more restrictions upon the dispatch of the SDF than certain Japanese policymakers had hoped, it did mark an expansion of Japan's military security role and firmly implanted the concept that Japan's contribution to international security should be linked to the dispatch of the SDF (Yamaguchi 1992: 166).

Japan as a "Normal" State?

The Gulf War exposed the lack of strategic vision for Japan's contribution to global and regional security, squeezing the government between competing international and domestic demands to maintain a minimalist defensive stance and to expand its military role. Japan's perceived inability to act decisively endangered its relations with its U.S. ally. At the same time, East Asian neighbors, particularly China and the two Koreas, feared the remilitarization of Japanese security policy. The outcome of the Gulf War, together with later North Korean and Taiwan regional crises, led to the search for a more proactive and expansive security role, even if it was conducted in incremental stages and within existing constitutional prohibitions.

The changing domestic political situation favored an expanded security role for Japan. The collapse of LDP one-party rule and the "1955 system" was in part engineered by Ozawa Ichirō, who wished to see the collapse also of the politically imposed postwar constraints on Japan's security role. Ozawa broke away from the LDP and created two short-lived coalition governments between August 1993 and June 1994, consisting of conservative splinter groups and the SDPJ. The SDPJ then entered a coalition with the LDP in June 1994. SDPJ leader Murayama Tomiichi (1994–1996) was elected prime minister, but the cost to the SDPJ was to break its own postwar taboo on security and accept the constitutionality of the SDF. One of the outcomes has been the SDPJ's abandonment by key Diet members and a general decline in its support base. The coalition lasted until June 1998, when it was replaced by LDP single-party government. The LDP has thus held power but since late 1998 was forced into another coalition with the

Kōmeitō Clean Government Party and the Conservative Party. The conservatives merged to form the New Frontier Party (NFP), led by Ozawa from 1996 onward. But the NFP dissolved by 1998, leaving Ozawa as the leader of the smaller conservative Liberal Party. Other former NFP and SDPJ splinter groups formed the centrist and main opposition Democratic Party of Japan.

These political machinations have had a profound impact on security debate. The return of the LDP, the rise of the DPJ, and the concomitant removal of the SDPJ ensured the constitutionality of the SDF, its overseas dispatch on PKOs, and the strengthening of the U.S.-Japan alliance. Security remains a controversial issue in Japan, and few are prepared to argue against the incremental expansion of Japan's military role or to challenge constitutional constraints or antimilitaristic norms. Nevertheless, Japan's politicians and bureaucratic policymakers are increasingly prepared to debate security issues in the open, and there is a strengthening body of opinion in Japan that argues that it should become a "normal" state.

This debate again reflects the influence of Ozawa, who sees Western developed nations as the benchmark and feels Japan should support the international community with forces in future military crises sanctioned by the UN (Hook and McCormack 2001: 39). The degrees of what constitutes "normality" varies, with moderates arguing for an expanded Japanese role taking heed of the full range of constitutional prohibitions, others arguing that for Japan to be truly normal it should seek to perform a full range of military functions without restrictions. The exact framework for Japan to fulfill this role is also the subject of intense debate. The majority of policymakers see the path to normalization as the gradual expansion of security responsibilities within the framework of the U.S.-Japan alliance. For others, the perpetuation of the alliance is key, but they wish for an equal role in the alliance less fettered by constitutional restraints. There also exist a minority of Gaullists who wish to see Japan break away from overdependence on the United States and see Japan as normal only if it assumes full responsibility for its own security. In turn, this has led some policymakers to look more closely at revisions to article 9 to free up and designate limits to military power. In recent years, the reinterpretation of constitutional prohibitions has become the center of the debate. Japan's self-imposed prohibition on the exercise of the right of collective self-defense is the central issue.

Continuity and Change in Security Policymaking

These debates have certainly penetrated the government itself and given momentum to the expansion of its military security role. MOFA retains responsibility for devising Japan's security policy, and, in line with the principle of civilian control, is cautious about ascribing the military too great a role in security planning, and especially wary about the commitment of Japanese forces to combat situations. MOFA has also been aware of the need for taking on greater security responsibilities and has sought to expand cooperation with the United States within constitutional limitations and without irreversibly committing to the U.S. strategy in East Asia. MOFA has also shown enthusiasm for the dispatch of the SDF on PKOs. Similarly, the JDA carefully oversees the SDF but has pushed for a greater regional role in support of the United States and in PKOs and bilateral military exchanges. The JDA's status has also grown since the institution in September 1996 of the more balanced formula for the U.S.-Japan SCC (the so-called 2+2), which includes the Japanese minister of foreign affairs and director general of the JDA alongside their U.S. counterparts.

The SDF is generally in favor of a more active security role. The MSDF's close working relationship with the U.S. Navy has led to closer cooperation in areas such as the patrolling SLOCs, logistical support for regional crises, and BMD. The ASDF also seeks a greater role in supporting U.S. power projection capabilities in regional contingencies, as well as the capabilities to support SDF PKOs. The GSDF has a less defined role resulting from the end of the Soviet threat. However, it still seeks closer cooperation with the United States and an expanded role in PKOs, as long as this does not mean dispatching to regions where they are exposed to combat situations for which they are not equipped. Japan's defense posture has been prompted by the strengthening of the role of the prime minister in security policy making. The prime minister's office and cabinet have been strengthened with the addition of a cabinet secretariat that places at their disposal security expertise that is less constrained by interjurisdictional disputes among ministries. This streamlining of the policy process facilitates swifter responses to international crises.

The pressure to assume an expanded military security role is thus growing domestically and internationally. Changes in Japanese security were put into motion with the publication in August 1994 of the report of the prime minister's Advisory Group on Defense; the Higuchi Report called for Japan to readapt security policy to the post–Cold War environment (Advisory Group on Defense Issues 1994). The report characterized the post–Cold War security environment as one of diverse and nonspecific problems, such as regional conflicts, the proliferation of WMD, and economic dislocation. The report identified the chief security concerns as the buildup of military capabilities in East Asia; confrontation on the Korean Peninsula; China's expansion of military power and tensions between China and Taiwan; destabilization in Cambodia; and the possibility that great power relations could deteriorate. The report recommended that Japan respond not only by strengthening its military cooperation with the United States but also by taking initiatives to increase SDF UN PKO activities and by promoting multilateral security dialogue in East Asia. The report, if fully implemented, would have produced a shift in Japanese military security policy toward greater multilateral cooperation.

In spite of these developments, the Japanese government attempted to maintain continuity. Japan has continued to adhere to constitutional constraints, to an incremental approach in the expansion of its military capabilities, and to the Yoshida doctrine, with a low-profile defense posture and dependence on the United States. Japan has gradually built up its own capabilities and experimented with multilateral security dialogues. It also attempted to hedge against entrapment and abandonment in U.S. security strategy in East Asia and unwanted conflict scenarios. Japanese policymakers have thus provided latent options within the individual and multilateral frameworks to provide alternatives to the U.S.-Japan alliance. Yet Japan's principal response has been to strengthen U.S.-Japan security cooperation, and it has become progressively harder for Japan to develop its own individual and multilateral frameworks as true alternatives.

Japan's Post–Cold War Security Threat Perceptions

Interstate and Intrastate Military Conflicts in Northeast Asia

The demise of the Soviet Union has eliminated the principal military threat that Japan faced in the Cold War. The Northern Territories continue to generate friction despite peace talks since 1997, but not enough friction to provoke military conflict. Instead the principal threat is the legacy of the Soviet weapons systems inherited by Russia. Russia's ballistic missile capabilities remain a concern, but more worrying is the decay of the Soviet Pacific Fleet's nuclear submarine force, which threatens to wreak environmental havoc in Northeast Asia. Japanese policymakers since the end of the Cold War have been preoccupied by a different set of military threats and been forced to search for different justifications for strengthening Japan's military capabilities and the U.S.-Japan alliance.

The source of threat given most prominence in Japan since the end of the Cold War is North Korea. Japanese policymakers have engaged North Korea through the utilization of economic power to moderate its security behavior. At the same time, they have identified a series of potential military threats, including its use of military brinkmanship to extract diplomatic and economic concessions from its neighbors and the United States. This could drag Japan into a conventional conflict on the Korean Peninsula. During the North Korean nuclear crisis of 1994, policymakers were aware that Japan's position in underpinning U.S. power projection capabilities through the provision of bases could lead to indirect involvement in a second Korean War. In addition, as tensions escalated, the United States began to request more active and direct support from Japan for any potential war effort, including logistical support (intelligence gathering, extra facilities for the repair of U.S. warships in Japan, and use of civilian harbors and airports) and the participation of the SDF in a naval blockade of the North.

The Japanese government, however, was unable to respond effectively to U.S. requests due to lack of research under the 1978 U.S.-Japan Defense Guidelines for Defense Cooperation relating to regional contingencies. This failure of military cooperation affected the U.S.-Japan alliance but led to the eventual strengthening of its operability with the revision of the Defense Guidelines.

Japanese policymakers also highlighted the risks of a direct conventional attack from North Korea. North Korea could launch guerrilla attacks on Japanese civilian nuclear power installations on the coast of the Sea of Japan. In March 1999, the SDF intercepted and fired upon two "suspicious ships," or *fushinsen,* in Japanese territorial waters. These *fushinsen* were believed to be North Korean vessels engaged in routine espionage missions. This incident was followed by the JCG's interception, pursuit, and sinking of another North Korean *fushinsen* in December 2001 (in Japanese and then Chinese waters).

Japanese anxieties are heightened by the North's suspected development of nuclear weapons and other WMD and its ballistic missile program. Japanese opinion is divided over whether the North has succeeded in developing a nuclear bomb, but the government does not wish to see a nuclear North Korea and has cooperated with the United States and South Korea to suppress its program through KEDO. Japan's security anxieties were further aggravated by North Korea's withdrawal from the NPT in 2003.

The North Korean missile threat and Japan's inherent vulnerability were demonstrated by the North's test-firing of a Nodong-1 in May 1994 and a Taepodong-1 in August 1998 (the "Taepodong shock"). The North may eventually be able to combine its nuclear and missile technologies to produce a nuclear strike force deliverable to Japan, even though the current belief of policymakers is that any nuclear device developed would be too great a payload for existing missile capabilities (Hughes 1996b: 83–84). Japan is also concerned with nontraditional threats, such as refugee flows, narcotics, and human security.

The mix of threats brought North Korea to the forefront of Japanese security concerns after the Cold War. But China may pose the greatest threat. North Korea does not yet pose a direct and serious challenge to the very existence of Japan. In contrast, China is perceived as presenting a far more dangerous challenge over the medium to long term.

Such challenges include China's quantitative and qualitative buildup of its armed forces since the Gulf War, an upgraded nuclear strike force, and its willingness to project military power in support of national interests. China could disrupt Japan's SLOCs with a small bluewater navy. China's actions in sending ships into Japan's EEZ around the Senkaku Islands has also been viewed as aggressive. Above all, the 1996 Taiwan Strait crisis raised Japanese suspicions. China test-fired ballistic missiles near Taiwan that landed within 60 kilometers of Japanese territorial waters around Okinawa. In the future China might be prepared to launch an invasion of Taiwan and to fight a major war with the United States to prevent a Taiwanese declaration of independence.

Japan in coping with the rise of China is faced with considerable security dilemmas. Japan could be caught in the middle of a tug-of-war between the United States and China—the most obvious scenario for this being a clash over the Taiwan issue. In this situation, Japan might be pulled dangerously toward one side or the other and enlisted in a political or military conflict it wishes to avoid. Japan's preferred strategy in dealing with a resurgent China in the post–Cold War period is clearly one of political and economic engagement. In this way, it can avoid the adversary security dilemma of turning China into a potential enemy, and the alliance security dilemma of becoming entrapped in U.S. military strategy toward China. Nevertheless, the strength of Japan's attachment to the U.S.-Japan alliance as the basis of its security and its apprehensions about China's growing power mean that it will also have to keep the United States on its side and avoid the alternative alliance security dilemma of being abandoned by the United States as a dependable ally in the event of another Taiwan crisis.

Hence, from the late-1990s onward, Japanese policymakers have been forced to perform a highly precarious balancing act between strengthening alliance ties with the United States while also attempting not to alienate China. The consequence of this Japanese "hedging" strategy toward China has been that, even though it is generally acknowledged among most policymakers that China is the greatest potential military threat to Japan, it is not openly identified as a threat to avoid unnecessary tensions. Instead, while Japan continues to strengthen its individual and bilateral military options in the event that China should emerge as a potential foe, it persists in identifying North Korea as the principal and most convenient source of threat and legitimization for the upgrading of its military power (Hughes 1999: 203).

Interstate and Intrastate Conflicts in Southeast Asia

Japan's principal security concern in Southeast Asia is the South China Sea. Japanese policymakers are concerned that if China were to assert territorial claims, it would disrupt vital SLOCs through to the Strait of Malacca and reinforce possible Chinese domination of the subregion (Lam 1996: 999). Hence, Japan has sought bilateral diplomacy, support for the U.S. presence and the ARF process, and an expanded military role in the subregion.

Japan's other concern is Cambodia. However, since the establishment of UNTAC and the coalition government in Cambodia, Japanese attention has shifted to state-building and intrastate security. Elsewhere in Southeast Asia, Japan has attempted to assuage interstate conflicts. Muslim separatist and tribal separatist movements in the Philippines and Burma could destabilize both states. Japan's greatest fear has been the disintegration of Indonesia resulting from the separatist movements in Aceh, Riau, South Sulawesi, and Irian Jaya, and especially East Timor. The Japanese government's preference is the preservation of the territorial integrity of the Indonesian state in order to secure the supply of raw materials and its SLOCs. Japan was hit by the disruption of LNG supplies from Aceh in 2001. Japan has thus provided economic assistance for state-building to successive Indonesian presidents, both authoritarian and democratic in character. But Japan was also compelled to accept the independence of East Timor and to support Aceh autonomy. Despite Japan's constitutional prohibitions on military power for intrastate security, the SDF has taken part in UN PKO activities in East Timor.

Societal Group and Individual Military Conflicts

Japan is also concerned with intrastate violence. Intercommunal violence harms human security in Indonesia and accentuates the centrifugal tendencies of the Indonesian state. In turn, Japan's response has once again been to emphasize the use of economic power for state-building efforts. Japan's interest in human security means that it has taken steps to tackle small-arms proliferation and the removal of landmines in Southeast Asia.

Organizational Group Military Conflicts

Terrorism is the main organizational group threat in the post–Cold War period. The JRA's revolutionary and communist-inspired terrorism has been virtually eliminated in the 1990s, but Aum Shinrikyō indicated in many ways the future shape of terrorism. Aum was principally a domestic terrorist group but was able to obtain conventional weapons, information on the development of WMD, and overseas financing (Hughes 1998). Moreover, its use of WMD demonstrated the increasing destructive potential of terrorism.

The Japanese government has been able to suppress Aum's activities, but similar terrorist concerns have emerged since 9/11. The "hyperterrorism" of Aum meant that Japan found common cause with the United States and UN to cooperate to expunge terrorism both globally and regionally. Japan has emphasized nonmilitary as well as military responses in the fight against terrorism. Japan has stressed the importance of economic power to assist state-building and to address the social unrest that can foster radical Islamism. Within constitutional limitations Japan has dispatched the SDF to support multilateral efforts against Al-Qaeda in the war on terror.

Japan's Military Security Policy in the Post–Cold War Period

Japan has adapted, albeit slowly, its individual military security policy to the post–Cold War security environment by revising existing military doctrines, devising new legislation, and acquiring new military hardware capabilities. At the same time, many adaptations of its individual capabilities were designed to strengthen the bilateral alliance with the United States.

NDPO Revision

Japanese policymakers' first attempt to tackle the new security complexities was the revision of the 1976 NDPO. The original NDPO was devised in the period of détente and set out the principles of Japan's defense policy alongside the military force structure to achieve them. The NDPO was criticized for rejecting the required defense force concept in favor of the standard defense force concept, thus underestimating the size of the forces necessary to counter the Soviet buildup in the Far East and that subsequently obliged Japan to embark on the qualitative and quantitative strengthening of the SDF to support the United States. By the end of the Cold War, the NDPO again came under attack for bequeathing a military force structure more suited to superpower conflict than the fluid security environment of the 1990s. The Advisory Group on Defense in 1994 fed innovative ideas to the NDPO. The revised NDPO unveiled in November 1995 highlighted the uncertain strategic situation around Japan, including the regional military buildup, the proliferation of WMD and ballistic missiles, religious and ethnic strife, terrorism, and natural disasters. In particular, it fixed the Korean Peninsula as the major concern. The NDPO also stressed the need to strengthen the U.S.-Japan alliance as well as bilateral and multilateral security dialogue, an enhanced SDF contribution to UN PKO, and the SDF countering terrorism.

However, the NDPO reflected the conservatism of the defense establishment and confirmed many traditional principles and patterns. The revised NDPO affirmed Japan's attachment to the principles of the standard defense force concept, exclusively defense-oriented defense, civilian control, and the three nonnuclear principles. Moreover, the NDPO retained the large numbers of interceptor aircraft, ASW warships, and main battle tanks that Japan had acquired during the Cold War. In addition, although the SDF gradually began to shift its deployments southward in the 1990s to deal with potential threats now concentrated around the Korean Peninsula, China, the South China Sea, and Japan's SLOCs, many forces remain stationed in northern Japan as during the Cold War.

Furthermore, the revised NDPO was formulated with an eye on strengthening the U.S.-Japan alliance. The promotion of Japan's role in multilateral security dialogue is predicated on the simultaneous strengthening of the bilateral alliance as the basis for this activity. The new NDPO thus makes heavy reference to the importance of the U.S.-Japan security alliance or "security system." It stresses the need for improved information exchange and planning consultations between Japan and the United States; joint research and exercises; equipment and technology exchange; and stationing U.S. forces in Japan. The new NDPO also overturns part of the defense doctrine in the event of direct aggression: Japan will seek from the outset to repel this with U.S. assistance. Finally, the revised NDPO emphasized the U.S.-Japan alliance by inserting a new clause stating that "should a situation arise in areas surrounding Japan [*shūhen*] which will have an important influence on national peace and security," then Japan will take appropriate steps to deal with this in line with constitutional and other military restrictions and through support for UN activities, and the "smooth and effective implementation of Japan-U.S. security arrangements" (Asagumo Shimbunsha 2002: 30; author's translation).

The clear intent was to demonstrate that Japan would seek proactively to support U.S. military forces for the security of Japan and the surrounding region. This carried over from the 1978 Defense Guidelines, paving the way for Japan to revise those guidelines and expand its potential role in supporting the United States to cope with regional contingencies (Funabashi 1999: 266), a role that it had not been able to fulfill during the 1994 North Korean nuclear crisis. Hence, the NDPO was a statement of Japan's individual security policy, increasingly being constructed within the context of the strengthening of the bilateral alliance. The NDPO has remained in place since 1995, but its lack of radicalism in terms of reshaping actual SDF capabilities has meant that the Japanese government has begun to consider another revision scheduled for 2004.

National Emergency Legislation

The North Korean nuclear crisis highlighted Japan's lack of planning and legal frameworks to cope with regional contingencies and the inability to remove obstacles to the deployment of the SDF to defend Japan from any type of external attack. Japanese memories of militarism, combined with the low probability of a large-scale invasion of the Japanese mainland during the Cold War, meant that the government was cautious about subverting the civilian sector for military need. In the event of a military attack on Japan, it was believed, SDF tanks would literally have to obey civilian traffic signals while responding to the crisis. The JDA since 1978 had conducted research into the possible creation of an emergency crisis legislation (*yūji hōsei*) to provide control over civilian property, buildings, electrical power networks, and transportation systems. However, the research failed to progress due to jurisdictional disputes among related ministries and antimilitaristic sentiment and then lost momentum by the early 1990s with the end of the Cold War and the decline of visible threats to Japan.

Japan's interest in the *yūji hōsei* was stimulated by the North Korean nuclear crisis, the Aum Shinrikyō sarin attack in 1995, and the Kobe earthquake of the same year, all of which revealed government deficiencies in crisis management (*kiki kanri*) and the lack of an appropriate legal framework. In particular, neither the SDF nor the police had sufficient legal mandates to defend against North Korean guerrilla or terrorist attacks against nuclear facilities. The absence of a legal framework would also make it difficult for the SDF to respond to U.S. requests for assistance in Japan itself and around its periphery in the types of regional contingencies envisaged under the revised U.S.-Japan Defense Guidelines. Consequently, the government resumed research into crisis legislation such as evacuating Japanese nationals from abroad, guarding coastal installations, and managing refugee flows. This research was impeded due to interjurisdictional disputes between the JDA and NPA, as well as concerns that *yūji hōsei* would be too controversial politically following the intense debates on the revised Defense Guidelines.

Japan once again returned to the issue of crisis legislation and finally submitted it to the Diet in April 2002. Momentum for the legislation was created by the events of 9/11, the North Korean gunboat incursion in December 2001, and apprehensions that the SDF was ill-equipped to respond to domestic terrorist and other international contingencies. The legislation was at first rejected in the Diet. Critics argued that conditions for mobilizing the SDF were too vague, possibly triggering SDF deployment in any scenario. In addition, the proposed legislation was viewed as biased toward U.S. power projection in regional contingencies. Consequently, it was criticized for concentrating more on complementing the revised Defense Guidelines than as serving for Japan's own individual defense. Critics also noted that the proposed legislation contained measures mainly for the SDF to engage in straight conventional war, rather than the types of terrorist and low-intensity conflicts that were anticipated. Finally, the extent of powers provided to the government to mobilize the SDF and to override civilian prerogatives were seen as too sweeping, including the right to fine or even imprison business owners that failed to cooperate during a military crisis. Japan's government was then forced to revise and resubmit the bills to the Diet, achieving passage in June 2003.

Japan's government further enhanced its crisis management powers by passing in October 2001 a new law that enabled the JCG to fire upon intruding vessels. The JCG is permitted to open fire on the condition that the intruder vessel represents a danger to peace, order, or security within Japan's territorial waters; that there is probability the ship's activity will be repeated if not dealt with; that the ship is suspected of preparing to commit serious crimes; and when prevention of the crime is impossible without stopping and searching the ship in question. The JCG subsequently used this new law to fire upon and ultimately sink the North Korean *fushinsen* in December of the same year.

Japan's Individual Military Capabilities

The 1995 revised NDPO has brought about a quantitative builddown in Japan's military capabilities, especially those oriented toward bipolar conflict. But this has been counteracted by the SDF's drive to build up its qualitative capabilities. Japan's economic problems since the early 1990s have constrained the defense budget. Japan's defense budget in total U.S. dollars continued to rise even into the mid-1990s, and by 2000, at U.S.$44 billion, it was the second largest in the world after the United States (International Institute for Strategic Studies 2001: 301). These figures are inflated by the strength of the Japanese yen. If Japan's defense budget is calculated in yen, it can be seen that since 1993 it has virtually stagnated (Hummel 1996: 140–142). Compared to the 1980s and early 1990s, when the annual increase was 5–7 percent, between 1993 and 1997 the rate slowed to 1–3 percent, and since then the increase has been almost zero (Asagumo Shimbunsha 2002: 301). The defense share of total government expenditures remained constant at around 6 percent throughout the 1990s and remained below the 1 percent limit on GDP. The size of Japan's defense budget and its purchasing power also has to be moderated by consideration that high personnel costs typically account for around 45 percent of the budget.

Despite these enhanced constraints, Japan has acquired new high-tech capabilities. Japan announced three further Mid-Term Defense Plans (Chūki Bōeiryoku Seibi Keikaku) for 1990–1995, 1996–2000, and 2001–2005. The GSDF under these plans has acquired the new and highly sophisticated M-90 main battle tank; the AH-1S and OH-1 antitank and ground attack helicopters; the UH-60JA multioperational helicopter; and the upgraded Hawk surface-to-air missile (SAM). It has also sought in the latest defense plan to improve equipment to deal with guerrilla incursions and nuclear, biological, and chemical warfare.

The MSDF has acquired three new Ōsumi-class transports ships. These ships do not carry helicopters but have flattop decks that enable landings of large helicopter transports. In addition, they have an integral dock in the stern for the operation of large hovercraft capable of transporting and landing tanks ashore. The MSDF categorizes this class of ship as designed for the support of GSDF UN PKOs. The flat deck, side-positioned superstructure, and profile (similar to light carriers) have aroused suspicions that it is the first step in Japan constructing a V/STOL aircraft carrier. The weakness of the decks on the Ōsumi-class ships prohibits such a role. The MSDF under the latest defense also plans to construct two DDH-destroyer helicopter carriers, mounting four helicopters for ASW and to assist in the evacuation of Japanese nationals and rescue from natural disasters. The MSDF also intends to acquire two additional Aegis-class destroyers necessary for air defense, a BMD system, and 200-ton high-speed missile patrol boats. The JCG for its part has now installed 30mm long-range machine guns on its patrol boats to counter intruder vessels.

The ASDF intends to upgrade its P-3C patrol aircraft, has introduced the F-2 fighter codeveloped with the United States, and has plans to develop a new transport aircraft to replace its existing C-1s. It also acquired Patriot

SAM batteries, upgrading them to the Patriot Advanced Capability-2 (PAC-2) antiballistic missile system. Japan as of 2001 has deployed twenty-four PAC-2 batteries and is currently upgrading launchers for mounting missiles as the PAC-3 BMD system, although no decision has yet been taken on the procurement of the actual missiles. In another significant move, the ASDF from 1999 onward has been permitted for the first time to acquire in-flight refueling capabilities. The ASDF is set to procure four tanker aircraft under the latest defense plan. It argues that they are necessary to expand the range of its transports engaged in UN PKOs and other international missions; to prolong the time that fighters can remain airborne and thus increase the efficient use of pilot time and fuel for takeoffs and landings; to enable the reduction of noise from frequent takeoffs and landings; and to allow aircraft to remain in the air when they are incapable of landing in poor weather conditions (Bōeichōhen 2001: 99).

The concern of many has been that in-flight refueling provides the ASDF with new power projection capabilities. The Japanese government has hinted it would take direct military action against threats to its security from neighboring states. For instance, JDA director general Norota Hōsei on 3 March 1999 argued that Japan could launch defensive air strikes against North Korean missile sites without contravening constitutional prohibitions. In January 2003 JDA director general Ishiba Shigeru stated Japan's right to strike North Korean missile bases. These comments were then taken as representing a new position for preemptive strikes and as a warning to North Korea not to undertake another missile test. However, the JDA in a 1999 white paper argued that this was a misinterpretation. The original position on this issue was formulated in the House of Representatives in 1954 in a pronouncement stating that in the event of "sudden and unjust harm" (*kinpaku fusei no higai*) inflicted upon Japan by means of a guided missile, then Japan, in line with its constitution, is permitted, using the most moderate degree of force possible, and when there is no other recourse, to defend against the missile by launching an attack on missile bases as within the boundaries of self-defense (Asagumo Shimbunsha 2000: 551). But this does not permit preemptive strikes. Sudden and unjust harm is judged to occur only after another country has taken steps to embark upon an action that would inflict damage. According to Japanese government definitions, preemptive strikes take place when the aggressor country is *feared* to be about to embark upon a damaging action; this rules out a Japanese strike under the definition of sudden and unjust harm. The comments of the two director generals did not in fact change Japan's position on preemptive strikes.

The SDF has also looked to improve its BMC4I capabilities to catch up with rapid developments in military technology and strategy heralded by the RMA. The three services of the SDF have deployed three separate command and control systems (MSDF the Maritime Operational Fleet [MOF];

ASDF the Base Air Defense Ground Environment [BADGE]; and GSDF the Ground Self-Defense Force Network). The maintenance of three systems complicates data-linking and exchange, operational coordination, and the ability to exploit new technology to respond more flexibly in real time. Moreover, the distinct BMC4I systems inhibit the SDF, especially the GSDF and ASDF, from effective cooperation with U.S. forces in conventional operations and in projected BMD architectures that require rapid data exchange between Japanese and U.S. command and control systems. Hence, under recent defense plans, the JDA sought to upgrade the BADGE system as the prime coordinator of Japanese air defense for a BMD system and to generally encourage closer integration between the three branches via the New Central Command System from 1996 onward, the Defense Information Infrastructure, and the Common Operating Environment for military computer systems (Bōeichōhen 2001: 103).

In addition, the Japanese government has sought to improve intelligence gathering and distribution capabilities. The JDA in 1997 established the Japan Defense Intelligence Headquarters (JDIH) (Jōhō Honbu) under the command of the Joint Staff Council to integrate all intelligence-gathering assets and improve the flow of information to the prime minister's office (Funabashi 1999: 114–115). The JDIH has a staff of 1,600 and consists of uniformed officers and JDA officials. Each of the SDF services has its own intelligence gathering division (GSDF, the Nibetsu Investigation Division; MSDF, the Fleet Intelligence Command; ASDF, the Intelligence Division and Tactical Reconnaissance Group). Intelligence capabilities are also vested in MOFA's Information and Analysis Bureau; the NPA, Metropolitan Police Department, and prefectural police security bureaus; and the MOJ's PSIA. But Japanese intelligence has been undercut by interjurisdictional squabbling, and the government is struggling to ensure greater sharing of information.

The government is also attempting to enhance Japan's access to information by developing spy satellites. Japan was reliant on information passed from the United States on North Korean missile test launches in 1994 and 1998. The Taepodong shock jolted the Japanese government into plans from 1998 onward to deploy four satellites, two optical and two with synthetic aperture radar (SAR). These were described as multipurpose information-gathering satellites that could be used not only for military purposes but also to monitor weather, natural disasters, and smuggling. The obfuscation of the prime military purpose was designed to circumvent the 1969 prohibition on the use of space for military purposes. Though satellites will not enable Japan to detect actual missile launches, they will enable it to distinguish changes in deployments on the ground. In May 1999, the Japanese government decided that the satellites would be developed indigenously to preserve Japan's military technology production capacity and to lessen its reliance on the United States. However, the government also admitted that many key components of the satellites will have to be procured from the United States and that it will require U.S. assistance for training personnel to analyze satellite information. Japan launched the first two satellites in March 2003 and established the Cabinet Satellite Intelligence Center with a staff of around 320, including 100 image analysts to process the data.

The outcome of this restructuring is mixed. On the one hand, the SDF retains many capabilities more suited to the Cold War. On the other, it has developed capabilities that provide greater flexibility on a range of interstate and intrastate military security challenges. The SDF is becoming better equipped in terms of legal frameworks, doctrine, and matériel to deal with low-intensity conflict such as terrorism. The SDF also developed the ability to engage in limited multilateral UN PKOs. Most important, the SDF is upgrading its ability to support U.S. power projection in the defense of Japan during regional conflicts. It maintains interceptor aircraft, ASW, early warning capabilities, and air defense and will possibly acquire a BMD system—all providing a shield for U.S. bases in Japan and to support U.S. forces acting on Japan's periphery. Hence, the U.S.-Japan alliance remains the key to understanding Japan's security policy even in the post–Cold War period.

Japan's Bilateral Military Security Policy in the Post–Cold War Period

The U.S.-Japan Alliance in Question

The end of the Cold War engendered major problems for the management and continuation of the U.S.-Japan alliance. During the Cold War, Japan and the United States had developed an asymmetric, but nevertheless effectively functioning, alliance relationship for the strategic circumstances of the time. Japan's relative weakness, domestic prohibitions and international structural constraints on its military strength, and the strategic considerations of the Yoshida Doctrine meant that its government and citizenry acquiesced in large part to depend on the United States for military security. The United States was content to defend Japan as a junior partner in the zone of interdependence in opposition to the zone of independence, and because of the access it offered to bases for power projection in East Asia against communism. In essence, Japan's concentration was on article 5 of the U.S.-Japan security treaty dealing with immediate defense of Japan, and U.S. concentration was on article 6 of the treaty dealing with regional contingencies.

The strategic bargain of the U.S.-Japan security treaty functioned due to the basic overlap of the two parties' perceived strategic interests—the common Soviet threat blurring the distinction between Japan's activities under the security treaty to provide for its own individual self-defense and providing support for the United States that could serve for the defense of its treaty partner and the East Asia region and thus be interpreted as an act of collective self-defense. Moreover, the belief among policymakers that the security fates of the United States and Japan were bound together in the face of the Soviet threat meant that the strategic bargain continued to hold into the late 1970s and 1980s, even as Japan became an economic superpower and strengthened its defense posture.

The division of labor established under the security treaty reflected the bargain—Japan developing defense capabilities to provide the shield for U.S. forces, the United States wielding the sword for regional power projection and countering of Soviet influence. Japan's integration under the security treaty could not be total due to constitutional prohibitions and wariness about entrapment in a regional conflict. Japan resisted research into regional contingencies as outlined in the 1978 Defense Guidelines, but Japan's commitment was sufficient to provide the United States with the defensive shield that it required during the Cold War. The treaty supported the interests of both partners to counter the common Soviet threat.

In the early post–Cold War period, however, the strategic bargain and commonality of interests was tested. The removal of the Soviet threat, combined with increased bilateral trade friction, undermined the political, military, and economic rationale of the U.S.-Japan alliance. In addition, a domestic political crisis emerged over renewed opposition to U.S. bases in Okinawa. Since the return of Okinawa to Japanese administration in 1972, around 60 percent of the 37,000 U.S. troops in Japan continued to be stationed in Okinawa, with U.S. bases accounting for close to 10 percent of the total land area of the prefecture. The necessity of this was questioned with the end of the Cold War, and long-term frustration in the prefecture reached a crisis point when a Japanese schoolgirl was raped by three U.S. servicemen in September 1995. In spite of official U.S. apologies for the incident and the arrest and imprisonment of the servicemen responsible, the incident prompted large-scale protests in Okinawa against the presence of U.S. bases. These protests were supported by the governor of Okinawa, Ōta Masahide, who was disinclined to allow the prefecture's land-use committee to force landowners to renew leases for land upon which U.S. bases were located, thereby threatening that, with the expiration of leases held by a group of around 3,000 antiwar activists, the presence of U.S. troops in Okinawa would become illegal. The largest demonstration, on 21 October 1995, was attended by 85,000, and protests continued until a prefectural referendum on 8 September 1996, in which a majority of residents voted for the realignment, consolidation, and reduction of U.S. bases. The alliance was badly shaken by this issue, and it has obliged the governments to reduce the burden of U.S. bases on Okinawa.

The potentially most destructive problem for the rationale of the alliance was an inability to deal with regional contingencies such as the North Korean nuclear crisis in 1994. The United States requested logistical support from

Japan when it appeared that a conflict could erupt on the Korean Peninsula, but the Japanese government simply had no definite answer on what it could provide. Again, the lack of preparedness to deal with such contingencies was the result of the overlapping and complementary, but nonetheless distinct, military planning and roles. Japan during the Cold War had been able to work in line with the principle of individual self-defense and the security treaty to cooperate with the United States as long as the Soviet Union represented a threat to both parties. During the post–Cold War period, the interests no longer necessarily overlapped. Japan faced no direct threat, and the United States was more concerned with the value of the security treaty for the bases that it provided to deal with article 6–type regional contingencies, which did not present themselves as necessarily impacting on Japan's security.

Japan was able to explore other possibilities to support the United States in regional contingencies, if they could be linked to Japan's security, finessing the prohibition on collective self-defense. However, Japan had taken few steps since the 1978 Defense Guidelines to carry out contingency-related research. The North Korean nuclear crisis thus exposed the essential lack of operability of the U.S.-Japan alliance to respond to regional contingencies.

Japanese policymakers became concerned that the United States might abandon the security treaty and Japan as an unreliable partner not worth defending; the United States was concerned that the alliance could crumble, thereby depriving the use of crucial bases and causing Japan to become a major security actor that could rival the United States or provoke a conflict itself. Both were forced to focus on rearticulating joint interests and on restoring military operability. The rationale was the revision of the Defense Guidelines for Defense Cooperation and the completion of research into regional contingencies.

Revision of the Japan-U.S. Guidelines for Defense Cooperation

The first moves to strengthen the U.S.-Japan alliance came from the U.S. side and the production of the EASR in February 1995. The major champion of the report was Joseph S. Nye Jr., a U.S. assistant secretary of defense who had become concerned that the drawdown of the U.S. military presence in East Asia was corroding the ability of bilateral networks to respond to regional contingencies. Nye pushed for the EASR to state that the United States would retain 100,000 troops in East Asia; he also fixed upon the rehabilitation of the U.S.-Japan alliance as one of the keystones of U.S. security strategy (Office of International Security Affairs 1995: 10). In turn, the so-called Nye initiative was conducted in coordination with Japan to restructure its security policy. The NDPO was revised with Nye's draft report in hand, which accounts for the heavy references made to the U.S.-Japan security arrangements in the 1995 version (Funabashi 1999: 265).

Afterward, Japan and the United States moved to revise the 1978 Defense Guidelines. Prime Minister Hashimoto Ryūtarō, following his February 1996 summit with President Bill Clinton, ordered an internal Japanese investigation into the necessity of revising the guidelines (Hughes 1999: 194–195). The outcome of the review (the Joint Declaration on Security: Alliance for the Twenty-First Century), announced on 17 April 1996 during Clinton's visit to Japan, reaffirmed the commitment to the common values of freedom, democracy, and human rights and stressed the importance of the bilateral alliance for the security of Japan and, for the first time, the entire Asia-Pacific. The joint declaration welcomed the maintenance of U.S. troops levels in Japan and the region, pledged Japan's continued HNS, and noted that Japan and the United States would cooperate in studying BMD. Simultaneously, the parties signed the Acquisition and Cross-Servicing Agreement (ACSA), enabling Japan to provide logistical support to the United States in peacetime exercises, international relief activities, and UN-led PKOs.

The central objective of the joint declaration was to state both sides' commitment to a review of the 1978 Defense Guidelines and research into cooperation in areas surrounding Japan that could influence peace and security. The governments then established the SCC to review the Defense Guidelines. The SCC held its first meeting in Hawaii in May 1996, produced a midterm progress report in September, and released the completed review in September 1997. The fields of cooperation are shown in Table 5.1 and include refugee flows, noncombat operations, the enforcement of economic sanctions, the use of SDF and civilian base facilities, rear-area support, and minesweeping—all items that the United States had requested but Japan had been unable to provide during the nuclear crisis in 1994. In April 1998, the Japanese government prepared a bill along with revisions to the SDF Law to create the legal framework. The bill was eventually passed by the Diet in May 1999.

The joint declaration and revised Defense Guidelines represent a significant upgrade of operability in responding to regional contingencies. The Defense Guidelines finally established the functional scope of U.S.-Japan cooperation for regional operations under the security treaty. In turn, the emphasis on the article 6 aspects of the alliance indicates that U.S.-Japan military cooperation is also expanding its geographical scope to concentrate on its role in providing for regional security more widely. This regionalization of the alliance was seen in the Joint Declaration with the statement that the alliance would now function for the security of the entire Asia-Pacific region. Japanese government policymakers maintain that the guidelines have not been designed to counter the threat from any specific country, and that the term *shūhen* used in the guidelines as well as the NDPO is situational rather than geographical. The government has argued that, while the new guidelines do contain a geographical element in the sense that the scope of their operation is likely to be relatively close to Japan, they do not involve a revision of Prime Minister Kishi's 1960 definition of the Far East

Table 5.1 Functions and Fields and Examples of Items of Cooperation in Areas Surrounding Japan Under the Revised 1997 Defense Guidelines

Functions and Fields	Examples of Items of Cooperation
Cooperation in activities initiated by either government	
Relief activities and measures to deal with refugees	• Transportation of personnel and supplies to the affected area. • Medical services, communications, and transportation in the affected area. • Relief and transfer operations for refugees, and provision of emergency materials to refugees.
Search and rescue	• Search and rescue operations in Japanese territory and at sea around Japan and information sharing related to such operations.
Noncombatant evacuation operations	• Information sharing and communication with and assembly and transportation of noncombatants. • Use of SDF facilities and civilian airports by U.S. aircraft and vessels for the transportation of noncombatants. • Customs, immigration, and quarantine of noncombatants upon entry into Japan. • Assistance to noncombatants in such matters as temporary accommodations, transportation, and medical services in Japan.
Activities for ensuring the effectiveness of economic sanctions for the maintenance of international peace and stability	• Inspection of ships based on UN Security Council resolutions for ensuring the effectiveness of economic sanctions and activities related to such inspections. • Information sharing.
Japan's support for U.S. forces' activities	
Use of facilities	• Use of SDF facilities and civilian airports and ports for supplies and other purposes by U.S. aircraft and vessels. • Reservation of spaces for loading/unloading of personnel and materials by the United States and of storage areas at SDF facilities and civilian airports and ports. • Extension of operating hours for SDF facilities and civilian airports and ports for use by U.S. aircraft and vessels. • Use of SDF airfields by U.S. aircraft. • Provision of training and exercise areas. • Construction of offices, accommodations, etc., inside U.S. facilities and areas.
Rear-area support	
Supply	• Provision of materials (except weapons and ammunition) and petroleum, oil, and lubricants (POL) to U.S. aircraft and vessels at SDF facilities and civilian airports and ports. • Provision of materials (except weapons and ammunition) and POL to U.S. facilities and areas.
Transportation	• Land, sea, and air transportation inside Japan of personnel, materials and POL. • Sea transportation to U.S. vessels on the high seas of personnel, materials, and POL. • Use of vehicles and cranes for transportation of personnel, vehicles, and POL.

(continues)

Table 5.1 continued

Functions and Fields	Examples of Items of Cooperation
Japan's support for U.S. forces' activities	
Rear-area support	
Maintenance	• Repair and maintenance of U.S. aircraft, vessels, and vehicles. • Provision of repair parts. • Temporary provision of tools and materials for maintenance.
Medical services	• Medical treatment of casualties inside Japan. • Transportation of casualties inside Japan. • Provision of medical supply.
Security	• Security of U.S. facilities and areas. • Sea surveillance around U.S. facilities and areas. • Security of transportation routes inside Japan. • Information and intelligence sharing.
Communications	• Provision of frequencies (including satellite communications) and equipment for communications among relevant U.S. and Japanese agencies.
Others	• Support for port entry/exit by U.S. vessels. • Loading/unloading of materials at SDF facilities and civilian airports and ports. • Sewage disposal, water supply, and electricity inside U.S. facilities and areas. • Temporary increase of workers at U.S. facilities and areas.
U.S.-Japan operational cooperation	
Surveillance	• Intelligence sharing.
Minesweeping	• Minesweeping operations in Japanese territory and on the high seas around Japan, as well as information and intelligence sharing on mines.
Sea and airspace management	• Maritime traffic coordination in and around Japan in response to increased sea traffic. • Air traffic control and airspace management in and around Japan.

Source: Bōeichōhen (2001). *Bōei Hakusho*. Tokyo: Ōkurashō Insatsukyoku, p. 168.

and the range of the security treaty. Kishi's definition first introduced the concept of *shūhen* to delimit the scope of the U.S.-Japan security treaty and was strongly geographical in nature due to its inclusion of the area north of the Philippines, South Korea, and Japan. However, the Japanese government's preference for the revised guidelines has stressed Kishi's additional statements at the time that definitions of *shūhen* are not necessarily geographically rigid or restrictive of the security treaty's range of action, and has posited that it is not possible to draw a firm geographical line to demarcate Japan's security interests.

This gradual shift in emphasis from geographical to situational definitions of *shūhen* carries two apparent advantages for Japan. First, it allows Japan based on the concept of situational need to expand the range of action of the U.S.-Japan alliance beyond the traditional geographical limits of the

Far East and security treaty as defined in 1960, and to encompass the entire Asia-Pacific region as envisaged in the U.S.-Japan Joint Declaration. Second, policymakers feel the concept of situational need introduces a valuable element of strategic ambiguity into the coverage of the U.S.-Japan security treaty, with the particular advantage of leaving vague the position of Taiwan and China as objects of the guidelines. In line with the 1960 definition of the Far East, Taiwan comes within the coverage of the U.S.-Japan security treaty, and the events of 1996 demonstrated that China-Taiwan tensions are still a major concern for the U.S.-Japan alliance. However, the policy of the United States and Japan appears to be to hedge against a possible military contingency involving China by strengthening the bilateral alliance, but also to avoid the designation of China as a threat for fear of antagonizing it and endangering the general policy of engagement. The concept of situational need seems to be ideally designed for this policy as it enables the United States and Japan to de-emphasize the clear cut geographical specification of Taiwan as part of *shūhen* and a concern of the U.S.-Japan security treaty and guidelines, but at the same time retains for the alliance the option to operate in the Taiwan Strait if necessary.

The revision of the Defense Guidelines contributed to the process of the reconfirmation (*saikakunin*), even redefinition (*saiteigi*), of the U.S.-Japan alliance and has restored the sense that it can respond to the post–Cold War security environment. Yet Japan's desire to strengthen the alliance has not been unconditional. Japan remains concerned about entrapment, so it maintains opt-out clauses in cooperation with the United States under the guidelines. This is a hedge against Japan becoming sucked into an unwanted conflict with China over Taiwan (Green 2001a: 84). Japan's ability to leave Taiwan and other contingencies vague cuts both ways. If Japan does not deem there to be sufficient situational need in a regional contingency, then it can define this as outside the scope of the guidelines and exercise the option not to support the United States. Clearly this is a difficult option because opting not to support the United States could jeopardize the alliance. Nevertheless, at the very least the United States cannot expect automatic Japanese alliance support in a conflict involving Taiwan and China, which restrains U.S. actions. Hence, Japan retains a degree of strategic independence.

Ballistic Missile Defense

If Japan has managed to avoid total integration into U.S. military strategy under the revised Defense Guidelines, then participation in BMD projects alongside the United States may tighten the alliance bonds irreversibly. Following the Cold War period and SDI, the United States maintained an interest in missile defense with research into a scaled-down system for Global Protection Against Limited Strikes between 1991 and 1993. The Clinton administration continued missile defense research with two separate programs (National Missile Defense [NMD] and Theater Missile Defense [TMD]). BMD is the term used in Japan to describe the TMD program. NMD was designed to defend the U.S. homeland from missile attack. The system envisaged the use of hit-to-kill technologies (hitting a bullet with a bullet) and ground-based interceptor or sea-based interceptor missiles to destroy incoming hostile ICBMs in the exo-atmosphere. TMD was designed to defend U.S. forces deployed overseas on allied or hostile territories by destroying SRBMs, MRBMs, and LRBMs in their midcourse and terminal phases. The Clinton administration was careful to distinguish between the two systems and to demarcate the capabilities of TMD systems as below the threshold of intercepting ICBMs because it wished to preserve the U.S.-Russia bilateral Anti-Ballistic Missile (ABM) Treaty of 1972, which limited the numbers of interceptors available to both sides to counter strategic missile strikes.

Clinton administration plans for TMD systems comprised four types of upper-tier exo-atmospheric and lower-tier endo-atmospheric weapon systems based on land and sea. Each member of the TMD family of systems essentially consists of three components: the actual interceptor missiles and the platforms to support them; sensors for the detection and tracking of missile launches; and BMC4I systems to pass information on launches to decisionmakers and then to execute the operation of the interceptor platform in response. The U.S. envisages the use of upper- and lower-tier TMD systems in combination to provide mutually reinforcing layers of protection to guard against "leakage" in the event of a major ballistic missile attack. The defended "footprint" of upper-tier systems is greater than that of lower-tier systems. Navy Theater-Wide Defense (NTWD) systems in the right conditions are able to defend an area as large as 2,000 kilometers in diameter against a ballistic missile with a range of 1,000 kilometers; the effectiveness of lower-tier systems is greater than upper-tier systems against shorter-range ballistic missiles. In addition, the combination of land- and sea-based systems offers differing advantages in mobility—the PAC-3 and Theater High-Altitude Area Defense (THAAD) systems can be loaded onto C-141 transport aircraft for rapid airlift to combat theatres, and the Navy Area Defense and NTWD systems take advantage of the sea mobility of Aegis-equipped cruisers and destroyers.

In terms of sensors, TMD systems employ individually or in combination ground-, sea-, air-, and space-based systems to track the trajectory of missiles from their midcourse onward. PAC-3 and THAAD systems are reliant principally on radar sets and ground-based radar; NAD and NTWD employ the Aegis War Fighting System and SPY-1B/D phased array radar mounted on warship weapons platforms. The existing SPY-1 B/D radar already has some capabilities to detect and track missile trajectories, and the United States is seeking to augment these with software upgrades to provide onboard and theatre "cueing" for interceptor missiles. These sources of tactical information can be supplemented by AWACS and E-2C surveillance aircraft equipped with infrared search and track (IRST). The effectiveness of these sensors is greatest in the detection and tracking of missiles from their postboost and midcourse phases onward. Nevertheless, all experts, including BMD contractors and U.S. and Japanese naval commanders, agree that space-based infrared sensors, and the early-warning tactical information that they provide in the detection of heat plumes from missiles in their boost phases and in calculating the exact launch point of missiles, are essential if a truly effective BMD/TMD system is to be constructed. The SPY-1 radar and Aegis system in their upgraded forms may be capable of tracking the trajectory of ballistic missiles, thus offering on their own a limited form of BMD. But the SPY-1B/D radar can only detect missiles that pass directly through its effective field of range and that are already midcourse. Hence, the ability of infrared space-based sensors to detect at the earliest possible time the launch point of missiles is invaluable in minimizing the area for the SPY-1B/D radar to search and in maximizing the time available. U.S. Defense Support Program (DSP) satellites and the planned U.S. Space-Based Infrared System High and Low (SBIRS) are uniquely capable of providing infrared early-warning information and external cueing. Given that a 1,000 kilometer–range ballistic missile has a boost phase lasting 70–110 seconds, and a total flight time of less than 10 minutes, the ability to access this infrared tactical information should greatly enhance the probability to cue up interceptor missiles with success.

In turn, sensor information concerning missile launches is transmitted and processed backward and forward through a BMC4^{I} system so that decisions and instructions concerning the response of the TMD weapons systems can be executed in real time. Spaced-based infrared tactical information will be fed into the BMC4^{I} system and accessed via the North American Aerospace Command (known by its acronym NORAD) and U.S. Space Command (SPACECOM). Though Japan has certain existing strengths in interceptor missiles and platforms, its need to access sensor and BMC4^{I} technology and information will influence the degree of its dependence on the United States in security planning.

The George W. Bush administration instigated several key changes in U.S. missile defense programs. The administration's outright commitment to deploy missile defense led to the U.S. withdrawal from the ABM Treaty. The U.S. unilaterally abrogated the ABM Treaty in December 2001 and declared its intention to deploy a multilayered missile defense system that integrates all existing research programs. Consequently, even though many key technologies of NMD and TMD systems remain the same, the United States no longer distinguishes between their architectures and has relabeled both under the concept of national missile defense. The U.S. has also abandoned the NAD program and renamed NTWD the Sea-Based Midcourse System (SBMS). SBMS is now regarded as part of the Midcourse Defense

Segment (MDS) of NMD, and THAAD and PAC-3 are part of the Terminal Defense Segment (TDS). The United States has added research into a Boost-Phase Intercept (BPI) system using sea- and air-mounted lasers as part of the Boost Defense Segment (BDS). BPI is advantageous in that it enables the destruction of missiles shortly after their launch, when their target size for radar is largest before the separation of booster rockets, and because any WMD payload will hopefully fall back across the territory from which the hostile missile is launched. The U.S. plan to remove the distinction between NMD and TMD and in favor of integrated BDS, MDS, and TDS systems has created additional problems for Japanese security strategy.

Proposals for U.S.-Japan cooperation on missile defense systems date to 1986 and the agreement of the Nakasone administration to participate in SDI research. This agreement became the basis for the U.S. Strategic Defense Initiative Office and prompted U.S. and Japanese private defense contractors to carry out a joint study on Western Pacific Missile Architecture for missile defense from December 1989 until April 1993. Meanwhile, U.S. and Japanese interest in BMD in the post–Cold War period continued to be driven by proliferation of ballistic missile capabilities globally and in East Asia. Japan upgraded its existing Patriot batteries to the PAC-2 ABM system.

In September 1993, the U.S. secretary of defense, Les Aspin, and Director General Nakanishi Keisuke agreed to establish the TMD Working Group, which met twelve times from December 1993 onward. This was followed in June 1994 by direct U.S. government proposals for bilateral collaboration with Japan on TMD. U.S. proposals were matched by the Advisory Group on Defense, which recommended U.S.-Japan cooperation in the development of TMD. The Japanese government established the specialist Bilateral Study on Ballistic Missile Defense under the SCC to investigate the technological feasibility of BMD systems; this group instituted regular meetings from January 1995 onward. In total, between 1995 and 1998 the government devoted ¥560 million for study costs into TMD weapon systems and sensor and BMC4^{I} systems as well as commissioning private Japanese defense contractors to investigate key technologies to improve native BMD capabilities. However, the Japanese government remained reticent about committing to cooperative research into BMD. Japan's commitment was assured by the Taepodong shock. The Japanese government approved joint research with the United States in December 1998, then signed an exchange of notes on research with the U.S. government in August 1999. Japan's interest increased following North Korea's withdrawal from the NPT in 2003 and rumors of another planned ballistic missile test over Japan.

Japan's interest in BMD extends to the introduction of PAC-3, and since early 2003 the JDA has indicated that it intends to request funds to purchase the upgraded system. Japan's main BMD efforts have concentrated on NTWD. Japan has agreed to undertake joint research into NTWD and four associated technologies: infrared seekers mounted in the nosecones of interceptor missiles to detect and pursue targets; the protection of infrared seekers from heat generated during flight from the atmosphere; kinetic interceptor warheads, or kinetic kill vehicles, for the direct destruction of ballistic missiles; and the second-stage rocket motor of the interceptor missile.

The NTWD BMD system and research into the development of the interceptor missile are attractive to Japanese policymakers for several reasons. The fact that NTWD is a relatively undeveloped BMD system is an opportunity to exploit Japan's world-class strengths in missile technology and to be involved from the early stages in acquiring new technologies. Japan also possesses many of the platforms for a NTWD system. The MSDF has already deployed four Aegis destroyers, with the procurement of two more planned for the new MTDP; and the ASDF deploys four E-767 AWACS, although they do not possess IRST capabilities. Hence, in terms of weapons platforms and seaborne and airborne sensors, the NTWD system represents the most cost-effective option, with any BMD system likely to run into billions of dollars in costs and already squeezing Japan's tight defense budget.

The Japanese government stresses that the BMD project (insisting on the distinction between the former U.S. TMD and current SBMS and TDS projects and Japan's own BMD for protecting Japanese national territory, including U.S. forces stationed in Japan) remains at the research stage (currently 2006–2007) and that separate government decisions will be necessary before development, production, and deployment. However, following the renewed nuclear crisis on the Korean Peninsula, Prime Minister Koizumi indicated in 2003 that Japan may "accelerate" its participation in BMD development with the United States.

If Japan were to consider moving ahead with a BMD system, it would have potentially radical strategic implications for Japan's defense posture and the security of East Asia. The first strategic implication is the potential worsening of Japan's adversary dilemma with China. Chinese officials have argued that a Japanese BMD or TMD system developed in conjunction with the United States would lead to the effective negation of China's nuclear deterrent (Johnston 1995: 73). The "spear" of the United States nuclear deterrent would be complemented by the "shield" of BMD, allowing Japan to enjoy deterrence by punishment and deterrence by denial. Chinese concerns may be justified. NTWD could have residual or upgradeable capabilities for countering China's longer-range ICBMs. China could overcome the negation of its strategic nuclear deterrent through countermeasures and the development of MIRVs designed to saturate and overwhelm BMD systems by force of numbers (Daalder et al. 2000: 15; O'Hanlon 1997: 186–187). However, NTWD and other BMD systems would still possess the capability to negate or severely circumscribe China's other SRBM capabilities unless China were to massively increase production of these missiles, a policy that China might consider given that IRBMs and SRBMs are relatively cheap to build compared to a BMD system.

For Chinese policymakers, a Japanese NTWD system would have significant ramifications for the Taiwan issue. Chinese IRBMs, such as the D-15 test-fired across the Taiwan Strait in March 1996, under China's worst-case scenario could be rendered useless if a Japanese NTWD system was deployed to protect Taiwan (Garrett and Glaser 1997: 395). China also fears the United States selling Taiwan BMD-capable Aegis destroyers. In this instance, China fears that the United States, Japan, and Taiwan would be equipped with identical and interoperable Aegis destroyers and BMD systems, making for a quasi-triple alliance against China.

Japan's reluctance to become directly embroiled in the Taiwan Strait means that Japan would be unlikely to contemplate the actual deployment of a Japanese NTWD in international waters to protect Taiwan. Japan would be more likely to use its BMD capabilities to provide indirect support for Taiwan's defense. First, Japan would have the capability to deploy its NTWD system to provide, in its own and international waters, antimissile cover for U.S. carrier and amphibious forces. Second, Japan would provide a missile shield for U.S. forces dispatched from bases in Japan to defend Taiwan (Christensen 2001: 21). These two forms of NTWD would lessen domestic concerns about breaching the prohibition against collective self-defense, although they would not prevent Japan from becoming further involved in a conflict.

The end result is that China has new suspicions about Japan's security intentions, with a new dilemma forming between Japan and China. In turn, the BMD project may accelerate Chinese upgrades to nuclear, ballistic missile, and conventional military capabilities, generating further momentum for a regional arms race.

The second implication is the potential for being entrapped by U.S. security strategy. Japan's cooperation in a BMD project would produce a deterioration in the security environment. At the same time, Japan's potential deployment of BMD risks direct involvement in conflicts alongside the United States. Japan is deficient in BMD technology compared to the United States. Its planned optical and SAR satellites lack the infrared capabilities necessary to detect and track hostile missile launches, and the SPY-1 radar on Aegis destroyers also lacks capabilities to track missiles and cue up interceptor missiles. Hence, Japan has no other choice but to secure access to information from U.S. DSP and SBIRS satellites. Japan is also deficient in BMC4^{I} technology. Japan's BADGE air defense system needs a total upgrade, the three services of the SDF have to integrate their command and control systems, and the SDF has to establish a BMC4^{I} that is capable of interconnection and data-linking with U.S. systems to ensure smooth access to satellite information. Japan's technological dependence on the United States, and the interlinking of its own command and control to the U.S. "system of systems," mean that Japan's security strategy could function as a subpart of U.S. regional and global strategies.

Japan, if it develops and deploys BMD, will in essence be acquiring a weapons system that cannot function without the active cooperation of the United States, even for homeland defense. Moreover, Japan would possess for the first time a weapons system with real-time defensive power. As noted above, Japan's ability to project defensive power with NTWD over 2,000 kilometers could lead to U.S. pressure to deploy MSDF during regional contingencies. Japan, due to the nature of the system's technology, will also be unable to shroud its defense posture in the type of strategic ambiguity and opt-out clauses included within the revised Defense Guidelines. The fact that Japan's security policymakers have less than ten minutes to respond to potentially hostile missile attacks means that they have to take decisions beforehand about whether or not to launch an interceptor missile. If a missile attack is imminent there is simply no time to procrastinate or to reverse a decision to launch an interceptor. Hence, the Japanese government has to give MSDF commanders in the field clear rules of engagement (ROE) to deal with preplanned scenarios that could commit Japan to a conflict. All of this involves planning by Japan for regional contingencies, much of which necessitates closer coordination with the United States and reveals the types of situations that would trigger Japanese support for the United States.

Furthermore, Japan's participation in BMD raises questions about civilian control and collective self-defense. Japan will have to devolve control of the BMD system and the exercise of military force away from civilian policymakers to military commanders if its defenses are to respond to missile threats. SDF commanders will need greater operational freedom to respond under fixed ROEs in a regional crisis, possibly providing them a freer hand to support U.S. forces. BMD will pressure Japan to reconsider collective self-defense. Japan's sharing of satellite information with the United States and the interlinking of their command and control systems will make it difficult to maintain the distinction between individual self-defense and collective self-defense.

The constitutional implications of BMD for Japan will be complicated by the recent changes in NMD architecture under the Bush administration. Japan attempted to maintain the distinction between its BMD system and U.S. NMD plans. This distinction was made easier by the previous separation of NMD and TMD under the Clinton administration, which enabled Japan to portray its TMD-like BMD system as purely for self-defense. However, the Bush administration's plans for incorporating all systems into one multilayered missile defense system raises the question as to whether Japan's BMD functions for the defense of Japan *and* the United States. In addition, the Bush administration's interest in BPI raises questions of collective self-defense. BPI can be used to intercept hostile Chinese ICBMs targeted at the U.S. mainland, but laser interceptor assets are likely to be deployed in Japan. This means that Japan would be an integral part and on the front line of any system designed for the defense of the United States. Therefore, BMD risks an arms race and heightened dilemmas with China and the United States.

Okinawa and Host-Nation Support

Policymakers tried to defuse the crisis over Okinawa by passing special legislation in April 1997 to ensure the provisional legality of U.S. bases while the prefecture's land-use committee continued deliberations, but also by establishing the Special Action Committee on Facilities and Areas in Okinawa (SACO) to look at reducing the size and number of U.S. bases. SACO issued a midterm report on 15 April 1996, timed to coincide with the visit of President Clinton to Japan. It recommended the return of the Futenma Marine Air Station at Ginowan and a 20 percent reduction in the land area of U.S. bases. This was followed by the committee's final report on 2 December 1996, which proposed that the Futenma facilities should be transferred to a floating heliport to be constructed off the coast of Okinawa. The huge estimated costs and the large economic stimulus package that the Japanese central government offered Okinawa demonstrated the lengths to which the Japanese government would go to keep a lid on the problem and prevent a larger political crisis centering on security issues.

Such initiatives have assuaged some ill feelings, but the problem still remains. Nago City, which indicated its willingness to accept the heliport site, rejected the project in a local referendum in December 1997; Governor Ōta confirmed opposition to the transfer of the Futenma facilities within Okinawa in February 1998. Inamine Keiichi defeated Ōta in the gubernatorial elections of November 1998 on a platform of accepting U.S. bases (Eldridge 2002). Inamine proposed plans for runways for military and civilian use to be built on a reclaimed reef near Nago City. The mayor of Nago accepted this new plan in 1999, and an agreement was reached between Okinawa and the Japanese government on the airstrip in August 2002. However, even six years after the original SACO report, the relocation of the air station is still not certain; Okinawa insists on a fifteen-year time limit for its operation, a condition that the U.S. military has not yet agreed to. The issue remains a political thorn.

Japan's negotiations on a new HNS arrangement with the United States have not been without difficulty. Since the mid-1990s Japan had assumed all the costs for civilian workers, fuel, heat, and lighting at U.S. facilities, and two-thirds of the total costs of stationing U.S. forces in Japan. The constraints of Japan's defense budget made for a potentially tough round of negotiations following the expiration of a special agreement for 1996–2001.

However, the belief of policymakers in the value of the alliance ensured that a new special agreement was signed in September 2000 for the period 2001–2006 extending the same terms to the United States.

The Future of the U.S.-Japan Alliance

The policymaking energy poured into the revised Defense Guidelines, the Okinawa issue, HNS, and extent BMD demonstrates the perceived importance of the bilateral alliance for the security of Japan and East Asia. Japan's strengthening of cooperation with the United States in article 6 contingencies can be seen to serve its own interstate security interests in Northeast Asia by ensuring that the alliance is able to check North Korean military brinkmanship and that it is able to hedge and counterbalance the rise of China as a regional power. The regionalization of the alliance, with Japan expanding its role as the shield for the U.S. sword, also has implications for Japan's security beyond Northeast Asia. Japan thereby reinforces the U.S. ability to smother potential conflicts along SLOCs in the South China Sea. In this sense, strengthening the operability of the alliance since the 1990s has contributed to Japanese and U.S. security and formed the security keystone for East Asia.

This justification for the revitalization of the alliance is not shared by all regional actors. During the revision of the Defense Guidelines, China condemned what it saw as an attempt to strengthen the alliance, constrain Chinese ambitions, and interfere in Taiwan. North Korea joined China's condemnation in even stronger terms. South Korea also expressed concerns that the revised Defense Guidelines were another step in encouraging Japan to take a more assertive military role. However, China recently has toned down attacks on Japan, fearful it would only drive it further into the arms of the United States. In the meantime, some states in Southeast Asia have expressed limited concerns about the revised Defense Guidelines and Japan's remilitarization; some showed mild approval as an important contribution to regional security.

The strengthening of the U.S.-Japan alliance is likely to remain controversial domestically and in the region. The appropriateness of the alliance to deal with the extant security agenda is questioned. The bilateral mechanism is designed to deal with interstate military conflict, but the regional security agenda is being driven by globalization and legacies of decolonization and bipolarization, issues that require essentially multilateral approaches. Many policymakers in the United States and Japan who support the alliance argue that it can also be a stable infrastructure for the growth of multilateral approaches.

However, others argue that U.S.-inspired bilateral frameworks are inherently antithetical to multilateralism, the patron-client relationships of asymmetrical alliances containing a "feudal" dynamic whereby clients are kept isolated from one another and therefore hindered in any attempt to organize collectively against the system of patronage (Leaver 2001: 31). The prospects for Japan establishing something more multilateral in nature remain questionable. The limitations of the alliance are evident as well in the increasing range and importance of intrastate security problems. The United States was prepared to offer only limited logistical support for international intervention in East Timor, and the U.S.-Japan alliance, although not designed for such a purpose, was not in the slightest degree adaptable to it despite the mantra that it functions as the bedrock of security infrastructure.

The growing range of intrastate security problems in East Asia will continue to raise doubts about the efficacy of the U.S.-Japan alliance. Nevertheless, the rise of China is likely to provide Japan and the United States with continuing grounds to strengthen the alliance. Indeed, the Bush administration line has continued to indicate its desire to upgrade the capabilities of the alliance. During the run-up to the U.S. presidential elections in October 2000, a study group organized by the Institute for National Strategic Studies, National Defense University, produced a report ("The United States and Japan: Advancing Toward a More Mature Partnership"). The study group was led by Joseph Nye and Richard Armitage, former assistant secretaries of defense. The security experts and former government officials in the group came from all political perspectives. The report focused attention on U.S. policymaking expectations and strengthening the alliance.

Specifically, the report reemphasized the importance of the U.S.-Japan alliance for regional and global strategy and that it should develop into something comparable to the U.S.-UK alliance (Institute for National Strategic Studies 2000: 2–5). The report urged improved cooperation in military technology exchange, BMD, and intelligence sharing. In addition, it noted that Japan's ban on the exercise of collective self-defense was a constraint. It is clear that many of the recommendations are materializing as official administration policy to contain China. And even though U.S. officials reiterate that it is a matter for the Japanese, removing the ban on collective self-defense would enable the smoother operation of the revised Defense Guidelines. If Japan is to move ahead with BMD, the exercise of collective self-defense will be vital to U.S.-Japan cooperation in a multilayered system.

Japanese policymakers need not fear they will be abandoned by the United States in the post–Cold War period, something that seemed a real possibility after the 1994 nuclear crisis. But at the same time, they remain wary of entrapment in U.S. security strategy, especially versus China. The caution in Japanese policy is evident in its reaction to U.S. calls for participation in the war on terrorism. Therefore, the alliance is growing stronger in the short term but is still fragile.

Japan's Bilateral Security Dialogue and Exchanges in East Asia

Japan has begun to investigate nonmilitary bilateral security linkages to supplement the relationship with the United States. The Japanese government announced officially for the first time in 1995 that it would augment security dialogue and CBMs with the states of East Asia. In fact, MOFA and the JDA had already begun to extend bilateral links in the late 1970s and 1980s to ASEAN states, South Korea, and China as part of the diversification (*tayōka*) of its security policy. Boxes 5.1–5.3 demonstrate the development and nature of these links. Japan's policy has varied in success. Japan has made significant progress in dispelling some of the suspicions concerning its remilitarization, especially since its participation in the UN PKO in Cambodia in 1993. Progress in Japan–South Korea security relations has also been remarkable, with a variety of personnel exchanges and training exercises since 1992. The bilateral dialogue has been pushed along by mutual concerns about the North Korean security threat and triangular U.S.–Japan–South Korea security cooperation. However, the Japan–South Korea relationship is still delicate, with South Korea canceling military exchanges after the textbook scandal.

In contrast, Sino-Japanese security dialogue has not progressed as rapidly. Bilateral dialogue has been hindered by Japanese concerns that China should increase the transparency of its defense budget, curb the export of missile technology in line with the Missile Technology Control Regime (MTCR), and cease nuclear weapons testing. Dialogue was suspended following the Tiananmen Square incident and again following China's 1995 nuclear tests. Japan has since resumed dialogue, but tensions over the revised Defense Guidelines and BMD have made progress difficult.

Japan's Multilateral Military Security Policy in the Post–Cold War Period

Japan, the ARF, and Multilateral Security Dialogue

Japan avoided proposals for any form of multilateral security dialogue during the period of the Cold War, fearful that such frameworks could undermine the bilateral security alliance ensuring stability in the past (Leifer 1996: 16–20, 23–24, 37–38; Nishihara 1994: 63–65). Even as late as July 1990 Prime Minister Kaifu Toshiki stated that it was too early for any type of multilateral security arrangement.

However, the principle of multilateral dialogue gained favor following Mikhail Gorbachev's visit to Japan in April 1991. That visit and the breakup of the Soviet Union in December 1991 indicated the possibility of improvement in Russo-Japanese relations and that the Soviet Union and Russia no longer threatened the alliance with the United States. Japan was

Box 5.1 Military Exchanges Between Japan and South Korea (ROK), 1979–2001

1979	
Jul. 25–26	Director General JDA visits ROK
1990	
Dec.	Director General JDA visits ROK
1994	
Apr. 26	Minister of National Defense ROK visits Japan
Nov. 9	1st Japan-ROK Defense Policy Working-Level Meeting (Seoul)
Dec. 20–23	ROK Navy training ship flotilla visits Japan
1995	
Feb.	Chairman of Joint Chiefs of Staff SDF visits ROK
Sept. 22	Director General JDA visits ROK
Oct.	2nd Japan-ROK Defense Policy Working-Level Meeting (Tokyo)
1996	
Jul. 12	Chief of Combined General Staff ROK visits Japan—talks with Director General JDA; Vice-Minister for Administrative Affairs JDA; Chairman of Joint Chiefs of Staff SDF
Sept. 2–6	MSDF training ship flotilla visits ROK
Sept. 23–24	Vice-Minister for Political Affairs JDA visits ROK
Oct. 16–19	3rd Japan-ROK Defense Policy Working-Level Meeting (Seoul)
Nov. 25–Dec. 3	Chief of Air Force Staff ROK visits Japan
Dec. 8–10	Chairman of Joint Chiefs of Staff SDF visits ROK
Dec. 12–15	ROK Navy training ship flotilla visits Japan
1997	
Apr. 28	Director General JDA visits ROK—explanation of Guidelines review
Jun. 12–13	Chief of Army Staff ROK visits Japan—talks with Director General JDA; Chairman of Joint Chiefs of Staff SDF
Jul. 13–17	Japan-ROK Joint Conference on Defense (Tokyo)
Aug. 8	4th Japan-ROK Defense Policy Working-Level Meeting
Sept. 2–6	Chief of Staff ASDF visits ROK

(continues)

Box 5.1 continued

Oct. 8–10	Deputy Director General of Defense Bureau JDA visits ROK—U.S.-Japan Guidelines review explanation
Oct. 27–Nov. 1	28 GSDF cadets visit ROK
1998	
Feb. 2–4	Chief of Staff ASDF visits ROK
Apr. 1	Head Officer of JDIH visits ROK
May 16–17	Chief of Defense Bureau JDA visits ROK—talks with National Defense Policy Adviser ROK
Jun. 25	5th Japan-ROK Defense Policy Working-Level Meeting (Seoul)
Jun. 26	1st Japan-ROK Security Dialogue (Seoul)—defense and foreign ministry bureau chief level
Jul. 9	Vice-Minister for Administrative Affairs JDA visits ROK
Oct. 12–16	MSDF flotilla visits ROK
1999	
Jan.	Director General JDA visits ROK
Jan. 6–8	Vice-Minister for Political Affairs JDA visits ROK
July	2nd Japan-ROK Security Dialogue
Aug.	MSDF and ROK Navy conduct joint search and rescue exercises in East China Sea
Sept.	6th Japan-ROK Defense Policy Working-Level Meeting
2000	
Mar. 14–17	Chairman of Joint Chiefs of Staff SDF visits ROK
May 22	Director General JDA and Minister of National Defense ROK talks (Tokyo)
Dec. 7–8	3rd Japan-ROK Security Dialogue
Dec. 8	7th Japan-ROK Defense Policy Working-Level Meeting (Seoul)
Dec. 27–28	Vice-Minister for Administrative Affairs JDA visits ROK
2001	
Apr. 20	Director General JDA and Minister of National Defense ROK talks (Seoul)

Source: Ministry of National Defense, Republic of Korea. (1998). *Defense White Paper 1998*. Seoul: Ministry of National Defense; Bōei Kenkyūjo (various years). *Higashi Ajia Senryaku Gaikan*. Tokyo: Ōkurashō Insatsukyoku; Bōeichōhen (various years). *Bōei Hakusho*. Tokyo: Ōkurashō Insatsukyoku.

Box 5.2 Military Exchanges Between Japan and ASEAN, 1988–2002

1988	
Jun.	Minister of Defense Indonesia visits Japan
Jun.–Jul.	Director General JDA visits Indonesia and Singapore
1989	
Jun.	Minister of Defense Singapore visits Japan
1990	
May	Director General JDA visits Malaysia
1991	
Apr.	Minister of Defense Philippines visits Japan
1992	
Oct.	Director General JDA visits Thailand and Cambodia
Nov.	Minister of Defense Singapore visits Japan
1994	
Nov.	Minister of Defense Thailand visits Japan
1996	
Jul.	Minister of Defense Singapore visits Japan
Sept. 24	Chief of Air Force Staff Indonesia visits Japan—talks with Vice-Minister for Administrative Affairs JDA, Chairman of Joint Chiefs of Staff SDF, Chief of Staff ASDF
Dec. 2–10	Chairman of Joint Chiefs of Staff SDF visits Singapore, Malaysia, Indonesia
1997	
Jan. 21–30	Vice-Minister for Administrative Affairs JDA visits Indonesia, Vietnam, Thailand, Singapore
Feb. 2–19	Chief of Staff MSDF visits Thailand, Malaysia
Mar.	Vice-Minister of Defense Vietnam visits Japan
Jul. 11–12	Vice-Minister for Political Affairs JDA visits Singapore
Jul. 13–17	Commander of Special Forces Indonesia visits Japan—talks with Minister of Foreign Affairs, Chairman of Joint Chiefs of Staff SDF
Aug. 27	Minister of Defense Singapore visits Japan

(continues)

Box 5.2 continued

1998	
Jan. 10	Director General JDA visits Vietnam
May 26	1st Japan-Thailand Defense Authority Meeting (Bangkok)
Jul. 6	Vice-Minister for Administrative Affairs JDA visits Singapore
Jul. 8	Vice-Minister for Administrative Affairs JDA visits Indonesia
Sept.	Vice Minister of Defense Singapore visits Japan
Nov.	Minister of Defense Vietnam visits Japan
Dec.	Minister of Defense Singapore visits Japan
1999	
Feb.	Supreme Commander of Thai Defense Forces visits Japan
May	MSDF training ship flotilla visits Vietnam
2000	
Jan. 11–18	Parliamentary Vice-Minister JDA visits Indonesia and the Philippines
May 2	Director General JDA and Minister of Defense Singapore talks (Singapore)
May 8	Director General JDA and Minister of Defense Vietnam talks (Hanoi)
2001	
Mar. 22	Director General JDA and Minister of Defense Malaysia talks (Tokyo)
Aug. 27	Director General JDA and Minister of Defense Philippines talks (Tokyo)
Sept. 5	Director General JDA and Minister of Defense Singapore talks (Tokyo)
Sept. 10	Director General JDA and Minister of Defense Indonesia talks (Jakarta)
2002	
Mar. 13–16	Vice-Minister for Administrative Affairs JDA visits Thailand

Source: Bōei Kenkyūjo (various years). *Higashi Ajia Senryaku Gaikan.* Tokyo: Ōkurashō Insatsukyoku; Bōeichōhen (various years). *Bōei Hakusho.* Tokyo: Ōkurashō Insatsukyoku.

Box 5.3 Military Exchanges Between Japan and China (PRC), 1985–2000

1985	
May	Vice-Minister for Political Affairs JDA visits ROK
1986	
May	Chief of Staff PLA visits Japan
1987	
May 29–Jun. 4	Director General JDA visits PRC
1994	
Mar. 1	1st Japan-PRC Security Dialogue
1995	
	2nd Japan-PRC Security Dialogue Chairman of Joint Chiefs of Staff SDF visits PRC
1996	
Aug. 20–23	Vice-Minister for Political Affairs JDA visits PRC 3rd Japan-PRC Security Dialogue
1997	
Mar. 15	4th Japan-PRC Security Dialogue
Mar. 24–29	Chief of Staff GSDF visits PRC
May 5–11	Chief of External Affairs Bureau Ministry of National Defense PRC visits Japan
Jun. 19	Vice-Minister for Administrative Affairs JDA visits PRC
Nov. 30–Dec. 2	Vice-Chief of Combined General Staff PLA visits Japan—talks with Director General JDA, Vice-Minister for Administrative Affairs JDA
1998	
Feb. 3–8	Minister of National Defense PRC visits Japan— talks with Director General JDA, agreement to promote military exchange with visits and exchanges
Mar. 25–28	Chief of Staff GSDF visits PRC
May 1–5	Director General JDA visits PRC— talks with Minister of National Defense
2000	
Apr. 3	Chief of General Staff of PLA visits Japan
Jun. 19–25	5th Japan-PRC Security Dialogue and Chief of Staff GSDF visits PRC (Beijing)
Nov. 2	Japan-PRC defense officials dialogue (Tokyo)

Source: Bōei Kenkyūjo (various years). *Higashi Ajia Senryaku Gaikan.* Tokyo: Ōkurashō Insatsukyoku; Bōeichōhen (various years). *Bōei Hakusho.* Tokyo: Ōkurashō Insatsukyoku.

also interested in multilateral security dialogue as a means to expand its regional role following the end of the Cold War, to help keep the United States engaged in the region, to reassure its East Asian neighbors about its future security intentions, and to engage China and maintain the territorial status quo in the South China Sea (Midford 2000: 379; Simon 1999: 87). Hence, Foreign Minister Nakayama Tarō at the July 1991 ASEAN-PMC proposed that in the future the meeting should become "a forum for political dialogue . . . designed to improve mutual security" among Asian states. Nakayama's proposal was greeted coolly by ASEAN states, but the proposal moved the United States toward official acceptance of the principle of multilateral dialogue by 1993 and became the basis for the July 1993 agreement to create the ARF.

Japan has taken a full role in ARF since the Nakayama proposal in 1991. The concept is an attractive one because it espouses cooperative security based on a structure of peaceful relations among members. In turn, it does not demand formal commitment to defend other members as with a collective self-defense arrangement like NATO. Thus, Japan's participation does not clash with its antimilitaristic and constitutional prohibitions, or with the U.S.-Japan security treaty. As a consequence, MOFA and JDA officials have taken part in ARF senior officials' meetings and intersessional meetings on PKOs and cochaired with Indonesia in 1997 intersessional support groups on CBMs. Japan also suggested the creation of an ASEAN secretariat to strengthen the role of the ARF chair in responding to regional crises. The Japan Institute of International Affairs (JIIA), a research institute affiliated with MOFA, has directed Japan's participation in CSCAP; it is the cochair of the North Pacific Working Group and has provided the largest slice of funding for CSCAP activities, including funding for North Koreans to attend CSCAP meetings. JIIA participates in the Trilateral Forum on North Pacific Security composed of researchers from Japan, the United States, and Russia. Japanese have participated as private individuals since 1993 in the Northeast Asia Cooperation Dialogue, involving Japan, the United States, South Korea, China, and Russia.

Meanwhile, the Japanese government has conducted regular Asia-Pacific security seminars since 1994, inviting uniformed officers from China, South Korea, Russia, the United States, and elsewhere to discuss regional security matters and CBMs. The SDF has participated in or sponsored multilateral security forums, including the Pacific Armies Management Seminar and the Western Pacific Navy Symposium, held in Japan in 2000 and 2002. The Japanese government dabbled with multilateral security concepts by suggesting a four-way dialogue on security between Japan, the United States, Russia, and China and that Japan and Russia could be added to the four-way peace talks over the Korean Peninsula to create a six-way peace framework. The director general of the JDA in March 2002 also suggested that the ARF could be complemented by a defense ministers' forum. APEC has served Japan as a type of multilateral security forum (Green 2001a: 216). Although it was never designed for this purpose, Japan has found it a useful forum to discuss issues such as East Timor and North Korea's missile program, placing the latter issue on the APEC statement of the 1999 Auckland summit. Japanese officials also entertain some hopes that the ASEAN+3 could develop some functions for regional security dialogue.

Japan's support for the ARF and other multilateral security frameworks is a transformation, but there are limits. Even though Japan has been influential in persuading the United States to back multilateral security dialogue, it has only contemplated such dialogue given the knowledge that the ARF process in no way threatens its existing bilateral relationship with the United States (Hook 1998: 182). Also, Japanese policymakers in the JDA and MOFA perceive the ARF to have only limited utility in security. This is because the ARF is a forum for cooperative dialogue rather than collective self-defense and due to Chinese objections that it has a limited mandate to discuss pressing security issues such as the Spratlys and Taiwan (Yamakage 1997: 302). Japanese policymakers also remain wedded to the U.S.-Japan security treaty as the foundation of Japan's security. In part, this is due to U.S. pressure for Japan not to expand its role in multilateral security bodies. The attempts by the Advisory Group on Defense in 1994 to prioritize multilateral security arrangements over the U.S.-Japan alliance were quashed by U.S. objections (Funabashi 1999: 231–238). More important, tensions surrounding Korea and Taiwan have affirmed for Japanese policymakers the indispensability of the bilateral relationship as a proven guarantee of security.

The most important developments in multilateral security dialogue and cooperation have taken place under the aegis of the United States. The trilateral dialogue between the United States, Japan, and South Korea in the form of the TCOG provides Japan greater input into Korean security affairs and is one manifestation of the growth of a "virtual" alliance among the three. Similarly, Japan has shown an interest in a U.S.-Australian proposal for trilateral dialogue in August 2001, resuscitating the idea of a JANZUS-type regional framework. TCOG and JANZUS are more advances in multilateralism in East Asia made possible with the consent of the United States. The United States retains the prime leadership role, and these frameworks are merely connecting different spokes in the U.S. hub. Japan is thus presented with a form of multilateralism that continues to bind it to the U.S.-Japan bilateral security treaty as the only viable framework. Japan and the United States promote multilateralism only in the sense of "bilateralism-plus" (Hughes and Fukushima 2003).

UN Disarmament and Nonproliferation Activities

Japan has long evinced the concept of UN-centered security policy. The preamble to the constitution, the U.S.-Japan security treaty, and the BNDP all note the importance of UN principles. Of course, the lack of faith in the

UN to fend off Soviet aggression during the Cold War compounded Japan's reliance on the U.S.-Japan security treaty and its aversion to other multilateral security frameworks. But even during the Cold War, Japan's policymakers attempted to utilize UN multilateral principles and frameworks at the global level to contribute to security regionally at the interstate and intrastate levels. At times, Japan's UN-centered efforts were in tune with the U.S. security relationship, particularly in regard to intrastate security measures that do not jar with Japan's commitment to the U.S.-Japan alliance and its contribution to interstate security. Moreover, Japan's cooperation in UN multilateral security efforts has often been something of a stalking horse to strengthen bilateral security efforts with the United States. At other times, though, Japan's commitment to the UN security agenda has generated incompatibility with the U.S. bilateral relationship and indicated that Japan continues to reserve a UN-centered multilateral option for security.

Japan has been an active supporter of UN initiatives for disarmament and nonproliferation. Japan's support and its own nonnuclear principles have been criticized as inconsistent and contradictory given that it depends on the U.S. nuclear umbrella for ultimate security (DiFilippo 2002: 164–167). In addition, Japan's plutonium recycling program and the occasional misjudged comments of policymakers raise suspicions that Japan will one day exercise a nuclear option. Nevertheless, Japan's position as the only state ever to experience direct atomic war meant it would be persistent in arguing for the control of nuclear weapons and other WMD. Japan signed the NPT in 1970 and ratified it in 1977. Japan's delayed ratification was a result of domestic dissatisfaction with the fact that the NPT legitimized the right of the United States and other nuclear states to preserve their nuclear arsenals and avoid disarmament, as well as by the concerns of Japan's nuclear industry that the NPT would bar Japan from developing peaceful nuclear technologies. Japan held out before agreeing to an indefinite extension of the NPT in 1993 for the same reasons, an attempt to pressure the existing nuclear powers to cut their arsenals. Japan thus objected to exempting nuclear powers from practical cuts under the NPT. But Japan vigorously supported the framework as the best available option to curb proliferation.

Japan has pressed North Korea to remain in the NPT prior to and since the 1994 nuclear crisis; its support for KEDO is a mechanism designed to uphold indirectly the NPT framework. Similarly, since the 1970s Japan has urged China to sign the NPT and thus contributed to China's eventual accession in 1992 (Drifte 1990: 37–39). Japan also demonstrated assiduous support for the Comprehensive Test-Ban Treaty (CTBT). The Japanese government reacted to China's nuclear tests in 1995 by freezing grant aid, and then to India's and Pakistan's nuclear tests in 1998 by freezing grant aid and yen loans. These actions were consistent with Japan's ODA Charter, which takes into account proliferation of WMD for ODA recipient status. Japan protested to France concerning its nuclear testing in 1996, and even to its U.S. ally over Congress's refusal to ratify the CTBT in 2000 (Green 2001a: 223). The Japanese government also worked for nuclear arms control at the intergovernmental level by convening an annual conference in Japan on disarmament issues and has been active in backing the establishment in 1998, following the South Asian nuclear tests, of the Tokyo Forum for Nuclear Non-Proliferation and Disarmament, which submitted recommendations to the UN Secretary-General.

Japan has contributed to WMD arms control through participation in the Chemical Weapons Convention (CWC), and to the nonproliferation of ballistic missiles through adherence to the MTCR. Yet Japan's history in the prewar period exposes it to criticism, and its potential joint development of BMD with the United States raises questions about ballistic missile proliferation in East Asia and a regional arms race.

Japan's support of the UN framework has been matched by efforts to control the spread of conventional weapons that fuel conflicts at the interstate and intrastate levels. Japan, in cooperation with the EU, launched in 1992 the UN Register of Conventional Arms, which invites governments in East Asia and elsewhere to submit information on large-scale armaments stockpiles and their export as a CBM. The Japanese government since 1995 has proposed and adopted resolutions in the UN calling for curbs on small-arms trafficking, which facilitates intrastate conflicts and civil wars. Japan convened the UN Conference on the Illicit Trade in Small Arms and Light Weapons in 2001 and provided U.S.$3.6 million for postconflict weapons collection. Japan's government views the initiative on small arms as part of a larger effort at conflict prevention and resolution advocated during the Group of Eight (G8) process.

Japan has been a stalwart supporter of efforts to ban antipersonnel landmines. Japan adopted in 1997 the Ottawa Convention prohibiting landmines and approached the United States to persuade it to sign the convention. Japan destroyed its last stocks of antipersonnel landmines in 2003 and in 2002 established a joint study group of MOFA, METI, the JDA, and the Ministry of Education, Culture, Sports, Science, and Technology to investigate new technological means for clearing landmines. Japan's efforts have involved the development of sensors and robotics to detect and remove antipersonnel landmines (Furuta 2003: 28–29) and plans to devolve this technology to NGOs involved in landmine disposal.

Finally, Japan's adherence to its own ban on the export of weapons, and its caution in power projection and WMD capabilities, a form of "unilateral arms control," has provided it with a degree of credibility when pushing for disarmament in East Asia and globally.

UN PKOs

Japan's first tentative steps toward participation in UN PKOs was the IPCL in June 1992 and the subsequent dispatch of noncombat reconstruction missions to Cambodia from September 1992 to September 1993. Japan's involvement in UNTAC represented the culmination of its attempts at peacebuilding in Southeast Asia since the late Cold War. Through the provision of ODA Japan supported the ASEAN states to resist Vietnam's occupation of Cambodia and its expansion of influence beyond Indochina during the Cold War. Japan took advantage of the strategic rapprochement among the Soviet Union, China, and the United States to play a role in reaching a final settlement of the Cambodia problem. Japan attempted to play a mediating role between ASEAN and Vietnam and sponsored the June 1990 Tokyo conference on Cambodia that produced a communiqué between Hun-Sen's government and Prince Norodom Sihanouk's faction, agreeing to an early cease-fire. Japan then provided diplomatic and economic support for the Paris Peace Conference in 1991 and the UNTAC process and sponsored the Ministerial Conference on the Rehabilitation and Reconstruction of Cambodia. Japan's government also made a decisive intervention in dealing with Hun-Sen's coup against Prince Norodom Ranariddh in 1997—promising the resumption of large-scale aid to the Cambodian government in return for Hun Sen's holdings of elections that then produced a new power-sharing arrangement (Green 2001a: 178). Japan's human contribution to UNTAC took the form of thirty-six civilian election observers, seventy-five civilian police officers, and 600 GSDF engineers for supply and reconstruction projects.

Following UNTAC, Japan participated in a number of UN PKO missions in Africa, the Middle East, and Latin America (Dobson 2003). Japan was not to participate in PKOs in East Asia again until the East Timor crisis in 1999. Japan was reluctant to dispatch the SDF to East Timor to avoid damaging diplomatic relations with Indonesia. The Japanese government was caught flatfooted by the scale of violence in East Timor, as well as the reaction of Australia, other states, and the UN in organizing an intervention force, and in many ways failed to respond to the challenge. Japan's principal contribution through the U.S.-Japan alliance had a minimal function in the case of East Timor. Japan's early diplomatic inaction was reinforced by its limited military capacity, the SDF being prohibited under the IPCL from dispatching troops to UN PKOs to areas where no cease-fire was in place. However, Japan did dispatch monitors in East Timor in 2001 and made available ASDF aircraft for transporting humanitarian aid. Following the conclusion of the elections, Japan since 2002 has dispatched 680 GSDF personnel for reconstruction activities—the largest SDF PKO contingent to date.

Japan is also beginning to consider putting into motion new developments in its PKO policy. In 2002 it unfroze provisions in the IPCL that limited its participation in core UN PKO activities and can now monitor cease-fires; patrol cease-fire zones; inspect, transport, and dispose weapons; and exchange prisoners. The Japanese government in 2002 formed the Advisory Group on International Cooperation for Peace composed of private experts and led by Akashi Yasushi, the former Undersecretary-General of the UN. The group's report called for more flexible interpretation of the five principles of the IPCL to facilitate faster SDF dispatch; the improvement of coordination among relevant government agencies; and the more efficient use of ODA to promote a seamless approach from conflict prevention to peace consolidation. All this indicates a possibly expanded commitment by Japan to UN PKOs in the future.

The War on Terror

Japanese participation in the post-9/11 war on terror is outside the scope of East Asia, the focus of this study. Nevertheless, Japan's reaction to the international crisis carries significant implications for its counterterrorism policies and future bilateral security arrangements with the United States in East Asia. Japan's policymakers decided early on that the events of 9/11 were of such magnitude that Japan was obligated to make a human contribution to combating terrorism.

The Japanese government swiftly passed the Anti-Terrorism Special Measures Law (ATSML) on 29 October, which enabled the dispatch in November of SDF units to support the campaign in Afghanistan. MSDF transports and destroyers, in combination with ASDF transport aircraft, were charged with providing refueling, logistical transport, medical, and maintenance support to U.S. and other forces in the Indian Ocean and Arabian Sea. The SDF's range of action was defined as including not only the sea and airspace of the Indian Ocean but also the territory along the coast and the supply lines stretching back to Japan, Australia, and the United States. Japan's response was quick; its rapid response and willingness to dispatch the SDF can be attributed to a number of factors. First, Japan was concerned that there should be no repeat of the Gulf War debacle and the perceived failure to make a human contribution to global security. Second, any failure by Japan to demonstrate solidarity could undermine political confidence in the U.S.-Japan alliance in East Asia. Third, there was genuine abhorrence at the events of 9/11, reinforced by the hyperterrorism of Aum Shinrikyō in 1995. However, many Japanese see terrorism as related to economic insecurity and state-building and thus diverge from the United States in the importance attached to military power as the ultimate solution.

Japan's government was highly concerned to take a proactive stance on SDF dispatch. Japanese policymakers, in designing the constitutional framework to legitimize SDF dispatch, took the decision to avoid the use of the readily available framework of the Japan-U.S. Defense Guidelines in favor of the new ATSML. Japan was motivated by an awareness that the revised Defense Guidelines were over- and underrestrictive in the case of Afghanistan. The revised Defense Guidelines were viewed as overrestrictive in the sense that the legitimization for their implementation could be provided only by military contingencies on Japan's periphery that if left unaddressed would lead to direct attack. Japan's government would have been hard-pressed to argue this in the case of the Afghan campaign and had already argued during the Defense Guidelines revision that the Indian Ocean was excluded from the functional definition of their geographical scope. In addition, Japanese policymakers envisaged the dispatch of the GSDF to provide medical care to refugees and U.S. personnel on the Pakistan-Afghanistan border, an activity that would have been blocked by the lack of such a provision in the revised Defense Guidelines that limited SDF support to the United States to sea and airspace. At the same time, the revised Defense Guidelines were underrestrictive in that if utilized in the case of the Afghan campaign they would have set new precedents for SDF activities beyond those that the Japanese government was willing to sanction. In particular, Japanese policymakers were concerned that willful stretching of the guidelines to meet the demands of the Afghan conflict would override government efforts to limit and retain control over the functional and geographical scope of U.S.-Japan military cooperation to obviate entrapment in regional contingencies. Consequently, Japan's policymakers, even while freeing up certain restrictions on SDF dispatch by avoiding the utilization of the revised Defense Guidelines, were ensuring that they kept intact existing constitutional prohibitions and a tight grasp on the operational scope of the SDF.

Japan's policymakers were faced with another set of constitutional problems. The United States and its partners had legitimized their own response to terrorism based on the rights of individual and collective self-defense rather than extant UN resolutions. Japan could not utilize the same basis, as it would have been a violation of its prohibition on the exercise of the right of collective self-defense. Japanese policymakers instead sought to legitimize the ATSML based on UN resolutions that identified the September 11, 2001, attacks as a threat to international peace and called upon all member states, and by implication Japan, to combat terrorism. Japan was then able to use these resolutions to provide a link to its own constitution to legitimize SDF dispatch. Japan did this by switching the emphasis from article 9 of the constitution to the preamble, which states that Japan should work with international society for the preservation of peace. Japan was then able to use the preamble to argue that it should support the UN and its resolutions to combat terrorism. In turn, Japan created a bridge between UN resolutions, its own constitution, and support for the United States, which itself had largely eschewed UN resolutions, arguing that its support was not just for the United States per se but for the international community as a whole. Japan's policymakers in devising the ATSML demonstrated ingenuity in expanding the potential for bilateral cooperation with the United States in the case of Afghanistan.

Nevertheless, Japan was also building in limits to its support for the United States in the war on terror by stressing that its actions were legitimized by the need for UN resolutions. Japanese policymakers attempted to maintain a distinction between the support that they provided in the context of the Afghan campaign and support in the context of East Asia. Japan's intent in providing different legal frameworks for the different contexts for SDF dispatch was to erect a constitutional firewall that would enable it to limit the precedent of the Afghan campaign and the extension of similar new forms of support to the United States in any type of East Asian or other regional contingency. Japan, despite being a willing supporter to combat terrorism in the case of Afghanistan, was seeking to limit its future military commitments.

Japan's position on the war in Iraq since 2003 has shown similar hedging. It declared its political support for the war, mindful of the need for U.S. support in East Asia to counter North Korea, but it did not provide any form of military support. In July 2003, Japan passed the Iraq Reconstruction Support Law enabling the SDF to be dispatched to Iraq on humanitarian and logistical support missions. Japan has further pushed the boundaries of its own military role and support for the United States, but again it placed limitations on its role by restricting SDF missions and predicating the law on relevant UN resolutions. In December 2003, the Japanese government finally stopped equivocating and confirmed SDF dispatch to Iraq despite its fear of being dragged into the conflict.

UN-Centered Activities and the Development of Individual, Bilateral, and Multilateral Security Options

Japan's involvement in UN military security activities constitutes an important contribution to the stability of East Asia. However, Japan's activity via the legitimacy of the UN in PKOs and the war on terror may impact its broader individual, bilateral, and multilateral security agenda. Japan has been motivated to support UN concepts of security due to principles of internationalism and its desire to uphold the status quo of the current interstate security system. Japan's role in PKOs should not be separated from the importance of upholding the bilateral security relationship with the United States. In certain ways multilateral UN PKOs have been used as stalking horses to advance bilateral cooperation with the United States. Hence, the IPCL was viewed by some as a means to accomplish the goal that was not possible at the time of the Gulf War: removing restrictions on the overseas dispatch of the SDF, then preparing the domestic and international conditions for SDF dispatch on non-UN missions, including support for U.S. forces in East Asia. Certainly the SDF has regarded UN PKOs as one form of preparation for a wider security role. Japan's role in PKOs has also been used to justify other changes in alliance arrangements. U.S.-Japan cooperation on BMD has been justified on the basis that a sea-mobile system could be used to provide air defense for U.S. forces engaged in UN operations against states with missile capabilities in the Persian Gulf, as in the 1991 Gulf War.

Japan's participation in the war on terror is another example of utilizing the UN to widen the role of the SDF in support of the United States. Japan as usual has taken steps to avoid entrapment, but policymakers are aware that the ATSML provides them with the option and operational experience to expand support for the United States in other theaters if they should decide to do so. Hence, the dispatch under the ATSML of the GSDF to territories to provide medical care for U.S. personnel is an important new provision that would complement the types of support already provided under the Defense Guidelines in East Asia.

Japan's involvement in PKOs and the war on terror may strengthen the bilateral security relationship with the United States but also may pull its security policy in other directions. Japanese policymakers do not perceive their UN-centered activities as yet a realization of the type of dependence on the UN for security as envisaged in the BPND; for the foreseeable future they will continue to focus on the U.S.-Japan security treaty. Japan's role in PKOs does, though, provide an alternative vision based on UN multilateralism. In addition, the war on terror has raised the intriguing prospect of collective security. Japan designed the ATSML by shifting the emphasis from article 9 to the preamble of the constitution. In this case article 9 is no longer providing a guide for *what Japan should do* to contribute to international security *and how it should do* it, but merely *how it should do* it in terms of restrictions on the use of force, while the legitimization for *what Japan should do* is now provided by the preamble.

Japan is potentially realizing Ozawa's concept of collective security, which would allow Japan to engage in any type of military activity including peace enforcement and full combat duties in international coalitions given UN authority. Arguably, the Japanese government inadvertently arrived at collective security and had little interest in participation in the range of UN security operations because it would distract Japan from its U.S. commitments. Still, if Japan were to choose collective security, UN-centered activities, it would lessen its dependence on the United States, allowing it to employ a wider range of military power and to achieve the status of a "normal" military state.

Conclusion: Japan as a "Normal" Military Power?

The end of the Cold War brought important changes in Japan's military security policy. Japanese concerns about the threats posed by North Korea, a resurgent China, interstate and intrastate conflict in Southeast Asia, and transnational terrorism have forced important changes in Japan's individual state, bilateral, and multilateral security frameworks. Japan's individual security framework has been characterized by the gradual restructuring of the SDF; the acquisition of new military hardware with possible power projection functions; and efforts to join the RMA and improve intelligence capabilities. Japan has made its first steps in multilateral security frameworks. It has maintained its support for UN arms control measures while participating for the first time in multilateral security dialogues via the ARF. Most notably, the 1992 IPCL enabled Japan to take part for the first time in UN PKOs in Cambodia and East Timor. Japan's response to the war on terror has seen it dispatch MSDF assets to the Indian Ocean to provide logistic support for the UN-sanctioned and U.S.-led campaign against Al-Qaida in Afghanistan.

But the principal thrust of Japan's military security policy has been concentrated on strengthening the U.S.-Japan alliance. The 1997 revised Defense Guidelines outlined for the first time the extent of Japan's logistic support for U.S. forces in the event of a regional military contingency. Japan's military doctrine defined by the NDPO stresses increasingly the importance of U.S.-Japan defense cooperation, and the SDF and U.S. forces are growing ever closer operationally. Japan by dispatching the SDF to the Indian Ocean in the war on terror also embarked on a learning process of how to fight in U.S.-led multilateral coalitions. In addition, Japan may be moving toward joint development with the United States of a BMD system, which will require closer integration than ever. BMD may finally tip Japan toward collective self-defense, which would lead to a radical transformation in Japan's military security policy and participation in nearly all forms of military operations, especially in cooperation with the United States.

All this indicates that the trajectory of Japan's military policy is toward becoming a "normal" military power. It is certain that there are influential elements of the Japanese and U.S. policymaking communities that are willing to see Japan assume a more normal military role by ending its ban on collective security and taking full part alongside in multilateral coalitions in East Asia and elsewhere.

However, even if Japan appears to be moving toward greater normality in military security affairs, it will not happen without resistance and careful self-evaluation in the context of East Asian security. Japan's policymakers are wary of entrapment in U.S. military strategy, and are hedging its commitments and erecting constitutional firewalls. Moreover, such reticence is reinforced by antimilitaristic norms in Japanese society.

Furthermore, Japan must consider whether a stronger military is the most efficacious option for security. The U.S. alliance serves interstate conflict, but it is limited in dealing with the East Asian security agenda concerned with intrastate instability. The economic roots of military insecurity in East Asia mean that Japanese policymakers may remain cautious about pursuing a normal role in military security if it detracts from the economic and environmental dimensions. Chapter 6 turns to the continuing role of these dimensions in Japan's comprehensive security policy.

6

Japan's Contemporary Economic and Environmental Security Policy

Japan has become a pioneer in developing concepts and practices of comprehensive security policy during the postwar era. Japanese security policy is multilevel (from the interstate level to the individual) and multidimensional (interconnecting the military, economic, and environmental dimensions). Japan's military defense posture has displayed greater multilateral comprehensive characteristics since the end of the Cold War. Japan's military doctrine and force structure are adapting to meet intrastate and nonstate security issues through counterterrorism activities and PKOs. Nevertheless, Japan's efforts are concentrated at the interstate level and channeled via the mechanism of the strengthened U.S.-Japan alliance. Japan as yet lacks the capabilities and motivation to develop a military security policy that would enable it to follow other developed powers to engage in a full range of interventionist activities.

Japan's limitations mean it must carve out a security role distinct from other states and based on conceptions of comprehensive security. First, Japan needs to compensate for its restricted military capabilities to address the full multilevel range of security issues in the military dimension. This requires alternative and nonmilitary means to address extant or potential military conflict issues at the individual, organization, societal, intrastate, and interstate levels. In many cases, this means deployment of economic power alone or in conjunction with military power, through bilateral or multilateral mechanisms, to address the root causes of military insecurity. Second, Japan needs to concentrate instead on those dimensions that are nonmilitary, where it may be better equipped to make a positive contribution. It is in the economic and environmental dimensions that Japan has attempted to make a distinct difference in the security of East Asia.

Japan's security policy must address economic and environmental dimensions. Japanese policymakers during the Cold War were highly conscious of the interlinkages between the economic and military security dimensions, and in turn the interlinkages of these dimensions with all levels of security. Japan viewed economic insecurity and its impact on individuals and societal groups as spilling over into intrastate and interstate military security. In addition, economic exclusion, disparity, rivalry, and dislocation, as well as environmental degradation, were security problems in their own right. Japan's response was often to deploy economic power through ODA, the promotion of private-sector trade, and FDI. In most cases, Japanese economic power was designed for engaging neighboring East Asian states to support internal social stability and state-building. Japan's hope was that state-building efforts would contribute to stability in East Asia. Japan was more reluctant to use economic power to contain neighboring states.

Japanese awareness of the interlinkages between military, economic, and environmental security was heightened by the onset of globalization. The liberalization of economies in many East Asian states in the sphere of interdependence, and the quickening integration of many states of the former sphere of independence, has brought new economic and social stresses with resultant security implications.

Japan's limitations as a military actor, and its concern at the chain reaction among military, economic, and environmental security, means that in the postwar era it has been forced to develop comprehensive traditions of security. The objective of this chapter is to investigate the degree to which Japan's security policy remains comprehensive following the end of the Cold War and the utility of Japan's approach to the existing regional security agenda. It argues that Japan follows comprehensive security in the economic and environmental dimensions and that in certain ways it has strengthened its commitment to comprehensive approaches. Indeed, it is arguable that Japan is well placed to develop an increasingly crucial and efficacious approach to regional security. However, this chapter also raises the question whether Japan is forgoing opportunities to fully exploit the potential of comprehensive security. Japan's declining ODA expenditures and doubts about economic engagement with China and North Korea signal that Japan may be losing faith in this approach and concentrating instead on the military security dimension.

Economic Security Threat Perceptions and Responses

Economic Exclusion: North Korea and Burma

Japan's principal economic security concern in terms of economic exclusion has been North Korea. Since the first nuclear crisis of 1994, Japan's government has understood that this is in part generated by the North's desperate economic situation and exclusion from the emerging regional economy (Hughes 1999: 110–111). Japan's response was the utilization of economic power and engagement to stabilize the regime and to moderate its security behavior. The Japanese government in 2001 extended 500,000 tons of food aid to North Korea bilaterally and multilaterally via UN agencies to assist famine relief. Japan has also been a consistent supporter of KEDO, providing U.S.$19 million of heavy fuel oil as a stopgap due to U.S. budget shortfalls in 1996, and pledging a total of U.S.$1 billion toward the costs of KEDO's administration and the construction of LWRs. As of 2001, Japan had already disbursed U.S.$293 million to KEDO (KEDO 2001: 14).

Japan has the potential to provide a massive infusion of economic assistance to North Korea through the normalization of diplomatic relations. Japan has yet to establish normal diplomatic ties with the North. The Japan-DPRK Pyongyang Declaration of 2002 produced an agreement that Japan would provide "economic cooperation" to the North, including grant aid and low-interest long-term loans. Japan in this agreement was following the precedent of bilateral normalization with South Korea in 1965, and, adjusting for inflation, the contemporary figure for Japanese aid to the North is estimated at between U.S.$5–10 billion. Japan's intention is to provide this assistance in the form of ODA that would be directed toward the reconstruction of key sectors of the North Korean economy, again following the precedent of Japan's economic assistance to the South that was instrumental in kick-starting its development in the 1960s.

Japan would thus open the way to increased private-sector contacts with the North. Japan's lack of normalized relations with North Korea, together with the North's own poor record in repaying its external debt and general image as a disruptive security influence, has undermined the confidence of private investors and traders in doing business with the North. However, greater Japanese government support for bilateral economic exchange following normalization would foster a stable business climate, activate private business ties among TNCs and small and medium-sized enterprises, and foster the North's integration into Northeast Asia. Japan and North Korea have considerable complementary economic assets in terms of the North's mineral and untapped energy resources, as well as the North's light manufacturing in areas such as textiles.

Japan thus has considerable economic capacity in the government and private spheres to help stabilize North Korea internally and enhance interdependence in East Asia. Japanese efforts would strongly complement the Sunshine Policy of South Korea. Nonetheless, it is also apparent that Japan continues to be reluctant to fully engage North Korea economically and that its efforts are restricted by domestic and international pressures. Japan–North Korea relations as of 2003 remain deadlocked over the issue of abducted Japanese citizens and the North's nuclear and missile programs. In this situation, Japan has tended to use its economic power to contain rather than engage the North. Japan's government has been resistant to defining food shortages in the North as a human security problem and to categorize them alongside other food aid in its ODA policy. In avoiding the securitization of this issue, the government has been able to demote the issue among its diplomatic and security concerns and to withhold food aid at critical junctures to pressure North Korea. Japan also threatened to cut funding to KEDO in 1998–1999 to protest the Taepodong-1 test and has used bilateral normalization talks and the promise of access to economic cooperation to pressure the North rather than induce it to moderate security behavior (Hughes 1999: 209). Japan's government has also contributed to blocking North Korea's entry into the ADB and IMF and thus its access to important sources of multilateral development finance. Hence, on balance it is arguable that Japan has used economic power more in the service of containment than engagement toward the North.

Japan's approach to Burma, another economically excluded and authoritarian regime in East Asia, contrasts this approach to North Korea. It also demonstrates a consistent attempt to utilize economic power to effect change in a state's security behavior. Japan since colonial rule and Burmese independence during World War II has continued to maintain relatively close relations. Japan's interest in postcolonial Burma was stimulated by commercial gain, in particular its rich energy and other natural resources (Steinberg 1993). However, Japan's interest in Burma has also been motivated by security interests and the belief that economic engagement and support for state-building are the most advantageous approaches to ensuring stability.

Since its colonial experience in Southeast Asia, Japan has been aware that the Burmese state is a fragile construct riven by ethnic divides. Burmese secessionism, the narcotics trade, migration, and environmental degradation are seen as testament to the failure of the "Burmese Way to Socialism" and the consequent weaknesses of the state's apparatus. Hence, Japanese policymakers have argued that encouraging developmentalism is an important means to bind the state together and that this, even if it involves a period of authoritarian government, will ultimately lead to more democratic forms of government.

Japan's policy toward Burma since the end of the Cold War must be viewed in this light. Japan was a major ODA donor to Burma until the establishment of the SLORC in 1998, but it then suspended its aid in reaction to the suppression of the prodemocracy movement. Japan did recognize the SLORC government following its promise to hold free elections, even announcing that it would resume ODA funding for approved projects. But Japan again suspended all ODA to Burma except humanitarian assistance following the house arrest of Aung San Suu Kyi in 1990. Following Aung San Suu Kyi's release from house arrest in 1995, Japan resumed limited grant aid for debt relief and other ODA on a case-by-case basis relating to basic human needs. Aung San Suu Kyi's rearrest in 2003 obliged Japan to once again consider cutting ODA. Japan's private sector, meanwhile, has maintained a small but important economic presence in Burma.

Japan has thus used ODA and private-sector links to engage Burma and to offer "carrots" to promote economic development and gradual political change (Hook and Zhang 1998: 1063). Japan has also sought greater political engagement with Burma. Prime Minister Hashimoto Ryūtarō made an official visit to Burma in 1997 and stated that "Japan does not feel international isolation is the optimal way for the improvement of the domestic situation in Myanmar. Rather, Japan thinks it important to give Myanmar incentives to behave in line with international norms by drawing it out as a member of the international community" (MOFA 1997). Japan also encouraged Burma's membership in ASEAN and in some senses has been following an approach of flexible engagement.

Whether Japanese policy will succeed is doubtful given the Burmese regime's reluctance to cede power to prodemocracy forces or embark on major economic reforms. Japan's limited extension of ODA means that its leverage over the regime is limited. Nonetheless, Japan's approach does demonstrate adherence to state-building and economic engagement as ways to address underlying problems of security in states such as Burma.

Japan's approach to Burma, though, also reveals contradictions in security policy. Japan's emphasis on "freedom from want" prior to "freedom from fear" means that it is in jeopardy of being seen to tolerate authoritarianism. Japan's desire to engage Burma is an instance where human security (defined as the material welfare of individuals) sits uncomfortably with the ongoing abuse of basic individual political rights.

Economic Disparity

Japan understands that economic disparities among and within states cause and compound security problems. Consequently, its ODA and economic policies support state-building and developmental objectives in the belief that they counteract instability. Japan's linkage of economic disparity, insecurity, and developmental policies was articulated by its sponsorship of the so-called G8 Miyazaki Initiatives for Conflict Prevention. The initiative stated that

> poverty, economic and social disparity, combined with complex ethnic and/or religious groups, can feed violent confrontations. It is therefore important that emphasis be placed on aid which contributes to poverty reduction and social development in order to achieve more equitable societies. . . . Japan will therefore provide strengthened assistance for human resources development and institutional building that will strengthen governance. . . . Japan places priority on its support for "governance" so as to build social systems that can appease antagonism among local communities and thus maintain long term peace and stability. In addition, Japanese aid will be allocated for projects which are implemented in regions of conflict and are of equal benefit to all parties, in order to encourage reconciliation and thereby prevent recurrence and/or aggravation of conflict. (MOFA 2000a: 3)

Japan's commitment to economic power to address interstate conflict can be seen in its support for ASEAN's subregional economic cooperation through the Initiative for ASEAN Integration (IAI). This initiative, launched in November 2000, aims to close the development gap between established members and newer entrants like Cambodia, Laos, Myanmar (Burma), and Vietnam (CLMV). Although not directly articulated as such, the IAI has a security rationale in that it is designed to alleviate potential causes of political, social, and economic strife among ASEAN members resulting from differential stages of development. Japan has provided assistance for the development of CLMV human resources and actively backed ADB funding for key ASEAN integration projects. Japan in 1995 hosted in Tokyo the Forum for Comprehensive Development in Indochina. Japan as an external power has obvious economic and security interests in Southeast Asia, and it hopes that increased political and economic interaction will result in a more effective regional security community.

Japanese interest extends to individual states within Southeast Asia. Japan has viewed intrastate separatist conflict and terrorism in the Mindanao area of the Philippines as partly the outcome of failure of the state's developmental agenda and the severe economic disparities imposed on Mindanao. The Japanese government in December 2002 unveiled the Support Package for Peace and Stability in Mindanao. It argued that strife in Mindanao had "aggravated the issue of poverty in the area, creating a hotbed of terrorism" (MOFA 2002a: 2). Moreover, it stressed that the conflict undermines opportunities for FDI and the development of the Philippines as a whole, thus reinforcing the cycle of poverty and conflict. Japan's ODA package for Mindanao was aimed to break this cycle by improving human resources and by providing basic needs such as medical care, rural development, and infrastructure. In this way, Japan's declared aim was to support the government efforts to fight poverty and terrorism simultaneously.

Japan's traditional policy toward Indonesia has been to support territorial integrity and to alleviate intrastate conflicts by strengthening developmental and state-building projects. Japan continues to provide large-scale ODA to restructure the Indonesian economy and state. It has also undertaken efforts to resolve the problem of Aceh separatism through the application of economic power. Japan, along with the United States and the World Bank, sponsored the Preparatory Conference on Peace and Reconstruction in Aceh in December 2002. It also argued that peace and stability could be consolidated only by economic reconstruction to alleviate social divisions.

Japanese policy with regard to East Timor changed during the late 1990s as it became clear that independence was inevitable and Indonesia's territorial integrity could not be guaranteed. Japan has contributed in noncombat terms stabilization through the deployment of the SDF on PKO reconstruction duties since 2002. Its prime role has been in economic reconstruction of the newly independent East Timor state through the pledge of U.S.$100 million in ODA bilaterally and multilaterally via the World Bank (Gorjão 2002: 770).

Japan's principal concerns in Northeast Asia relate to China. Japan's engagement policy to promote economic reform, to stabilize China internally, and to bring China into the regional and global economic community has led to rapid economic growth. This is a testament to the success of Japanese policy, but it has also presented new problems. On the one hand, China's economic rise is a challenge to Japan's position as economic superpower. On the other hand, China's dash for economic development, and the domestic economic disparities that emerged as a result, raised questions about social and political stability and how this may impact China's internal and external security behavior. Japan has become anxious about the economic disparities among China's coastal and inland regions and among different strata of society. The unspoken fear is that the exacerbation of poverty, internal migration flows, and crime rates could plunge China into internal social and political chaos with unpredictable consequences for its security behavior and relations with Japan.

In reaction to China's economic transformation, Japan has been obliged to switch toward improving living standards and human resources in the inland regions. Japan has used its new multiyear loan for sustainable agricultural development in rural areas to alleviate poverty and to provide medical facilities, in addition to dealing with environmental degradation.

Economic Rivalry: Water and Food Resources

Japan has shared the view that rivalry over water and food resources, often exacerbated by globalization and rapid economic growth, can cause human insecurity and interstate conflict. Child health and potential conflict conditions are paramount concerns. Prime Minister Koizumi Junichirō announced at the World Summit on Sustainable Development in Johannesburg in August 2002 an initiative to continue providing safe and reliable drinking water supplies and to promote model water development projects. The Koizumi Initiative was made in conjunction with the U.S.-Japanese Partnership to Provide Safe Water and Sanitation to the World's Poor. Japan also hosted the Third World Water Forum in Osaka, Kyoto, and Shiga in March 2003 to facilitate cooperation on sustainable water resource development. Japan in 1999 disbursed a total of U.S.$794 million to drinking water projects in Africa and East Asia, supplying around 20 million people (Ministry of Land, Infrastructure, and Transport 2003: 3). Other projects were devoted to improving water management in China and the Mekong Basin.

Rivalry over agricultural food resources and fish stocks are major human security concerns and potential sources of interstate conflict. Competition for maritime food resources impacts Japan and regional security and has been reinforced by the history of disputes over fishing rights with neighboring Northeast Asian states. The Japanese government has attempted to alleviate frictions by concluding fishing rights agreements. The Japan-China Fisheries Agreement was negotiated in November 1997 and came into force in June 2002. Both states agreed to establish a joint fisheries commission that would manage fishing operations in areas where EEZs overlap. Japan and South Korea concluded a new agreement in 1998 that permits fishing within set catch limits in both of their national EEZs in the Sea of Japan. Japan signed an agreement with Russia in February 1998 permitting Japanese fishing vessels to operate safely within the Russian-controlled waters of the Northern Territories, which Japan still claims as its sovereign territory and EEZ.

Nonetheless, Japan experiences periodic tensions over fishing resources. For instance, the Japanese government in August 2001 protested when Russia allowed South Korean fishing vessels into the waters around the Northern Territories in contravention of its sovereign claims and EEZ. Tensions rose when Japan and South Korea threatened to close access to fishing grounds in their respective EEZs. The dispute was settled in December 2001 when Japan agreed to allow limited South Korean fishing in its EEZ in return for the South forgoing the right to fish around the Northern Territories.

Economic Rivalry: Energy

Japan as a resource-poor state has suffered energy security vulnerabilities throughout the modern era. Japanese anxieties about the severance of oil supplies from the United States and the British Empire in the prewar era contributed to its decision to initiate the Pacific War and to expand southward to gain control of oil fields in Southeast Asia. Similarly, Japan's energy insecurities were highlighted by the first oil shock of 1973. Japan, a potential target for an Arab oil embargo along with other industrialized states, responded by dispatching diplomatic missions to the Middle East, by pledging new ODA for the region, and by stating its willingness to defy the U.S. policy of noncooperation with the Organization of the Petroleum Exporting Countries (OPEC) and the organization of a consumers' cartel.

Japan since then has sought to improve its energy security situation through a variety of means. Japan continues to rely on oil for approximately 56 percent of its total energy, and 77 percent of its oil supplies are derived from the Middle East. Hence, Japan has maintained a policy of resource diplomacy (*shigen gaikō*), using ODA to build closer relations with the Arab world and Middle East. It has provided economic support to the Palestinian Authority and courted the Gulf States. Japan's Arabian Oil Company, backed by the government, lost concessions in Saudi Arabia in February 2000. But the Japanese government concluded an agreement in March 2002 to enable the company to continue drilling in Kuwait, and since November 2000 it has been negotiating with Iran to gain concessions in the Azadegan oil field.

Japan hedges against oil dependency and vulnerability by building stockpiles of oil and diversifying its supply sources. Japan has 170 days of domestic reserves to draw upon in the event of another oil crisis in the Middle East.

Japan has sought to diversify the source of supplies through exploitation of fields in Southeast Asia and in the Russian Far East. For example, the Japan-Russia Joint Action Plan announced in January 2003 states that both sides will press ahead with the construction of the 3,800-kilometer Siberia-Pacific Ocean oil pipeline from Angarsk to Nahodka and energy projects on Sakhalin Island.

Japan's diversification led to an increase in the use of coal, LNG, and nuclear energy and the search for sources that are geographically dispersed yet closer to home. Japan uses coal for about 17 percent of its total energy and procures more than 50 percent of supplies from Australia. Its use of LNG has risen to about 11 percent of total energy consumption, with about two-thirds being imported from Indonesia. Japanese concerns about interruptions to its oil supplies from Aceh in the 1990s help explain its keen interest in supporting the peace process there.

Between 1985 and 1996, Japan roughly doubled its use of nuclear power to around 12 percent of total energy usage, making it the third largest national user of nuclear energy after the United States and France (Fujii 2000: 65–68). Japan's declared aim is to raise this proportion of nuclear energy to around 45 percent by 2010. Japan is engaged in a program to achieve complete nuclear fuel recycling by burning MOX in LWRs and advanced thermal reactors. This program involves the development of fast-breeder reactors; an increase in domestic nuclear reprocessing capabilities; and the stockpiling of considerable amounts of plutonium, estimated at around 16 tons in 1995 (Katahara 1997: 57). Japan's obvious aim is to arrive at total energy independence and security by removing the need to utilize imported uranium and other energy supplies (Samuels 1998: 55).

Energy shortfalls in East Asia can generate conditions for conflict. China's growing demand for external energy resources from East Asia and the Middle East is a particular concern. China could become a major competitor in regional and global energy markets and even seek control over potential oil resources around the Spratlys and the Senkakus, all of which would disrupt Japan's SLOCs and draw both states into conflict. Japan has witnessed firsthand the destabilizing effects of energy shortages in North Korea.

Japan thus promotes its own experiences in dealing with energy insecurities. In March 2002 it convened in Tokyo the Seminar on Energy Security in Asia. Japan expressed its intention to share technology with East Asian states on petroleum stockpiling. Following the seminar, Japan's Agency for Natural Resources and Energy initiated bilateral discussions in East Asia concerning the future establishment of mechanisms to share petroleum stockpiles in the event of large price increases in oil supplies (*Asahi Shimbun*, 17 March 2001: 2). In September 2002, Japan also hosted in Osaka the Eighth International Energy Forum to enhance cooperation among energy consumers and producers and to improve the operation of energy markets. Japan through ODA has encouraged East Asian states to diversify energy supplies. Japan bilaterally and via multilateral organizations provided financing for hydroelectric power schemes in China and Indonesia, as well as hydroelectric and thermal power schemes in Vietnam. In terms of nuclear energy, Japan has made a major contribution through KEDO.

Japan has thus sought to guarantee its own and the region's energy security. Japan's policy is not without problems. Japan's support for KEDO has been conditional on North Korea's observance of the 1994 Agreed Framework. In 1998, by threatening to withhold funding for LWR construction, Japan actually sought to increase the North's energy insecurities. Moreover, Japan's nuclear recycling program has raised concerns about environmental impacts and nuclear weapons. Japan's large stockpiles of plutonium have led to suspicions that it might retain the option of constructing nuclear weapons. Japan's reliance on the U.S. nuclear umbrella and its own antimilitaristic principles make such an option hard to envisage. Japan has also displayed transparency in abiding by IAEA safeguards for its nuclear program. However, as long as Japan continues to dispose of large stockpiles of plutonium, speculation about the acquisition of nuclear weapons will continue (Kim 1996).

Economic Dislocation

Japan understands that economic crises threaten the welfare of individuals and societal groups and that social unrest may aggravate intra- and interstate insecurity. Japan in the contemporary era has viewed the onset of globalization and the 1997 financial crisis as major economic and security challenges and designed its crisis management policies to address interrelated issues.

In response to the financial crisis, Japan agreed to host in Tokyo in August 1997 an IMF meeting of regional finance ministers. This meeting succeeded in raising U.S.$16 billion in emergency funding for Thailand, with Japan contributing the largest share (U.S.$4 billion). Japan proposed in late September 1997 a U.S.$100 billion Asian Monetary Fund (AMF) as a regional financial surveillance and loan facility to suppress future crises. However, Japan's proposal was vetoed in large part by the United States and China, which were suspicious that the AMF proposal was an attempt to exert leadership over the region. Moreover, the United States and IMF objected to the AMF proposal because it purported to offer loans on softer conditions and to undermine the discipline of IMF austerity programs. Japan was undeterred and unveiled in October 1998 the U.S.$30 billion New Miyazawa Initiative. The initiative enabled Japan to provide financial assistance to states in East Asia, both bilaterally and multilaterally via the ADB, with softer conditions than IMF loans. Japan provided financial and technical support for the Chiang Mai initiative of March 2000, which sought to establish a currency swap among East Asian states to prevent financial crises.

Japan's motives to provide financial assistance can be explained by a variety of reasons, and its jostling for increased influence over the region vis-à-vis the United States and China should not be discounted (Hughes 2000a). For Japan, however, there was also a security imperative. Japanese policymakers perceived that financial meltdowns in East Asia would lead to economic collapse, undermine developmental and state-building projects, impose major social costs on their citizens, and generate intrastate and individual human insecurity.

Japanese predictions were borne out by the experience of Indonesia and IMF programs. Strict IMF conditionalities insisting on the removal of government subsidies for basic health and medicine led to social and political unrest. IMF conditionality and restructuring programs were seen as tampering with the Indonesian political economy just when a strong state was needed to prevent disintegration. Japan agreed with much of the structural reforms to prevent financial crises but viewed them as longer-term measures to be implemented once the immediate crisis had abated (Inada 2001: 120). For these reasons, Japan insisted that financial assistance be provided to Indonesia and other Southeast Asian states on softer conditions so that they could weather the worst political and security problems.

Japan's financial assistance to East Asia through the IMF, ADB, and Miyazawa Initiative was thus directed toward the stabilization of state economies and to strengthen their resilience to global and regional economic shocks. Japan's assistance to Indonesia possibly came too late and was insufficient. But its assistance to Thailand and Malaysia contributed to overall stabilization. Japan's assistance was also directed toward the social impacts of financial crisis, locating such problems firmly within the emerging human security agenda. In contrast to initial IMF programs, the Miyazawa Initiative allocated U.S.$150 million for assistance to the socially vulnerable, including medicine and public health care. Japan also provided U.S.$750 million and U.S.$60 million for immediate poverty relief to Indonesia and the Philippines in 1999, as well as 750,000 tons of rice aid for Indonesia that same year (Suehiro 2001: 248). In the aftermath of the 1997 crisis, Japan allocated ODA to fund the construction of social safety nets to prevent poverty and associated political implications among large sections of Southeast Asian society in a future financial crisis (Suehiro 2001: 227).

Migration

Migration and unregulated population movements are triggered by a combination of economic exclusion, disparities, and dislocation and political instability. In certain instances, economic instability may be the primary motivation for individuals, leading to their status as economic migrants. In other instances, political instability provides refugee status. However, in many cases these motivations and statuses overlap, providing a dual character of economic refugees. For governments, this has complicated the task of distinguishing migrants who are entitled to economic assistance and residency.

Japan's government has identified migration as part of the regional security agenda. It has focused on refugee problems as a human security issue and prefers to separate this from the issue of economic migration within, to, and from Japan itself. Japan has made a significant contribution toward humanitarian assistance for refugees in East Asia. Japan is the second largest donor to the United Nations High Commissioner for Refugees (UNHCR) and the WFP and is a major donor to the International Committee of the Red Cross (MOFA 2000b). MOFA introduced a grant scheme for Japanese NGO emergency relief projects (known as the Direct Fund); and the Ministry of Public Management, Home Affairs, Posts, and Telecommunications operates the Postal Savings for International Voluntary Aid to fund Japanese NGO support for refugees in the field. Japanese NGOs have assisted returning refugees in East Timor in reconstruction, health care, education, and food production. The Japanese government in February 2002 provided U.S.$2.5 million via the UN Trust Fund for Human Security to support UNDP and UNICEF activities for the resettlement of displaced persons in Maluku and Aceh.

Japan's identification of population movements as a security problem, and its support for refugee relief, have been an important contribution to East Asian security. Nevertheless, Japan's policy does have inconsistencies, particularly if human security criteria do not match government policy. Japan's ability to pick and choose which population movements it defines as security problems is demonstrated by its reaction to North Korean asylum-seekers. Japan and China became embroiled in a diplomatic dispute following the entry of Chinese police into the Japanese consulate in Shenyang on 8 May 2002 to expel North Korean asylum-seekers. Japan's initial protests were directed more toward the infringement of diplomatic privileges than concern for the fate of the asylum-seekers themselves. Official Japanese policy toward North Korean asylum-seekers in China prior to the Shenyang incident had been to refuse entry into consulates and embassies. Japan and China eventually resolved the dispute by allowing them to travel to South Korea. Japan's refusal to provide asylum to North Koreans would seem to undercut its human security agenda.

This demonstrates Japan's reluctance to treat the problem of North Korean refugees as a human security issue in the same way as other refugee issues in East Asia. Japanese policymakers fear that internal economic and political collapse in the North and any conflict on the peninsula could lead to outflows of refugees to Japan. In this instance, population flows would be the result of political instability and economic exclusion. The former would lead to political refugee status, the latter to protection under the human security agenda. However, the Japanese government has been reluctant to articulate the North Korean security threat in this manner and prefers to place it on the military security agenda. In this way Japan can legitimize the strengthening of the Japan-U.S. alliance. It has been stated that North Korean refugees in Japan could be armed and seek common cause with other North Korean residents to incite internal strife (Hughes 1999: 93).

Japan's inconsistencies between its human security criteria and its responses to security problems generated by population movements are revealed by its treatment of migrant labor within the domestic economy. Japan from the mid-1980s onward has become a major destination for unregulated migrant labor from East Asian states such as Malaysia, Thailand, the Philippines, South Korea, and China. In many cases, these are purely economic migrants seeking employment and higher wages and planning to return to stable economic circumstances in home states. However, they are also driven to Japan by economic exclusion, disparity, and dislocation. Moreover, upon reaching Japan many take up employment under dangerous conditions. Many female migrant workers come to Japan to work in the sex industry and face exploitation by organized crime groups.

The question is whether Japan should devote resources to the welfare and dignity of migrant workers as a human security issue. The Japanese government has no intention of acknowledging economic migration to Japan as a problem of human security. If anything, unregulated migration is treated as a problem of societal security for the Japanese people themselves to be handled by the police. By not defining migration flows as a security problem, the Japanese government can fix their priority on the policy agenda and retain control over migration. The only area where human security is seen to touch upon economic migration is the issue of human smuggling.

Transnational Organized Crime

Globalization has spurred the growth of transnational organized crime through technology and the global movement of commodities, money, information, and people. MOFA argues that transnational organized crime challenges the "safety of civil society and undermines the rule of law and market economy, which are the basis for the peace and prosperity of society" (MOFA 2000c). Japan's NPA shares a similar view of the interconnections between globalization, transnational crime, and the destabilization of societies (Keisatsuchō 2001: 216; Kadono 1999: 119). MOFA has identified transnational crime as a threat by placing it on Japan's comprehensive and human security agenda. Moreover, since 9/11 Japanese authorities have emphasized linkages between transnational organized crime and funding for terrorist networks.

Japan's recognition of the issue has engendered a new policy response. Transnational issues by definition operate outside national borders and sovereignty. Japan's policymakers have come to the realization that greater international cooperation through bilateral and multilateral frameworks is thus essential.

Japan has focused upon crimes committed by migrants in Japan, as well as human smuggling, arms smuggling, money laundering, narcotics trafficking, and high-tech crime in Japan and across East Asia. Japanese policymakers view these as important problems because they immediately and directly impact Japan's own security.

As the number of migrant workers in Japan increases, so has the proportionate number of crimes committed by foreigners. Japan has intercepted illegal migrants, particularly originating from China, who attempt to slip into its territory by sea. Japanese authorities have confiscated larger amounts of illegal firearms, most manufactured in the United States, China, and Russia. Japan's drug problem has escalated in recent years, with the majority of narcotics produced externally. Japan's supply of ATS, its main drug of choice, comes in large part from China and North Korea; heroin from Thailand, Russia, and from China via Hong Kong; and cocaine from Colombia and Bolivia. Japanese concerns about drug smuggling from North Korea have been shown by the fact that its customs authorities in 1997 seized from a North Korean ship 154 pounds of Chinese-produced methamphetamines with an estimated street value of U.S.$95 million. Japanese officials seized another 440 pounds of methamphetamines in January 1999. This shipment had been offloaded to Japanese crime groups by a North Korean vessel disguised as a fishing boat. In May 1999, a shipment of 100 kilograms of the synthetic drug philopon, similar to speed and destined for Japan, was intercepted in South Korea (Noland 2000: 120).

Japan's police authorities see evidence of links between organized crime groups in Japan (*bōryokudan* or Yakuza) and migrant laborers, with the latter acting as agents for the former. In addition, Japanese *bōryokudan* have increased cooperation with organized crime groups elsewhere, such as the Chinese triads, the Russian mafia, and Colombia drug cartels (Keisatsuchō 2001: 221). Japanese and external transnational crime groups have been engaged in human smuggling, the illegal import of firearms, and narcotics trafficking (Dupont 2001: 154). Taken together, illicit activities originating externally but entering Japan, and the links between Japanese and external organized crime groups, indicate that Japan has become increasingly vulnerable to transnational crime since the end of the Cold War.

Japan has responded by supporting initiatives at the global and regional levels. Japan signed the UN Convention Against Transnational Organized Crime (UNTOC) and its three related protocols on migrant smuggling, people trafficking (including forced labor and prostitution), and the illicit manufacture and trafficking of firearms in November 2000 and May 2001, respectively. Japan has been active in G8 anticrime measures. NPA officials chaired the G8 Senior Experts Group on Transnational Organized Crime (the Lyon Group), which was formed after a 1996 summit. Japan was reportedly active in encouraging cooperation between G8 members and East Asian states with regard to UNTOC. Japan's hosting of the G8 Kyūshū-Okinawa summit in 2001 enabled it to place the issues of ATS and high-tech crime on the leaders' communiqué. The Japanese government then hosted the G8 Government Private Sector High Level Meeting on High-Tech Crime in Tokyo in May 2001, which aimed to involve nonstate private actors in a range of anticrime steps in areas such as telecommunications data (MOFA 2002b: 137–138). Japan is also a member of the international Financial Action Task Force (FATF), with its secretariat located at the Organization for Economic Cooperation and Development (OECD); it seeks to counter money laundering.

At the regional level, Japan sponsored the Asia-Pacific Group on Money Laundering meeting held in Tokyo in 1999, a regional derivative of the FATF (Keisatsuchō 2001: 234). It then sponsored the Asia-Pacific Symposium on Trafficking Persons in 2000, and the Asia-Pacific Law Enforcement Conference against Transnational Crime in Tokyo in 2001. According to MOFA, this conference attracted more than 230 high-ranking officials from thirty states and territories, mostly from the region (MOFA 2002b: 137). Japan also cosponsored with Indonesia in May 2000 and with Australia in January 2003 seminars addressing the issues of the illicit trafficking of small arms in East Asia and in the Pacific Islands.

Japan has stepped up cooperation with regional police forces through multilateral and bilateral frameworks. It has provided training for law enforcement officials through the United Nations, Asia, and Far East Institute for the Prevention of Crime and the Treatment of Offenders. The deputy director of the NPA attended a Japan South Korea–China–Russia police chiefs' conference in South Korea in October 2000. Japanese academics and NPA officials have taken part in CSCAP's Working Group on Transnational Crime, with particular interest in exchanging information on combating high-tech crime. The NPA has already established close working links with Hong Kong, Singapore, and Taiwan police authorities (Okawara and Katzenstein 2001: 174). It also began forging links with China's police, initiating a regular director-level discussion forum that brings officials from the NPA, MOJ, MOFA, MOF, and JCG together with their Chinese counterparts (Keisatsuchō 2001: 235).

Japan's transnational crime prevention efforts go beyond improving law enforcement. Reflecting Japanese traditions of comprehensive security and the understanding that economic disparity and poverty drive insecurity, Japan has addressed economic factors that are behind the supply of narcotics. Hence, Japan since 1998 has provided U.S.$1.2 million to the

United Nations Drug Control Program (UNDCP) and grant aid to the government of Burma for the development of alternative crops to narcotics (MOFA 2002b: 138). Japan has allocated part of this funding from its Trust Fund for Human Security and also funded programs for public health care and drug demand reduction in the Wa Special Region of Burma.

Japan is thus becoming more active beyond its borders in grappling with transnational crime, exploiting existing multilateral frameworks and forging new ones. As for policy inconsistencies, the government is prepared to define people trafficking as a general security problem but is less willing to apply human security criteria to economic migrants smuggled into Japan.

Japanese attempts to deal with inflows of ATS from North Korea also appear inconsistent. On the one hand, economic dislocation leads to the production and export of narcotics. On the other, Japan refuses to recognize that this may also be a motivation for North Korea's behavior and has been reluctant to extend its economic power to alleviate the North's economic predicament and to lessen the regime's need to rely on narcotics smuggling.

Piracy

Japan is reliant on the security of SLOCs for economic vitality and so has become concerned about piracy. According to a 2001 survey by Japan's Ministry of Land, Infrastructure, and Transport (see Table 6.1), piracy involving Japanese shipping worldwide increased. The majority of cases were reported in East Asia (around 75 percent); Southeast Asia accounted for close to 100 percent of cases. MOFA reports that the number of cases involving use of guns and knives is on the increase (MOFA 2001a), and several Japanese have been physically injured in pirate attacks. Most incidents involve robbery, but the theft of entire ships and their cargoes is also common.

MOFA provides a number of notorious cases of piracy involving vessels in recent years (MOFA 2001a). In September 1997, the M/V *Tenyu* disappeared after departing from Sumatra in Indonesia bound for Inchon in South Korea. The ship was later discovered in the Jiangsu Province in China, but its crew and cargo of aluminum ingots are still missing. In October 1999, the M/V *Alondra Rainbow* was attacked after departing Sumatra bound for Miike in Japan. The ship's crew, including the Japanese captain and chief engineer, were later rescued in Thailand after having been set adrift in the Sea of Andaman for ten days with little food or water. In February 2000, the M/V *Global Mars* was attacked near Phuket after departing Malaysia for India. The crew was eventually rescued in Thailand. The ship was later seized by Chinese authorities in Guangdong Province.

Japan has attempted to respond to piracy in a comprehensive fashion. As Esaki Tetsuma, senior secretary of state for foreign affairs, noted at the April 2000 Regional Conference on Combating Piracy and Armed Robbery Against Ships:

Table 6.1 Reports of Armed Robbery and Hijacking Piratical Incidents Toward Japanese-Related Shipping, 1989–2001

	1989	1990	1991	1992	1993	1994	1995	1996	1997	1998	1999	2000	2001	Total
Number of piratical incidents	1	4	3	7	2	8	8	11	18	19	39	31	10	166
Number of injured persons														
(Japan citizens)		1 (1)			1 (1)		1	2	1	16 (1)	1	1	1	25 (3)
Region of occurrence														
East Asia	1	4	8	7	1	6	5	10	12	14	28	22	4	122
(Southeast Asia)	(1)	(4)	(8)	(7)	(0)	(6)	(2)	(8)	(12)	(14)	(27)	(22)	(4)	(115)
Indian Ocean						1	1		1	1	6	5	3	18
Africa					1			1	2	4	1			9
South America						1	2				1	3	3	10
Other									3		3	1		7
Navigation state														
Sailing	1	3	4	2		4	2	2	5	6	6	5		40
At anchor		1	3	4	2	4	5	6	9	5	24	16	7	86
Arriving at shore							1	3	4	6	8	10	3	35
Unknown		1	1							2	1			5
Type of piratical incident														
Robbery						4	2	2	9	12	15	12	3	59
Theft and grand larceny						4	6	7	9	7	24	18	7	82
Unknown								2				1		3

Source: Japanese Shipowners' Association, "Kaizoku Kōi ni kan suru chōsa kekka ni tsuite" (Results of survey on pirate behavior), www.jsanet.or.jp/d2–3.html.

> We need to recognise fully that the problem of piracy must not be viewed solely as a matter of maritime law enforcement, but as part of our efforts to counter transnational organised crimes that emerge against the background of various social and economic problems. It is essential to adopt a comprehensive approach based on this understanding when pursuing regional cooperation on measures to combat piracy. . . . [S]ocial factors such as poverty and high unemployment rates caused by, among other things, the impact of the currency and economic crises that broke out in the summer of 1997 is said to lie in the background of maritime robberies in Asia. (MOFA 2000d)

Japan has thus viewed ODA to Southeast Asia as part of a comprehensive security package to deal with piracy and has provided aid for poverty countermeasures in regions where piracy is frequent. At the same time, Japanese policymakers argued that piracy is related to weaknesses in maritime law enforcement and that greater global and regional cooperation in these areas is necessary. In particular it has viewed reduced U.S. and Soviet naval activity in East Asia as one cause.

Japan has encouraged discussion of piracy issues at UNCLOS meetings, as well as cooperation with International Maritime Organization (IMO) conventions on piracy. Japan has also shown considerable leadership in responding to piracy at the regional level through multilateral and bilateral frameworks. It proposed at the ASEAN-Japan summit in Manila in November 1999 that East Asian coast guard agencies should meet to discuss piracy. This initiative led to the Regional Conference on Combating Piracy and Armed Robbery Against Ships held in Tokyo on 27–28 April 2000. This was the first regional conference on piracy and involved maritime policy authorities and representatives of shipowners' associations from seventeen states and territories, including Japan, South Korea, China, Hong Kong, Indonesia, Brunei, Malaysia, Burma, Philippines, Singapore, Thailand, Vietnam, India, Sri Lanka, and Bangladesh. The conference adopted the Tokyo Appeal, which recognized the common importance of the issue and the need to adopt countermeasures. In addition, the conference adopted the Model Action Plan to Combat Piracy and Armed Robbery Against Ships for surveillance of ships, reporting incidents to relevant authorities, cooperation among governments, and information exchange and analysis. The action plan was complemented by the adoption of Asia Anti-Piracy Challenges 2000, a document that expressed the intention to carry out the principles of the plan and to increase cooperation multilaterally and bilaterally (Kaijō Hoanchō 2000: 20). Japan stressed that it would seek to provide support in areas such as training and technology (Japanese Shipowners' Association 2003).

Japan followed up this conference by dispatching a government survey team to the Philippines, Malaysia, Singapore, and Indonesia on 19–26 September 2000. This team was made up of members of MOFA, the Ministry of Land, Transport, and Infrastructure, the JCG, and the Japan International Cooperation Agency (JICA). These officials planned further regional dialogue to counter piracy; human resource exchange and technical training that could be provided by Japan; and coordinated antipiracy patrols. The immediate outcome was an experts' meeting in Malaysia in November 2000 and the acceptance of foreign students at the JCG Academy from April 2001 onward.

Japan then proposed at the ASEAN+3 summit in Singapore in November 2000 a second regional conference on piracy, resulting in the Asian Cooperation Conference on Combating Piracy and Armed Robbery Against Ships that was held in Tokyo on 4–5 October 2001. The conference was attended by the ASEAN+3 states, Hong Kong, India, Sri Lanka, Bangladesh, and IMO and IMB representatives. It reiterated the importance of the problem and that regional cooperation was indispensable at the government and private-sector levels. Japan followed up this conference by pushing through a proposal at the ASEAN+3 summit in Brunei in November 2001 that participating states should form a working group of government experts to study the formation of a regional antipiracy cooperation agreement (MOFA 2001a).

Japan's antipiracy initiatives have not gone unopposed in East Asia. China's suspicion is that Japan may be utilizing the issue to justify the expansion of its naval presence, to compensate for any decline of U.S. patrols, and to prevent Chinese influence over SLOCs in Southeast Asia. China thus applied the brakes to many of Japan's multilateral and region-wide antipiracy initiatives in the ASEAN+3. The issue of piracy, in contrast to previous years, did not receive a great deal of attention at the November 2002 ASEAN+3 summit. In part this was due to the preoccupation with terrorism following 9/11, as well as China's go-slow attitude to Japanese led initiatives on piracy.

Such suspicions may have some validity. The JDA's National Institute for Defense Studies in the late 1990s conducted research into the possibility of the MSDF antipiracy patrols (known as ocean peacekeeping operations) in cooperation with Southeast Asian states (*Yomiuri Shimbun*, 4 February 1999). If the MSDF were to engage in this activity, it would involve a major expansion beyond its usual 1,000-nautical-mile patrol range first set in 1980 as part of Japan's military support for the U.S. Navy. ASEAN states are believed to have encouraged Japan's efforts not only to protect against piracy but also as a first step in engaging Japan as a potential maritime power in the subregion to counter Chinese influence in the South China Sea (Chanda 2000: 29; Graham 2003: 261–262).

Japan is certainly keen to undertake CBMs to improve cooperation with ASEAN and to exert regional leadership; this may be seen as maritime law enforcement or as projecting military power. Nevertheless, Japan remains conscious of sensitivities concerning its maritime role in Southeast Asia and has moved with caution. Japan has taken note of China's unease by involving it in all regional counterpiracy initiatives and by discussing the issue within ASEAN+3 rather than through the Japan-U.S. alliance. Moreover, Japan has limited antipiracy patrols to the JCG only, realizing that involvement of the MSDF would be provocative.

Japan has still made important progress in contributing to the suppression of piracy, especially through bilateral frameworks. In March 2001, Japan launched a joint study group in cooperation with Indonesia and the IMB to strengthen Japanese shipping companies' defense measures against piracy (MOFA 2002b: 138). JCG vessels visited Singapore, the Philippines, and Thailand in August, October, and December 2001 and conducted joint training exercises with the coast guards of those states, as well as patrols in international waters (*Nihon Keizai Shimbun,* 27 January 2001: 13). At the Japan-Philippines summit of December 2001, President Gloria Macapagal-Arroyo requested that Japan provide multipurpose ships to the Philippines Coast Guard; and in November 2002 the two states held joint coast guard training exercises that involved armed JCG personnel storming a hijacked vessel.

Japan has thus taken a purposeful if cautious leadership role against piracy in East Asia. It is aware that its leadership will be limited by Chinese and other regional suspicions. Added to this, all regional states will be reluctant to cooperate with certain and perhaps the most effective antipiracy measures, such as hot pursuit across territorial boundaries, if these are seen to undermine sovereignty.

Environmental Security Threat Perceptions and Responses

Natural Disasters

Japan, vulnerable to natural disasters itself, has long taken an interest in disaster prevention and relief as part of security policy in East Asia. Japan since the early 1980s has identified natural disasters as an element of its comprehensive security policy. In the post–Cold War era, Japan has continued to suffer from floods, landslides, volcanic activity, tidal waves, and earthquakes. The threat of earthquakes was illustrated by the Hanshin-Awaji earthquake of 17 January 1995, which claimed 4,571 lives and injured 14,678 (Kobe City 2003). One of the main justifications and areas of public support for the SDF has been its success in disaster relief operations (Hook 1996: 112–113).

The security impact of natural disasters is multiplied in many East Asian states that are less well equipped to deal with such contingencies.

MOFA argues for natural disaster prevention and relief because disasters can become more complex and implicate human security issues such as infectious diseases and refugee flows (MOFA 2003a). Japan as part of its disaster relief program passed in September 1987 the Law Concerning the Dispatch of Japan Disaster Relief Teams (JDRT). JDRTs, usually consisting of NPA, JCG, JICA, and SDF personnel, can be dispatched within one or two days to provide humanitarian and medical assistance. Japan has provided ODA for disaster relief via the UN and bilaterally. For instance, in East Asia Japan provided U.S.$200,000 for earthquake disaster relief in Yunan Province in China in November 1998; U.S.$500,000 of grant aid and a JDRT for earthquake disaster relief in Taiwan in September 1999; a JDRT medical team for earthquake disaster relief in Indonesia in June 2000; U.S.$100,000 for flood assistance in Cambodia in September 2001; assistance for volcanic damage in Papua New Guinea in August 2002; aid for floods in Burma in September 2002; and U.S.$150,000 for earthquake relief in the Xinjiang Uygur Autonomous Region of China in February 2003. Japan's efforts have taken form in technical training in areas such as volcanic and seismic detection. Its recognition that some natural disasters, especially floods, are precipitated by mismanagement of the environment has meant that it has also devoted ODA resources to projects to control soil erosion and sediment accumulation.

Japan's role is an important contribution to stability in the region and as a means to avert human security risks. It also provides Japan an important nonmilitary security role readily accepted within the region. Japan's policy is not without inconsistencies. Most notable is its limited contribution to natural disaster relief efforts in North Korea. In part, flooding and food shortages in North Korea since the mid-1990s have been due to the regime's mismanagement of agricultural policy, which has caused soil erosion. Japan responded with periodic provision of food aid. Nevertheless, it has not consistently provided food aid in every instance, and much of Japan's disaster relief has been held hostage to political relations between the states.

Infectious Diseases and HIV/AIDS

Japan fixed upon infectious diseases and HIV/AIDS as a major component of its human security agenda in the post–Cold War period. Former prime minister Mori Yoshirō, head of Japan's delegation to the UN Special Session on HIV/AIDS in June 2001, argued that "the rapid spread of HIV/AIDS poses a threat to human security and greatly hinders the efforts of developing countries to reduce poverty, advance social and economic development, and gain stability" (MOFA 2001b). Japan recently overcame highly infectious diseases such as tuberculosis and malaria. Japan's position as a developed economy has contributed to its low incidence of HIV/AIDS compared to other East Asian states. Nevertheless, in 1999 there were reported to be 10,000 adults with HIV and 1,900 with AIDS; the incidence of new cases is believed to be rising (Brandt 2001: 13).

Japan supported initiatives to respond to parasitic and infectious diseases at the global and regional levels. At the 1998 G8 Summit in Birmingham in 1998, Prime Minister Hashimoto Ryūtarō (1996–1998) proposed the establishment of human resource and research centers in Africa and East Asia to improve cooperation with G8 states in combating parasitic diseases in these continents. The UN and Japanese government sponsored the second Tokyo International Conference on African Development (TICAD II) in October 1998, which then agreed to establish one of these centers in Thailand. Japan at the Kyūshū-Okinawa G8 Summit in 2000 proposed the Okinawa Infectious Diseases Initiative, which aimed to provide U.S.$3 billion to improve cooperation against infectious diseases through improved public health care, human resource development, research, and education relating to diseases (MOFA 2002b: 87–88). Japan's initiative contributed to the UN Special Session on HIV/AIDS in 2001, which led to an agreement at the July 2001 Genoa G8 summit for the establishment of the Global Fund to Fight AIDS, Tuberculosis, and Malaria (GFTAM). GFTAM functions as a private-sector foundation for the prevention and treatment of these diseases. In June 2001, Japan pledged U.S.$200 million to GFTAM, close to 10 percent of the fund's total budget.

Japan in East Asia has expressed concern about the HIV/AIDS epidemic in China and has made the response to infectious diseases one of the new priorities of its ODA program there. Elsewhere in the region, Japan extended ODA via its Trust Fund for Human Security to deal with HIV/AIDS in Thailand. Japan since March 2003 has dispatched JDRTs to Vietnam, Taiwan, and China (the latter funded from the Human Security Trust Fund) to provide medical assistance for an outbreak of SARS.

Environmental Destruction

MOFA identifies environmental destruction as a human security issue, arguing in 2002 that "global environmental problems have emerged as potential threats to the existence of all humanity" and that "the advancement of environmental diplomacy has increased the number of voices calling for new approaches such as emphasizing the life and health of individual human beings from the perspective of human security" (MOFA 2002b: 134). In addition, the Initiatives for Sustainable Development (ISD) Towards the Twenty-First Century, announced in June 1997 at the UN General Assembly Special Session on the Environment and Development (UNGASS), identifies the linkage between environmental degradation and human security as one of the guiding components of Japan's environmental philosophy. Japan replaced the ISD in August 2002 with the Environmental Conservation Initiative for Sustainable Development (EcoISD); it also professed human security to be one of the key principles of environmental policy.

Japan has good reason to be concerned about environmental destruction, being directly threatened by pollution resulting from rapid economic growth in China. Growing public consciousness of environmental issues, and a desire to play a larger international role in the post–Cold War period, have also spurred attempts to respond to global and regional environmental challenges (Matsumura 2000; Ohta 2000: 102–108). Japan was historically perceived as a denier of environmental security due to the export of its own pollution problems to the region. Japan's environmental diplomacy and protection measures today offer an important alternative security role as a potential supplier of environmental security. This role is one that is less controversial for Japan due to its nonmilitary nature. But Japan's environmental policies are not without controversy.

Japan's interest in environmental threats and security is reflected in domestic principles and legislation following the end of the Cold War. Japan's ODA Charter in 1992 committed the government to provide assistance for environmental conservation and identified the environment as an overall ODA priority issue. Japan's Basic Environment Law, passed in 1993, mandated the government to promote international cooperation to deal with global environmental issues such as marine pollution, global warming, and biodiversity (Imura 1994: 355).

In turn, Japan launched and supported environmental initiatives via individual state, bilateral, and multilateral frameworks, attempting to acquire status as an "environmental superpower." In 1991, METI proposed the Green Aid Plan, concentrating on reductions in energy consumption and air pollution. In July 1993, Japan and the United States established the Common Agenda for Cooperation in Global Perspective, including cooperation for coral reef, forest, swampland, and ocean preservation (Ohta 2000: 115). The 1997 ISD and 2002 EcoISD sought to provide ODA to support efforts in developing states to meet targets on air and water pollution, as well as the conservation of nature and global warming, while seeking to maintain economic growth.

Japan hosted the Third Conference of the Parties (COP3) to the Framework Convention on Climate Change in Kyoto in December 1997, which then produced the Kyōto Protocol and agreements on quantitative reductions and mechanisms for the reduction of greenhouse gases. In line with the ISD and the Kyōto Protocol, Japan sought to provide ODA for environmental protection capacity-building in developed states. This includes training 3,000 personnel from developing states in the areas of air pollution, waste disposal, energy-saving technologies, and forest conservation and afforestation; loans for the implementation of environmental technologies; and the dispatch of Japanese personnel for information sharing and technology on environmental protection (Ohta 2000: 114–115). Japan has also been a major contributor to the Global Environment Facility. This multilateral body operated by the World Bank, UNDP, and the United Nations Environmental Programme is designed to assist in the management of climate change, biodiversity, international waters, and the ozone layer. Japan has provided roughly one-fifth of the total budget between 1998 and 2001, a sum equivalent to the total contribution of the United States. Similarly, Japan has been the second largest contributor after the United States to the Multilateral Fund for the Implementation of the Montreal Protocol on implementing ozone protection measures (MOFA 2002b: 135–136). Japan furthermore hosts a UN Environmental Program International Environment Technology Center.

Japan's response to environmental pollution has focused on China. Research indicates that China produces two-thirds of SO_2 emissions and half of all NO_x emissions in East Asia and that 38 percent of Japan's acid rain deposits come from China (Wong 2001: 204). Japan, facing the threat to human health from growing Chinese acid raid depositions, has thus begun to reorient its bilateral ODA program to deal with transborder pollution. Japan and China signed the Environmental Protection Cooperation Agreement in March 1994, and in the same year METI's Green Aid Plan began to extend aid for the transfer of clean coal technologies to China (Green 1999: 169). The Ministry of International Trade and Industry (MITI) also explored providing similar technologies to China's inner provinces (*Asahi Shimbun,* 25 January 2001: 3). Japanese ODA funded the establishment in Beijing in 1996 of the U.S.$100 million Center for Sino-Japanese Friendship and Environmental Protection, which hosts Chinese and overseas organizations working on environmental issues in China. Exchanges of Japanese and Chinese experts led to the establishment of the Comprehensive Forum on Environmental Cooperation, with meetings of local government officials, academics, private corporations, and NGOs from May 1996 onward. The Sino-Japanese summit in 1997 produced the agreement on Japan-China Environmental Cooperation Towards the Twenty-First Century. This agreement consisted of two major elements. The first is the Japan-China Environmental Development Model Cities Plan, under which bilateral committees of experts recommend air pollution and acid rain control measures to the Chinese cities of Guiyan, Dalian, and Chongqing. Japan's intention is to provide ODA for pollution control measures for these cities as model examples for other cities in China. The second element is the Project for Improvement in Environmental Information Networks to assist the exchange of information within China on antipollution measures.

These bilateral efforts have been reinforced by Japan's sponsorship of multilateral frameworks to counter acid rain. Japan from 1993 onward initiated a series of expert symposiums involving China, South Korea, Indonesia, and other East Asian states. In March 1998 it hosted the First Intergovernmental Meeting on the Acid Deposition Network in East Asia, which agreed to establish the Acid Deposition Monitoring Network in East Asia (EANET). In 2000, Japan's Acid Deposition and Oxidant Research Center in Niigata was designated as the Network Center for EANET.

Japan has other pollution concerns, like the leakage of radiation from 190 Russian submarines currently awaiting decommission in Vladivostok. The risk of radiation leaks can result from the gradual sinking of submarines at dock, or accidents during removal and storage of nuclear material from their reactors (Glosserman 2002). Russia possesses the technological capabilities but not the budgetary resources to safely dispose of its rusting submarine fleet. Japan proposed an initiative in 1993, and then signed a bilateral accord with Russia in 1999, to provide ¥16 billion of financial assistance for submarine decommissioning. However, the agreement remained in abeyance due to Russia's concerns over military secrets and its lack of organizational capacity to implement the program. Japan was finally able to resume the program as part of the Japan-Russia Action Plan announced at a bilateral summit in January 2003.

Japan's response to the 1997 Indonesian forest fires was to dispatch two JDRT missions to provide medical support and firefighting expertise. Added to this, Japan provided firefighting equipment and smoke protection masks.

Japanese policies created to deal with transborder environmental pollution have been matched by growing efforts to protect ecosystems in East Asia. Japan has been responsible for considerable environmental destruction from its massive importation of forestry products from Southeast Asia. Japan is the largest importer of tropical hardwoods in the world, and the majority comes from Southeast Asia (Wong 2001: 147). Japanese private corporate investment and government ODA have played a role in commercial logging and deforestation in the Philippines, Indonesia, and Malaysia (Wong 2001: 163–164). Japan's concern over declining supplies of tropical hardwoods in the subregion prompted a change of official government policy to emphasize reforestation, afforestation, and forestry conservation. Japan has hosted the International Tropical Timber Organization (ITTO) headquarters in Yokohama since 1995, established under the auspices of the UN as an international commodity agreement focusing on arresting deforestation. EcoISD placed new emphasis on forestry conservation. Japan hosted the first meeting of the Asia Forest Partnership in Tokyo in 2002, a new body to promote sustainable forestry management in East Asia through measures such as combating illegal logging, fire prevention, and reforestation.

Japan's efforts in the field of climate change include its sponsorship of the Kyōto Protocol. Following COP3 in 1997, Japan participated in a series of discussions culminating in COP6 in November 2000, which outlined measures necessary for the implementation of the Kyōto Protocol, including international emissions trading and sinks. COP6 did not reach agreement and was suspended until July 2001. In the meantime, the United States announced that it would not support the Kyōto Protocol because developing states were not mandated to restrict greenhouse emissions gases to quantified levels. Japan attempted to persuade the United States in bilateral discussions to support the protocol, but to no avail. Japan pressed ahead with other parties and formally accepted it in June 2002.

Japan's roles in the Kyōto Protocol and other environmental issues affecting East Asia demonstrate that it has exercised leadership in an important nonmilitary security role. Nevertheless, criticisms can be leveled against Japan's environmental security policy in terms of its philosophy and execution.

The Japanese approach to environmental protection is implanted with the belief in sustainable development. It continues to view the environment as a natural resource that can and should be exploited for developmental needs; the application of technology is the means to ensure the balance between environmental protection and economic growth. Japan's ODA policies have very much been characterized by technological solutions to environmental problems, particularly technology transfer and training in developing states in East Asia. Japan also placed more emphasis on improving the management of natural resources such as forests rather than strict preservation without human interference. Its interest in hosting the ITTO ensured that Japan retained influence over conservation debates relating to tropical forestry and that the region's forests remained open for human exploitation (Wong 2001: 174–176). Similarly, Japan's measures to combat acid rain in China stress technology as the means to assuage the worst excesses of rapid development, but they never undercut economic growth as a root cause of environmental insecurity.

Japan's support for sustainable development is understandable given its experience of development and the belief that security in East Asia has to be rooted in developmentalism. Japan is proposing that East Asian states need to experience industrialization and growth, then to counter environmental problems through technology. The Japanese approach may indeed work for the security of the region in terms of economic growth and conserving certain types of environmental resources. However, copying the Japanese example may also mean a loss of biodiversity. For instance, Japan's deforestation and reforestation processes left sustainable timber estates and "factory forests" rather than coherent forest ecosystems. Moreover, the Japanese government needs to consider whether the scale of economic growth and environmental destruction under way in East Asia is so overwhelming that it may never be possible for states to follow Japan's lead to "get dirty, get rich, and get clean."

Finally, Japan's execution of its environmental protection policies is subject to inconsistencies and implementation problems. Japan's assistance for Russian nuclear submarine decommissioning is an important contribution to reducing radiation damage to the environment. However, Japan's own transport by ship of MOX fuel to the UK and France for reprocessing threatens a major ecological disaster in the event of an accident or terrorist hijacking at sea. Japan also faces problems over the short term in implementing its ODA due to interministerial rivalries and due to cuts in the ODA budget that will hamper environmental diplomacy.

Conclusion: Japan as a Multidimensional Security Actor

Japan has retained and continued to act upon its conceptions of comprehensive security during the post–Cold War period. Japan's limitations as a military actor, coupled with its recognition of the growing impact of globalization on the stability of states in East Asia and the region, have meant that it has persisted and further developed many important initiatives in the economic and environmental dimensions of security.

Japan has recognized the insecurity generated by economic exclusion and has attempted to engage North Korea and Burma. The problem of economic disparity has occupied Japanese policymakers especially with regard to China. Japan has enacted a number of initiatives to deal with economic rivalry over water, food, and especially energy resources. It has paid great attention to the human and interstate security implications of economic dislocation in Southeast Asia following the 1997 financial crisis. Japan has also taken important steps to shape individual, bilateral, and multilateral responses to the economic security problems of migration, organized crime, and piracy. Japan with regard to the last two has shown a new impulse to work multilaterally with regional partners.

In the environmental dimension, Japan has to some extent fulfilled its ambitions to become an environmental superpower. Japan has been active in responding to natural disasters and infectious diseases across the region. In addition, it has promoted initiatives to deal with environmental degradation and the destruction of the biosphere, assuaging its image as a threat to environmental security in the region.

Japan's contribution to regional security in the economic and environmental dimensions must be judged as a success. Its policy has displayed many multilevel and multidimensional characteristics. Japan has laid out a multiactor approach by involving nonstate actors, such as NGOs in environmental conservation and TNCs in the prevention of transnational crime and piracy. Japan has thus made a distinct and important contribution to the security of East Asia. In many ways it has been a leader in these fields. Its policy is comprehensive.

Japan's security policy in these dimensions is not without problems. It has been inconsistent in the types of problems that it chooses to identify and not to identify in security terms. Japan is reluctant to treat food shortages and asylum-seekers from North Korea as human security problems; it tends to draw an artificial distinction between migration within East Asia as a security issue and migration to Japan as a nonsecurity issue; and it promotes environmental protection for human exploitation without fully addressing the costs for biodiversity.

Even more important, its capacity to continue pursuing this comprehensive security agenda for the foreseeable future is in doubt. Chapter 7 considers Japan's shrinking ODA budget as undermining its ability to pursue economic solutions to existing security problems.

7

Conclusion: The Trajectory of Japanese Security Policy

The objective of this book is to outline and evaluate the trajectory and effectiveness of Japan's comprehensive security policy in East Asia from the Cold War to the post–Cold War period. It began by outlining an analytical framework to capture the complexity of global and regional security issues and that could be applied to test the extent, consistency, relevance, and effectiveness of Japan's security policy in East Asia. The book sketched a conception of security that included multiple actors from sovereign states, including nonstate actors, societal groups, individuals, and organizations. All these actors are potential consumers, deniers, and suppliers of security. This conception involves multiple dimensions from the military, economic, and environmental spheres. In turn, all these levels and dimensions are fully interpenetrated with each other to produce a complex schemata of security.

Thus the challenge for contemporary security policy globally and across regions is to respond to intermingling issues such as high- and low-intensity unconventional and conventional military conflicts among state, intrastate, and nonstate actors; economic exclusion, disparity, rivalry, and dislocation; migration, organized crime, and piracy associated with economic integration and disintegration; and of natural and manmade disasters, infectious diseases, and environmental destruction. This requires policy frameworks from the individual sovereign state, bilateral alliances, and cooperation; multilateral alliances, organizations, regimes, and dialogues; and a wide range of capabilities from military to political and economic power. In sum, Chapter 1 presented a complex and comprehensive security agenda, requiring similarly comprehensive policy responses involving multiple actors, multiple dimensions, and multiple frameworks and forms of power.

Next this scheme was applied to East Asia during the Cold War and post–Cold War period. Chapters 2 and 3 showed that East Asia exhibits a similar complexity in its security dynamics. The region is characterized by interstate conflict among superpowers, great powers, and regional powers relating to geostrategic rivalries and territorial disputes in Northeast and Southeast Asia. The region's security agenda was influenced by intrastate conflicts centering on insurgency, irredentism, and separatism; societal and individual military conflicts such as ethnic and political strife; and organizational group conflicts involving terrorism. The economic dimension is complex, with problems of insecurity related to the economic exclusion of North Korea and Burma; economic disparities in China and Southeast Asia; economic rivalry for many food, marine, and energy resources; and the financial crisis of 1997, producing economic dislocation and problems of human and intrasecurity in Southeast Asia. East Asia is faced with a host of environmental security problems, such as deforestation, desertification, the exhaustion of natural resources, transboundary pollution, the destruction of biodiversity, and climate change.

Chapters 2 and 3 also explained the dynamics of the political economy and the causation of problems. The analysis of the East Asian regional agenda was combined with a historical and political economy approach that traced the three overlapping processes of decolonization, bipolarization, and globalization. These processes have been responsible for the generation, shaping, and prolonging of military, economic, and environmental security problems. In the military dimension, much superpower and great power conflict has been driven by the contest between and adjustment to different forms of organizing individual state and regional economic life. In addition, conflict involving regional powers has often been driven by the desire to obtain economic resources and development; and intrastate conflict has been generated by weak states that seek to achieve legitimacy through economic development and state-building. The roots of economic exclusion, disparity, rivalry, and dislocation are clear; environmental destruction is also a process propelled by economic competition. Therefore, East Asia's security agenda is complex and comprehensive. But to effectively address these concerns, comprehensive security policies employ military and economic power.

Chapter 4 began to test these arguments about the comprehensive nature and political economy causation of insecurity in East Asia and the utility of Japan's security policy in mounting an effective response. It outlined Japan's fundamental conceptions of security that straddle the prewar and postwar eras. It argued that Japan has long had a multilevel conception of security that incorporates state and nonstate actors. The chapter also argued that Japan has a multidimensional view of security that emphasizes the importance of economic power alongside military power and is a means of resolving not just economic and environmental security problems but also military problems. The embodiment of this multilevel and multidimensional conception of security is the articulation of human security in the post–Cold War period; particularly for this study is its articulation of comprehensive forms of security policy from the 1980s onward.

The book then examined Japan's security policy in the military, economic, and environmental dimensions and the track record of implementing balanced and comprehensive approaches to security during the Cold War. In the military dimension, Japan's security policy was characterized by the incremental buildup of independent military capabilities, the gradual strengthening of alliance ties with the United States, and the avoidance of multilateral security frameworks. Nevertheless, Japan remained wary of military power for security ends and entanglement in U.S. security strategy. Its principal security contribution was thus limited and indirect via the mechanism of the U.S.-Japan alliance, designed to prevent interstate conflict. Japan made its direct contribution to regional security through the use of economic power. Its comprehensive security conceptions meant that it became engaged in efforts to support state-building and economic development programs of newly emergent states in Northeast and Southeast Asia. Japan saw this as the key to alleviating many economic as well as military security problems on the interstate, intrastate, and nonstate levels. In this sense, Japan's security policy became comprehensive and oriented toward addressing the causal factors of regional insecurity. In turn, Japan's approach provided the conceptions and practices of comprehensive security that would serve it well during the post–Cold War period.

Chapter 5 took up the issue of Japan's security policy in East Asia during the post–Cold War period. It argued that Japan become a more active and direct military player in regional security affairs, matched by greater experimentation and flexibility in the type of security role that it was prepared to fulfill. Japan augmented its individual state military capabilities but also sought a role in UN PKOs to contribute to the resolution of intrastate conflict. Japan also showed an interest in multilateral and bilateral security cooperation with other states in the region for the first time. Nevertheless, the principal thrust of Japan's policy efforts in the military dimension came through continued and deepened bilateral cooperation with the United States. Japan through the revision of the Japan-U.S. Defense Guidelines strengthened its potential support for the United States in regional military contingencies. Japan's growing interest in BMD may further tighten bilateral cooperation. Japan's support for the United States has not been unconditional, and it still remains wary of entanglement in U.S. regional and global strategies. Japan looks to alternative options to cooperation, as shown by its strategic ambiguity over the scope of the revised Defense Guidelines, its caution over BMD, and its active but guarded response to the war on terror. However, the principal trend is toward greater integration of Japanese and U.S. military forces, which could quicken as Japan becomes concerned about the immediate military threat from North Korea and greater long-term threat from China. Japanese debates over the exercise of the right of collective self-defense may finally push Japan toward becoming a "normal" military power in East Asia.

Whether a normal military role fostered by the U.S.-Japan alliance will provide Japan a more effective role in East Asian security is open to question. The U.S. military presence can lead to the suppression, if not resolution, of a range of interstate conflicts. But the functions of the alliance in dealing with intrastate security are less clear. Moreover, Japan's adherence to U.S.-centered bilateralism inhibits the growth of potential multilateral frameworks that could contribute to regional security.

Chapter 6 looked at the trajectory and effectiveness of Japan's economic and environmental security policies after the end of the Cold War. It argued that Japan has in many ways continued to stand upon and to expand its commitment to comprehensive notions of security policies in these two dimensions. Japan used economic power to engage the economically excluded regimes in North Korea and Burma; worked to alleviate economic disparities regionwide and within individual states such as China, Indonesia, and the Philippines; outlined initiatives to alleviate friction over economic resources; and worked at the macro- and microeconomic levels to address security issues resulting from the 1997 financial crisis. Japan took the lead in organizing much of the region's response to transnational crime and piracy. In the environmental dimension, Japan took on a leadership role in articulating and fashioning a response to problems of natural disasters, infectious diseases, and environmental pollution and destruction. Japan's security policy in the economic and environmental dimensions is comprehensive. It has attempted to tackle a range of issues and has employed a range of economic capabilities across individual state, bilateral, and multilateral frameworks.

Japan's comprehensive security policy, though, is problematic at times. Japan has shown a propensity for arbitrary and inconsistent labeling of human security problems and therefore the security agenda to which it is mandated to respond. Japan is reluctant to treat the North Korean famine as a human security problem but was willing to do so in the case of Southeast Asia after the financial crisis. It views migration within East Asia as a potential human security issue, but migration to Japan itself as a straight policing problem. And Japan aims to contribute to the protection of the regional environment but is also one of the biggest threats to biodiversity.

Japan's Trajectory and Effectiveness as a Security Actor in East Asia and Globally

Japan throughout the Cold War and post–Cold War period pursued a comprehensive security policy. It attempted to balance its military contribution to security in East Asia with a commitment to the economic and environmental dimensions and has sought to articulate this approach in the post–Cold War period with concepts such as human security. Japan has attempted to employ nonstate actors such as NGOs and TNCs in the service of its security policy; used military and economic power to reinforce each other, with a predilection for economic power to address sources of insecurity in all dimensions; and used a variety of individual state, bilateral, and multilateral frameworks to deploy this power, leaning toward bilateral frameworks in the military dimension, and toward individual state and multilateral frameworks in the economic and environmental dimensions.

Japan's comprehensive activity across all these dimensions invites us to reconsider its presence as an important security actor in East Asia. Japan's contribution to the stability of the region should surely not be underrated. Even if Japan has not been a proactive and direct actor in military affairs, it has compensated for this through the use of economic power.

Moreover, Japan has been more than a prominent and innovative security actor; its contributions have been relevant and distinctly effective. Many of the root causes of insecurity in East Asia can be ascribed to the overlapping processes of decolonization, bipolarization, and globalization. These gave rise to sovereign state units characterized by internal and external economic weaknesses and engaged in state-building projects to overcome these problems. Japan recognized how processes of political economy underlie the regional security agenda, and its comprehensive security agenda is singularly well designed to support the security aspirations of many states in the region. Japan's security policy has not been without problems, especially in backing authoritarian regimes and their territorial integrity, which can lead to the contravention of human security policy. But Japan's utilization of economic power as part of its comprehensive security policy has been oriented toward the most pressing security needs in the region. Therefore, Japan has made an important difference to the stability of East Asia.

The need to reevaluate Japan's efficacy as a security actor in East Asia also raises questions about its security role globally, particularly the wider utility of comprehensive security policy. Although it is beyond the scope of this book to investigate Japan's security role beyond East Asia, it is important to note that Japan's conceptions of comprehensive security have relevance and application in other regional contexts. Japan's support for economic stabilization and state-building in East Asia through policies of comprehensive security is part of a security agenda that will increasingly arise in other regions. Japan and other developed states are already engaged in supporting state-building in the wake of the war on terror in the Middle East. The continuing impact of globalization means that this will become an increasingly important activity in other regions. Hence, even though Japan has often been underappreciated as a security actor due to its limited military contribution to global security, it may be the case that in the post-9/11, postglobalized world Japan has developed the most efficacious approach to achieving security through economic power.

Japan and the Future of Comprehensive Security

Japan's traditional approach to regional and global security is relevant to the unfolding regional and global security agenda. Thus it is ironic that Japan may be moving away from this approach over the long term. The trajectory of Japan's military security is toward becoming a "normal" state, that is, using its military capabilities to support the U.S.-Japan alliance and U.S. regional and global military strategies. Japanese policymakers have poured tremendous energy into the military dimensions of Japan's security policy during the post–Cold War period. At the same time, Japan's commitment to use economic power for security ends is increasingly questioned. Japan since 2000 has cut its ODA budget, and it chopped ODA to China by 25 percent in 2001. In part this reflects Japan's own economic malaise and budgetary pressures, but in part it also reflects a crisis of confidence in the effectiveness of ODA to respond to political and security issues generated by the rise of actors such as China. Japan's ODA cuts may force it to use ODA in a more focused and efficient manner. Japan may pay special attention to peacebuilding and funding NGOs with local expertise to implement small-scale and more flexible projects, instead of emphasizing the big-ticket infrastructure items.

But the cuts in ODA also reflect a gradual retreat from using economic power for security ends and, possibly, using economic power as the principal means to contribute to regional security. As Japan becomes a "normal" military actor in East Asia, and as its use of economic power shrinks, the comprehensive security agenda will tilt toward the military dimension. In the end, Japan may be seen more as a military security actor than as an economic security actor. In this instance, Japan might receive greater attention as a major security actor, a status for which many policymakers have yearned. But this could erode the comprehensive notions of security that contributed so much to the security agenda throughout the postwar period and that have provided Japan with its current relevant, distinct, and effective role in East Asian security.

Acronyms

ABC	atomic/biological/chemical
ABM	Anti-Ballistic Missile [Treaty]
ACSA	Acquisition and Cross-Servicing Agreement
ADB	Asian Development Bank
AMF	Asian Monetary Fund
APEC	Asia-Pacific Economic Cooperation
ARF	ASEAN Regional Forum
ASDF	Air Self-Defense Force
ASEAN	Association of Southeast Asian Nations
ASEAN-ISIS	ASEAN Institutes of Strategic and International Studies
ASEAN-PMC	ASEAN postministerial conference
ASW	antisubmarine warfare
ATS	amphetamine-type stimulants
ATSML	Anti-Terrorism Special Measures Law
AWACS	Airborne Warning and Control System
BADGE	Base Air Defense Ground Environment
BCP	Burmese Communist Party
BDS	Boost Defense Segment
BMC4I	battlefield management, command, control, communications, computers, and intelligence
BMD	Ballistic Missile Defense
BPI	Boost-Phase Intercept
BPND	Basic Policy on National Defense
CBM	confidence- and security-building measure
CCP	Chinese Communist Party
CINCPAC	Commander-in-Chief of the Pacific Command
CLMV	Cambodia, Laos, Myanmar, and Vietnam
COP3	Third Conference of the Parties
CPM	Communist Party of Malaya
CPP	Cambodian People's Party
CSCA	Conference on Security Cooperation in Asia

CSCAP	Council for Security Cooperation in the Asia Pacific
CSCE	Council for Cooperation and Security in Europe
CTBT	Comprehensive Nuclear Test-Ban Treaty
CWC	Chemical Weapons Convention
DMZ	Demilitarized Zone
DPJ	Democratic Party of Japan
DPP	Democratic Progressive Party
DPRK	Democratic People's Republic of Korea
DSP	Defense Support Program
EANET	Acid Deposition Monitoring Network in East Asia
EASR	East Asian Strategic Review
EcoISD	Environmental Conservation Initiative for Sustainable Development
EEZ	Exclusive Economic Zone
EU	European Union
FATF	Financial Action Task Force
FDI	Foreign Direct Investment
FS-X	Fighter Support Experimental
G8	Group of Eight
GAM	Gerakan Aceh Merdeka
GDP	gross domestic product
GFTAM	Global Fund to Fight AIDS, Tuberculosis, and Malaria
GSDF	Ground Self-Defense Forces
HNS	host-nation support
IAEA	International Atomic Energy Agency
IAI	Initiative for ASEAN Integration
ICBM	intercontinental ballistic missile
IMB	International Maritime Bureau
IMF	International Monetary Fund
IMO	International Maritime Organisation
INTERFET	Intervention Force in East Timor
IPCL	International Peace Cooperation Law
IPE	international political economy
IR	international relations
IRBM	intermediate-range ballistic missile
IRST	infrared search and tracking
ISD	Initiatives for Sustainable Development
IT	information technology
ITTO	International Tropical Timber Organization
JCG	Japan Coast Guard
JDA	Japan Defense Agency
JDIH	Japan Defense Intelligence Headquarters
JDRT	Japan Disaster Relief Teams
JICA	Japan International Cooperation Agency

JIIA	Japan Institute of International Affairs
JRA	Japanese Red Army
JSC	Joint Staff Council
JSP	Japan Socialist Party
KEDO	Korean Peninsula Energy Development Organization
KMT	Kuomintang
LDP	Liberal Democratic Party
LNG	liquefied natural gas
LRBM	long-range ballistic missile
LWR	lightwater reactor
MAD	Mutually Assured Destruction
MDS	Midcourse Defense Segment
METI	Ministry of Economy, Trade, and Industry
MILF	Moro Islamic Liberation Front
MIRV	multiple independently targetable reentry vehicle
MNLF	Moro National Liberation Front
MOF	Maritime Operational Fleet
MOF	Ministry of Finance
MOFA	Ministry of Foreign Affairs
MOJ	Ministry of Justice
MOX	mixed oxide
MPF	Maritime Patrol Force
MRBM	medium-range ballistic missile
MSDF	Maritime Self-Defense Force
MTCR	Missile Technology Control Regime
NAM	Non-Aligned Movement
NATO	North Atlantic Treaty Organization
NDPO	National Defense Program Outline
NEP	New Economic Policy
NFP	New Frontier Party
NGO	nongovernmental organization
NIDL	New International Division of Labor
NIES	Newly Industrialized Economies
NMD	National Missile Defense
NPA	National Police Agency
NPA	New People's Army
NPRF	National Police Reserve Force
NPT	Non-Proliferation Treaty
NSA	National Safety Agency
NSC	National Security Council
NSF	National Safety Force
NTWD	Navy Theater-Wide Defense
ODA	Official Development Assistance
OECD	Organization for Economic Cooperation and Development

OPEC	Organization of the Petroleum Exporting Countries
OSCE	Organization for Security and Cooperation in Europe
PAC	Patriot Advanced Capability
PKI	Partai Komunis Indonesia
PKOs	peacekeeping operations
PLA	People's Liberation Army
PRC	People's Republic of China
PSIA	Public Security Investigation Agency
PULO	Pattani United Liberation Organization
RIMPAC	Rim of the Pacific
RMA	Revolution in Military Affairs
ROC	Republic of China
ROE	rules of engagement
ROK	Republic of Korea
SACO	Special Action Committee on Facilities and Areas in Okinawa
SAM	surface-to-air missile
SAR	synthetic aperture radar
SARS	severe acute respiratory syndrome
SBIRS	Space-Based Infrared System High and Low
SBMS	Sea-Based Midcourse System
SCAP	Supreme Command Allied Powers
SCC	Security Consultative Committee
SDF	Self-Defense Forces
SDI	Strategic Defense Initiative
SDPJ	Social Democratic Party of Japan
SEATO	Southeast Asia Treaty Organisation
SEZ	Special Economic Zone
SLOC	sea lines of communication
SLORC	State Law and Order Restoration Council
SO_2	sulfur dioxide
SRBM	short-range ballistic missile
TAC	Treaty of Amity and Cooperation
TCOG	Trilateral Coordination and Oversight Group
TDS	Terminal Defense Segment
THAAD	Theater High-Altitude Area Defense
TICAD	Tokyo Conference on African Development
TMD	Theater Missile Defense
TNC	transnational corporation
TRADP	Tumen River Area Development Program
UN	United Nations
UNCLOS	United Nations Convention on the Law of the Sea
UNDCP	United Nations Drug Control Programme
UNDP	United Nations Development Programme

UNGASS	UN General Assembly Special Session on the Environment and Development
UNHCR	United Nations High Commissioner for Refugees
UNICEF	United Nations Children's Fund
UNTAC	United Nations Transitional Authority Cambodia
UNTAET	United Nations Transitional Authority East Timor
UNTOC	United Nations Convention against Transnational Organized Crime
V/STOL	vertical/short takeoff and landing
WFP	World Food Programme
WHO	World Health Organization
WMD	weapons of mass destruction
WTO	World Trade Organization
ZOPFAN	Zone of Peace, Friendship, and Neutrality

References

Abbot, Jason, and Neil Renwick. (1999a). "Piratical Violence and Maritime Security in Southeast Asia," *Security Dialogue* 30(2): 183–196.

———. (1999b). "Pirates? Maritime Piracy and Societal Security in Southeast Asia," *Pacifica Review* 11(1): 7–24.

Acharya, Amitav. (1992). "Regionalism and Regime Security in the Third World: Comparing the Origins of the ASEAN and GCC," in Brian L. Job (ed.), *The Insecurity Dilemma: National Security of Third World States,* Boulder: Lynne Rienner, pp. 143–164.

———. (1993). *A New Regional Order in Southeast Asia: ASEAN in the Post–Cold War Era.* London: Brassey's for the International Institute for Strategic Studies.

———. (2000). *The Quest for Identity: International Relations of Southeast Asia.* Singapore: Oxford University Press.

———. (2001a). *Constructing a Security Community in Southeast Asia: ASEAN and the Problem of Regional Order.* London: Routledge.

———. (2001b). "Human Security: East Versus West," *International Journal* (Summer 2001): 442–460.

Advisory Group on Defense Issues. (1994). *The Modality of the Security and Defense Capability of Japan: The Outlook for the Twenty-First Century.* Tokyo: Ōkurashō Insatsukyoku.

Akamatsu, K. (1962). "A Historical Pattern of Economic Growth in Developing Countries," *The Developing Economies,* reproduced in Peter Drysdale and Luke Gower (eds.), *The Japanese Economy,* part 1. London: Routledge, 1998, pp. 3–23.

Alagappa, Muthiah. (1995). "Contestation and Crisis," in Muthiah Alagappa (ed.), *Political Legitimacy in Southeast Asia: The Quest for Moral Authority.* Stanford: Stanford University Press, pp. 54–65.

Alexander, Ronni. (1999). "Jendā to anzen hoshō: nani ga mondai ka" [Gender and Security: What Is the Issue?], in Takeda Isami and Naya Masatsugu (eds.), *Shinanzen Hoshō no Kōzu* [The New Security Structure]. Tokyo: Keisō Shobō, pp. 54–79.

Allison, Graham, and Gregory T. Treverton, eds. (1992). *Rethinking America's Security: Beyond Cold War to New World Order.* New York: W. W. Norton.

Alperovitz, Gar. (1994). *Atomic Diplomacy: Hiroshima and Potsdam.* London: Pluto.

Andreas, Peter. (2002). "Transnational Crime and Economic Globalization," in Mats Berdal and Mónica Serrano (eds.), *Transnational Crime and International Security: Business as Usual?* Boulder: Lynne Rienner, pp. 37–52.

Andrews-Speed, Philip, Xuanli Liao, and Roland Danreuther. (2002). *The Strategic Implications of China's Energy Needs*. Adelphi Paper 346. Oxford: Oxford University Press.

Anwar, Dewi Fortuna. (2001). "Insurgencies and Communal Conflicts: Governance and Security in Indonesia's Plural Societies," in Andrew H. Tan and J. D. Kenneth Boutin (eds.), *Non-Traditional Security Issues in Southeast Asia*. Singapore: Institute of Defence and Strategic Studies, pp. 349–376.

Arase, David. (1995). *Buying Power: The Political Economy of Japan's Foreign Aid*. Boulder: Lynne Rienner.

Asagumo Shimbunsha. (2000). *Bōei Handobukku 2000* [Defense Handbook 2000]. Tokyo: Asagumo Shimbunsha.

———. (2001). *Bōei Handobukku 2001*. Tokyo: Asagumo Shimbunsha.

———. (2002). *Bōei Handobukku 2002*. Tokyo: Asagumo Shimbunsha.

Asano, R. (2000). "Gunji dokutorinu no henyō" [Transformations in Military Doctrine], in Takagi Seichirō (ed.), *Datsureisenki no Chūgoku Gaikō to Ajia Taiheiyō* [China's Post–Cold War Diplomacy in the Asia-Pacific]. Tokyo: Nihon Kokusai Mondai Kenkyūjo, pp. 23–52.

Asian Development Bank. (2001). *Asian Environment Outlook 2001*. Manila: Asian Development Bank.

Ayoob, Mohammed. (1995). *The Third World Security Predicament: State Making, Regional Conflict, and the International System*. Boulder: Lynne Rienner.

Baker, Richard W., and Charles E. Morrison. (2000). *Asia Pacific Security Outlook 2000*. Tokyo: Japan Center for International Exchange.

Baldwin, David. (1995). "Security Studies and the End of the Cold War," *World Politics* 48(1): 117–141.

———. (1997). "The Concept of Security," *Review of International Studies* 23(5): 5–26.

Ball, Desmond. (1993–1994). "Arms and Affluence: Military Acquisitions in the Asia-Pacific," *International Security* 18(3): 78–112.

———. (2000). *The Council for Security Cooperation in the Asia-Pacific: Its Record and Its Prospects*. Canberra Papers on Strategy and Defence no. 139. Canberra: Australian National University.

Ballistic Missile Defense Organization. (1999). *Summary of Report to Congress on the Utility of Sea-Based Assets to National Missile Defense*. Washington, D.C.: Ballistic Missile Defense Organization.

Barrett, Brendan F., and Riki Therivel. (1991). *Environmental Policy and Impact Assessment in Japan*. London: Routledge.

Beasley, W. G. (1987). *Japanese Imperialism 1894–1945*. Oxford: Clarendon.

Berger, Thomas U. (1998). *Cultures of Antimilitarism: National Security in Germany and Japan*. Baltimore: Johns Hopkins University Press.

Bermudez, Joseph S. (2001). *The Armed Forces of North Korea*. London and New York: I. B. Tauris.

Bōei Kenkyūjo. (various years). *Higashi Ajia Senryaku Gaikan* [East Asia Strategic Overview]. Tokyo: Ōkurashō Insatsukyoku.

Bōei Mondai Kenkyūjo. (2000). *Nihon no Bōei Yoku Wakaru* [Understanding Japan's Defense]. Tokyo: Nihon Kajo Shuppan.

Bōeichōhen. (1995). *Bōei Hakusho* [Defense of Japan White Paper]. Tokyo: Ōkurashō Insatsukyoku.

———. (1999). *Bōei Hakusho*. Tokyo: Ōkurashō Insatsukyoku.

———. (2000). *Bōei Hakusho*. Tokyo: Ōkurashō Insatsukyoku.

———. (2001). *Bōei Hakusho*. Tokyo: Ōkurashō Insatsukyoku.

———. (2002). *Bōei Hakusho*. Tokyo: Zaimushō Insatsukyoku.

Booth, Ken. (1979). *Strategy and Ethnocentrism.* London: Croom Helm.

———. (1991a). "Introduction the Interregnum: World Politics in Transition," in Ken Booth (ed.), *New Thinking About Strategy and International Security.* London: HarperCollins, pp. 1–28.

———. (1991b). "Security in Anarchy: Utopian Realism in Theory and Practice," *International Affairs* 67(3): 527–545.

———. (1991c). "Security and Emancipation," *Review of International Studies* 17: 313–326.

Braddick, Christopher W. (2001). "The Waiting Game: Japan-Russia Relations," in Inoguchi Takashi and Purnendra Jain (eds.), *Japanese Foreign Policy Today.* London: Macmillan, pp. 209–225.

Brandt, Don. (2001). *The Approaching Storm: HIV/AIDS in Asia Special Report.* Monrovia, CA: World Vision.

Breslin, Shaun. (1997). "The China Challenge? Development, Environment, and National Security," *Security Dialogue* 28(4): 497–508.

Bridges, Brian. (1993). *Japan and Korea in the 1990s: From Antagonism to Adjustment.* Aldershot, UK: Edward Elgar.

Buzan, Barry. (1984). "Economic Structure and International Security: The Limits of the Liberal Case," *International Organization* 38(4): 597–564.

———. (1991a). *People, States and Fear: An Agenda for International Security Studies in the Post-Cold War Era.* New York: Harvester Wheatsheaf.

———. (1991b). "New Patterns of Global Security in the Twenty-First Century," *International Affairs* 67(3): 431–451.

———. (1994). "The Post–Cold War Asia-Pacific Security Order: Conflict or Cooperation?" in Andrew Mack and Stuart Harris (eds.), *Pacific Cooperation: Building Economic and Security Regimes in the Asia-Pacific Region.* Boulder: Westview, pp. 130–151.

Buzan, Barry, and Gerald Segal. (1994). "Rethinking East Asian Security," *Survival* 36(2): 3–21.

Buzan, Barry, Ole Waever, and Jaap de Wilde. (1998). *Security: A New Framework for Analysis.* Boulder: Lynne Rienner.

Cable, Vincent. (1995). "What Is International Economic Security?" *International Affairs* 71(2): 305–324.

Calder, Kent E. (1988). *Crisis and Compensation: Public Policy and Political Stability in Japan, 1949–1986.* Princeton, NJ: Princeton University Press.

———. (1996). "Asia's Empty Gas Tank," *Foreign Affairs* 75(2): 55–69.

———. (1997). *Asia's Deadly Triangle: How Arms, Energy, and Growth Threaten to Destabilise the Asia-Pacific.* London: Nicholas Brealey Publishing.

Callahan, Mary P. (1995). "Myanmar in 1994: New Dragon or Still Dragging?" *Asian Survey* 35(2): 201–208.

Camilleri, Joseph A. (1994). "The Asia-Pacific in the Post-Hegemonic World," in Andrew Mack and Stuart Harris (eds.), *Pacific Cooperation: Building Economic and Security Regimes in the Asia-Pacific Region.* Boulder: Westview, pp. 180–208.

———. (2000). *States, Markets, and Civil Society in Asia-Pacific, Volume 1: The Political Economy of the Asia-Pacific Region.* Cheltenham, UK: Edward Elgar.

Candio, Patrick, and Roland Bleiker. (2001). "Peacebuilding in East Timor," *Pacific Review* 14(1): 63–84.

Capie, David, and Amitav Acharya. (2002). "A Fine Balance: U.S. Relations with Southeast Asia Since 9/11," paper presented at conference on "United States-Asia Relations Today: A New 'New' World Order?" CERI, Paris, 2–4 December 2002, pp. 1–26.

Chalk, Peter. (1999). "Political Terrorism in Southeast Asia," in Carolina G. Hernandez and Gina R. Pattugalan (eds.), *Transnational Crime and Regional Security in the Asia-Pacific*. Manila: Institute for Strategic and Development Studies, pp. 187–206.

———. (2000). "'Grey Area Phenomen' and Human Security," in William T. Tow, Ramesh Thakur, and In-Taek Hyun (eds.), *Asia's Emerging Regional Order: Reconciling Traditional and Human Security*. Tokyo, New York, and Paris: United Nations University Press, pp. 124–141.

Chanda, Nayan. (2000). "Foot in the Water," *Far Eastern Economic Review,* 9 March 2000, pp. 28–29.

Chandler, David P., et al. (1987). *In Search of Southeast Asia*. Honolulu: Hawaii University Press.

Chapman, J. M. W., I. T. M. Gow, and R. Drifte. (1983). *Japan's Quest for Comprehensive Security: Defence, Diplomacy, Dependence*. London: Pinter.

Christensen, Thomas J. (2001). "Posing Problems Without Catching Up: China's Rise and Challenges for U.S. Security Policy," *International Security* 25(4): 5–40.

Chu, Yun-Han. (1999). "Surviving the East Asian Financial Storm: The Political Foundation of Taiwan's Economic Resilience," in T. J. Pempel (ed.), *The Politics of the Asian Crisis*. Ithaca: Cornell University Press, pp. 184–202.

Clamor, Maria Concepcion. (1999). "Terrorism in the Philippines and Its Impact on Regional Security," in Carolina G. Hernandez and Gina R. Pattugalan (eds.), *Transnational Crime and Regional Security in the Asia-Pacific*. Manila: Institute for Strategic and Development Studies, pp. 207–230.

Clutterbuck, Richard. (1994). *Terrorism in an Unstable World*. London: Routledge.

Coker, Christopher. (2002). *Globalisation and Insecurity in the Twenty-First Century: NATO and the Management of Risk*. Adelphi Paper 345. Oxford: Oxford University Press.

Commission on Global Governance. (1995). *Our Global Neighbourhood*. Oxford: Oxford University Press.

Commission on Human Security. (2003). *Human Security Now*. New York: Commission on Human Security.

Contreras, Antonio P. (2000). "Forest Policy in Southeast Asia: Implications for ASEAN and Asia-Europe Cooperation," in Carolina G. Hernandez and Gill Wilkins (eds.), *Population, Food, Energy, and the Environment: Challenges for Asia-Europe Cooperation*. Manila: Council for Asia-Europe Cooperation, pp. 343–364.

Cotton, James. (1999). *ASEAN and the Southeast Asian "Haze": Challenging the Prevailing Modes of Regional Engagement*. Canberra: Australian National University.

Cox, Robert W. (1996). "Multilateralism and World Order," in Robert W. Cox with Timothy J. Sinclair, *Approaches to World Order*, Cambridge: Cambridge University Press, pp. 494–423.

Cumings, Bruce. (1984). "The Origins and Development of the Northeast Asian Political Economy: Industrial Sector, Product Cycles, and Political Consequences," *International Organization* 38(1): 1–40.

———. (1990). *The Origins of the Korean War, Volume 2: The Roaring of the Cataract*. Princeton, NJ: Princeton University Press.

Cusimano, Maryann K. (2000). "Beyond Sovereignty: The Rise of Transnational Problems," in Maryann K. Cusimano (ed.), *Beyond Sovereignty: Issues for a Global Agenda*, Boston and New York: Bedford/St. Martin's, pp. 1–43.

Daalder, Ivo H., James M. Goldgeier, and James M. Lindsay. (2000). "Deploying NMD: Not Whether, but How," *Survival* 42(1): 6–28.

Dalby, Simon. (1997). "Contesting an Essential Concept: Reading the Dilemmas in Contemporary Security Discourse," in Keith Krause and Michael C. Williams (eds.), *Critical Security Studies*. Minneapolis: University of Minnesota Press, pp. 3–31.
Deans, Phil. (2000). "Contending Nationalisms and the Diaoyutai/Senkaku Dispute," *Security Dialogue* 31(1): 119–131.
Deudney, Daniel. (1990). "The Case Against Linking Environmental Degradation and National Security," *Millennium* 19(3): 461–476.
Devetak, Richard. (1996). "Critical Theory," in Scott Burchill and Andrew Linklater (eds.), *Theories of International Relations*. London: Macmillan, pp. 145–178.
Dibb, Paul, David D. Hale, and Peter Prince. (1998). "The Strategic Implications of Asia's Economic Crisis," *Survival* 40(2): 5–26.
DiFilippo, Anthony. (2002). *The Challenges of the U.S.-Japan Military Arrangement: Competing Security Transitions in a Changing International Environment*. Armonk, NY: M. E. Sharpe.
Dobson, Hugo. (2003). *Japan and UN Peackeeping: New Pressures and New Responses*. London: Routledge.
Dower, John. (1986). *War Without Mercy: Race and Power in the Pacific War*. London: Faber and Faber.
Downs, Erica Strecker, and Philip C. Saunders. (1998–1999). "Legitimacy and the Limits of Nationalism: China and the Diaoyu Islands," *International Security* 23(3): 114–146.
Doyle, Michael W. (1986). "Liberalism and World Politics," *American Political Science Review* 80(4): 1151–1169.
Drifte, Reinhard. (1983). "Diplomacy," in J. M. W. Chapman, Reinhard Drifte, and I. T. M. Gow, *Japan's Quest for Comprehensive Security: Defence, Diplomacy, Dependence*. London: Pinter, pp. 81–142.
———. (1986). *Arms Production in Japan: The Military Applications of Civilian Technology*. London: Westview.
———. (1990). *Japan's Rise to International Responsibilities: The Case of Arms Control*. London: Athlone.
———. (2002). *Japan's Security Relations with China Since 1989*. London: Routledge.
Dunn, David J. (1991). "Peace Research Versus Strategic Studies," in Ken Booth (ed.), *New Thinking About Strategy and International Security*. London: Harper Collins, pp. 56–71.
Dupont, Alan. (1998). *The Environment and Security in Pacific Asia*. Adelphi Paper 319. Oxford: Oxford University Press.
———. (1999). "Transnational Crime, Drugs, and Security in East Asia," *Asian Survey* 39(3): 433–455.
———. (2001). *East Asia Imperilled: Transnational Challenges to Security*. Cambridge: Cambridge University Press.
Dziedzic, Michael J. (1990). "The Transnational Drug Trade and Regional Security," *Survival* 31(6): 533–548.
Ebata, Kensuke. (1999). *Anzen Hoshō to wa Nani ka?* [What Is Security Policy?] Tokyo: Heibonsha Shinsho.
Eberstadt, Nicholas. (1999). *The End of North Korea*. Washington, D.C.: AEI.
Edström, Bert. (1999). *Japan's Evolving Foreign Policy Doctrine: From Yoshida to Miyazawa*. London: Macmillan.
Elbe, Stefan. (2002). "HIV/AIDS and the Changing Landscape of War in Africa," *International Security* 27(2): 159–177.
Eldridge, Robert. (2002). *Okinawa and U.S.-Japan Relations in the Twenty-First Century: Bilateral and Trilateral Approaches to a Sounder Okinawa Policy*. Tokyo: RIPS.

Elliott, Lorraine. (2000). "Environmental Security," in William T. Tow, Ramesh Thakur, and In-Taek Hyun (eds.), *Asia's Emerging Regional Order: Reconciling Traditional and Human Security.* Tokyo, New York, and Paris: United Nations University Press, pp. 157–176.

Emmerson, Donald K. (2001). "Goldilocks's Problem: Rethinking National Security and Sovereignty in Asia," in Sheldon W. Simon (ed.), *The Many Faces of Asian Security.* Lanham, MA: Rowman and Littlefield, pp. 89–114.

Evans, Michael. (2000). "Implications of the Revolution in Military Affairs Debate: Lessons from America and Australia," unpublished paper presented at 8th Working Group, Council for Security Cooperation in the Asia-Pacific, Kuala Lumpur, Malaysia, 20 October 2000.

Ferro, Marc. (2000). *Colonization: A Global History.* London: Routledge.

Flynn, Steven E. (2000). "The Global Drug Trade Versus the Nation State: Why the Thugs Are Winning," in Maryann K. Cusimano (ed.), *Beyond Sovereignty: Issues for a Global Agenda.* Boston and New York: Bedford/St. Martin's, pp. 44–66.

Foot, Rosemary. (1988–1989). "Nuclear Coercion and the End of the Korean Conflict," *International Security* 13(3): 92–112.

Freedman, Lawrence. (1998). *The Revolution in Strategic Affairs.* Oxford: Oxford University Press.

Fujii, Hideaki. (2000). "Japan," in Paul B. Stares (ed.), *Rethinking Energy Security in East Asia.* Tokyo and New York: Japan Center for International Exchange, pp. 59–78.

Fukushima, Akiko. (1999). *Japanese Foreign Policy: The Emerging Logic of Multilateralism.* London: Macmillan.

Funabashi, Yōichi. (1991–1992). "Japan and the New World Order," *Foreign Affairs* 70(5): 58–74.

———. (1994). "Introduction: Japan's International Agenda in the 1990s," in Yōichi Funabashi (ed.), *Japan's International Agenda.* New York: New York University Press, pp. 1–27.

———. (1999). *Alliance Adrift.* New York: Council on Foreign Relations.

Furuta, Katsuhisa. (2003). "Japan Promises New Technologies to Clear Antipersonnel Landmines," *Look Japan* 48(562): 28–29.

Gaimushōhen. (2001). *Gaikō Seisho 2001* [Diplomatic Bluebook 2001]. Tokyo: Zaimushō Insatsukyoku.

Gallagher, Michael G. (1994). "China's Illusory Threat to the South China Sea," *International Security* 19(1): 169–194.

Gallicchio, Marc. (2001). "Occupation, Dominion, and Alliance: Japan in American Security Policy, 1945–1969," in Akira Iriye and Robert A. Wampler (eds.), *Partnership: The United States and Japan, 1951–2001.* Tokyo: Kodansha International, pp. 115–134.

Galtung, Johan. (1969). "Violence, Peace, and Peace Research," *Journal of Peace Research* 3: 167–191.

Ganesan, N. (2001). "Illegal Fishing and Illegal Migration in Thailand's Bilateral Relations with Malaysia and Myanmar," in Andrew H. Tan and J. D. Kenneth Boutin (eds.), *Non-Traditional Security Issues in Southeast Asia.* Singapore: Institute of Defence and Strategic Studies, pp. 507–527.

Gao, Shixian. (2000). "China," in Paul B. Stares (ed.), *Rethinking Energy Security in East Asia.* Tokyo and New York: Japan Center for International Exchange, pp. 43–58.

Garrett, Banning, and Glaser, Bonnie. (1997). "Chinese Apprehensions About the Revitalization of the U.S.-Japan Alliance," *Asian Survey* 37(4): 383–402.

George Mulgan, Aurelia. (1997). "The U.S.-Japan Security Relationship in a New Era," in Denny Roy (ed.), *The New Security Agenda in the Asia-Pacific Region.* London: Macmillan, pp. 140–169.

Giarra, Paul S., and Akihisa Nagashima. (1999). "Managing the New U.S.-Japan Security Alliance: Enhancing Structures and Mechanisms to Address Post–Cold War Requirements," in Michael J. Green and Patrick M. Cronin (eds.), *The U.S.-Japan Alliance: Past, Present, and Future.* New York: Council on Foreign Relations, pp. 94–113.

Gilpin, Robert. (2000). *The Challenge of Global Capitalism: The World Economy in the Twenty-First Century.* Princeton, NJ: Princeton University Press.

Gleick, Peter H. (1993). "Water and Conflict: Fresh Water Resources and International Security," *International Security* 18(1): 79–112.

Glosserman, Brad. (2002). "Russia's New Nuclear Threat," Pacific Forum CSIS, PacNet, 17 October 2002.

Godement, Francois. (1997). *The New Asian Renaissance: From Colonialism to the Post–Cold War.* London: Routledge.

Godson, Roy, and Phil Williams. (1998). "Strengthening Cooperation Against Transnational Crime," *Survival* 40(3): 66–88.

Godwin, Paul H. B. (1996). "From Continent to Periphery: PLA Doctrine, Strategy, and Capabilities Towards 2000," *China Quarterly* 146: 464–487.

Goh, Evelyn. (2001). "The Hydro-Politics of the Mekong River Basin: Regional Cooperation and Environmental Security," in Andrew H. Tan and J. D. Kenneth Boutin (eds.), *Non-Traditional Security Issues in Southeast Asia.* Singapore: Institute of Defence and Strategic Studies, pp. 468–506.

Gorjão, Paulo. (2002). "Japan's Foreign Policy and East Timor, 1975–2002," *Asian Survey* 42(5): 754–771.

Gow, Ian T. M. (1983). "Japan's Postwar Military Establishment," in J. M. W. Chapman, Reinhard Drifte, and I. T. M. Gow, *Japan's Quest for Comprehensive Security: Defence, Diplomacy, Dependence.* London: Pinter, pp. 20–55.

Graham, Euan. (2003). *The Security of Japan's Sea Lanes 1940–2003: "A Matter of Life and Death"?* unpublished Ph.D. diss., Australian National University.

Gray, Colin. (1999). "Clausewitz Rules, OK?" *Review of International Studies* 25 (Special Edition): 161–182.

Green, Michael J. (1995). *Arming Japan: Defence Production, Alliance Politics, and the Postwar Search for Autonomy.* New York: Columbia University Press.

———. (1999). "Managing Chinese Power: The View from Japan," in Alastair Iain Johnston and Robert S. Ross (eds.), *Engaging China: The Management of an Emerging Power.* London: Routledge, pp. 152–175.

———. (2001a). *Japan's Reluctant Realism: Foreign Policy Challenges in an Era of Uncertain Power.* New York: Palgrave.

———. (2001b). "The Search for an Active Security Partnership: Lessons from the 1980s," in Akira Iriye and Robert A. Wampler (eds.), *Partnership: The United States and Japan, 1951–2001.* Tokyo: Kodansha International, pp. 135–160.

Green, Michael J., and Patrick M. Cronin (eds.). (1999). *The U.S.-Japan Alliance: Past, Present, and Future.* New York: Council on Foreign Relations.

Gurtov, Mel. (2002). *Pacific Asia? Prospects for Security and Cooperation in East Asia.* Lanham, MD: Rowman and Littlefield.

Haacke, Jürgen. (2003). *ASEAN's Diplomatic and Security Culture: Origins, Development, and Prospects.* London: RoutledgeCurzon.

Haggard, Stephan. (2000). *The Political Economy of the Asian Financial Crisis.* Washington, D.C.: Institute for International Economics.

Hara, Kimie. (1998). *Japanese-Soviet/Russian Relations Since 1945: A Difficult Peace*. London: Routledge.
———. (1999). "Rethinking the 'Cold War' in the Asia-Pacific," *Pacific Review* 12(4): 515–536.
Harada, Chikahito. (1997). *Russia and North-East Asia*. Adelphi Paper 310. Oxford: Oxford University Press.
Harrison, Selig E. (ed.). (1996). *Japan's Nuclear Future: The Plutonium Debate and East Asian Security*. Washington, D.C.: Carnegie Endowment for International Peace.
Heginbotham, Eric. (2002). "The Fall and Rise of Navies in East Asia: Military Organizations, Domestic Politics, and Grand Strategy," *International Security* 27(2): 86–125.
Heginbotham, Eric, and Richard J. Samuels. (1998). "Mercantile Realism and Japanese Foreign Policy," *International Security* 22(4): 171–203.
Helleiner, Eric. (1990). "Money and Influence: Japanese Power in the International Monetary and Financial System," in Kathleen Newland (ed.), *The International Relations of Japan*. London: Macmillan, pp. 23–44.
Henderson, Jeannie. (1999). *Reassessing ASEAN*. Adelphi Paper 328. Oxford: Oxford University Press.
Henry L. Stimson Center Working Group Report. (2000). *Theater Missile Defenses in the Asia-Pacific Region*. Washington, D.C.: Henry L. Stimson Center.
Hernandez, Carolina. (1996). "Controlling Asia's Armed Forces," in Larry Diamond and Marc F. Plattner (eds.), *Civil-Military Relations and Democracy*. Baltimore and London: Johns Hopkins University Press, pp. 66–80.
Hernandez, Carolina G., Jorge V. Tigno, and Crisline G. Torres. (2000). "The Asian Overview: Population, Food, Energy, and the Environment," in Carolina G. Hernandez and Gill Wilkins (eds.), *Population, Food, Energy, and the Environment: Challenges for Asia-Europe Cooperation*. Manila: Council for Asia-Europe Cooperation, pp. 119–139.
Hewison, Kevin. (1997). "Thailand: Capitalist Development and the State," in Garry Rodan, Kevin Hewison, and Richard Robison, *The Political Economy of Southeast Asia*. Melbourne: Oxford University Press, pp. 93–120.
Higgott, Richard, and Richard Robison with Kevin J. Hewsion and Gary Rodan. (1985). "Theories of Development and Underdevelopment: Implications for Southeast Asia," in Richard Higgott and Richard Robison (eds.), *Southeast Asia: Essays in the Political Economy of Structural Change*. London: Routledge and Kegan Paul, pp. 16–61.
Hill, Hal, and Yun-Peng Chu. (2001). "An Overview of the Key Issues," in Yun-Peng Chu and Hal Hill (eds.), *The Social Impact of the Asian Financial Crisis*. Cheltenham, UK: Edward Elgar, pp. 1–25.
Hitchcox, Linda. (1994). "Relocation in Vietnam and Outmigration: The Ideological and Economic Context," in Judith M. Brown and Rosemary Foot (eds.), *Migration: The Asian Experience*. London: Macmillan, pp. 202–220.
Homer-Dixon, Thomas. (1994). "Environmental Scarcities and Violent Conflict," *International Security*, 19(1): 5–40.
Hook, Glenn D. (1996a). "Japan and the Construction of the Asia-Pacific," in Andrew Gamble and Anthony Payne (eds.), *Regionalism and World Order*. London: Macmillan, pp. 169–206.
Hook, Glenn D. (1996b). *Militarization and Demilitarization in Contemporary Japan*. London: Routledge.
———. (1998). "Japan and the ASEAN Regional Forum: Bilateralism, Multilateralism, or Supplementalism," *Japanstudien*, 10: 159–188.

Hook, Glenn D., and Gavan McCormack. (2001). *Japan's Contested Constitution: Documents and Analysis*. London: Routledge.
Hook, Glenn D., Julie Gilson, Christopher W. Hughes, and Hugo Dobson. (2001). *Japan's International Relations: Politics, Economics, and Security*. London: Routledge.
Hook, Steven W., and Guang Zhang. (1998). "Japan's Aid Policy Since the Cold War: Rhetoric and Reality," *Asian Survey* 38(11): 1051–1066.
Horii, Kenzō. (1991). "Disintegration of the Colonial Economic Legacies and Social Restructuring in Malaysia," *Developing Economies* 29(4): 281–313.
Hughes, Christopher W. (1996a). "Japan's Subregional Security and Defence Linkages with ASEAN, South Korea, and China in the 1990s," *Pacific Review* 9(2): 229–250.
———. (1996b). "The North Korean Nuclear Crisis and Japanese Security," *Survival* 38(2): 79–103.
———. (1998). "Japan's Aum Shinrikyō, the Changing Nature of Terrorism, and the Post–Cold War Security Agenda," *Pacifica Review* 10(1): 39–60.
———. (1999). *Japan's Economic Power and Security: Japan and North Korea*. London: Routledge.
———. (2000a). "Japanese Policy and the East Asian Currency Crisis: Abject Defeat or Quiet Victory?" *Review of International Political Economy* 7(2): 219–253.
———. (2000b). "Japan's 'Strategy-less' North Korea Strategy: Shifting Policies of Dialogue and Deterrence and Implications for Japan–U.S.–South Korea Security Cooperation," *Korean Journal of Defense Analysis* 12(2): 153–180.
———. (2001). "Conceptualizing the Globalization-Security Nexus in the Asia-Pacific," *Security Dialogue* 32(4): 407–421.
———. (2002). "Tumen River Area Development Programme (TRADP): Frustrated Microregionalism as a Microcosm of Political Rivalries," in Shaun Breslin and Glenn D. Hook (eds.), *Microregionalism and World Order*. Basingstoke, UK: Palgrave Macmillan, pp. 115–143.
Hughes, Christopher W., with Akiko Fukushima. (2003). "Japan-U.S. Security Relations: Toward 'Bilateralism Plus'?" in Ellis S. Krauss and T. J. Pempel (eds.), *Beyond Bilateralism: The U.S.-Japan Relationship in the New Asia-Pacific*. Stanford: Stanford University Press, pp. 55–86.
Hummel, Hartwig. (1996). "Japan's Military Expenditures After the Cold War: The 'Realism' of the Peace Dividend," *Australian Journal of International Affairs* 50(2): 137–155.
Huntington, Samuel P. (1976). *No Easy Choice: Political Participation in Developing Countries*. Cambridge, MA: Harvard University Press.
Hutchinson, Jane. (1997). "Pressure on Policy in the Philippines," in Garry Rodan, Kevin Hewison, and Richard Robison, *The Political Economy of Southeast Asia*. Melbourne: Oxford University Press, pp. 64–92.
Huxley, Tim. (2000). *Defending the Lion City: The Armed Forces of Singapore*. Crow's Nest, Australia: Allen and Unwin.
———. (2002). *Disintegrating Indonesia? Implications for Regional Security*. Adelphi Paper 349. Oxford: Oxford University Press.
Huxley, Tim, and Susan Willett. (1999). *Arming East Asia*. Adelphi Paper 329. Oxford: Oxford University Press.
Igarashi, Takeshi. (1990). "Keizai taikoku no kadai" [The Economic Great Power Issue], in Takeshi Igarashi (ed.), *Nihon no ODA to Kokusai Chitsujo* [Japan's ODA in the International Order]. Tokyo: Nihon Kokusai Mondai Kenkyūjo, pp. 3–24.

Imura, Hidefumi. (1994). "Japan's Environmental Balancing Act: Accommodating Sustained Development," *Asian Survey* 34(4): 355–368.

Inada, Jūichi. (2001). "Sekai Ginkō IMF no kōzō chōsei rejīmu to Nihon no seiksaku: Betonamu to Indoneshia no jirei" [The World Bank's and IMF's Structural Adjustment Regime and Japanese Policy: The Cases of Vietnam and Indonesia], in Shimomura Yasutami and Inada Jūichi (eds.), *Ajia Kinyū Kiki no Seiji Keizaigaku* [The Political Economy of the Asian Financial Crisis]. Tokyo: Nihon Kokusai Mondai Kenkyūjo, pp. 117–144.

Institute for National Strategic Studies. (2000). *The United States and Japan: Advancing Toward a Mature Partnership*. INSS Special Report. Washington, D.C.: National Defense University.

International Institute for Strategic Studies. (2001). *The Military Balance, 2001–2002*. Oxford: Oxford University Press.

Iokibe, Makoto. (2000). "Sengo Nihon gaikō no kōzō" [The Structure of Japan's Postwar Diplomacy], in Iokibe Makoto (ed.), *Sengo Nihon Gaikō shi* [Japan's Postwar Diplomatic History]. Tokyo: Yūhikakusha, pp. 1–20.

Japan External Trade Organization (JETRO). (various years). *Sekai to Nihon no Bōeki* [World and Japanese Trade]. Tokyo: JETRO.

Japanese Shipowners' Association. (2003). "Asia Anti-Piracy Challenges 2000," www.jsanet.or.jp/e2–3/pi2–2–3.html.

Jayasuriya, Kanishka. (2001). "Southeast Asia's Embedded Mercantilism in Crisis: International Strategies and Domestic Coalitions," in Andrew H. Tan and J. D. Kenneth Boutin (eds.), *Non-Traditional Security Issues in Southeast Asia*. Singapore: Institute of Defence and Strategic Studies, pp. 26–53.

Johnson, Chalmers. (1982). *MITI and the Japanese Miracle: The Growth of Industrial Policy, 1925–1975*. Stanford: Stanford University Press.

———. (1987). "Political Institutions and Economic Performance: The Government-Business Relationship in Japan, South Korea, and Taiwan," in Frederic C. Deyo (ed.), *The Political Economy of the New Asian Industrialism*. Ithaca: Cornell University Press, pp. 136–164.

———. (2000). *Blowback: The Costs and Consequences of American Empire*. New York: Owl Books.

Johnston, Alastair Iain. (1995). "China's New 'Old Thinking': The Concept of Limited Deterrence," *International Security* 20(3): 5–42.

Kadono, Nario. (1999). "How Can We Fight Twenty-First Century Crime? International Cooperation Against Transnational Crime," in Carolina G. Hernandez and Gina R. Pattugalan (eds.), *Transnational Crime and Regional Security in the Asia-Pacific*. Manila: Council for Security Cooperation in the Asia-Pacific, Institute for Strategic and Development Studies, pp. 119–125.

Kaijō Hoanchō. (2000). *Kaijō Hoan Hakusho* [Maritime Safety White Paper]. Tokyo: Ōkurashō Insatsukyoku.

Kaldor, Mary. (2001). *New and Old Wars: Organized Violence in a Global Era*. Cambridge: Polity.

Kamiya, Matake. (1997). "Ajia Taiheiyō ni okeru jūsōteki anzen hoshō kōzō ni mukatte: takokukan kyōchō taisei no genkai to Nichibei anpo taisei no yakuwari" [Toward a Multi-Layered Security Structure in the Asia-Pacific: The Current Status of Multilateral Cooperation and the Role of the U.S.-Japan Security System], *Kokusai Seiji* [International Politics] 115: 144–160.

———. (2000). "Japanese Foreign Policy Toward Northeast Asia," in Inoguchi Takashi and Purnendra Jain (eds.), *Japanese Foreign Policy Today*. New York: Palgrave, pp. 226–250.

Katahara, Eiichi. (1990). *The Politics of Japanese Defence Policy-Making, 1975–1989*, unpublished Ph.D. diss. Griffith University, Australia.

———. (1997). "Japan's Plutonium Policy: Consequences for Non-Proliferation," *Nonproliferation Review* (Fall): 53–61.

———. (2001). "Japan: From Containment to Normalization," in Muthiah Alagappa (ed.), *Coercion and Governance: The Declining Political Role of the Military in Asia.* Stanford: Stanford University Press, pp. 69–91.

Katzenstein, Peter J. (1996a). "Introduction: Alternative Perspectives on National Security," in Peter J. Katzenstein (ed.), *The Culture of National Security: Norms and Identity in World Politics.* New York: Columbia University Press, pp. 1–32.

———. (1996b). *Cultural Norms and National Security: Police and Military in Postwar Japan.* Ithaca: Cornell University Press.

Katzenstein, Peter J., and Nobuo Okawara. (1993). "Japan's National Security: Structures, Norms, and Policies," *International Security* 17(4): 84–118.

———. (2002). "Japan, Asian-Pacific Security, and the Case for Analytical Eclecticism," *International Security* 26(3): 153–158.

Katzenstein, Peter J., and Yutaka Tsujinaka. (1991). *Defending the Japanese State: Structures, Norms, and Political Response to Terrorism and Violent Social Protest in the 1970s and 1980s.* Ithaca: Cornell University Press.

Keddell, Joseph P., Jr. (1993). *The Politics of Defense in Japan: Managing Internal and External Pressures.* Armonk, NY: M. E. Sharpe.

Keisatsuchō. (2001). *Keisatsu Hakusho* [Police White Paper]. Tokyo: Ōkurashō Insatsukyoku.

Khong, Yuen Foong. (1997). "ASEAN and the Southeast Asian Security Complex," in David A. Lake and Patrick M. Morgan (eds.), *Regional Orders: Building Security in a New World,* pp. 318–339.

Khoo, Boo Teik. (1997). "Democracy and Authoritarianism in Malaysia Since 1957," in Anek Laothamatas (ed.), *Democratization in Southeast and East Asia.* Singapore: Institute of Southeast Asian Studies, pp. 46–76.

Kim, Taewoo. (1996). "Japanese Ambitions, U.S. Constraints, and South Korea's Nuclear Future," in Selig S. Harrison (ed.), *Japan's Nuclear Future: The Plutonium Debate and East Asian Security.* Washington, D.C.: Carnegie Endowment for International Peace, pp. 87–109.

Kimura, Hiroshi. (1998). *Islands or Security? Japanese-Soviet Relations Under Brezhnev and Andropov.* Kyoto: International Research Center for Japanese Studies.

———. (2000). *Distant Neighbours, Volume 1: Japanese-Russian Relations Under Brezhnev and Andropov.* New York and London: M. E. Sharpe.

Kindleberger, Charles. (2001). *Manias, Panics, and Crashes: A History of Financial Crises.* New York: John Wiley and Sons.

Klare, Michael T. (1988). "The New Interventionism: Low Intensity Warfare in the 1980s and Beyond," in Michael T. Klare and Peter Kornbluh (eds.), *Low Intensity Warfare: Counterinsurgency, Proinsurgency, and Antiterrorism in the Eighties.* New York: Pantheon Books.

Kobe City. (2003). "The Great Hanshin-Awaji Earthquake Statistics and Restoration Progress," www.city.kobe.jp/cityoffice/06/013/report/1–2.html.

Kohli, Athul. (1999). "Where Do High Growth Political Economies Come From? The Japanese Lineage of Korea's 'Developmental State,'" in Meredith Woo-Cumings (ed.), *The Developmental State.* Ithaca and London: Cornell University Press, pp. 93–136.

Kojima, Reiitsu. (2000). "Kankyō seisaku rekishi" [The History of Environmental Policy], in Kojima Reiitsu (ed.), *Gendai Chūgoku no Kōzō Hendō 6. Kankyō: Seichō e no Seiyaku to Naru* [Changes in Modern China's Structure 6. Environment: Becoming a Constraint on Growth]. Tokyo: Tōkyō Daigaku Shuppankai, pp. 7–66.

Korean Peninsula Energy Development Organization (KEDO). (2001). *KEDO 2001 Annual Report*. New York: KEDO.

Kurusu, Kaoru. (2001). "Ningen anzen hoshō: shuken kokka shisutemu no henyō to gabanansu" [Human Security: The Sovereign State System's Transformation and Governance], in Akenaya Tatsuo and Ochiai Tarō (eds.), *Atarashii Anzen Hoshō no Shiza* [Perspectives on New Security]. Tokyo: Aki Shobō, pp. 113–149.

Lam, Pang Er. (1996). "Japan and the Spratlys Dispute: Aspirations and Limitations," *Asian Survey* 36(10): 995–1010.

Leaver, Richard. (2001). "The Meanings, Origins, and Implications of the 'Howard Doctrine,'" *Pacific Review* 14(1): 15–34.

Lebra, Joyce C. (1977). "The Significance of the Japanese Military Model for Southeast Asia," in Joyce C. Lebra (ed.), *Japanese Trained Armies in Southeast Asia: Independence and Volunteer Forces in World War II*. New York: Columbia University Press, pp. 167–184 [reproduced in Wolf Mendl, ed., *Japan and Southeast Asia, Volume 1: From the Meiji Restoration to 1945*. London: Routledge, 2001].

Lee, Shin-wa. (2000). "Safeguarding the Environment: An Agenda for Cooperation in South Korea, Northeast Asia and Beyond," in Carolina G. Hernandez and Gill Wilkins (eds.), *Population, Food, Energy, and the Environment: Challenges for Asia-Europe Cooperation*. Manila: Council for Asia-Europe Cooperation, pp. 182–218.

Leifer, Michael. (1983). "The Security of Sea-Lanes in Southeast Asia," *Survival* 25(1): 16–24.

———. (1995). *Dictionary of the Modern Politics of Southeast Asia*. London: Routledge.

———. (1996). *The ASEAN Regional Forum: Extending ASEAN's Mode of Security*. Oxford: Oxford University Press.

———. (2000a). "The Changing Temper of Indonesian Nationalism," in Michael Leifer (ed.), *Asian Nationalism*. London: Routledge, pp. 153–169.

———. (2000b). *Singapore's Foreign Policy: Coping with Vulnerability*. London: Routledge.

Li, Kai. (2000). "The Impact of Expanding Population and Economic Growth on the Demand for and Supply of Both Grain and Energy with Environmental Concerns in the People's Republic of China: A Medium Term Outlook," in Carolina G. Hernandez and Gill Wilkins (eds.), *Population, Food, Energy, and the Environment: Challenges for Asia-Europe Cooperation*. Manila: Council for Asia-Europe Cooperation, pp. 140–181.

Liew, Leong. (2000). "Human and Economic Security: Is There a Nexus?" in William T. Tow, Ramesh Thakur, and In-Taek Hyun (eds.), *Asia's Emerging Regional Order: Reconciling Traditional and Human Security*. Tokyo, New York, and Paris: United Nations University Press, pp. 192–208.

Lin, Cheng-yi. (1997). "Taiwan's South China Sea Policy," *Asian Survey* 37(4): 323–339.

Lintner, Bertil. (1999). *Burma in Revolt: Opium and Insurgency Since 1948*. Chiang Mai: Silkworm Books.

Lowi, Miriam R. (1993). "Bridging the Divide: Transboundary Resource Disputes and the Case of the West Bank Water," *International Security* 18(1): 113–188.

Mackinlay, John. (2002). *Globalisation and Insurgency*. Adelphi Paper 352. Oxford: Oxford University Press.

Maeda, Tetsuo. (2000). *Zainichi Beigun Kichi no Shushi Kessan* [Calculating the Costs of U.S. Bases in Japan]. Tokyo: Chikuma Shinsho.

Maley, William. (2000). "Refugees and Forced Migration as a Security Problem," in William T. Tow, Ramesh Thakur, and In-Taek Hyun (eds.), *Asia's Emerging Regional Order: Reconciling Traditional and Human Security*. Tokyo, New York, and Paris: United Nations University Press, pp. 142–156.

Matsumura, Hiroshi. (2000). *Japan and the Kyoto Protocol: Conditions for Ratification*. London: Royal Institute of International Affairs.

Maull, Hanns. (1989). "Energy and Resources: The Strategic Dimensions," *Survival* 31(6): 500–518.

Mazaar, M. J. (1995). *North Korea and the Bomb: A Case Study in Non-Proliferation*. London: Macmillan.

McCardle, Hamish, Jonathan Boxhall, Juan Ronderos, and Rino A. Francisco. (2000). "Cybercrime and Its Effects on the Asia-Pacific Region," unpublished paper presented to CSCAP Transnational Crime Working Group, Bangkok, Thailand, October 2000.

McDougall, Derek. (2001). "Regional Institutions and Security: Implications of the 1999 East Timor Crisis," in Andrew H. Tan and J. D. Kenneth Boutin (eds.), *Non-Traditional Security Issues in Southeast Asia*. Singapore: Institute of Defence and Strategic Studies, pp. 166–196.

McFarlane, John. (2001). "Transnational Crime and Asia-Pacific Security," in Sheldon W. Simon (ed.), *The Many Faces of Asian Security*. Lanham, MD: Rowman and Littlefield, pp. 197–229.

McNally, Christopher A., and Charles A. Morrison (eds.). (2001). *Asia-Pacific Security Outlook 2001*. Tokyo and New York: Japan Center for International Exchange.

Mendl, Wolf. (1995). *Japan's Asia Policy: Regional Security and Global Interests*. London: Routledge.

Midford, Paul. (2000). "Japan's Leadership Role in East Asian Security Multilateralism: The Nakayama Proposal and the Logic of Reassurance," *Pacific Review* 13(3): 367–397.

Milne, R. S., and Diane K. Mauzy. (1999). *Malaysian Politics Under Mahathir*. London: Routledge.

Ministry of Foreign Affairs (MOFA). (1997). "Japan's Position Regarding the Situation in Myanmar," www.mofa.go.jp/region/asia-paci/myanmar/myanmar.html.

———. (2000a). "The Significance of the 'G-8 Miyazaki Initiatives for Conflict Prevention.' Action from Japan on Conflict and Development: Japanese Development Cooperation for Conflict Prevention," www.g-8kyushu-okinawa.go.jp/e/theme/action.html.

———. (2000b). "Refugee Assistance," www.mofa.go.jp/policy/un/pamph2000/refugee.html.

———. (2000c). "Measures by the International Community and Japan to Combat Transnational Organized Crime," www.mofa.go.jp/policy/I_crime/measure0011.html.

———. (2000d). "Opening Speech by Mr. Tetsuma Esaki, Senior State Secretary for Foreign Affairs Regional Conference on Combating Piracy and Armed Robbery Against Ships," www.mofa.go.jp/policy/piracy/speech0004.html.

———. (2001a). "Present State of the Piracy Problem and Japan's Efforts," www.mofa.go.jp/policy/piracy/problem0112.html.

———. (2001b). "Statement by Former Prime Minister Yoshiro Mori at the United Nations Special Session on HIV/AIDS," www.mofa.go.jp/policy/pop_aids/session0106/state.html.

———. (2002a). "Support Package for Peace and Stability in Mindanao," www.mofa.go.jp/region/asia-paci/philippine/pv0212/mindanao.html.

———. (2002b). *Diplomatic Bluebook 2002*. Tokyo: MOFA.
———. (2003). "Emergency Assistance Responding to Requests from Damaged Countries and International Organizations," www.mofa.go.jp/policy/oda/category/disaster/emergency.html.
Ministry of Land, Infrastructure, and Transport, Japan. (2003)."The Third World Water Forum: Japan's ODA," www.mlit.go.jp/tochimizushigen/mizsei/wwf3/eng/measures.html.
Ministry of National Defence, Republic of Korea. (1998). *Defense White Paper 1998*. Seoul: Ministry of National Defence.
Mitchell, Bernard, and John Ravenhill. (1995). "Beyond Product Cycles and Flying Geese: Regionalization, Hierarchy, and the Industrialization of East Asia," *World Politics* 47(2): 171–209.
Mochizuki, Mike M. (1997). "American and Japanese Strategic Debates: The Need for a New Synthesis," in Mike M. Mochizuki (ed.), *Toward a True Alliance: Restructuring U.S.-Japan Security Relations*. Washington, D.C.: Brookings Institution, pp. 43–82.
Murata, Kōji. (2000). "Do the New Guidelines Make the Japan-US Alliance More Effective?" in Nishihara Masashi (ed.), *The Japan-U.S. Alliance: New Challenges for the Twenty-First Century*. Tokyo and New York: Japan Center for International Exchange, pp. 19–38.
Muroyama, Yoshimasa. (1992). *Nichibei Anpo Taisei* [The U.S.-Japan Security System]. Tokyo: Yūhikaku.
Murphy, Anne Marie. (1999). "Indonesia and Globalization," *Asian Perspective* 23(4): 229–260.
Myers, Norman. (1993). *Ultimate Security: The Environmental Basis of Political Stability*. New York: W. W. Norton.
Nagashima, Akihisa. (2001). "Collective Self-Defense and the Japan-U.S. Alliance," *Japan Echo* 28(5): 30–35.
Nakai, Yoshifumi. (2000). "Policy Coordination on Taiwan," in Nishihara Masashi (ed.), *The Japan-U.S. Alliance: New Challenges for the Twenty-First Century*. Tokyo and New York: Japan Center for International Exchange, pp. 71–102.
Narine, Shaun. (1997). "ASEAN and the ARF: The Limits of the 'ASEAN Way,'" *Asian Survey* 37(10): 961–976.
National Defense Panel. (1997). *Transforming Defense: National Security in the Twenty-First Century*, Washington, D.C.: National Defense Panel.
Naughton, Barry. (1999). "China: Domestic Restructuring and a New Role in Asia," in T. J. Pempel (ed.), *The Politics of the Asian Crisis*. Ithaca: Cornell University Press, pp. 203–223.
Naya, Masatsugu. (1999). "Keizai anzen hoshōron no igi to sono tenkai" [Economic Security Policy's Meaning and Development], in Takeda Isami and Naya Masatsugu (eds.), *Shinanzen Hoshō no Kōzu* [The Structure of New Security Policy]. Tokyo: Keisō Shobō, pp. 82–114.
Nester, William R. (1992). *Japan and the Third World: Patterns, Power, Prospects*. New York: St. Martin's.
———. (1996). *Power Across the Pacific: A Diplomatic History of American Relations with Japan*. London: Macmillan.
Nishihara, Masashi. (1994). "Ajia Taiheiyō chiiki to takokukan anzen hoshō kyōryoku wakugumi: ASEAN Chiiki Fōramu o chūshin ni" [The Asia-Pacific Region and the Framework for Multilateral Security Cooperation: Focusing on the ASEAN Regional Forum], *Kokusai Mondai* [International Affairs] 470: 16–28.
Nishihara, Masashi (ed.). (2000). *The Japan-U.S. Alliance: New Challenges for the Twenty-First Century*. Tokyo and New York: Japan Center for International Exchange.

Nishihara, Masashi, and Jitsuo Tsuchiyama. (1998). *Nichibei Dōmei Q & A 100* [U.S.-Japan Alliance Q & A 100]. Tokyo: Akishobō.

Noland, Marcus. (2000). *Avoiding the Apocalypse: The Future of the Two Koreas*. Washington, D.C.: Institute for International Economics.

Oberdorfer, Don. (1997). *The Two Koreas: A Contemporary History*. London: Warner Books.

O'Hanlon, Michael. (1997). "Theater Missile Defense and the US-Japan Alliance," in Mike M. Mochizuki (ed.), *Toward a True Alliance: Restructuring U.S.-Japan Security Relations*. Washington, D.C.: Brookings Institution, pp. 149–178.

———. (1998). "Stopping a North Korean Invasion: Why Defending South Korea Is Easier Than the Pentagon Thinks," *International Security* 22(4): 135–170.

———. (2000a). *Technological Change and the Future of War*. Washington, D.C.: Brookings Institution.

———. (2000b). "Why China Cannot Conquer Taiwan," *International Security* 25(2): 51–86.

Ohta, Hiroshi. (2000). "Japanese Environmental Foreign Policy," in Inoguchi Takashi and Purnendra Jain (eds.), *Japanese Foreign Policy Today*. London: Macmillan, pp. 96–121.

Okawara, Nobuo, and Peter J. Katzenstein. (2001). "Japan and Asian-Pacific Security: Regionalization, Entrenched Bilateralism, and Incipient Multilateralism," *Pacific Review* 14(2): 165–194.

Ōnō, Kenichi, and Kōjirō Sakurai. (2000). *Higashi Ajia no Kaihatsu Keizaigaku* [The Economics of East Asia's Development]. Tokyo: Yūhikaku Aruma.

Orr, Robert M. (1990). *The Emergence of Japan's Foreign Aid Power*. New York: Columbia University Press, 1990.

Osius, Ted. (2002). *The U.S.-Japan Security Alliance: Why It Matters and How to Strengthen It*. Westport, CT: Praeger.

Ōtake, Hideo. (1983). *Nihon no Boei to Kokunai Seiji* [Japan's Defense and Domestic Politics]. Tokyo: Sanichi Shobō.

Ozawa, Ichirō. (1993). *Nihon Kaizō Keikaku* [Blueprint for a New Japan]. Tokyo: Kōdansha.

Paik, Jin-Hyun, and Anthony Bergin. (2000). "Maritime Security in the Asia-Pacific," in William T. Tow, Ramesh Thakur, and In-Taek Hyun (eds.), *Asia's Emerging Regional Order: Reconciling Traditional and Human Security*. Tokyo, New York, and Paris: United Nations University Press, pp. 177–191.

Painter, David S., and Melvyn P. Leffler. (1994). "Introduction: The International System and the Origins of the Cold War," in Melvyn P. Leffler and David S. Painter (eds.), *Origins of the Cold War: An International History*. London: Routledge, pp. 1–12.

Paris, Roland. (2001). "Human Security: Paradigm Shift or Hot Air?" *International Security* 26(2): 87–102.

Paul, Linda M. B. (1999). "Strategic, Legal, and Political Initiatives for Cooperative Maintenance of Law and Order at Sea," in Sam Bateman (ed.), *Maritime Cooperation in the Asia-Pacific: Current Situation and Prospects*. Canberra Papers on Strategy and Defence no. 132. Canberra, Strategic and Defence Studies Centre, pp. 121–143.

Pempel, T. J. (1997). "Transpacific Torii: Japan and the Emerging Asian Regionalism," in Peter J. Katzenstein and Takashi Shiraishi (eds.), *Network Power: Japan and Asia*. Ithaca: Cornell University Press, pp. 47–82.

———. (1999). "The Developmental Regime in a Changing World Economy," in Meredith Woo-Cumings (ed.), *The Developmental State*. Ithaca and London: Cornell University Press, pp. 137–181.

Pharr, Susan. (1993). "Japan's Defensive Foreign Policy and the Policies of Burden Sharing," in Gerald L. Curtis (ed.), *Japan's Foreign Policy*. New York: M. E. Sharpe, pp. 235–263.

———. (1994). "Japanese Aid in the New World Order," in Craig C. Garby and Mary Brown Bullock (eds.), *Japan: A New Kind of Superpower?* Ithaca: Johns Hopkins University Press, pp. 159–180.

Pirages, Dennis, and Paul Runci. (2000). "Ecological Interdependence and the Spread of Infectious Diseases," in Maryann K. Cusimano (ed.), *Beyond Sovereignty: Issues for a Global Agenda*. Boston and New York: Bedford/St. Martin's, pp. 177–197.

Potter, David. (1994). "Assessing Japan's Environmental Aid Policy," *Pacific Affairs* 67(2): 200–215.

Prime Minister's Commission on Japan's Goals in the Twenty-First Century. (2000). *Japan's Goals in the Twenty-First Century, the Frontier Within: Individual Empowerment and Better Governance in the New Millennium*. Tokyo: Office for Prime Minister's Commission on Japan's Goals in the Twenty-First Century.

Putzel, James. (2000). "Social Capital and the Imagined Community: Democracy and Nationalism in the Philippines," in Michael Leifer (ed.), *Asian Nationalism*. London: Routledge, pp. 170–186.

Ravenhill, John. (2001). *APEC and the Construction of Pacific Rim Regionalism*. Cambridge: Cambridge University Press.

Reese, David. (1998). *The Prospects for North Korea's Survival*. Adelphi Paper 323. Oxford: Oxford University Press.

Rix, Alan. (1993). *Japan's Foreign Aid Challenge: Policy Reform and Aid Leadership*. London: Routledge.

Robison, Richard. (1985). "Class, Capital, and the State in New Order Indonesia," in Richard Higgott and Richard Robison (eds.), *Southeast Asia: Essays in the Political Economy of Structural Change*. London: Routledge and Kegan Paul, pp. 295–335.

———. (1997). "Politics and Markets in Indonesia's Post-Oil Era," in Garry Rodan, Kevin Hewison, and Richard Robison, *The Political Economy of Southeast Asia*. Melbourne: Oxford University Press, pp. 29–63.

Robison, Richard, Richard Higgott, and Kevin Hewison. (1987). "Crisis in Economic Strategy in the 1980s: The Factors at Work," in Richard Robison, Kevin Hewison, and Richard Higgott (eds.), *Southeast Asia in the 1980s: The Politics of Economic Crisis*. Sydney: Allen and Unwin, pp. 1–15.

Romm, Joseph J. (1993). *Redefining National Security: The Non-Military Aspects*. New York: Council on Foreign Relations.

Rose, Caroline. (1998). *Interpreting History in Sino-Japanese Relations*. London: Routledge.

Rothschild, Emma. (1995). "What Is Security?" *Daedulus* 124(3): 53–98.

Roy, Denny. (1998). *China's Foreign Relations*. Basingstoke, UK: Macmillan.

Salameh, Mandouh G. (1995–1996). "China, Oil, and the Risk of Regional Conflict," *Survival* 37(4): 133–146.

Samuels, Richard J. (1991). "Reinventing Security: Japan Since Meiji," *Daedalus* 120(4): 47–68.

———. (1994). *Rich Nation, Strong Army: National Security and the Technological Transformation of Japan*. Ithaca: Cornell University Press.

———. (1998). "Sources and Uses of Energy," in Patrick Heenan (ed.), *The Japan Handbook*. London and Chicago: Fitzroy Dearborn, pp. 48–58.

Schaller, Michael. (1985). *The American Occupation of Japan: The Origins of the Cold War in Asia*. Oxford: Oxford University Press.

———. (1997). *Altered States: The United States and Japan Since the Occupation.* Oxford: Oxford University Press.
Scholte, Jan Aart. (1997). "Global Capitalism and the State," *International Affairs* 73(3): 427–452.
Sebata, Takao. (1998). *Bōei Keikaku no Taikō to Nihchibei Gaidorain: Bōei Seisaku Kettei no Kanryō Seijiteki Kōsatsu* [Japan National Defense Program Outline and the U.S.-Japan Defense Guidelines: Defense Decisionmaking and the Intersection of Bureaucracy and Politics]. Tokyo: Bokutaku Shakan.
Segal, Gerald, and David S. Goodman. (1994). *China Deconstructs.* London: Routledge.
Shambaugh, David. (1999–2000). "China's Military Views the World: Ambivalent Security," *International Security* 24(3): 52–79.
Shearer, David. (1998a). *Private Armies and Military Intervention.* Adelphi Paper 316. Oxford: Oxford University Press.
———. (1998b). "Outsourcing War," *Foreign Policy* 112: 68–81.
Sherwin, Martin J. (1994). "The Atomic Bomb and the Origins of the Cold War," in Melvyn P. Leffler and David S. Painter (eds.), *Origins of the Cold War: An International History.* London: Routledge, pp. 77–94.
Shiraishi, Masaya. (1990). *Japan's Relations with Vietnam, 1951–1987.* Ithaca: Cornell University Press.
Shiraishi, Takashi. (2000). *Umi no Teikoku: Ajia o dō Kangaeru ka* [Empire of the Sea: How Should We Think About Asia?]. Tokyo: Chūkō Shinsho.
Shouchuan, Asuka-Zhang. (2000). "Regional Environmenal Cooperation in Northeast Asia," in Carolina G. Hernandez and Gill Wilkins (eds.), *Population, Food, Energy, and the Environment: Challenges for Asia-Europe Cooperation.* Manila: Council for Asia-Europe Cooperation, pp. 218–250.
Sigal, L. V. (1998). *Disarming Strangers: Nuclear Diplomacy with North Korea.* Princeton, NJ: Princeton University Press.
Simon, Sheldon W. (1978). "The ASEAN States: Obstacles to Security Cooperation," *Orbis: A Journal of World Affairs* 22(2): 415–434.
———. (1999). "Multilateralism and Japan's Security Policy," *Korean Journal of Defense Analysis* 11(2): 79–96.
Singapore Institute of International Affairs. (2001). *Special Report: Sovereignty and International Intervention.* Singapore: Singapore Institute of International Affairs.
Singer, P. W. (2001/2002). "Corporate Warriors: The Rise of the Privatized Military Industry and Its Ramifications for International Security," *International Security* 26(3): 186–220.
Skeldon, Ronald. (1999). "Migration in Asia After the Economic Crisis: Patterns and Issues," *Asia-Pacific Population Journal* 14(3): 3–24.
Smith, Hazel. (1999). "'Opening' Up by Default: North Korea, the Humanitarian Community, and the Crisis," *Pacific Review* 12(3): 453–478.
Soeya, Yoshihide. (1998). "Japan: Normative Constraints Versus Structural Imperatives," in Muthiah Alagappa (ed.), *Asian Security Practice: Material and Ideational Influences.* Stanford: Stanford University Press, pp. 198–233.
Sōgō Anzen Hoshō Gurūpu. (1980). *Sōgō Anzen Hoshō Senryaku* [Comprehensive Security Policy]. Tokyo: Ōkurashō Insatsukyoku.
Sorensen, Theodore C. (1990). "Rethinking National Security," *Foreign Affairs* 69(3): 1–18.
Spero, Joan Edelman. (1997). *The Politics of International Economic Relations.* London: Routledge.
Stares, Paul B. (1996). *Global Habit: The Drug Problem in a Borderless World.* Washington, D.C.: Brookings Institution.

———. (2000a). "Introduction," in Paul B. Stares (ed.), *The New Security Agenda: A Global Survey*. Tokyo and New York: Japan Center for International Exchange, pp. 11–22.
———. (2000b). "Introduction and Overview," in Paul B. Stares (ed.), *Rethinking Energy Security in East Asia*. Tokyo and New York: Japan Center for International Exchange, pp. 19–41.
Steinberg, David I. (1993). "Japanese Economic Assistance to Burma: Aid in the Tarenagashi Manner?" in Bruce M. Koppel and Robert M. Orr (eds.), *Japan's Foreign Aid: Power and Policy in a New Era*. Boulder: Westview, pp. 135–162.
Storry, Richard. (1979). *Japan and the Decline of the West in Asia, 1894–1943*. London: Macmillan.
Strange, Susan. (1994). *States and Markets*. London: Pinter.
———. (1996). *The Retreat of the State*. Cambridge: Cambridge University Press.
Stubbs, Richard. (1994). "The Political Economy of the Asia-Pacific Region," in Richard Stubbs and Geoffrey R. D. Underhill (eds.), *Political Economy and the Changing Global Order*. London: Macmillan, pp. 366–377.
———. (2001). "Performance Legitimacy and 'Soft Authoritarianism,'" in Amitav Acharya, B. Michael Frolic, and Richard Stubbs (eds.), *Democracy, Human Rights, and Civil Society in South East Asia*. Toronto: Joint Centre for Asia-Pacific Studies, pp. 37–54.
Sudo, Sueo. (2002). *The International Relations of Japan and Southeast Asia: Forging a New Regionalism*. London: Routledge.
Suehiro Akira. (2001). "Nihon no aratna Ajia kanyo: chiteki seisaku shien wa kanō ka" [Japan's New Engagement with Asia: Is It Possible to Support a Regional Policy?], in Suehiro Akira and Yamakage Susumu (eds.), *Ajia Seiji Keizairon: Ajia no Naka no Nihon o Mezashite* [The Political Economy of the Asian Financial Crisis]. Tokyo: NTT Shuppan.
Sukma, Rizal. (2001). "The Achenese Rebellion: Secessionist Movement in Post-Suharto Indonesia," in Andrew H. Tan and J. D. Kenneth Boutin (eds.), *Non-Traditional Security Issues in Southeast Asia*. Singapore: Institute of Defence and Strategic Studies, pp. 377–409.
Sumi, Kazuo. (1995). *ODA Enjo no Genjitsu* [ODA's Current Situation]. Tokyo: Iwanami Shoten.
Takahashi, Susumu, and Kenji Nakamura. (1979). "Peace Research in Post-War Japan," in Japan Peace Research Group (ed.), *Peace Research in Japan, 1978–1979*. Tokyo: Tokyo University Press, pp. 7–34.
Takemura, Masayoshi. (1994). *Chīsakutomo Kirari to Hikaru Kuni Nihon* [A Small but Bright Shining Country]. Tokyo: Kōbun Shobō.
Takubo, Tadae. (1999). *Nihon no Ryōdo: Somo Somo Kokka wa Nani ka* [Japan's Territories: What Is a Nation?]. Tokyo: PHP.
Tanaka, Akihiko. (1991). *Nicchū Kankei, 1945–1990* [Japan-China Relations, 1945–1990]. Tokyo: Tokyo Daigaku Shuppankai.
———. (1995). "The Domestic Context: Japanese Politics and UN Peacekeeping," in Selig S. Harrison and Masashi Nishihara (eds.), *UN Peacekeeping: Japanese and American Perspectives*. Washington, D.C.: Carnegie Endowment for International Peace, pp. 89–105.
———. (1997). *Anzen Hoshō: Sengo 50nen no Mosaku* [Security Policy: The Fifty-Year Search in the Postwar Period]. Tokyo: Yomiuri Shimbunsha.
Tay, Simon S. C. (1999). "Preventive Diplomacy and the ASEAN Regional Forum: Principles and Possibilities," in Desmond Ball and Amitav Achrya (eds.), *The Next Stage: Preventive Diplomacy and Security Cooperation in the Asia-Pacific*. Canberra: Australian National University, pp. 93–116.
Thakur, Ramesh. (2000). "Human Security Regimes," in William T. Tow, Ramesh

Thakur, and In-Taek Hyun (eds.), *Asia's Emerging Regional Order: Reconciling Traditional and Human Security*. Tokyo, New York, and Paris: United Nations University Press, pp. 229–255.

Thomas, Caroline. (1987). *In Search of Security: The Third World in International Relations*. Brighton, UK: Wheatsheaf.

Tickner, J. Ann. (1992). *Gender in International Relations: Feminist Perspectives on Achieving Global Security*. New York: Columbia University Press.

———. (1995). "Re-Visioning Security," in Ken Booth and Steve Smith (eds.), *International Relations Theory Today*. Cambridge: Polity, pp. 175–197.

Tow, William T. (1999). *Assessing U.S. Bilateral Security Alliances in the Asia-Pacific's 'Southern Rim': Why the San Francisco System Endures*. Stanford: Asia Pacific Research Center, Stanford University.

———. (2001a). "Alternative Security Models: Implications for ASEAN," in Andrew H. Tan and J. D. Kenneth Boutin (eds.), *Non-Traditional Security Issues in Southeast Asia*. Singapore: Institute of Defence and Strategic Studies, pp. 257–285.

———. (2001b). *Asia-Pacific Strategic Relations: Seeking Convergent Security*. Cambridge: Cambridge University Press.

Trocki, Carl A. (1999). *Opium, Empire, and the Global Political Economy*. London: Routledge.

Tsuru, Shigeto. (1999). *The Political Economy of the Environment: The Case of Japan*. London: Athlone.

Ui, Jun. (1989). "Pollution Export," in Shigeto Tsuru and Helmut Weidner (eds.), *Environmental Policy in Japan*. Bonn, Germany: Edition Sigma, pp. 395–412.

Ullman, Richard. (1983). "Redefining Security," *International Security* 8(1): 129–153.

Umbach, Frank. (1998). "Financial Crisis Slows but Fails to Halt East Asian Arms Race-Part One," *Jane's Intelligence Review*, August, pp. 23–27.

Unger, Jonathan. (1996). "Introduction," in Jonathan Unger (ed.), *Chinese Nationalism*. London: M. E. Sharpe, pp. ix–xviii.

United Nations Development Programme. (1994). *Human Development 1994*. Oxford: Oxford University Press.

United Nations, Office of Drug Control and Crime Prevention. (2001). *Global Illicit Drug Trends 2001*. New York: United Nations Publications.

U.S. Department of Defense. (1999). *The Security Situation in the Taiwan Strait*. Washington, D.C.: U.S. Department of Defense.

———. (2001). *Quadrennial Defense Review*. Washington, D.C.: U.S. Department of Defense.

U.S. Department of Defense, Office of International Security Affairs. (1995). *United States Strategy for the East Asia-Pacific Region*. Washington, D.C.: U.S. Department of Defense.

Vagg, Jon. (1995). "Rough Seas? Contemporary Piracy in Southeast Asia," *British Journal of Criminology* 33(1): 63–80.

Valencia, Mark J. (1995). *China and the South China Sea Disputes*. Adelphi Paper 298. Oxford: Oxford University Press.

———. (1997). "Energy and Insecurity in East Asia," *Survival* 39(3): 85–106.

———. (2001). "Building Confidence and Security in the South China Sea: The Way Forward," in Andrew H. Tan and J. D. Kenneth Boutin (eds.), *Non-Traditional Security Issues in Southeast Asia*. Singapore: Institute of Defence and Strategic Studies, pp. 528–569.

Van Creveld, Martin. (1991). *The Transformation of War*. New York: Free Press.

Van Ness, Peter. (1999). "Globalization and Security in East Asia," *Asian Perspective* 23(4): 315–342.

Vatikiotis, Michael R. J. (1998). *Indonesian Politics Under Suharto: The Rise and Fall of the New Order.* London: Routledge.

Väyryen, Raimo. (1999). "Multilateral Security: Common, Co-Operative, or Collective?" in Michael G. Schechter (ed.), *Future Multilateralism: The Political and Social Framework.* Tokyo and New York: United Nations University Press, pp. 55–65.

Vogel, Ezra. (1986). "Pax Nipponica?" *Foreign Affairs* 64(4): 752–767.

Waever, Ole. (1995). "Securitization and Desecuritization," in Ronnie D. Lipschutz (ed.), *On Security.* New York: Columbia University Press, pp. 46–86.

Walt, Stephen M. (1991). "The Renaissance of Security Studies," *International Studies Quarterly* 35(2): 211–239.

Wan, Ming. (1995–1996). "Japan and the Asian Development Bank," *Pacific Affairs* 68(4): 509–528.

Wan, Ming. (2001). *Japan Between Asia and the West: Economic Power and Strategic Balance.* New York: M. E. Sharpe.

Wang, James C. F. (1995). *Contemporary Chinese Politics: An Introduction.* Englewood Cliffs, NJ: Prentice Hall.

Wang, Jianwei, and Xinbo Wu. (1998). *Against U.S. or with U.S.? The Chinese Perspective of America's Alliances with Japan and Korea.* Stanford: Asia-Pacific Research Center, Stanford University.

Watanabe, Akio. (2001). "Japan's Position on Human Rights in Asia," in Javed S. Maswood (ed.), *Japan and East Asian Regionalism.* London: Routledge, pp. 68–89.

Weatherbee, Donald E. (2001). "Environment, Development, and Security in Southeast Asia," in Sheldon W. Simon (ed.), *The Many Faces of Asian Security.* Lanham, MD: Rowman and Littlefield, pp. 141–163.

Wee, Vivienne, and Kanishka Jayasuriya. (2002). "New Geographies and Temporalities of Power: Exploring the New Fault Lines of Southeast Asia," *Pacific Review* 15(4): 475–496.

Weeks, Stanley. (1999). "Existing Maritime Cooperation Agreements in the Asia-Pacific Region," in Sam Bateman (ed.), *Maritime Cooperation in the Asia-Pacific: Current Situation and Prospects.* Canberra Papers on Strategy and Defence no. 132. Canberra: Strategic and Defence Studies Centre, pp. 1–17.

Weeks, Stanley B., and Charles A. Meconis. (1999). *The Armed Forces of the USA in the Asia-Pacific Region.* London: I. B. Tauris.

Weiner, Myron. (1995). "Security, Stability, and International Migration," in Sean M. Lynn-Jones and Steven E. Miller (eds.), *Global Dangers: Changing Patterns of International Security.* Cambridge, MA: MIT Press, pp. 183–218.

Welfield, John. (1970). *Japan and Nuclear China: Japanese Reactions to China's Nuclear Weapons.* Canberra: Australian National University Press.

———. (1988). *An Empire in Eclipse: Japan in the Postwar American Alliance System.* London: Athlone.

Welsh, Bridget. (1999). "Malaysia and Globalization: Contradictory Currents," *Asian Perspective* 23(4): 261–286.

Whiting, Allen S. (1997). "ASEAN Eyes China: The Security Dimension," *Asian Survey* 37(3): pp. 299–322.

Wilkinson, Paul. (1988). "Trends in International Terrorism and the American Response," in Lawrence Freedman, Christopher Hill, Adam Roberts, R. J. Vincent, Paul Wilkinson, and Philip Windsor, *Terrorism and International Order.* London: Routledge, pp. 38–47.

Wirth, David. (2000). "Globalizing the Environment," in Maryann K. Cusimano (ed.), *Beyond Sovereignty: Issues for a Global Agenda.* Boston and New York: Bedford/St. Martin's, pp. 198–216.

Wong, Anny. (2001). *The Roots of Japan's International Environmental Policies.* New York and London: Garland.

Woolley, Peter J. (1996). "Japan's 1991 Minesweeping Operation: An Organizational Response," *Asian Survey* 36(8): 804–817.

World Bank. (1993). *The East Asian Miracle: Economic Growth and Public Policy.* Oxford: Oxford University Press.

World Health Organization (WHO). (2003). *Severe Acute Respiratory Syndrome (SARS): Status of the Outbreak and Lessons for the Immediate Future.* Geneva: WHO.

Yahuda, Michael. (1996). *The International Relations of the Asia-Pacific, 1945–1995.* London: Routledge.

Yamaguchi Jirō. (1992). "The Gulf War and the Transformation of Japanese Constitutional Politics," *Journal of Japanese Studies* 18(1): 155–172.

Yamakage, Susumu. (1997). "Japan's National Security and Asia Pacific's Regional Institutions in the Post–Cold War Era," in Peter J. Katzenstein and Takashi Shiraishi (eds.), *Network Power: Japan and Asia.* Ithaca: Cornell University Press, pp. 275–308.

Yamashita, Masamitsu, Susumu Takai, and Shūichirō Iwata. (1994). *TMD: Seniki Dandō Missairu Bōei* [TMD: Theater Missile Defense]. Tokyo: TBS Buritanika.

Yasutomo, Denis T. (1986). *The Manner of Giving: Strategic Aid and Japanese Foreign Policy.* Lexington, MA, and Toronto: Lexington Books.

Yue, Chia Siow, and Shamira Bhanu. (1999). "Human Security Dimensions of the Asian Financial Crisis: A Compendium of Research Materials," in Japan Center for International Exchange/Institute for Southeast Asian Studies (ed.), *The Asian Crisis and Human Security.* Tokyo: JCIE/ISEAS.

Zamzam, Mohd Jafaar. (2000). "ASEAN," in Paul B. Stares (ed.), *Rethinking Energy Security in East Asia.* Tokyo and New York: Japan Center for International Exchange, pp. 117–140.

Zhao, Quansheng. (1993). *Japanese Policy-Making: The Politics Behind the Politics, Informal Mechanisms, and the Making of China Policy.* Oxford: Oxford University Press.

Index

About the Book

Long constrained as a security actor by constitutional as well as external factors, Japan now increasingly is called to play a greater role in stabilizing both the Asia-Pacific region and the entire international system. *Japan's Security Agenda* explores the country's diplomatic, political, military, and economic concerns and policies within this new context.

Hughes looks closely at the security issues facing Japanese policymakers: among them, remnants of Cold War conflicts, the proliferation of weapons of mass destruction, transnational terrorism, organized crime, piracy, economic dislocation, financial crises, and environmental disasters. He then examines Japan's response to these problems in the military, economic, and environmental spheres, as well as its key security relationships.

Does Japan's multidimensional and comprehensive approach to security policy offer a viable alternative paradigm to that of the traditional U.S. and European military-dominated model? Hughes's theoretical and empirical illustrations demonstrate the benefits and drawbacks to such an approach in an era of globalization.

Christopher W. Hughes is senior research fellow in the Centre for the Study of Globalisation and Regionalisation at the University of Warwick. He is author of *Japan's Economic Power and Security: Japan and North Korea* and coauthor of *Japan's International Relations: Politics, Economics and Security*.